LIPSTICK TRACES

A SECRET

HISTORY

OF THE

TWENTIETH

CENTURY

GREIL MARCUS . . . .

faber and faber

First published in 1989 in *Oral Review* by Secker &
Warburg Ltd
Published in this edition in 2001
by Faber and Faber Limited
3 Queen Square London WC1N 3AU

Greil Marcus is hereby identified as author of this
work in accordance with Section 77 of the Copyright,
Designs and Patents Act 1988

A CIP record for this book is available from the British
Library

ISBN 0-571-21288-3

2 4 6 8 10 9 7 5 3 1

To John Rockwell,
who got me started.

To the Firesign Theater and
Monty Python's Flying Circus,
who got me through it.

CONTENTS

. . . . *LIPSTICK TRACES*

PROLOGUE

From inside a London tea room, two well-dressed women look with mild disdain at a figure in the rain outside. "It's that shabby old man with the tin whistle!" says one. A battered fedora pulled down over his eyes, the man is trying to make himself heard: "I yam a antichrist!" "It is," reads the caption to this number of Ray Lowry's comic-strip chronicle of the adventures of has-been, would-be pop savior Monty Smith, "seventeen long years since Monty was spotted in the gutter outside Malcolm MacGregor's Sex 'n' Drugs shop . . ."

Years long enough: but as I write, Johnny Rotten's first moments in "Anarchy in the U.K."—a rolling earthquake of a laugh, a buried shout, then hoary words somehow stripped of all claptrap and set down in the city streets—

I AM AN ANTICHRIST

—remain as powerful as anything I know. Listening to the record today—listening to the way Johnny Rotten tears at his lines, and then hurls the pieces at the world; recalling the all-consuming smile he produced as he sang—my back stiffens; I pull away even as my scalp begins to sweat. "When you listen to the Sex Pistols, to 'Anarchy in the U.K.' and 'Bodies' and tracks like that," Pete Townshend of the Who once said, "what immediately strikes you is that *this is actually happening*. This is a bloke, with a brain on his shoulders, who is actually saying something he *sincerely* believes is happening in the world, saying it with real venom, and real passion. It touches you, and it scares you—it makes you feel uncomfortable. It's like somebody saying, 'The Germans are coming! And there's no way we're gonna stop 'em!'"

It is just a pop song, a would-be, has-been hit record, a cheap commodity, and Johnny Rotten is nobody, an anonymous delinquent whose greatest achievement, before that day in 1975 when he was spotted in Malcolm McLaren's Sex boutique on King's Road in London, had been to occasionally irritate those he passed on the street. It is a joke—and yet the voice that carries it remains something new in rock 'n' roll, which is to say something new in postwar popular culture: a voice that denied all social facts, and in that denial affirmed that everything was possible.

It remains new because rock 'n' roll has not caught up with it. Nothing like it had been heard in rock 'n' roll before, and nothing like it has been heard since—though, for a time, once heard, that voice seemed available to anyone with the nerve to use it. For a time, as if by magic—the pop magic in which the connection of certain social facts with certain sounds creates irresistible symbols of the transformation of social reality—that voice worked as a new kind of free speech. In countless new throats it said countless new things. You couldn't turn on the radio without being surprised; you could hardly turn around.

Today those old voices sound as touching and as scary as they ever did—partly because there is an irreducible quality in their demands, and partly because they are suspended in time. The Sex Pistols were a commercial proposition and a cultural conspiracy, launched to change the music business and make money off the change—but Johnny Rotten sang to change the world. So did some of those who, for a time, found their own voices in his. In the small body of work they left behind, you can hear it happen. Listening, you can feel yourself respond: "This is actually happening." But the voices remain suspended in time because you can't look back and say, "This actually happened." By the standards of wars and revolutions, the world did not change; we look back from a time when, as Dwight D. Eisenhower once put it, "Things are more like they are now than they ever were before." As against the absolute demands so briefly generated by the Sex Pistols, nothing changed. The shock communicated by the demands of the music becomes a shock that something so seemingly complete could, finally, pass almost unnoticed in the world of affairs: "This was actually not happening." Music seeks to change life; life goes on; the music is left behind; that is what is left to talk about.

The Sex Pistols made a breach in the pop milieu, in the screen of received cultural assumptions governing what one expected to hear and how one expected to respond. Because received cultural assumptions are hegemonic propositions about the way the world is supposed to work—ideological constructs perceived and experienced as natural facts—the breach in the pop milieu opened into the realm of everyday life: the milieu where, commuting to work, doing one's job in the home or the factory or the office or the mall, going to the movies, buying groceries, buying records, watching television, making love, having conversations, not having conversations, or making lists of what to do next, people actually lived. Judged according to its demands on the world, a Sex Pistols record had to change the way a given person performed his or her commute—which is to say that the record had to connect that act to every other, and then call the enterprise as a whole into question. Thus would the record change the world.

Elvis Costello recalled how it had worked back when he was still Declan McManus, a computer operator waiting for his train to Central London. It was 2 December 1976, the day after the Sex Pistols appeared on a television talk show to promote the record that was to change the world: "'God, did you see the Sex Pistols on TV last night?' On the way to work, I was on the platform in the morning and all the commuters were reading the papers when the Pistols made headlines—and said FUCK on TV. It was as if it was the most awful thing that ever happened. It's a mistake to confuse it with a major event in history, but it was a great morning—just to hear people's blood pressure going up and down over it." It was an old dream come true—as if the Sex Pistols, or one of their new fans, or the commuters beside him, or the television itself, had happily rediscovered a formula contrived in 1919, in Berlin, by one Walter Mehring, and then tested the formula to the letter, word for word save for the name of the game:

    ??? What is DADAyama ???
    DADAyama is
    to be reached from railroad stations only by a double somersault
    Hic salto mortale /
    Now or never /
    DADAyama makes
    the blood boil like it
    enrages the crowd
    in the melting pot /
    (partly bullfight arena—partly Red Front meeting—partly
    National Assembly)—
    1/2 gold plate—1/2 silver-plated iron
    plus surplus value

$$\frac{\text{\hspace{3cm}}}{\infty} = \text{Everyday life}$$

Echoing each other across half a century, Costello and Mehring raise the question that shapes this book: is it a mistake to confuse the Sex Pistols' moment with a major event in history—and what is history anyway? Is history simply a matter of events that leave behind those things that can be weighed and measured—new institutions, new maps, new rulers, new winners and losers—or is it also the result of moments that seem to leave nothing behind, nothing but the mystery of spectral connections between people long separated by place and time, but somehow speaking the same language? To fix a precious disruption, why is it that both Mehring and Costello find themselves talking about train platforms and blood pressure? The happenstance of specific words in common is an accident, but it might suggest a real affinity. The two men are talking about the same thing, looking for words to make disruption precious; that may not be an accident at all. If the language they are speaking, the impulse they are voicing, has its own history, might it not tell a very different story from the one we've been hearing all our lives?

THE QUESTION

The question is too big to tackle now—it has to be put aside, left to find its own shape. What it leaves behind is music; listening now to the Sex Pistols' records, it doesn't seem like a mistake to confuse their moment with a major event in history. Listening to "Anarchy in the U.K." and "Bodies," to Elvis Costello's *This Year's Model*, to the Clash's "Complete Control," to the Buzzcocks' "Boredom," X-ray Spex's "Oh Bondage Up Yours!" and *Germfree Adolescents*, Essential Logic's "Wake Up," the Raincoats' "Fairytale in the Supermarket," Wire's *Chairs Missing*, the Mekons' "Never Been in a Riot," Joy Division's "An Ideal for Living" and *Unknown Pleasures*, the Slits' "Once upon a time in a living room," the Gang of Four's "At Home He's a Tourist" and "Return the Gift," the Au Pairs' "Kerb Crawler," Kleenex's "Ü" and (after Kimberly-Clark forced the band to change its name) Liliput's "Split" and "Eisiger Wind," to the Adverts' *Crossing the Red Sea with the Adverts* (on the sleeve, a smear of color around a photo collage of a public housing complex and a white billboard with the words "Land of Milk and Honey" running in bureaucratic type: the sound was millenarian from the beginning, certain to lead the listener into the promised land, or forty years in the wilderness)—listening now, and listening especially to *The Roxy London WC 2 (Jan-Apr 77)*, a shoddy live album where behind table talk and breaking glass one can hear various groups of public speakers which before Johnny Rotten announced himself as an antichrist had not existed even in the minds of those who made them up—listening to this relatively small body of work, now exiled to cut-out bins, bargain racks, collectors' sales, or flea markets—I feel a sense of awe at how fine the music was: how irreducible it remains.

What remains irreducible about this music is its desire to change the world. The desire is patent and simple, but it inscribes a story that is infinitely complex—as complex as the interplay of the everyday gestures that describe the way the world already works. The desire begins with the demand to live not as an object but as a subject of history—to live as if something actually depended on one's actions—and that demand opens onto a free street. Damning God and the state, work and leisure, home and family, sex and play, the audience and itself, the music briefly made it possible to experience all those things as if they were not natural facts but ideological constructs: things that had been made and therefore could be altered, or done away with altogether. It became possible to see those things as bad jokes, and for the music to come forth as a better joke. The music came forth as a no that became a yes, then a no again, then again a yes: nothing is true except our conviction that the world we are asked to accept is false. If nothing was true, everything was possible. In the pop milieu, an arena maintained by society at large both to generate symbols and to defuse them, in the only milieu where a nobody like Johnny Rotten had a chance to be heard, all rules fell away. In tones that pop music had never produced, demands were heard that pop music had never made.

Because of Johnny Rotten's ludicrous proclamation—in one sense, he was from his first recorded moment a shabby old man in the rain trying to get out his crazy words ("I want to destroy pass–ers–by," croaks the Antichrist, reading from his smudgy broadsheet; you give the bum a wide berth)—teenagers screamed philosophy; thugs made poetry; women demystified the female; a nice Jewish girl called Susan Whitby renamed herself Lora Logic and took the stage of the Roxy in a haze of violence and confusion. Everyone shouted past melody, then rhyme, then harmony, then rhythm, then beat, until the shout became the first principle of speech—sometimes the last. Old oaths, carrying forgotten curses, which themselves contained buried wishes, were pressed into seven-inch pieces of plastic as a bet that someone would listen, that someone would decipher codes the speakers themselves didn't know they were transmitting.

I began to wonder where this voice came from. At a certain time, beginning in late 1975, in a certain place—London, then across the U.K., then spots and towns all over the world—a negation of all social facts was made, which produced the affirmation that anything was possible. "I saw the Sex Pistols," said Bernard Sumner of Joy Division (later, after the band's singer killed himself, of New Order). "They were terrible. I thought they were great. I wanted to get up and be terrible too." Performers made fools of themselves, denounced their ancestors, and spit on their audiences, which spit back. I began to wonder where these gestures came from. It was, finally, no more than an art statement, but such statements, communicated and received in any form, are rare. I knew a lot about rock 'n' roll, but I didn't know about this. Did the voice and the gestures come out of nowhere, or were they sparked? If they were sparked, what sparked them?

A TWENTY

A twenty-year-old stands before a microphone and, after declaring himself an all-consuming demon, proceeds to level everything around him—to reduce it to rubble. He denies the claims of his society with a laugh, then pulls the string on the history of his society with a shift of vowels so violent that it creates pure pleasure. He reduces the fruits of Western civilization to a set of guerrilla acronyms and England's green and pleasant land to a block of public housing. "We have architecture that is so banal and destructive to the human spirit that walking to work is in itself a depressing experience. The streets are shabby and tawdry and litter-strewn, and the concrete is rain-streaked and graffiti-strewn, and the stairwells of the social-engineering experiments are lined in shit and junkies and graffiti. Nobody goes out of their rooms. There is no sense of community, so old people die in despair and loneliness. We've had a lowering of the quality of life"—so said not Johnny Rotten as he recorded "Anarchy in the U.K." in 1976, but "Saint Bob" Geldof (first runner-up for the 1986 Nobel Peace Prize because of his work organizing pop-music campaigns to fight African famine) as he repeated the social critique of "Anarchy in the U.K." in 1985. Reduced to a venomous stew, that was what the song had said—except that as the Sex Pistols performed it, you heard not woe but glee.

> Is this the em pee el ay
> Or is this the yew dee ay
> Or is this the eye rrrrr ay
> I thought it was the yew kay
> Or just
> Another
> Country
> Another council tenancy!

It was the sound of the city collapsing. In the measured, deliberate noise, words tumbling past each other so fast it was almost impossible to tell them apart, you could hear social facts begin to break up—when Johnny Rotten rolled his *r*'s, it sounded as if his teeth had been ground down to points. This was a code that didn't have to be deciphered: who knew what the MPLA was, and who cared? It sounded like fun, wrecking the world. It felt like freedom. It was the freedom, after hearing the news that a San Diego teenager named Brenda Spenser had, because she didn't like Mondays, opened fire on her high school and killed three people, to write a song celebrating the event—as Bob Geldof had once done.

"I Don't Like Mondays" was a hit; in the United States it might have made number one, save for Brenda Spenser's superseding right to a fair trial. Too bad—wasn't a song like "I Don't Like Mondays" what "punk," which is what the putatively nihilist music generated by the Sex Pistols would be called, was all about? All about what? In the course of an interview, Bob Geldof's version of "Anarchy in the U.K.," like the explanations Johnny Rotten offered interviewers in 1976 and 1977, is perfectly rational: on record, both flesheater Johnny and Saint Bob call up the words of surrealist Luis Buñuel—who, Pauline Kael notes, "once referred to some of those who praised *Un Chien Andalou* as 'that crowd of imbeciles who find the film beautiful or poetic when it is fundamentally a desperate and passionate call to murder.'"

It is a question of nihilism—and "Anarchy in the U.K.," a

fan might like to think, was something different: a negationist prank. "'Anarchy in the U.K.' is a statement of self-rule, of ultimate independence, of do-it-yourself," said Sex Pistols manager Malcolm McLaren, and whatever that meant (do what yourself?), it wasn't nihilism. Nihilism is the belief in nothing and the wish to become nothing: oblivion is its ruling passion. Its best depiction is in Larry Clark's *Tulsa*, his photographic memoir of early 1960s youths spiking themselves to death with speed rather than becoming what they already look like: local Charley Starkweathers and Caril Fugates. Nihilism can find a voice in art, but never satisfaction. "This isn't a play, Larry," one of Clark's needle buddies told him after he'd taken one too many pictures. "This is real fuckin' life." "So other people didn't think it was a play," Clark recalled years later, "but I did"—even though he'd been in it, using a shutter timer to shoot the blood running down his own arm.

Nihilism means to close the world around its own self-consuming impulse; negation is the act that would make it self-evident to everyone that the world is not as it seems—but only when the act is so implicitly complete it leaves open the possibility that the world may be nothing, that nihilism as well as creation may occupy the suddenly cleared ground. The nihilist, no matter how many people he or she might kill, is always a solipsist: no one exists but the actor, and only the actor's motives are real. When the nihilist pulls the trigger, turns on the gas, sets the fire, hits the vein, the world ends. Negation is always political: it assumes the existence of other people, calls them into being. Still, the tools the negationist seems forced to use—real or symbolic violence, blasphemy, dissipation, contempt, ridiculousness—change hands with those of the nihilist. As a negation, "Anarchy in the U.K." could be rationally translated in interviews: seeking to prove that the world is not as it seems, the negationist recognizes that to others the world is as it seems to be. But by the time of "Holidays in the Sun," the Sex Pistols' fourth and last single, issued in October 1977, just a month short of a year after "Anarchy in the U.K.," no such translations were offered, or possible.

By that time, countless new groups of public speakers were issuing impossible demands, and the Sex Pistols had been
banned across the U.K. Waving the bloody shirt of public decency, even public safety, city officials canceled their shows;
chain stores refused to stock their records. Cutting "Anarchy
in the U.K." out of the market just as it was reaching its audience, EMI, the Sex Pistols' first label, dropped them after the
televised "fuck" that made Declan McManus' day, recalled the
records, and melted them down. Patriotic workers refused to
handle "God Save the Queen," the follow-up single, a three-
minute riot against Elizabeth II's silver jubilee; A&M, the
band's second label, destroyed what few copies were produced.
Finally released on Virgin, the Sex Pistols' third label, "God
Save the Queen" was erased from the BBC charts and topped
the hit parade as a blank, thus creating the bizarre situation
in which the nation's most popular record was turned into contraband. The press contrived a moral panic to sell papers, but
the panic seemed real soon enough: the Sex Pistols were denounced in Parliament as a threat to the British way of life,
by socialists as fascist, by fascists as communist. Johnny Rotten was caught on the street and slashed with a razor; another
band member was chased down and beaten with an iron bar.

The group itself had become contraband. In late 1975, when
the Sex Pistols first appeared, crashing another band's concert
and impersonating the opening act, the plug was pulled after
ten minutes; now to play in public they were forced to turn up
in secret, under a false name. The very emptiness of the terrain they had cleared—the multiplication of new voices from
below, the intensification of abuse from above, both sides fighting for possession of that suddenly cleared ground—had
pushed them toward self-destruction, into the silence of all
nihilist noise.

It was there from the start—a possibility, one of the alleys
leading off the free street. There was a black hole at the heart
of the Sex Pistols' music, a willful lust for the destruction of

values that no one could be comfortable with, and that was why, from the start, Johnny Rotten was perhaps the only truly terrifying singer rock 'n' roll has known. But the terror had a new cast at the end: certainly no one has yet seen all the way to the bottom of "Holidays in the Sun," and probably no one ever will.

They had begun as if in pursuit of a project: in "Anarchy in the U.K." they had damned the present, and in "God Save the Queen" they had damned the past with a curse so hard that it took the future with it. "NO FUTURE"—

> NO FUTURE
> NO FUTURE
> NO FUTURE FOR YOU
> NO FUTURE
> NO FUTURE
> NO FUTURE
> NO FUTURE FOR ME

—so went the mordant chant as the song ended. "No future in England's dah-rrrreeming!": England's dream of its glorious past, as represented by the Queen, the "moron," the nation's basic tourist attraction, linchpin of an economy based on nothing, salve on England's collective amputee's itch for Empire. "We're the future," Johnny Rotten shouted, never sounding more like a criminal, an escaped mental patient, a troglodyte—"Your future." Portrayed in the press as heralds of a new youth movement, with "God Save the Queen" the Sex Pistols denied it; every youth movement presents itself as a loan to the future, and tries to call in its lien in advance, but when there is no future all loans are canceled.

The Sex Pistols were after more than an entry in the next revised edition of a sociology text on Britain's postwar youth subcultures—just what more, one could perhaps have learned from a fragment that made up part of the collage on the back sleeve of the Clash's first record, "White Riot"/"1977": "that there is, perhaps, *some* tension in society, when perhaps overwhelming pressure brings industry to a standstill or barricades to the streets years after the liberals had dismissed the notion as 'dated romanticism,'" some unidentified person had written at some unidentified time, "the journalist invents the theory that this constitutes a clash of generations. Youth, after all, is not a permanent condition, and a clash of generations is not so fundamentally dangerous to the art of government as would be a clash between rulers and ruled." So maybe that was what the Sex Pistols were after: a clash between rulers and ruled. As the number-two London punk band, the Clash's pop project was always to make sense of the Sex Pistols' riddles, and this made sense—except that a single listening to "God Save the Queen" dissolved whatever sense it made.

The consumptive disgust in Johnny Rotten's voice ("We love our Queen / We mean it, man / God *save*"—that was the end of the line), the blinding intransigence of the music, so strong it made intransigence into a self-justifying, all-encompassing new value: as a sound, "God Save the Queen" suggested demands no art of government could ever satisfy. "God *save*"—the intonation said there was no such thing as salvation. A guitar lick ripped the song and whoever heard it in half.

What was left? Mummery, perhaps: with "Pretty Vacant," their third single, the Sex Pistols had risen from graves hundreds of years cold as Lollards, carriers of the ancient British heresy that equated work with sin and rejected both. Work, the Bible said, was God's punishment for Original Sin, but that was not the Lollards' bible. They said God was perfect, men and women were God's creation, so therefore men and women were perfect and could not sin—save against their own perfect nature, by working, by surrendering their God-given autonomy to the rule of the Great Ones, to the lie that the world was made for other than one's perfect pleasure. It was a dangerous creed in the fourteenth century, and a strange idea to find in a twentieth-century pop song, but there it was, and who knew what buried wishes it might speak for?

"We didn't know it would spread so fast," said Bernard Rhodes, in 1975 one of Malcolm McLaren's co-conspirators at the Sex boutique, later the manager of the Clash. "We didn't have a manifesto. We didn't have a rule book, but we were hoping that . . . I was thinking of what I got from Jackie Wilson's 'Reet Petite,' which was the first record I ever bought. I didn't need anyone to describe what it was all about, I knew it . . . I was listening to the radio in '75, and there was some expert blabbing on about how if things go on as they are there'll be 800,000 people unemployed by 1979, while another guy was saying if that happened there'd be chaos, there'd be actual—anarchy in the streets. *That* was the root of punk. One *knew* that."

Socialists like Bernard Rhodes knew it; it was never clear what Malcolm McLaren or his partner Jamie Reid, before Sex an anarchist publisher and poster artist, thought they knew. Unemployment in the U.K. had reached an unimaginable one million by the time "Pretty Vacant" was released in July 1977, and the punk band Chelsea summed up the social fact with the protest single "Right to Work." But Johnny Rotten had never learned the language of protest, in which one seeks a redress of grievances, and speaks to power in the supplicative voice, legitimating power by the act of speaking: that was not what it was about. In "Pretty Vacant" the Sex Pistols claimed the right not to work, and the right to ignore all the values that went with it: perseverance, ambition, piety, frugality, honesty, and hope, the past that God invented work to pay for, the future that work was meant to build. "Your God has gone away," Johnny Rotten had already sung on "No Feelings," the flipside of the first, abortive pressing of "God Save the Queen"—"Be back another day." Compared to Rhodes's sociology, Johnny Rotten spoke in unknown tongues. With a million out of work the Sex Pistols sat in doorways, preened and spat: "We're pretty / Pretty vacant / We're pretty / Pretty vacant / We're pretty / Pretty vacant / And we don't care." It was their funniest record yet, and their most professional, sounding more like the Beatles than a traffic accident, but Johnny Rotten's lolling tongue grew sores for the last word: like the singles before it, "Pretty Vacant" drew a laugh from the listener, and then drove it back down the listener's throat.

So that was the project—God and the state, the past, present, and future, youth and work, all these things were behind the Sex Pistols as they headed to the end of their first and last year on the charts. All that was left was "Holidays in the Sun": a well-earned vacation, albeit geopolitical and world-historical, sucking up more territory than the Sex Pistols had set foot on, and more years than they had been alive.

THE SLEEVE

The sleeve was charming: on the front was a borrowed travel-club comic strip, depicting happy tourists on the beach, in a nightclub, cruising the Mediterranean, celebrating their vacations in speech balloons Jamie Reid had emptied of advertising copy and filled with the words Johnny Rotten was singing on the plastic—"A cheap holiday in other people's misery!" On the back was a perfect family scene, dinnertime, a photograph Reid annotated with little pasted-on captions: "nice image," "nice furniture," "nice room," "nice middle age lady," "nice middle aged man," "nice food," "nice photo," "nice young man," "nice young lady," "nice gesture" (the nice young man is holding the hand of the nice young lady), "nice little girl" (she's sticking out her tongue), and even, at the bottom, "nice sleeve." "I don't want a holiday in the sun," Johnny Rotten began. "I want to go to the new Belsen."

He went. Off he goes to Germany, the marching feet of package-tour tourists behind him, drawn by the specter of the Nazi extermination camp that, for the British, serves as Auschwitz does for Americans: a symbol of modern evil. "I wanna see some history," he says, but history is out of reach; now Belsen is not in Germany at all, but part of something called "East Germany," less a place than an ideological construct, and so Johnny Rotten finds himself at the foot of the Berlin Wall, the ideological construct symbolizing the division between the two social systems that rule the world, a world that is more like it is now than it ever was before.

Johnny Rotten stands at the Berlin Wall. People are staring at him, and he can't stand it; the sound of marching feet grows louder, and he can't stand that either. As the band behind him spins into a frenzy, he begins to scream: he wants to go over the wall. Is that where the real Nazis are? Is East Berlin what the West will look like in the no-future he's already prophesied? He can't stop himself: he wants to go under the wall. He seems not to know what he's singing, but the music presses on, squeezing whoever might hear it like Poe's shrinking closet. The shifts in Johnny Rotten's voice are lunatic: he can barely say a word before it explodes in his mouth. Part of the terror of the song is that it makes no apparent sense and yet drags you into its absurdity and strands you there: time and place are specific, you could plot your position on a map, and you'd be nowhere. The only analogue is just as specific, and just as vague.

IN 1924

In 1924 a forty-two-year-old North Carolina lawyer named Bascom Lamar Lunsford recorded a traditional ballad called "I Wish I Was a Mole in the Ground"—how traditional, no one knows. A reference to "the Bend," a turn-of-the-century Tennessee prison, might fix the piece in a given time and place, but the reference could have been added long after the piece came into being; all that was certain was the measured count of Lunsford's banjo, the inexorable cadence of his voice. The song, the music said, predated whoever might sing it, and would outlast whoever heard it.

"I Wish I Was a Mole in the Ground" wasn't an animal song, like "Froggy Went A-Courtin'" or "The Leatherwing Bat." It was an account of everyday mysticism, a man dropping his plow, settling onto the ground, pulling off his boots, and summoning wishes he will never fulfill. He lies on his back in the sun:

> Oh, I wish I was a mole in the ground
> Yes, I wish I was a mole in the ground
> Like a mole in the ground I would root that mountain down
> And I wish I was a mole in the ground

Now what the singer wants is obvious, and almost impossible to comprehend. He wants to be delivered from his life and to be changed into a creature insignificant and despised. He wants to see nothing and to be seen by no one. He wants to destroy the world and to survive it. That's all he wants. The performance is quiet, steady, and the quiet lets you in: you can listen, and you can contemplate what you are listening to. You can lie back and imagine what it would be like to want what the singer wants. It is an almost absolute negation, at the edge of pure nihilism, a demand to prove that the world is nothing, a demand to be next to nothing, and yet it is comforting.

This song was part of the current that produced rock 'n' roll—not because a line from it turned up in 1966 in Bob Dylan's "Memphis Blues Again," but because its peculiar mix of fatalism and desire, acceptance and rage, turned up in 1955 in Elvis Presley's "Mystery Train." In that founding statement he tipped the balance to affirmation, concealing the negative but never dissolving it, maintaining the negative as the principle of tension, of friction, which always gave the yes of rock 'n' roll its kick—and that was the history of rock 'n' roll, up to October 1977, when the Sex Pistols happened upon the impulse to destruction coded in the form, turned that impulse back upon the form, and blew it up. The result was chaos: there was nowhere to lie down and no time to contemplate anything. This was actually happening. The Sex Pistols left every band in the world behind them for the last minute of "Holidays in the Sun": Johnny Rotten was climbing, digging with his hands, throwing pieces of the wall over his shoulder, crying out his inability to understand more of the story than you do, damning his inability to understand what, in 1924, Bascom Lamar Lunsford had accepted he could not understand.

What is happening? It sounds as if Hitler's legions have risen from the dead, taking the place of nice tourists, nice East German bureaucrats, nice West German businessmen—or as if Nazis have jumped out of the skins of the capitalists and communists who replaced them. Johnny Rotten is drawn like an iron filing to a magnet—but he slows down, stops, tries to think. If Buñuel had damned those who found his movie beautiful or poetic when it was fundamentally a call to murder, much of the twentieth-century has been taken up with the attempt to prove that the beautiful, the poetic, and the call to murder are all of a piece—and in the last seconds of "Holidays in the Sun," Johnny Rotten seemed to understand this. His incessant shout of "I DON'T UNDERSTAND THIS BIT AT ALL!" as the song headed to a close may have been his way of saying so, of saying that he didn't want to understand it: his way of saying that when he looked into the void of the century, he found the void looking back. Johnny Rotten went through the wall; "please don't be waiting for me," he said. The song ended.

Buñuel Reference

His aim, one can believe, was to take all the rage, intelligence, and strength in his being and then fling them at the world: to make the world notice; to make the world doubt its most cherished and unexamined beliefs; to make the world pay for its crimes in the coin of nightmare, and then to end the world—symbolically, if no other way was open. And that, for a moment, he did.

Thus did the Sex Pistols end the world, or anyway their own. The followup news was dissolution, murder, suicide—and though in each case the facts were formally logged in the relevant civil and criminal courts, who can tell if the events took place in the realm where people actually live more than in the symbolic realm of the pop milieu? As a double, the nihilist holds the negationist's dope; usually they rent the same rooms, and sometimes they pay the same bills. Usually the coroner—be it fan, epigone, critic, or best friend—cannot tell the difference by looking at the corpse. The Sex Pistols were a scam, a bid for success through scandal, for "cash from chaos," as one of Malcolm McLaren's slogans had it; they were also a carefully constructed proof that the whole of received hegemonic propositions about the way the world was supposed to work comprised a fraud so complete and venal that it demanded to be destroyed beyond the powers of memory to recall its existence. In those ashes anything would be possible, and permitted: the most profound love, the most casual crime.

THERE IS

There is an alchemy at work. An unacknowledged legacy of desire, resentment, and dread has been boiled down, melted down, to yield a single act of public speech that will, for some, overturn what they have taken for granted, thought they wanted, decided to settle for. It was, it turned out, a twisted story.

This book is about a single, serpentine fact: late in 1976 a record called "Anarchy in the U.K." was issued in London, and this event launched a transformation of pop music all over the world. Made by a four-man rock 'n' roll band called the Sex Pistols, and written by singer Johnny Rotten, the song distilled, in crudely poetic form, a critique of modern society once set out by a small group of Paris-based intellectuals. First organized in 1952 as the Lettrist International, and refounded in 1957 at a conference of European avant-garde artists as the Situationist International, the group gained its greatest notoriety during the French revolt of May 1968, when the premises of its critique were distilled into crudely poetic slogans and spray-painted across the walls of Paris, after which the critique was given up to history and the group disappeared. The group looked back to the surrealists of the 1920s, the dadaists who made their names during and just after the First World War, the young Karl Marx, Saint-Just, various medieval heretics, and the Knights of the Round Table.

My conviction is that such circumstances are primarily odd. For a gnomic, gnostic critique dreamed up by a handful of Left Bank cafe prophets to reappear a quarter-century later, *to make the charts*, and then to come to life as a whole new set of demands on culture—this is almost transcendently odd.

CONNECTIONS

Connections between the Sex Pistols, dada, the so grandly named Situationist International, and even forgotten heresies are not original with me. In the early days of London punk, one could hardly find an article on the topic without the word "dada" in it: punk was "like dada," everybody said, though nobody said why, let alone what that was supposed to mean. References to Malcolm McLaren's supposed involvement with the spectral "SI" were insider currency in the British pop press, but that currency didn't seem to buy anything.

Still, all this sounded interesting—even if for me "dada" was barely a word, only vaguely suggesting some bygone art movement (Paris in the Golden Twenties? something like that); even if I'd never heard of the Situationist International. So I began to poke around, and the more I found, the less I knew. All sorts of people had made these connections, but no one had made anything of them—and soon enough my attempt to make something of them led me from the card catalogue at the university library in Berkeley to the dada founding site in Zurich, from Gil J Wolman's bohemian flat in Paris to Michèle Bernstein's seventeenth-century parsonage in the south of England, from Alexander Trocchi's junkie pad in London back to books that had stood on library shelves for thirty years before I checked them out. It took me to microfilm machines unspooling the unambiguous public speech of my own childhood—and it is queer to crank through old newspapers for the confirming date of some fragment of a private obsession one hopes to turn into public speech, to be distracted by the ads, made so clumsy and transparent by time, to feel that, yes, the past is another country, a nice place to visit but you wouldn't want to live there, to happen upon the first dispatches on the overthrow of the Arbenz government in Guatemala, to read the dead news as if it were a crummy parody of CIA disinformation, and then to pick up the day's paper and follow the consequences: faces, says the reporter in 1984, three decades after Arbenz passed into microfilm, now removed from questionable citizens by means of bayonets, then hung on trees to dry into masks. Time marches on.

This was no heroic quest; some of those books deserved to sit for another thirty years. More than anything it was play, or an itch that needed to be scratched: the pursuit of a real story, or the pursuit of a non sequitur for the pleasures only a non sequitur can bring. Research makes time march forward, it makes time march backward, and it also makes time stand still. Two years and ten thousand miles later, I had before me the first numbers of *Potlatch*, a Lettrist International newsletter that was given away in Paris in the mid-1950s; in its mimeographed pages, "criticism of architecture" was presented as the key to the criticism of life. Renamed "M. Sing-Sing," the great architect Le Corbusier was damned as a "builder of slums." His Radiant City was dismissed as an authoritarian experiment in social engineering, a huddle of "vertical ghettos" and tower-block "morgues": the true function of Le Corbusier's celebrated "machines for living," one read in *Potlatch*, was to produce machines to live in them. "Decor determines gestures," said the LI; "we will build passionate houses." With a megalomania that belied its smudgy typescripts, the LI was writing words that "Anarchy in the U.K." would put in Bob Geldof's mouth—that was easy enough to imagine. But remembering my Guatemalan time travels in the microfilm room, I wondered what, if anything, it meant for the Sex Pistols' story that in the summer of 1954 the *Potlatch* writers (Gil J Wolman, Michèle Bernstein, the four others who at that moment were putting their names on the pages) had fixed on the CIA's ouster of the reformist Arbenz as a central social fact, as a metaphor—a means to the language of the "old world" they said they were going to destroy, of the "new civilization" they said they were going to create.

Here were prescient versions of the next week's news, as *Potlatch* brought Saint-Just back from the guillotine to render a "judgment in advance" on Arbenz's refusal to arm Guatemalan workers against the inevitable coup ("Those who make a revolution by halves only dig their own graves")—plus incomprehensible references to the Catharist heretics of thirteenth-century France and the latest discoveries in particle physics. And here too was the first note of what would become a recurrent situationist theme: the idea of "the vacation" as a sort of loop of alienation and domination, a symbol of the false promises of modern life, a notion that as CLUB MED—A CHEAP HOLIDAY IN OTHER PEOPLE'S MISERY would become graffiti in Paris in May 1968, and then, it seemed, turn into "Holidays in the Sun." "Following Spain or Greece, Guatemala can now count itself among those countries suitable for tourism," the LI wrote coolly, noting that the firing squads of the new government were already cleaning the streets of Guatemala City. "Someday we hope to make the trip."

THE QUESTION

The question of ancestry in culture is spurious. Every new manifestation in culture rewrites the past, changes old maudits into new heroes, old heroes into those who should have never been born. New actors scavenge the past for ancestors, because ancestry is legitimacy and novelty is doubt—but in all times forgotten actors emerge from the past not as ancestors but as familiars. In the 1920s in literary America it was Herman Melville; in the rock 'n' roll 1960s it was Mississippi bluesman Robert Johnson of the 1930s; in the entropic Western 1970s it was the carefully absolutist German critic Walter Benjamin of the 1920s and 1930s. In 1976 and 1977, and in the years to follow, as symbolically remade by the Sex Pistols, it was, perhaps, dadaists, lettrists, situationists, and various medieval heretics.

Listening to the records, it was hard to tell. Looking at the connections others had made and taken for granted (check a fact, it wasn't there), I found myself caught up in something that was less a matter of cultural genealogy, of tracing a line between pieces of a found story, than of making the story up. As it emerged out of the shadow of known events it was a marginal story, each manifestation claiming, in its brief moment, the whole world, and then relegated to a long number in the Dewey decimal system. Though almost silence as against the noise of wars and revolutions, it was a story seemingly endemic to the century, a story that repeatedly speaks and repeatedly loses its voice; it was, it seemed, a voice that only had to speak to lose itself.

As I tried to follow this story—the characters changing into each other's clothes until I gave up trying to make them hold still—what appealed to me were its gaps, and those moments when the story that has lost its voice somehow recovers it, and what happens then. Long before I tracked down *Potlatch*, I'd come across an advertisement for it, titled "The Gilded Legend," dated 1954, a page in *Les Lèvres nues*, a slick-paper, Belgian neo-surrealist review. "The century has known a few great incendiaries," the ad read. "Today they're dead, or finishing up preening in the mirror . . . Everywhere, youth (as it calls itself) discovers a few blunted knives, a few defused bombs, under thirty years of dust and debris; shaking in its shoes, youth hurls them upon the consenting rabble, which salutes it with its oily laugh." Promising that *Potlatch* knew a way out of this dead end, the LI publicist was talking about what fragments remained of surrealist knives and dada bombs; now it seems to me that the Lettrist International (just a few young people who for a few years banded together under that name in a search for a way to amuse themselves, to change the world) was itself a bomb, unnoticed in its own time, which would explode decades later as "Anarchy in the U.K." and "Holidays in the Sun."

Such a claim is not so much an argument about the way the past makes the present as it is a way of suggesting that the entanglement of now and then is fundamentally a mystery. *Potlatch*, as it described itself, drew "its title from the name, used among the Indians of North America, of a pre-commercial form of the circulation of goods, founded on the reciprocity of sumptuary gifts"; the "non-saleable goods such a free bulletin can distribute are previously unpublished desires and questions, and only their thorough analysis by others can constitute a return gift." This book grew out of a desire to come to grips with the power of "Anarchy in the U.K." as music, to understand its fecundity as culture; it may be that the key to those questions is not that the Sex Pistols could have traced their existence to the LI's gift, but that, blindly, they returned the gift—and in a form those who first offered it, aesthetes who would have been appalled to see their theories turned into cheap commodities, would never recognize. If "Anarchy in the U.K." truly did distill an old, forgotten social critique, that is interesting; if, in a new "potlatch," in a conversation of a few thousand songs, "Anarchy in the U.K." brought that critique to life—that is something far more than interesting.

This story, if it is a story, doesn't tell itself; once I'd glimpsed its outlines, I wanted to shape the story so that every fragment, every voice, would speak in judgment of every other, even if the people behind each voice had never heard of the others. Especially if they hadn't; especially if, in "Anarchy in the U.K.," a twenty-year-old called Johnny Rotten had rephrased a social critique generated by people who, as far as he knew, had never been born. Who knew what else was part of the tale? If one can stop looking at the past and start listening to it, one might hear echoes of a new conversation; then the task of the critic would be to lead speakers and listeners unaware of each other's existence to talk to one another. The job of the critic would be to maintain the ability to be surprised at how the conversation goes, and to communicate that sense of surprise to other people, because a life infused with surprise is better than a life that is not.

My wish to make sense of the outline I began with became a wish to make sense of the confusion the outline immediately produced: to make sense of such cryptic pronouncements, mysteries blithely claiming all the weight of history, as that made by Marxist sociologist Henri Lefebvre in 1975—

to the degree that modernity has a meaning, it is this: it carries within itself, from the beginning, a radical negation—Dada, this event which took place in a Zurich cafe.

Or that of the situationists in 1963: "The moment of real poetry brings all the unsettled debts of history back into play." Was that line, I wondered, a clue to the promise of the Berlin dadaists in 1919?

dada is the only savings bank that pays interest in eternity.

Or to the appeal of the Sex Pistols' most famous slogan, "NO FUTURE"? To the no-future chill in the face of lettrist Serge Berna as he posed for the camera in 1952? To the manifesto of one Guy-Ernest Debord, running a few pages on in the same obscure volume that carried Berna's portrait: "The art of the future will be the overthrow of situations, or nothing"? Or to the boast the situationists left behind in 1964:

While present-day impotence rambles on about the belated project of "getting into the twentieth century," we think it is high time to put an end to the *dead time* that has dominated this century, and to finish the Christian era with the same stroke. Here as elsewhere, it's a matter of breaking the bounds of measurement. Ours is the best effort so far to *get out* of the twentieth century.

We are already a long way from a pop song—but a pop song was supposed to be a long way from "I am an antichrist." We are already at a point where an appeal to rock 'n' roll will tell us almost nothing worth knowing, though this is, finally, a rock 'n' roll story. Real mysteries cannot be solved, but they can be turned into better mysteries.

VERSION ONE . . . .

THE LAST

SEX PISTOLS

CONCERT

GOD SAVE THE <u>LIBRARY</u>

WHERE THE <u>MONEY</u> IS THE FIRST

NO FUTURE
<u>←</u>

NO FUTURE FOR YOU
<u>___</u>

FUCKING DESK RESERVE

THE LAST SEX PISTOLS CONCERT

His teeth were ground down to points. So one heard, when Johnny Rotten rolled his *r*'s; when in 1918 draft dodger Richard Huelsenbeck told a polite Berlin audience gathered to hear a lecture on a new tendency in the arts that "We were for the war and Dadaism today is still for war. Life must hurt—there aren't enough cruelties"; when in 1649 the Ranter Abiezer Coppe unfurled his *Fiery Flying Roll* ("Thus saith the Lord, *I inform you, that I overturn, overturn, overturn*"); when in 1961 the Situationist International issued a prophecy, a "warning to those who build ruins: after the town planners will come the last troglodytes of the slums and the ghettos. They will know how to build. The privileged ones from the dormitory towns will only know how to destroy. Much can be expected from the meeting of these two forces: it will define the revolution."

So one heard when Johnny Rotten rolled his *r*'s; so one might have heard, anyway.

IN 1975

In 1975 a teenager who would be called Johnny Rotten turned himself into a living poster and paraded down London's King's Road to World's End—the end of the street—with "I HATE" scrawled above the printed logo of a Pink Floyd t-shirt. He dyed what was left of his chopped-off hair green and made his way through the tourist crowds spitting at hippies, who tried to ignore him. One day he was pointed out to a businessman who was attempting to put together a band. The drummer remembered the teenager's audition, which took place in front of a jukebox, the boy mouthing the words to Alice Cooper's

"Eighteen": "We thought he's got what we want. Bit of a lunatic, a front man. That's what we was after: a front man who had definite ideas about what he wanted to do and he'd definitely got them. And we knew straight away. Even though he couldn't sing. We wasn't particularly interested in that because we were still learning to play at the time."

It may be that in the mind of their self-celebrated Svengali, King's Road boutique owner Malcolm McLaren, the Sex Pistols were never meant to be more than a nine-month wonder, a cheap vehicle for fast money, a few laughs, a touch of the old épater la bourgeoisie. He had recruited them out of his store, found them a place to rehearse, given them a ridiculously offensive name, preached to them about the emptiness of pop music and the possibilities of ugliness and confrontation, told them they had as good a chance as anyone to make a noise, told them they had the right. If all else failed they could be a living poster for his shop, which always needed a new poster: before settling on Seditionaries in 1977, McLaren called his store Let It Rock in 1971, when it sold Teddy Boy clothes and old 45s; Too Fast to Live Too Young to Die in 1973, when it sold biker clothes and youth-gang accessories; Sex in 1974, when it sold bondage gear, nonmarital aids, and "God Save Myra Hindley" t-shirts commemorating the woman who along with Ian Brady had in 1963 and 1964 committed the Moors Murders—child murders, which Hindley and Brady recorded on tape as an art statement. It may also be that in the mind of their chief theorist and propagandist, 1960s art student and had-been, would-be anarchist provacateur Malcolm McLaren, the Sex Pistols were meant to set the country on its ear, to recapture the power McLaren had first glimpsed in Jerry Lee Lewis' "Great Balls of Fire" ("I'd never seen anything like it," he said once, recalling a fellow pupil singing the song at a grammar-school talent show. "I thought his head was going to come off"), to finally unite music and politics, to change the world. Thrilled by the May 1968 revolt in France, McLaren had helped foment solidarity demonstrations in London and later sold t-shirts decorated with May '68 slogans—even if, in

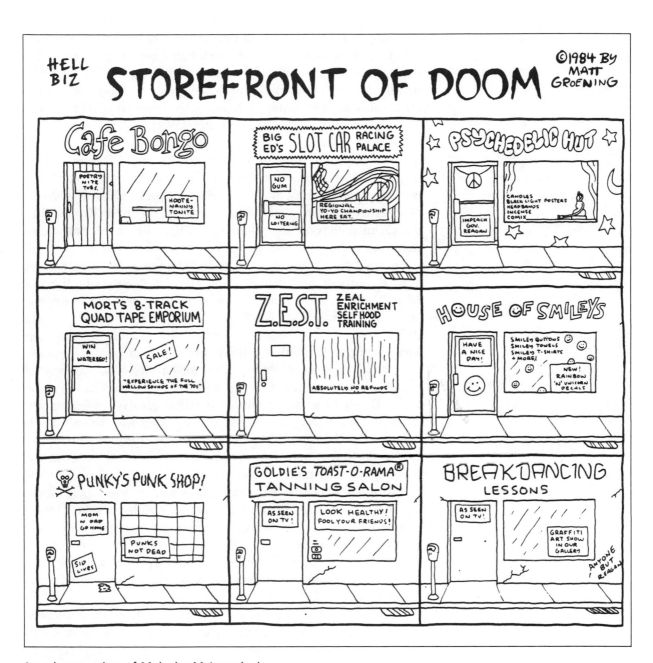

American version of Malcolm McLaren's shop

his shop, "I TAKE MY DESIRES FOR REALITY BECAUSE I BE-LIEVE IN THE REALITY OF MY DESIRES," the slogan of the En-ragés, the tiny cabal of students that began the uprising, mainly helped closeted businessmen work up the nerve to buy McLaren's rubber suits. McLaren would sell anything: in late 1978, after ex-Sex Pistols bassist Sid Vicious was arrested for the murder of Nancy Spungen, his girlfriend, McLaren rushed out "I'M ALIVE—SHE'S DEAD—I'M YOURS" Sid Vicious t-shirts (to help raise money for Vicious' defense, McLaren said). But not long before, he'd been carrying around copies of Christo-pher Gray's *Leaving the 20th Century*, the first English-lan-guage anthology of situationist writings, which he and Jamie Reid had helped publish in 1974.

He tried to get people to read it. "It's just a little more than a 20th century interpretation of Marxist essays on alienated labor," said Peter Urban, manager of the Dils, a Los Angeles punk band "into class war" (their first single was "I Hate the Rich," the principal result of which was a tune by the rival Vom, "I Hate the Dils"). "It's a little of that," said McLaren, "but it is very, very strong. The good thing about it was all those slogans you can take up without being party to a move-ment. Being in a movement often stifles creative thinking and certainly, from the point of view of a young kid, the ability to announce yourself . . . That's the greatest thing, that it allows you to do that. There is a certain aggression and arrogance in there that's exciting . . ." Old hat, said Urban, ignoring the in-teresting conclusions McLaren was drawing, and ignoring too the sticker on the cover of the book, which carried a quote from a review by John Berger: "one of the most lucid and pure political formulations of the '60s." "Lost Prophets," Berger's re-view was titled; had the rest of it been somehow squeezed onto the sticker, it could have taken the conversation even farther afield, or closer to home.

The conversation was appearing in the May 1978 issue of *Slash*, an L.A. punk magazine; the number, a note on the con-tents page read, was "dedicated to the handful of *enragés* (French for maniacs, fanatics, crazies) who, ten years ago, tried to change life." The dedication was illustrated with "une jeunesse que l'avenir inquiète trop souvent" (a youth disturbed too often by the future), a once-famous poster by the May '68 art-student collective Atelier populaire: it showed a young woman with her head covered in surgical gauze and a safety pin jamming her lips closed. After ten years, with May '68 all but forgotten in the United States, this was true archaeology. It was an odd return to strange times, when apparently trivial disruptions on a university campus in the Paris suburbs had begun a chain reaction of refusal—when first students, then factory workers, then clerks, professors, nurses, doctors, athletes, bus drivers, and artists refused work, took to the streets, threw up barricades, and fought off the police, or turned back upon their workplaces, occupied them, fought off their unions, and transformed their workplaces into laboratories of debate and critique, when the walls of Paris bled with unusual slogans—when ten million people brought a signal version of modern society to a standstill. "In the confusion and tumult of the May revolt," Bernard E. Brown wrote in *Protest in Paris*, his unique academic account of May '68, "the slogans and shouts of the students were considered expressions of mass spontaneity and individual ingenuity. Only afterward was it evident that these slogans"—

REVOLUTION CEASES TO BE THE MOMENT IT BECOMES NEC-ESSARY TO BE SACRIFICED FOR IT   IT IS FORBIDDEN TO FORBID   NEITHER GODS NOR MASTERS   DOWN WITH THE ABSTRACT, LONG LIVE THE EPHEMERAL   AFTER GOD, ART IS DEAD   DOWN WITH A WORLD WHERE THE GUAR-ANTEE THAT WE WON'T DIE OF STARVATION HAS BEEN PUR-CHASED WITH THE GUARANTEE THAT WE WILL DIE OF BOREDOM   CLUB MED, A CHEAP HOLIDAY IN OTHER PEO-PLE'S MISERY   DON'T CHANGE EMPLOYERS, CHANGE THE EMPLOYMENT OF LIFE   NEVER WORK   CHANCE MUST BE SYSTEMATICALLY EXPLORED   RUN, COMRADE, THE OLD WORLD IS BEHIND YOU   BE CRUEL   THE MORE YOU CONSUME THE LESS YOU LIVE   LIVE WITHOUT DEAD TIME, INDULGE UNTRAMMELED DESIRE   PEOPLE WHO

TALK ABOUT REVOLUTION AND CLASS STRUGGLE WITHOUT
REFERRING EXPLICITLY TO EVERYDAY LIFE, WITHOUT UN-
DERSTANDING WHAT IS SUBVERSIVE ABOUT LOVE AND POS-
ITIVE ABOUT THE REFUSAL OF CONSTRAINTS, HAVE
CORPSES IN THEIR MOUTHS   UNDER THE PAVING STONES,
THE BEACH!

—"were fragments of a consistent and seductive ideology that
had virtually all appeared in situationist tracts and publications . . . Mainly through their agency there welled up in the
May Revolt an immense force of protest against the modern
world and all its works, blending passion, mystery, and the
primeval." "This explosion," said President Charles de Gaulle
in the June speech with which he recaptured power, "was provoked by a few groups in revolt against modern society,
against consumer society, against technological society,
whether communist in the East or capitalist in the West—
groups, moreover, which do not know what they would put in
its place, but which delight in negation." "The Beginning of an
Epoch," proclaimed the lead article in the twelfth and last
number of the journal *Internationale situationniste* in 1969.
"The death rattle of the historical irrelevants," said Zbigniew
Brzezinski.

In 1978, when Brzezinski was national security adviser to
the president of the United States and "The Beginning of an
Epoch" was, in English, a badly translated, smudgy pamphlet
long out of print, *Slash* readers were expected to recall the un-
scheduled holiday of May '68 approximately as dimly as they
might recall Gary "U.S." Bonds's small 1965 hit "Seven Day
Weekend." The reader was to look casually at the blind reference of the Atelier populaire poster, and then to superimpose
the best-known Sex Pistols graphic, Jamie Reid's photo-collage
for "God Save the Queen," which featured H.R.H. Elizabeth II
with a safety pin through her lips; out of the ether of unmade
history, connections were supposed to tumble like counters in a
slot machine. "The revolutionary hopes of the 1960s, which
culminated in 1968," John Berger wrote in 1975,

are now blocked or abandoned. One day they will break out again, transformed, and be lived again with different results. I mean only that; I am not prophesying the difference. When that happens, the Situationist programme (or anti-programme) will probably be recognized as one of the most lucid and pure political formulations of that earlier, historic decade, reflecting, in an extreme way, its desperate force and privileged weakness.

As manager of the Dils, Peter Urban would not have been interested in such sentimental meanderings. There was a world to win, he told McLaren, tactics to be formulated, ideology to be fixed, and anyway . . . McLaren cut him off. "So, Peter, how come you're managing a band with a name like a pickle? Or a dildo, what's the controversy there?"

The Sex Pistols had sparked the Dils; when I saw them play in 1979, they were a helpless imitation, nothing more. By the time Nancy Spungen was stabbed to death, the Sex Pistols had sparked new bands all over the world, and more of them than anyone could count were doing things no one in rock 'n' roll had done before. But as an above-ground group—a commercial possibility, an international scandal—the Sex Pistols lasted little longer than nine months: they saw the release of their first record on 4 November 1976, and ceased to exist as much more than an asset in a lawsuit on 14 January 1978, when, immediately following the last show of their single American tour, Johnny Rotten quit the band, claiming that McLaren, in his lust for fame and money, had betrayed everything the Sex Pistols ever stood for. And what was that? For guitarist Steve Jones, an illiterate petty criminal, and drummer Paul Cook, a sometime electrician's helper, it was girls and good times. For original bassist Glen Matlock, former art student and Sex shop clerk, it was pop music. For Sid Vicious, the junkie who replaced him, it was pop stardom. As for Johnny Rotten, he would say many different things (including, after the fall: "Steve can go off and become Peter Frampton"—he didn't; "Sid can go off and kill himself"—he did; "Paul can go back to being an electrician"—he may still), and, one suspected, had yet to say what he meant.

Atelier populaire poster, May 1968

Sex Pistols flyer by Jamie Reid, 1977

THE SEX PISTOLS

The Sex Pistols called their final performance the worst of their career, but to the five thousand people packed into San Francisco's Winterland Ballroom on 14 January 1978, that performance was as close to Judgment Day as a staged event can be—and not because many had seen the leaflets evangelists were distributing outside: "There's a Johnny Rotten in each of us, and he doesn't need to be liberated—*he needs to be crucified!*"

That would have been old news to Johnny Rotten; one of his publicity photos showed him nailed to a cross. In London the subculture generated by the Sex Pistols and their first followers had already been pronounced dead by those whose business it is to make such pronouncements: a once-secret society diffused by headlines and tourism. Or was it that, in the beginning, punk was indeed a sort of secret society, dedicated not to the guarding of a secret but to its pursuit, a society based on a blind conviction that there was a secret to be found? Was it that once the secret was seemingly discovered, once punk became an ideology of protest and self-expression—once people knew what to expect, once they understood just what they would get when they paid their money, or what they would do to earn it—the story was ready for its footnotes?

In the United States, primitive enclaves had formed across the country (nightclubs, fanzines, record stores, a half-dozen high school students here, a trio of artists there, a girl locked in her room staring at her new haircut in the mirror)—though perhaps less in response to the thrill of hearing $10 import copies of the banned "Anarchy" single than to newspaper and TV features about London teenagers mutilating their faces with common household objects. Real discoveries were taking place, out of nothing ("The original scene," said a founder of the Los Angeles punk milieu, "was made of people who were taking chances and operating on obscure fragments of information"); for some, those discoveries, a new way of walking and a new way of talking, would dramatize the contradictions of everyday existence for years to come, would keep life more interesting than it would have otherwise been.

"Now it's time for audience participation," Joe Strummer of the Clash said from the stage in late 1976. "I want you all to tell me what exactly you're doing here." As they waited for the Sex Pistols to take the stage at Winterland, probably a lot of people wondered what they were doing there—wondered why their expectations were so confused, and so fierce. In all the stories coded in that moment, at least one was simply musical; compared to everything the music secretly contained, that story was almost silent, but I will tell that story first.

HAVE YOU

"Have you seen the Sex Pistols?" Joe Strummer whispered to Graham Parker one night in early 1976—it was as if he were passing on a rumor so unlikely he was afraid to raise his voice. They were part of the London "pub rock" scene (Parker chasing echoes of Wilson Pickett and the Temptations, Strummer looking for Chuck Berry and Gene Vincent): one more abortive attempt to bring the bloated music of the 1970s back to basics. "No," said Parker. "The Sex Pistols?" "Whole new thing, man," said Strummer. "Whole new thing."

Straight away, Strummer quit his rock revival band to form the Clash: "Yesterday I thought I was a crud," he would later say he said to friends who asked him why. "Then I saw the Sex Pistols, and I became a king." It's a good story, too good to be true, but it was true in the music, and never more so than in the music of the Slits. They were the first all-female punk band: four teenagers who hadn't the slightest idea of how to do anything but climb onto a stage and shout. They said "Fuck you"; it meant "Why not." It was the sound, Jon Savage wrote long after the fact, of people discovering their own power.

ALL THE SLITS

All the Slits really left behind is an object screaming with muteness: a nameless lp in a blank bootleg sleeve. I like to think the disc is called "Once upon a time in a living room," but there's no way to be sure; with phrases scrawled at random across the label in lieu of titles, you have to decide the names of the songs from the choices offered. "A Boring Life," then: once the music starts I've never tried to understand a word.

One Slit giggles; a second asks, "You ready?," another answers *"Ready?"* as if she never could be, then the fourth returns the giggle like Alice diving down the rabbit hole: "Ah, ah, OH NOOOOO—" It's the last sound you hear at the crest of a roller coaster, and in the dead pause that follows you have time to remember Elvis in Sam Phillips' Sun studios in 1955, setting up "Milkcow Blues Boogie" with a little rehearsed dialogue ("Hold it, fellas! That don't *move* me! Let's get real, real *gone* for a change!"), except that the Slits' dialogue is too trivial to have been rehearsed, let alone lead anywhere, and then the silence is collapsed by an unyielding noise. This compressed drama—embarrassment to anticipation, hesitation to panic, silence to sound—is what punk was all about.

The Slits were Ari Up, lead singer; Palmolive, drums; Viv Albertine, guitar; Tessa, bass. The *Rolling Stone Rock Almanac* entry for 11 March 1977: "The Slits make their stage debut, opening for the Clash at the Roxy in London . . . [They] will have to bear the double curse of their sex and their style, which takes the concept of enlightened amateurism to an extreme . . . The Slits will respond to charges of incompetence by inviting members of the audience on stage to play while the four women take to the floor to dance." A line from an old Jamaican 45 comes to mind—from Prince Buster's "Barrister Pardon," the finale to his Judge Dread trilogy, the tale of an avenger come from Ethiopia to rid the Kingston slums of its rude-boy hooligans. Across three singles he sentences teenage murderers to hundreds of years in prison, jails their lawyers when they have the temerity to appeal, reduces everyone in the courtroom to tears, then sets everyone free and highsteps down from the bench to lead the crowd in a cakewalk: "I am the judge, but I know how to dance." With "A Boring Life," the Slits judged every other version of rock 'n' roll: "Milkcow Blues Boogie," "Barrister Pardon," the crummy official records they themselves would make after their moment had passed.

Nothing could keep up with it. Shouting and shrieking, out of guitar flailings the group finds a beat, makes a rhythm, begins to shape it; the rhythm gets away and they chase it down, overtake it, and keep going. Squeaks, squeals, snarls, and whines—unmediated female noises never before heard as pop music—course through the air as the Slits march hand in hand through a storm they themselves have created. It's a performance of joy and revenge, an armed playground chant; every musical chance is taken, and for these women playing the simplest chord was taking a chance: their amateurism was not enlightened.

"No more rock 'n' roll for you / No more rock 'n' roll for me," goes a drunken moan elsewhere on the record, echoing the Sex Pistols' chorus for no-future—some unidentified man was singing, maybe a guy running the tape recorder, but it was the Slits' affirmation that whatever they were doing, they wouldn't call it rock 'n' roll. This was music that refused its own name, which meant it also refused its history—from this moment, no one knew what rock 'n' roll was, and so almost anything became possible, or impossible, as rock 'n' roll: random noise was rock 'n' roll, and the Beatles were not. Save for the buried productions of a few cult prophets—such American avatars as Captain Beefheart, mid-1960s garage bands like Count Five or the Shadows of Knight, the Velvet Underground and the Stooges of the late 1960s, the New York Dolls and Jonathan Richman and the Modern Lovers of the early 1970s, and the reggae voice of gnostic exile—punk immediately discredited the music that preceded it; punk denied the legitimacy of anyone who'd ever had a hit, or played as if he knew how to play. Destroying one tradition, punk revealed a new one.

Slits flyer, 1978

Looking back, it remains possible to take this version of the rock 'n' roll story for the truth, as the whole story—not because the music punk discredited was worthless, but because what little remains of the Slits' music allows you to imagine that the sound they made communicated more completely and more mysteriously than the most carefully crafted work of anyone who came before or after. "A Boring Life," heard as it was made in 1977 or heard a decade later, rewrites the history of rock 'n' roll.

IT'S SAID

It's said that in the 1950s fifteen thousand black vocal groups made records. I don't know if this is true; when I first came across the figure, my eyes bugged out. Punk made it credible.

Only the smallest fraction of those groups would have been heard by the public, though all would have been bent on the public—on fame and money, and on the sensation that if only in the fantasy utopia of a three-minute record, this was the momentary empowerment of people who never before had reason to think anyone might be interested in what they sounded like, or what they had to say. It was a surge of new voices unprecedented in the history of popular culture, and along with other forms of early rock 'n' roll—the sophisticated rhythm and blues of Ray Charles and Clyde McPhatter's Drifters, the rockabilly of Elvis, Carl Perkins, and Jerry Lee Lewis, the mad irruptions of Little Richard, the savvy teen anthems of Chuck Berry, the suprises of noisemakers like the Monotones—this event marked the transformation of popular music all over the world. "I must speak to a boy named Elvis Presley," said the headmistress of a London comprehensive academy in 1956, "because he has carved his name on every desk in the school."

The next major event in rock 'n' roll—the emergence of the Beatles in Liverpool and London between 1962 and 1963, powered by the black rock of James Brown, Motown in Detroit,

"*IT WAS SO* wonderful to have rediscovered at what was already an advanced age the sort of feelings I first had when I heard Little Richard and Elvis Presley as a kid. It was exciting, but there was an element of fear as well—you thought, 'Can this be real?' You went to the gigs and there was a feeling that you were participating in something that had come from another planet, it seemed so remarkable that it was happening at all."

—BBC disc jockey John Peel, 1986, on London punk, 1976

and Stax in Memphis—produced no such cacophony. Countless new bands recorded, but once revitalized the music was soon dominant and entrenched across the West; linked to the social revolt of American blacks, then to the international rebellion of white youth, rock 'n' roll grew self-important. Hailed as art, it grew self-conscious. The spirit that brought the sound to the attention of the world in the first place—the eagerness to do absolutely anything to get heard that still leaps out of so many 1950s 45s, or for that matter out of so many third-rate 1964 Beatle imitations—was replaced by a cult of wisdom, responsibility, and virtuosity.

Bypassed the first time around by hundreds of tiny independent labels, from the mid-1960s the major record companies covered the major artists and built a center; idiosyncratic music, a concept that would have made no sense at all in 1956, soon sounded merely cranky. By 1967, a pop year organized around the Beatles' *Sgt. Pepper's Lonely Hearts Club Band*, rock 'n' roll was governed by an ideology of affirmation, creativity, and novelty. Almost everything sounded hopeful, significant, and new, but in fact the music was imploding. Almost everything was aimed at the center, and the spinning center threw off whatever was not. End-of-the-decade warnings—the Beatles' "A Day in the Life," the Rolling Stones' *Let It Bleed*, Bob Dylan's *John Wesley Harding*, the Velvet Underground's *White Light/White Heat*, John Lennon's *Plastic Ono Band*, Sly and the Family Stone's *There's a riot goin' on*, the post-*Riot* wave of disillusioned, politicized black pop—were ignored even by those who made them. The music business moved toward rationalization; the process was almost complete by 1975, when leisure-service conglomerates had concentrated record sales in the hands of corporations hardly more numerous than American auto manufacturers. "Entertainment isn't a suspension of belief," Michael Ventura wrote in 1985, "but a suspension of values. It may even be said that this is the *meaning* of 'entertainment' as it is practiced among us: the relief of suspending values with which we are tired of living and frightened of living without . . . To go from a job you don't like to watching a screen on which others live more intensely than you . . . this is American life, by and large"; Ventura could as easily have said modern life. In 1977, in its annual report, Warner Communications, then the leading leisure-service corporation, had already faced the problem:

Entertainment has become a necessity. The statement seems unsupportable: can entertainment be necessary in the sense that food, clothing and shelter are necessary? . . . the problem in the above statement is not with the word "necessary," but with the word "entertainment." As recently as twenty years ago, "entertainment"—diversion, amusement—would have served adequately to describe the vast majority of movies, television, radio, popular print and recorded sound. But today the word seems inadequate, outdistanced by events. The role of these media is now far more various and crucial than the pleasurable passing of time. In their mechanical operations . . . the media [have remained] essentially the same. Yet in their personal and social usefulness, they are utterly changed . . . The pace of world industrialization that has steadily accelerated since the 19th century is widely believed to have effected a severe challenge to individual identity: an increasingly efficient and standardized world jeopardizes personal freedom, importance and opportunity, with a consequent sensation of disenfranchisement of self.

This is what, in 1956, Harold Rosenberg meant when he spoke of "proletarianization": the "process of depersonalization and passivity" brought on by modern social organization, the extension of "the psychic condition of the nineteenth-century factory worker" into the totality of twentieth-century society. "Demoralized by their strangeness to themselves and by their lack of control over their relations with others," Rosenberg said, "members of every class surrender themselves to artificially constructed mass egos that promise to restore their links with the past and future." In 1977 Warner Communications did not see things so bleakly:

Having allowed technology to create the problem, man has begun using technology to redress it. With the exponentially increased availability of all forms of communication, the media of "entertainment" have been pressed into service to provide the individual with models of experience, opportunities for self-recognition, and the ingredients of identity . . . The movement of information—at many rates of speed, to many kinds of people—is the business of Warner Communications. And the phenomenal growth of our company, along with other leaders in the field, reflects a marriage of culture and technology unprecedented in history, and a commensurate revolution in the human sense of self.

THE WORLD

The Penguins, one of 15,000 black vocal groups to make records in the 1950s

The world had prospered despite the disappearance of the Jordan Motor Car Company, makers of the Jordan Playboy, the most glamorous American automobile of the 1920s; presumably the world could get along without the equivalent of fifteen thousand doo-wop groups making records. With the market hugely expanded and organized from the top down, record sales boomed, even though the flush economy of the 1960s was giving way to an irrational, shrinking economy that mocked traditional values, be they the pre-rock values of work-hard-and-save-your-money or the already traditional 1960s values of don't-work-and-get-it-while-you-can. The plague hit the U.K. before the U.S.A., which would take a couple of years to catch up. It is no accident that *The Ice Age*, Margaret Drabble's novel about the economic and social collapse of Britain, peopled with characters who actively welcomed depression as a relief from anxiety, appeared at the same time as the Sex Pistols. Both sought a purchase on a world in which society's promises were no longer kept, and in which those who believed they would be kept were swiftly exposed as fools.

Bills for war or social planning came due, Arabs with oil began dealing with the West like Westerners with guns once dealt with Arabs, unemployment rose, inflation soared, capital dried up. The world promised in the 1950s ("What do *you* want?" read a British ad in 1957. "Better and cheaper food? Lots of new clothes? A dream home with the latest comforts and labour-saving devices? A new car . . . a motor-launch . . .

a light aircraft of your own? Whatever you want, it's coming your way—plus greater leisure for enjoying it all. With electronics, automation and nuclear energy, we are entering on the new Industrial Revolution which will supply our every need . . . quickly . . . cheaply . . . abundantly"), a world apparently on the verge of realization in the 1960s, seemed like a cruel joke by 1975. Based less on concrete suffering than on blocked expectations, panic set in; so did the urge to seek revenge. Drabble wrote:

All over the nation, families who had listened to the news looked at one another and said, "Goodness me," or "Whatever next," or "I give up," or "Well, fuck that," before embarking on an evening's viewing of colour television, or a large hot meal, or a trip to the pub, or a choral society evening. All over the country, people blamed other people for the things that were going wrong—the trades unions, the present government, the miners, the car workers, the seamen, the Arabs, the Irish, their own husbands, their own wives, their own idle good-for-nothing offspring, comprehensive education. Nobody knew whose fault it really was, but most people managed to complain fairly forcefully about somebody; only a few were stunned into honourable silence. Those who had been complaining for twenty years about the negligible rise in the cost of living did not, of course, have the grace to wish they had saved their breath to cool their porridge, because once a complainer always a complainer, so those who had complained most when there was nothing to complain about were having a really wonderful time now.

MAINSTREAM

Mainstream rock 'n' roll, by 1975 nearly all-white and middle-class, continued to play out its string to rhythms that were nothing if not passively congruent. "Adventure" and "risk" had been watchwords, finally cant words, of the 1960s, an era which had itself become cant, "the sixties." Now the deaths, breakdowns, and burnouts attendant upon the struggles and experiments of those times were converted into the cant watchword of the 1970s: "survival."

Queer as the word might seem as a definition of choices open to people who were white, middle-class, and relatively young—for it was almost exclusively to such people that the word was applied—it proved impossible to resist. Through the magic of ordinary language, "survival" and its twin, "survivor," wrote the 1960s out of history as a mistake and translated the 1970s performance of any act of personal or professional stability (holding a job, remaining married, staying out of a mental hospital, or simply not dying) into heroism. First corrupted as a reference to those "survivors" of "the sixties" who were now engaged in "real life," the word contained an implacable equation: survival was real life.

Soon enough, anyone whose material or physical existence was patently not in jeopardy could claim the title of survivor, and to be named a survivor was to receive the highest praise. The idea grew arms and legs. Intimations of aggression crept in: ads for a new line of suitcases, "The Survivor," made it plain that what was at stake was the survival of the fittest—in the jungle of the new economy, nothing else mattered. The idea conquered ontology as it overran ethics. "Garp is a survivor," wrote a fan of John Irving's novel *The World According to Garp*, knowing full well that Irving's hero is shot to death at the age of thirty-three. Here was the ultimate victory of the idea over its word: the dead survivor.

The notion of what in 1976 Bruno Bettelheim called "a completely empty survivorship," where "survival is all, it does not matter how, why, what for," invaded every form of discourse. Bettelheim was writing about the new philosophical sanctification of "survival," as opposed to even a fantasy of resistance, in Nazi extermination camps: according to such arguments as Lina Wertmuller's film *Seven Beauties* and Terrence Des Pres's camp-study, *The Survivor*, he said, "the only thing that is really important, is life in its crudest, merely biological form . . . we must 'live beyond compulsions of culture' and 'by the body's crude claims.'" One had to live, in other words, according to a dictatorship of necessity, not beyond culture but before it, and as Hannah Arendt once wrote, the dictates of the body were inimical to freedom: when survival took precedence, "freedom had to be surrendered to the urgency of the life process itself." In 1951 in *The Rebel*, Albert Camus retold a different story—

Ernst Dwinger in his *Siberian Diary* mentions a German lieutenant—for years a prisoner in a camp where cold and hunger were almost unbearable—who constructed himself a silent piano with wooden keys. In the most abject misery, perpetually surrounded by a ragged mob, he composed a strange music audible to him alone

—a story, Camus said, of an "harmonious insurrection." But Camus was no longer fashionable; neither were cold and hunger or the "state of constant want and acute misery" Arendt meant by "necessity." Language turned inside out, so that culture was a compulsion, necessity a luxury, survival an affluent sensibility, and thus the creed of survivalism was embraced most eagerly not by those suffering privation, but by rock stars. You could read the new ideology off the record titles: *Survivor*, *Rock and Roll Survivor*, "You're a Survivor," *I Survive*, "Soul Survivor," *Street Survivors*, *Survival*, *Surviving*, "I Will Survive," on and on into endless redundancy—in almost every case signifying the offerings of performers who should have been stunned into an honorable silence years before, but who now found themselves granted the dispensation to purvey their wares forever and, what is more, to celebrate the act as a moral triumph, a triumph that devalued any effort to pursue adventure and risk. The exchange of a guarantee of dying of boredom for a guarantee of not dying of hunger was a good deal—the only game in town.

NOW

Now identified with those who had the money and the corporate affiliations to secure the most sophisticated and arcane tools, rock 'n' roll became an old story: a parody of the time had a rock star demanding that his label fund the recording of his next album in outer space, but it didn't come off as a parody. Rock 'n' roll became an ordinary social fact, like a commute or a highway construction project. It became a habit, a structure, an invisible oppression.

A mythical era even as it unfolded, the sixties were based in the belief that since everything was true, everything was possible. Among rock stars, that utopian ideology was by the 1970s reduced to a well-heeled solipsism. On the terms of the barefoot solipsism of extermination camp survival, even a fantasy of resistance—which by its nature almost had to be a fantasy of collectivity, of solidarity—was utopian; insisting on the sensitivity of the individual as the source of all value, rock stars made a utopia out of solipsism. Like movie stars, they had made so much money that they remained untouched by and uninterested in what was happening in the world, and their renderings of a life of ease or of small problems proved attractive to a very large audience. There was no need for change; "change" began to seem like an old-fashioned, sixties word. The chaos in society at large called for a music of permanence and reassurance; in the pop world, time stood still. For years that seemed like decades, you could turn on the radio with the assurance that you would hear James Taylor's "Fire and Rain," Led Zeppelin's "Stairway to Heaven," the Who's "Behind Blue Eyes," Rod Stewart's "Maggie May." It was all right; they were good songs.

SOME PEOPLE

Some people began to lose their taste for surprise; others had never known it. "People pay to see others believe in themselves," Kim Gordon of the New York punk band Sonic Youth wrote in 1983. "On stage, in the midst of rock 'n' roll, many things happen and anything can happen, whether people come as voyeurs or come to submit to the moment." Such words would not have been written in the mid-1970s, when people paid to see others believe that others believed in them. As the concerts of the time ended, fans stood up, lit matches, held them high: they were praying.

It was 1974. Malcolm McLaren was briefly in the United States, managing the New York Dolls, then on their last legs. They had wandered into his shop, played him their records; he'd laughed. "I couldn't believe how anybody could be so bad," he said long after, citing the moment as the inspiration for the Sex Pistols. "The fact that they were so bad suddenly hit me with such force that I began to realize, 'I'm laughing, I'm talking to these guys, I'm looking at them, and I'm laughing with them'; and I was suddenly impressed by the fact that I was no longer concerned with whether you could play well. Whether you were able to even know about rock 'n' roll to the extent that you were able to write songs properly wasn't important any longer . . . The Dolls really impressed upon me that there was something else. There was something wonderful. I thought how brilliant they were to be this bad."

No doubt a year later McLaren would be playing Dolls records for the Sex Pistols, just as two decades before Sam Phillips had played old blues records for his new rockabilly singers. A banner McLaren painted up and hoisted over the Dolls' last stages captured the dead time they never escaped: "WHAT ARE THE POLITICS OF BOREDOM?"

IT WAS

It was, once removed, a situationist slogan. "Boredom is always counterrevolutionary," the situationists had liked to say. McLaren's question mark was his way of asking how much power might be secreted in the slogans he put such stock in; to find the answer, you had to use the slogans. "Boredom is always counterrevolutionary"—the line was typical of the situationist style, of its voice, a blindside paradox of dead rhetoric and ordinary language floated just this side of non sequitur, the declarative statement turning into a question as you heard it: what does this mean?

You already know, the situationists had answered: all you lack is the consciousness of what you know. Our project is nothing more than a seductive, subversive restatement of the obvious: "Our ideas are in everyone's mind." Our ideas about how the world works, about why it must be changed, are in everyone's mind as sensations almost no one is willing to translate into ideas, so we will do the translating. And that is all we have to do to change the world.

Boredom, to the situationists, was a supremely modern phenomenon, a modern form of control. In feudal times and for the first century of the Industrial Revolution, drudgery and privation produced numbing fatigue and horrible misery, no mystery, just a God-given fact: "In Adam's fall so sinned we all," and as for those few who knew neither fatigue nor misery, it was easier for a camel to pass through the eye of a needle than for a rich man to enter heaven. As the situationists saw modernity, limited work and relative abundance, city planning and the welfare state, produced not happiness but depression and boredom. With God missing, people felt their condition not exactly as a fact, but simply as a fatalism devoid of meaning, which separated every man and woman from every other, which threw all people back upon themselves. I'm not happy—what's wrong with me?

Fatalism is acceptance: "Que sera, sera" is always counter-revolutionary. But as the situationists understood the modern world, boredom was less a question of work than of leisure. As they set out in the 1950s work seemed to be losing its hold on life; "automation" and "cybernetics" were wonderful new words. Leisure time was expanding—and in order to maintain their power, those who ruled, whether capitalist directors in the West or communist bureaucrats in the East, had to ensure that leisure was as boring as the new forms of work. More boring, if leisure was to replace work as the locus of everyday life, a thousand times more. What could be more productive of an atomized, hopeless fatalism than the feeling that one is deadened precisely where one ought to be having fun?

The eight men and women who gathered in the Italian town of Cosio d'Arroscia on 27 July 1957 to found the Situationist International pledged themselves to intervene in a future they believed to be on the verge of banishing both material necessity and individual autonomy. Modern technology had raised the specter of a world in which "work"—employment, wage labor, whatever tasks were performed because someone else said they had to be—might soon be no more than a fairy tale out of the Brothers Grimm. In a new world of unlimited leisure each individual might construct a life, just as in the old world a few privileged artists had constructed their representations of what life could be. It was an old dream, the dream of the young Karl Marx—every man his own artist!—but those who owned the present saw the future far more clearly than any of the sodden leftist sects claiming Marx's legacy. Those who ruled were reorganizing social life not merely to maintain their control, but to intensify it; modern technics was a two-edged sword, a means to the domination of the free field of abundance and leisure that revolutionaries had fantasized for five hundred years. Thus boredom. Misery led to resentment, which sooner or later found its rightful target, those who ruled. Boredom was a haze, a confusion, and finally the ultimate mode of control, self-control, alienation perfected: a bad conscience.

In modern society, leisure (What do I want to do today?) was replaced by entertainment (What is there to see today?). The potential fact of all possible freedoms was replaced by a fiction of false freedom: I have enough time and money to see whatever there is to see, whatever there is to see others do. Because this freedom was false, it was unsatifying, it was boring. Because it was boring, it left whoever was unsatisfied to contemplate his or her inability to respond to what, after all, was a hit show. It's a good show, but I feel dead: my God, what's wrong with me? It was leisure culture that produced boredom—produced it, marketed it, took the profits, reinvested them. So the world was going to be changed, announced the first number of *Internationale situationniste* in June 1958, *"because we don't want to be bored . . .* raging and ill-informed youth, well-off adolescent rebels lacking a point of view but far from lacking a cause—boredom is what they all have in common. The situationists will execute the judgment contemporary leisure is pronouncing against itself."

The situationists saw boredom as a social pathology; they looked for its negation among sociopaths. In the pages of their journal, lunatic criminals and rioters without manifestos sometimes seem like the only allies the writers are willing to embrace. The situationists meant to define a stance, not an ideology, because they saw all ideologies as alienations, transformations of subjectivity into objectivity, desire into a power that rendered the individual powerless: "There is no such thing as situationism," they said for years. The world was a structure of alienations and ideologies, of hierarchies and bureaucracies, each of which they saw as a version of the other; thus they celebrated a madman's slashing of a famous painting as a symbolic revolt against a bureaucratically administered alienation in which the ideology of the masterpiece reduced whoever looked at it to nothing. In the same way, they understood the responsible parade monitor who tried to keep people in check during a march against the Vietnam War as a bureaucratic ideologue enforcing a split between desire and comportment—and as much the enemy as General William Westmoreland, or for that matter Ho Chi Minh. Both the painting and the war were hit shows; whether a visit to the museum or a march in the street, both turned the spending of free time into the consumption of repression. The masterpiece convinced you that truth and beauty were someone else's gift from God, the protest in favor of the struggle of the Vietnamese that revolution was a fact of someone else's life. Neither could ever be yours, and so you left each show diminished, with less than you had brought to it. That, the situationists said again and again, was why the show had to be stopped, and could be: just as the tiny humiliations inflicted by the parade monitor were the essence of oppression, a fanatic's exemplary act could prove that liberty was within everyone's grasp.

The situationists announced themselves as revolutionaries, interested only in freedom, and freedom can mean the license to do anything, with consequences that are indistinguishable from murder, theft, looting, hooliganism, or littering—phenomena that, lacking anything better, the situationists were almost always ready to embrace as harbingers of revolution. But freedom can also mean the chance to discover what it is you truly want to do: to discover, as Edmund Wilson wrote in Paris in 1922, "for what drama one's setting is the setting." That too was what the situationists meant by leisure—and it was a lust not simply to discover but to create that drama that drove a twenty-five-year-old Parisian named Guy-Ernest Debord to gather artists and writers from France, Algeria, Italy, Denmark, Belgium, England, Scotland, Holland, and West Germany into the Situationist International in 1957. In 1975, with the defunct SI no more than a legend to a few one-time 1960s art students and student radicals, that drama was what McLaren was still seeking. What were the politics of boredom?

DEBORD

Debord wrote "Theses on the Cultural Revolution" for the first number of *Internationale situationniste*: "Victory," he said, "will be for those who know how to create disorder without loving it." As empty of disorder as rock 'n' roll was in 1975, McLaren understood that it remained the only form of culture the young cared about, and at thirty in 1975, he clung to a sixties definition of young—youth was an attitude, not an age. For the young everything flowed from rock 'n' roll (fashion, slang, sexual styles, drug habits, poses), or was organized by it, or was validated by it. The young, who as legal phantoms had nothing and as people wanted everything, felt the contradiction between what life promised and what it delivered most keenly: youth revolt was a key to social revolt, and thus the first target of social revolt could be rock 'n' roll. Connections

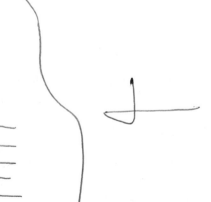

FOR A DIGNIFIED AND EFFECTIVE DEMONSTRATION

Brought to you by the ALL-LONDON UNITED ALLIANCE OF SOCIALIST CAUCUSES to whom the following are signatories: G.L.C., London Labour Party, T.U.C., S.W.P., W.R.P., I.M.G., C.N.D., Ecology Party, Y.C.L., and B.F.

CORRECT

INCORRECT

We welcome everyone to today's demonstration, which we hope will be amongst the biggest London has seen for many years. We are confident that the vast majority of you will keep intact your dignity. A disciplined rally is essential if we are to avoid discrediting ourselves in the eyes of the public and losing the approval of the police. We want to give the media no reason to condemn our campaign by pointing to any over-imaginative acts. To this end, we call on everyone to obey the dictates of the stewards who will be found alongside the police. They will be acting in your interests. They are sensible people — please be sensible with them. Beware of troublemakers — some may be in the crowd with you. If you see any do not hesitate to summon stewards or the police, who, we must remember, are our brothers in work. Comrades! Even in a socialist society we shall still need Specialists-In-Order to combat hooligans and deviants. While it's true that nowadays the police are occasionally over-zealous in their protection of privilege, property, and the violence of the world market, the best way of dealing with this is by demanding public accountability through elected local government or some other representation of sub-missive community. In the meantime we should recognize that they will only listen to our complaints if we conduct ourselves in the correct manner.

RESPECT FOR THE DEAD

Our tactics are those to which the greatest number can conform with the least difficulty. They require no more than your presence and a minimum of participation. All that we ask is that you recreate the conditions of your work. Remember! It's numbers that count; the boredom you feel is also imposed by the demo on everyone else. Each demonstrator must be equivalent to and replaceable by any other. Just like our old friend, the commodity. Please bear in mind that love and marriage go together like a horse and carriage. OK?

We therefore ask you to comply with the following simple rules:

1. Exactly one hundred to a line, each rank to be one yard clear of the line in front. No lounging please.
2. Wait for the initiative of the official loud-speakers before repeating the correct slogans, always recognisable by their format. For example: "X – IN! . . . Y – OUT!" or "WHAT DO WE WANT? – SOMETHING! . . . WHEN DO WE WANT IT? – WHENEVER YOU GET ROUND TO GIVING IT TO US!". Kindly check that all Extra-Parliamentary slogans recognise the ultimate sovereignty of Parliament. If you have any doubts, consult our easy-to-read list of DEMONSTRATION SLOGANS DO's & DON'Ts:–

CHANT		DO NOT CHANT
Cheap Fares Now!	NOT	Helicopters on Demand!
Victory to Fares Fight!	NOT	Total Contestation!
No Return to the '30s!	NOT	No Adventure for the '80s!
Slogans are jolly good fun!	NOT	Bollocks to Demands of our Enemies!
Baaaaaaaaaaaaaa!	NOT	Riot for Romance!

3. The left-hand side of the rally has been designated a 'No Smoking' area. Demonstrators are respectfully asked to comply with this request.
4. If you see any impatient extremists please inform us immediately. They are easily distinguishable by the following kinds of sectarian individualism:

a) Inventing unofficial slogans such as "Kenny is a Cop!", "Neither Left, Right, nor Centre!" or "Revolution is the Festival of the Depressed!" or some other aggressive utopian rubbish.

b) Departing from the prescribed site of the demo for the purpose of indulging in manual waltzes through shop windows and the wilful destruction of saleable goods. Take care to note that Piccadilly, offering gold-drenched shops and fine vistas of the commodity, is a holiday of sheer temptation you should avoid.

c) Making unauthorised alterations to luxury cars.

d) Using banner poles in an extravagantly exhuberant manner.

e) Smoking excessively long cigarettes or 'joints'.

f) Drinking looted alcohol.

coordinated ferocity

g) Suggesting that demonstrators should band together in groups of fifty or more in order to spread disruption of traffic as widely as possible. For example, by the continuous use of zebra crossings, standing around chatting in the middle of the road or arranging obstacles to prevent the free flow of carbon monoxide, lead, cop cars, and tension-producing noises through our streets.

h) Any clever, erotic, or playful expression of individual or group initiative.

Anonymous situationist-inspired leaflet, London, early 1980s

CLOCKWORK FUTILITY

5. During the rally you are urged to clap your favourite speakers. Please confine your enthusiasm to 15 secs per point made in the middle of a speech and a maximum of 30 secs at the end of one. Please do not interrupt with shouts of "BORING"!

6. Always remember to smile at the press cameras and adopt a suitably militant stance even when you feel pissed off with the whole business.

7. If you are uncertain whether a particular mode of behaviour is orderly or not, just do what everybody else is doing. Should any unconventional urges remain do not hesitate to discuss them with one of our stewards. They will be only too pleased to refer you to the appropriate specialist, whether G.P. or S.W.P.

8. At the end of the demo please do not dawdle. Failure to make your way home quickly could result in you missing the sight of yourself on TV.

This leaflet is brought to you courtesy of the ALL-LONDON UNITED ALLIANCE OF SOCIALIST CAUCUSES.

The following have refused to sign this leaflet:

The vandals of St Saviours Primary School who refused to accept their discipline quietly and who wrecked their compulsory prison, causing one sobbing teacher to lament "These youngsters have hardly left their cradles, but they are threatening to take over the school".

The rioters at Bydgoszcz Prison in Poland who fought Communist Party hacks, State Police, and Solidarity union officials, all allied in defence of the walls of the prison against the townspeople who were helping prisoners escape.

The ASLEF traindrivers who avoid wage slavery as much as possible, preferring dancing and drinking to sacrificing themselves to a job which mainly involves transporting other slaves so that they may perpetuate the futility of it all.

The black and white joyriding youth of Clapham who used CB radios for the fun of organising efficient looting.

The Deptford New Cross Marchers of a year ago who in anger and audacity broke away from the march in order to re-distribute wealth in the Bond Street area.

The Toxteth and Southall youths who shouted down Left Labour activists patronising enough to characterize the riots as "understandable but inexcusable".

The truckdrivers of Cleveland, USA, who took over the local distribution of food, medicine, and other necessities, by themselves and without mediation, for over 3 weeks.

---

the road is an arm of the law...

grasping everywhere for the pollution of money

STREET INCREDIBILITY
not permitted

could be made. If one could show that rock 'n' roll, by the mid-1970s ideologically empowered as the ruling exception to the humdrum conduct of social life, had become simply the shiniest cog in the established order, then a demystification of rock 'n' roll might lead to a demystification of social life.

To structure the situation in this way took real imagination, even genius—it doesn't matter whose it was. In the past, rock 'n' roll as a version of revolt had always been seen by its fans as a weapon or, more deeply, as an end in itself, self-justifying: a momentary version of the life everyone would live in the best of all possible worlds. Pete Townshend, in 1968:

Mother has just fallen down the stairs, dad's lost all his money at the dog track, the baby's got TB. In comes the kid with his transistor radio, grooving to Chuck Berry. He doesn't give a shit about mom falling down the stairs . . . It's a good thing that you've got a machine, a radio that puts out rock and roll songs and it makes you groove through the day. That's the game, of course: When you are listening to a rock and roll song the way you listen to "Jumpin' Jack Flash," or something similar, that's the way you should really spend your whole life.

So McLaren heard when a fellow student got up to sing "Great Balls of Fire"—in 1958, the act itself was a negation of social facts. But when rock 'n' roll had become just another social fact, this was self-defeating, even on the level of the next good song. By 1975, Townshend's Candideisms removed rock 'n' roll from the social realities that gave the music its kick. In 1958, even in 1968, a simple rock 'n' roll performance could open up questions of identity, justice, repression, will, and desire; now it was organized to draw such questions into itself and make them disappear.

Who could say that "Fire and Rain," "Stairway to Heaven," "Behind Blue Eyes," and "Maggie May" were not affirmations of freedom as they were made, and oppressions as they were used? Only those who refused to believe that the affirmation where freedom is grasped is rooted in a negation where freedom is glimpsed—and those people did not include McLaren and the Sex Pistols. Thus they damned rock 'n' roll as a rotting corpse: a monster of moneyed reaction, a mechanism for false consciousness, a system of self-exploitation, a theater of glamorized oppression, a bore. Rock 'n' roll, Johnny Rotten would say, was only the first of many things the Sex Pistols came to destroy. And yet because the Sex Pistols had no other weapons, because they were fans in spite of themselves, they played rock 'n' roll, stripping it down to essentials of speed, noise, fury, and manic glee no one had touched before.

They used rock 'n' roll as a weapon against itself. With all instruments but guitar, bass, drums, and voice written off as effete, as elitist accoutrements of a professionalist cult of technique, it was a music best suited to anger and frustration, focusing chaos, dramatizing the last days as everyday life, ramming all emotions into the narrow gap between a blank stare and a sardonic grin. The guitarist laid down a line of fire to cover the singer, the rhythm section put both in a pressure drop, and as a response to what was suddenly perceived as the totalitarian freeze of the modern world the music could seem like a version of it. It was also something new under the sun: a new sound.

IT'S THE OLDEST

It's the oldest hype in the book—and the page that can't be footnoted. After thirty years of rock 'n' roll there are plenty of footnotes: collectors' albums that allow a listener to go back in time, enter the studio that no longer exists, and hear the new sound as it was discovered, flubbed, or even denied. It is a displacing experience.

In Chicago in 1957, trying to cut "Little Village," bluesman Sonny Boy Williamson and his white producer get into an argument over just what, exactly, constitutes a village—an argument resolved only when Williamson shouts, "Little *village*, motherfucker! You name it after yo' mammy if you like!" As a footnote, this explains why Williamson proceeds to take up much of the song with a discussion of what distinguishes a village from a hamlet, a town, or a city; it also explains a great deal about the evolution of the master-slave relationship. In Memphis in 1954, guitarist Scotty Moore responds to a slow, sensual early take of "Blue Moon of Kentucky" by calling nineteen-year-old Elvis Presley a nigger; three years later in the same spot, Jerry Lee Lewis and Sam Phillips engage in an hysterical donnybrook over the question of rock 'n' roll as music of salvation or damnation. These moments explain most of American culture.

In 1959 in New Orleans, Jimmy Clanton, much loathed over the years as a classic example of the white pretty boy who forced authentic black rockers into oblivion, begins "Go, Jimmy, Go," his most loathsome hit. He pauses: "Bop bop bop ba da da," he lilts to the control booth. "Am I singing Mickey Mouse enough yet?" "A little bit more!" comes the answer. "Geez, I'm not Frankie Avalon," says Clanton, just before turning himself into Frankie Avalon. This explains that Clanton's heart was in the right place.

Again in Chicago in 1957, Chuck Berry is about to make another run at "Johnny B. Goode." "Take three!" shouts the producer. "Gotta be good!" Berry and his band lean into the tune, but the opening passage—in the version that made the charts, the most deliciously explosive opening in rock 'n' roll— isn't there. The structure is there, the chords, the notes, everything one could write down on a lead sheet, but the music is battened by a queer languor, a hesitation, a hedged bet. Then one changes records and listens to "Johnny B. Goode" as it has been on the radio since 1958: those notes and chords have grown into a fact that throws off all footnotes. They hit.

And one can listen to *The Great Rock 'n' Roll Swindle*, a two-record documentary of the rise and fall of the Sex Pistols, orchestrated by Malcolm McLaren to prove that the panicky adventures he and the band lived out were part of a plot he had scripted long in advance. The idea this set of footnotes means to get across is that the story of the Sex Pistols—the sudden gulp of social life into the throat of a hunched boy calling himself an antichrist—was from the beginning conceived and delivered as a mere shuck, McLaren's little joke on the world. If Johnny Rotten really meant it when he railed "We *mean* it, man!" in "God Save the Queen," then the joke was on him, or on anyone who believed what he said.

It's a good try. Released in 1979, a year after the Sex Pistols had ceased to be, *The Great Rock 'n' Roll Swindle* includes a lumbering "God Save the Queen Symphony" with fey narration, various depressing post-Sex Pistols rave-ups by the then nearly late Sid Vicious, "Anarchy in the U.K." done in the manner of Michel Legrand and sung entirely in French by one Jerzimy, and a medley of Pistols hits by a happy-feet disco group. Both the French and disco numbers are actually quite appealing: "Pretty Vacant" recast as elevator music is not an uninspired fantasy. But McLaren's effort to show up the Sex Pistols as a con (the secret at the heart of the secret society turns out to be a shaggy-dog story) is blown up by the inclusion of several real Sex Pistols recordings: "Belsen Was a Gas" from the final performance in San Francisco, a sore-throat alternate take of "Anarchy," versions of the Who's "Substitute" and the Monkees' "Stepping Stone," and a combination of "Johnny B. Goode" and Jonathan Richman's "Road Runner."

The last number sounds like a rehearsal—not a rehearsal for a recording session or a concert, but for the idea of the Sex Pistols itself. You can hear them reaching back for the most primitive rock 'n' roll voice in order to destroy the smug self-parody rock 'n' roll had become; at the same time, you can hear them reinventing the music out of whole cloth.

The band heads into "Johnny B. Goode," but Johnny Rotten doesn't know, or won't sing, the words; once past Deep-down-in-Lweezeeanna all he can come up with are squawks, spew, birdcalls. "Ah, fuck, it's *awful*," he moans, but the musicians charge on and take hold of the song. "I *hate* songs like that," Rotten announces: "Stop it, stop it! It's *torture!*" The band won't stop, so finally he screams them down: "AAAAAAAAAAAAH!" They slow the pace. "Is there anything else we can do," he asks hopelessly—and then up from his synapses comes "Road Runner." The association is right: both

> **"'SEX PISTOLS'** *meant to me the idea of a pistol, a pinup, an young thing. A better-looking assassin."*
>
> —Malcolm McLaren, 1988

"Johnny B. Goode" and "Road Runner" are elemental rock statements, the former a founding myth, the story of a little country boy who could play a guitar just like ringing a bell, the latter pretty much an account of listening to him, an account of how good it felt.

The band makes the tiny switch to the second song, and Rotten panics. "I don't know the words," he says. "I don't know how it starts, I've forgotten it!" There is such weary embarrassment in his voice you're afraid he's going to run out of the studio. "Stop it, stop it," Rotten cries again. A thuggish cynicism is fighting the desperation in his voice and losing, the band hasn't stopped for a second, and he gives it one more try: "What's the first line?" And so drummer Paul Cook, courtesy of Jonathan Richman, as the latter wrote at eighteen, in Boston in 1969, calls back: "One, two, three, four, five, six." That is the first line of "Road Runner." With the words in his head, Johnny Rotten, not yet Anarchy or Antichrist, just a kid making new culture out of old chords, takes off.

AS RICHMAN

As Richman finally recorded it, "Road Runner" was the most obvious song in the world, and the strangest. He surfaced around 1970, performing as someone you'd never notice if he weren't standing on a stage making you watch; his themes were traditional (cars, girls, the radio), but with an overlay of moment-to-moment, quotidian realism that made the traditional odd. He sang about standing in line at the bank, falling in love with the teller (or maybe just feeling sorry for her, trying to decide if he'd rather be the teller or the person waiting for her to raise her eyes and not see who she was looking at). He sang about hating hippies, because they wore attitudes like shades, so complete in their smugness, so complete they never noticed *anything*, because they cut themselves off from everything that was good and alive and wonderful about the modern world.

Richman's music did not sound quite sane. When I went to see him play in 1972, his band—the Modern Lovers, which is what he's always called whatever band he's played with—was on stage; nothing was happening. For some reason I noticed a pudgy boy with short hair wandering through the sparse crowd, dressed in blue jeans and a white t-shirt on which was printed, in pencil, "I LOVE MY LIFE." Then he climbed up and played the most shattering guitar I'd ever heard. "I think this is great," said the person next to me. "Or is it terrible?"

"I didn't start singing or playing till I was 15 and heard the Velvet Underground," Richman said years later. "They made an *atmosphere*, and I knew then that I could make one too!" He got sanction: Richman signed with Warner Bros., which had hired John Cale, late of the Velvet Underground, as a staff producer, and it was Cale who was assigned to produce Jonathan Richman—Adam went into the studio with God.

The album they made was not released, and the band dissolved. "Road Runner" was just hearsay until 1975, when Richman assembled a few new Modern Lovers in Berkeley and recorded the song one last time; the tune saw the light of day on an otherwise forgettable sampler of local bands, and from then on it was a classic. Nothing could have been more unassuming: just bass, snare drum, and strummed guitar for the start, it sounded like a combination of a 1954 Sun Records tuneup and a 1967 Velvet Underground demo. Like Rod Stewart's "Every Picture Tells a Story"—a cataclysm, and for most of its seven minutes no more than drums, bass, and acoustic guitar—"Road Runner" said that the power of rock 'n' roll was all in its leaps from one moment to the next, in the impossibility of the transitions.

"One, two, three, four, five, six." One-two / One-two-three-*four* is the traditional rock kickoff; in 1976 and 1977, with punk flying, a flat "One-two-three-four" would be the punk signpost. The punk rejection of the opening "One-two" meant that punk was ready to dispense with any warmup, with history; Richman's addition of "five-six" meant that he wasn't ready, that he was taking a deep breath, that he was gearing up for a charge no one had made before.

"Road runner, road runner / Going faster miles an hour / Gonna drive by the Stop 'n' Shop / With the radio on." Choking on pleasure, on a teenager's nostalgia for the previous day, Richman proceeded to turn wish into fact. He did drive past the Stop 'n' Shop; but first, to make sure, he walked past the Stop 'n' Shop, and concluded that he liked driving past the Stop 'n' Shop much better than walking past the Stop 'n' Shop, because he could have the radio on.

From there Richman drove into delight, then into reverie. He "felt in touch with the modern world"; he "felt in love with the modern world." He "felt like a road runner." He left Boston, headed out on Route 128: there were no limits. He punched the radio and heard 1956; "It was patient in the bushes, next to '57!"

The band hammered down, James Brown-style, and then Richman pulled back like Jerry Lee Lewis in the middle of "Whole Lotta Shakin' Goin' On"—the message first shouted now whispered, reflective, spooky. He was on Route 128. It was cold, dark, he smelled the pine trees, he heard them as he rushed by with the radio on, he caught a glimpse of neon that was colder still—the modern world he was looking for. The band roared back, and Richman talked to the band about what he was seeing. "Now, what do you think about that, you guys?" "RADIO ON," they answered him, and that was what he wanted to hear: "Good! We got the AM—" "RADIO ON," the band said. "I think we got the power, got the magic now—" "RADIO ON." "We got the feelin' of the modern world—" "RADIO ON." "We got the feelin' of the modern sound—" "RADIO ON."

Richman took one more deep breath—and every time I listen to this performance, I smile at what comes next. Every phrase of the song that's come before, the most conventional narrative of an experience millions of people have had in any seamless teenage night, is broken down and recreated. Every phrase is reduced to single words, each word shuffled out of its phrase, verse and chorus broken into a shamanistic incantation, the chorus, left whole, fighting to keep up with the versifier's incomprehensible rhythm and somehow succeeding, even though by now the words are barely words at all, just Burma Shave signs flashing by too fast to read. There is a sudden increase in pressure:

The sound, of the modern radio, feelin' when it's late RADIO ON at night we got the sound of the modern lonely when it's cold outside RADIO ON got the sound of Massachusetts when it's blue and white RADIO ON cause out on Route 128 on the dark and lonely RADIO ON I feel alone in the cold and lonely RADIO ON I feel uh I feel alone in the cold and lonely RADIO ON I feel uh I feel alone in the cold and neon RADIO ON I feel alive I feel a love I feel alive RADIO ON I feel a rockin' modern love I feel a rockin' modern live RADIO ON I feel a rockin' modern neon sound modern Boston town RADIO ON a modern sound modern neon modern miles around RADIO ON I say a road runner once a road runner twice RADIO ON ah ah very nice road runner gonna go home now yea RADIO ON road runner go home oh yes road runner go home—

In an act of pure violence, he breaks the pace. Returning to a conventional rock signature, it's the violence of waking from a dream: "Here we go, now / We're gonna drive him home, you guys / Here we go—" And the band hammers down again, twice three times, twice four times:

> That's right!
> Again!
> Bye Bye!

THE SEX PISTOLS

The Sex Pistols never went that far. Johnny Rotten ran through the tune as if it were a crack in the pavement waiting to break his mother's back: he stepped on it and kept going. He called back to the band: "Do we know any other fucking songs we can do?"

JOHNNY B. GOODE

"Johnny B. Goode" had the best beginning in rock 'n' roll, but the Sex Pistols couldn't play it. "Road Runner" had the best ending, and the Sex Pistols didn't have to play it—all they had to do was swallow it. What Jonathan Richman did with words, the Sex Pistols did with sound.

They found a corrosive momentum in the given rhythm that exploded all expectations, making everything that came before, be it the Velvet Underground's 1967 "Heroin," the Stooges' 1969 "No Fun," the New York Dolls' 1974 "Human Being," even Captain Beefheart's 1969 *Trout Mask Replica*, even "Road Runner," seem rational: planned and executed. The Sex Pistols' sound was irrational—as a sound, it seemed to make no sense at all, to make nothing, only to destroy, and this is why it was a new sound, and why it drew a line between itself and everything that came before it, just as Elvis Presley did in 1954 and the Beatles did in 1963, though nothing could be easier, or more impossible, than to erase those lines with a blur of footnotes.

A lot of people—fans of Chuck Berry, the Beatles, James Taylor, the Velvet Underground, Led Zeppelin, the Who, Rod Stewart, or the Rolling Stones—didn't think this was music at all, or even rock 'n' roll; a smaller number of people thought it was the most exciting thing they'd ever heard. "It was the first taste of rock & roll excitement I ever got," Paul Westerberg of the Replacements said in 1986—ten years after, it was still a story worth telling. "The Sex Pistols made you feel like you knew them, that they weren't above you. It was obvious that they didn't know what they were doing and they didn't care. I was a much better guitar player years ago. I'd sit there and learn the scales, the whole bit. I learned all the slide solos from the Allman Brothers' *At Fillmore East*. I'd put the record on and turn it down to 16 rpm so I could transpose the solos. But then the Sex Pistols came along and said, 'You don't need nothin'. Just play it.'" And what Westerberg said, so said countless other people—describing what they were now allowed to play and what they were now allowed to hear.

The music business was not destroyed. Society did not fall, and a new world did not come into being. If, as Dave Marsh wrote, punk was "an attempt to eliminate the hierarchy that ran rock—ultimately, to eliminate hierarchy, period," it did neither. You could still turn on the radio with the assurance that, on most stations, you would hear "Behind Blue Eyes," "Stairway to Heaven," and "Maggie May"—with the radio terrorized backward by punk, you could hear these songs more often than ever before. But over the next few years, far more than fifteen thousand groups of people made records. They made a blind bet that someone might be interested in what they sounded like or what they had to say, that they themselves might be interested. Some were bent on fame and money, and some were not; some wanted most of all a chance to announce themselves, or anyway to change the world.

Tiny independent labels, most no more than a post-office box and a typed letterhead, sprouted like mushrooms. "Suddenly," read the liner notes to *Streets*, the first collection of U.K. punk singles, "we could do anything." It was a surge of new voices unprecedented in the geopolitics of popular culture—a surge of voices that, for a time, made a weird phrase like "the geopolitics of popular culture" seem like a natural fact.

THE ADVERTS

The Adverts' "One Chord Wonders" takes place right on the verge of the punk moment. The Sex Pistols have cleared the ground—burned it up. There's nothing left but the city standing as if nothing has happened, a patch of smoking dirt in the middle of the city, in the middle of that a lettered piece of wood that in the haze looks as much like a for-rent sign as a condemnation notice: you can't tell if it reads "FREE STREET" or "FIRE SALE."

The people circling the empty space don't know what to do next. They don't know what to say; everything they're used to talking about has been parodied into stupidity as the old words rise in their mouths. Their mouths are full of bile: they're drawn to the void, but they hold back. "Rozanov's definition of nihilism is the best," situationist Raoul Vaneigem had said in 1967 in *Traité de savoir-vivre à l'usage des jeunes générations* (Treatise on Living for the Young Generations, known in English as *The Revolution of Everyday Life*): "'The show is over. The audience get up to leave their seats. Time to collect their coats and go home. They turn round . . . No more coats and no more home.'" That's where they are.

A girl and three boys take the first steps. They enter the black terrain like two-year-olds set down on familiar concrete at the edge of a field of grass—will it hurt? Feeling the lightness of the grass beneath their feet, they run, and as they run a double fantasy possesses them: the crowd smiles, tenses, joins them; it flinches, and stones them to death.

It's the chance of a lifetime. The four grab hold of the wooden sign, break it into pieces, and begin to beat on them: they make a narrow, channeled noise. It's a noise that acknowledges no listeners, connects only to itself: it's random, then focused, helpless, then cruel. That the four can't keep time with each other makes time move so fast it seems to stop: freeze. No one can get out of this moment, and so the four hammer out the common fantasy that possessed them when they first moved toward each other, ages before. The music pulls against itself, the first two or three lines of each verse violent, cynical, present, the next two almost drifting away into a split-second reverie of doubt, regret, a sense of chances already taken and blown, a tense of future past. Only the momentum of the music holds it together.

> I wonder what we'll play for you tonight
> Something heavy, something light
> Something
> To set your soul alight
>
> I wonder how we'll answer when you say
> WE DON'T LIKE YOU! GO AWAY!
> Come back
> When you've learned to play

I wonder what we'll do when things go wrong
When we're halfway
Through our favorite song
We look up
And the audience is gone

"THE WONDERS DON'T CARE!" shout three of the group, "We don't give a damn!" answers the last one, and they press on like that, ten, twenty times, back and forth, but as with the verses the double chorus is opposed to itself: the three singers hard and certain, their chant never varying in tone or speed, the isolated voice hard too at first, then mournful, then despairing, then leaving the cadence as the other side of the chorus marches on in lockstep—that single voice rises, twists almost out of the music, discovers hints of a melody in the banging rhythm, abandons the melody and turns into a scream that comes from deep in the body, then buries itself in a greater noise.

THE SPACE

The space wasn't altogether empty. There was that sign, and attached to the sign was a string that, once pulled, turned the world inside out. As people in the Roxy heard the Adverts, or the two girls and three boys who made up X-ray Spex, or the balding teenage Beckett fan who sang for the Buzzcocks—all people who had climbed out of the Sex Pistols' first audiences—there was a reversal of perspective, of values: a sense that anything was possible, a truth that could be proven only in the negative. What had been good—love, money, and health—was now bad; what had been bad—hate, mendicity, and disease—was now good. The equations ran on, replacing work with sloth, status with reprobation, fame with infamy, celebrity with obscurity, professionalism with ignorance, civility with insult, nimble fingers with club feet, and the equations were unstable. In this new world, where suicide was suddenly a code word for meaning what you said, nothing could be more hip than a corpse, but the affluent survivors you saw on the street every day, the ones you had paid to see in concert halls the day before, were walking corpses. Punk factored the equation with the instinctive apprehension of an old argument: "The only objective way of diagnosing the sickness of the healthy," Theodor Adorno wrote three decades earlier in *Minima Moralia*, "is by the incongruity between their rational existence and the possible course their lives might be given by reason. All the same, the traces of illness give them away: their skin seems covered by a rash printed in regular patterns, like a camouflage of the inorganic. The very people who burst with proofs of exhuberant vitality could easily be taken for prepared corpses, from whom news of their not-quite-successful decease has been withheld for reasons of population policy." In other words, the only good survivor was a dead survivor.

Since heroes were frauds and poverty riches, both murderers and deformity were privileged: had Myra Hindley or the Hunchback of Notre-Dame entered the Roxy the crowd would have boosted them onto the stage. Entertainment was posited as boredom and boredom as the categorical imperative, the destroyer of values, precisely what the new entertainer, shaking her falsity as a sign of authenticity, had to turn into something else: for an hour, for the length of a single song, just a moment within it, the source of values.

There were no more coats, so people began to dress in rips and holes, safety pins and staples through flesh as well as cloth, to wrap their legs in plastic bin liners and trash bags, to drape their shoulders in remnants of curtains and couch coverings left on the street. Following the lead of McLaren's designs for the Sex Pistols and the Clash, people painted slogans up and down their sleeves and pants legs, across jackets, ties, and shoes: the names of favorite bands and songs, passwords like "ANARCHY" or "RIOT," phrases more cryptic ("WHERE IS DU-RUTTI?", "YOUR ON THE NEVER NEVER"), or a noisy, cut-up zeitgeist: "WE AN'T PROUD PUNKS ONE big MESS, like something else SCHOOL'S A RIP OFF straights out of it all, everywhere if you dont we will include 1/4!," the whole scored with a giant X.

"There couldn't have been more than a hundred real punks in all of England then," Lora Logic, in early 1977 the saxophonist for X-ray Spex, said in 1980 of the group's first performance; her working word was "real." There was no more home, so she left hers—left behind the pink uniform she'd worn to her good private school, which, she realized too late, was a mistake, because it would have looked just right on stage. Along with her, the rest of the "real punks," more than a hundred, the two or three or ten in every town in Britain by early 1977, changed the picture of social life.

Punk began as fake culture, a product of McLaren's fashion sense, his dreams of glory, his hunch that the marketing of sado-masochistic fantasies might lead the way to the next big thing. "The art of the critic in a nutshell," Walter Benjamin wrote in 1925–26 in *One-Way Street*: "to coin slogans without betraying ideas. The slogans of an inadequate criticism peddle ideas to fashion." This was Benjamin's careful absolutism—the pre-pop, anti-pop conviction that you can't have it both ways. It was an absolutism an anarchist gold digger like McLaren could have never shared, and didn't have to. In a milieu shaped by the enervation of the pop scene, crushing youth unemployment, IRA terrorism spreading from Belfast to London, growing street violence between British neo-Nazis, colored English, socialists, and the police, punk became real culture.

The way in which punk sound did not make musical sense made social sense: in a few short months, punk came together as a new set of visual and verbal signs, signs that were both opaque and revelatory, depending on who was looking. By its very unnaturalness, its insistence that a situation could be constructed and then, as an artifice, escaped—the graffiti now creeping up from wrecked clothes onto faces, into slashed, dyed hair and across holes in the hair that went to the skull—punk made ordinary social life seem like a trick, the result of sado-masochistic economics. Punk drew lines: it divided the young from the old, the rich from the poor, then the young from the young, the old from the old, the rich from the rich, the poor from the poor, rock 'n' roll from rock 'n' roll. Rock 'n' roll once again became a new story: something to argue about, to search for, to prize and reject, something to hate, something to love. Once again, rock 'n' roll became fun.

FOR REASONS

For reasons the two or three or ten could not articulate beyond songs and screeds (each one, at first, lifted from a Sex Pistols single or interview), everything was now a matter of ugliness, evil, and error, of repulsion, repression, and bondage—sex, love, family, education, pop music, the star system, government, guitar solos, labor, welfare, shopping, traffic, advertising—and everything was all of a piece. The inane radio jingle you heard too many times a day fed into a totality: to get that jingle off the air, you somehow understood, the radio had to be changed, which meant that society had to be changed. The totality came back on the fragment: enough Myra Hindleys, you could imagine in some right-side lobe that knew nothing of language but everything of what language couldn't say, and there would be no more jingles.

Shopping, traffic, and advertising as world-historical insults integrated into everyday life as seductions—in a way, punk was most easily recognizable as a new version of the old Frankfurt School critique of mass culture, the refined horror of refugees from Hitler striking back at the easy vulgarity of their wartime American asylum; a new version of Adorno's conviction, as set out in *Minima Moralia*, that as a German Jewish intellectual in flight from the Nazis to the land of the free he had traded the certainty of extermination for the promise of spiritual death. But now the premises of the old critique were exploding out of a spot no one in the Frankfurt School, not Adorno, Herbert Marcuse, or Walter Benjamin, had ever recognized: mass culture's pop cult heart. Stranger still: the old critique of mass culture now paraded as mass culture, at the least as protean, would-be mass culture. If punk was a secret society, the goal of every secret society is to take over the

Lora Logic,
1979

world, just as the goal of every rock 'n' roll band is to make everyone listen.

Probably no definition of punk can be stretched far enough to enclose Theodor Adorno. As a music lover he hated jazz, likely retched when he first heard of Elvis Presley, and no doubt would have understood the Sex Pistols as a return to Kristallnacht if he hadn't been lucky enough to die in 1969. But you can find punk between every other line of *Minima Moralia*: its miasmic loathing for what Western civilization had made of itself by the end of the Second World War was, by 1977, the stuff of a hundred songs and slogans. If in the Sex Pistols' records all emotion is reduced to the gap between a blank stare and a sardonic grin, in Adorno's book all emotion is compressed into the space between curse and regret—and on that field, the slightest reach toward compassion or creation can take on a charge of absolute novelty; along with every sort of fraud and swindler, negation empowers the smallest gesture. The negationist, Raoul Vaneigem wrote, is "like Gulliver lying stranded on the Lilliputian shore with every part of his body tied down; determined to free himself, he looks about keenly: the smallest detail of the landscape, the smallest contour of the ground, the slightest movement, everything becomes a sign on which his escape may depend." When life is recast in these terms, when domination is posited, when a mere gesture, a new way of walking, can signify liberation, one result is an almost limitless opportunity for popular art.

Minima Moralia was written as a series of epigraphs, of ephemeralities, each severed block of type marching relentlessly toward the destruction of whatever intimations of hope might appear within its boundaries, each paragraph headed by an impotent oath, a flat irony, each (chosen at random) a good title for a punk 45: "Unfair intimidation," "Blackmail," "Sacrificial Lamb," "They, the People." After 1977 a spoken-rant lp could have been made into an album called *Big Ted Says No* and it would have made perfect pop sense, and for that matter it did: listen to *Metal Box* by PiL, Johnny Rotten's post-Sex

Pistols band, read *Minima Moralia* as you listen, and see if you can tell where one leaves off and the other begins.

What Adorno's negation lacked was glee—a spirit the punk version of his world never failed to deliver. Walking the streets as pose and fashion, Adorno's prophecies were suffused with happiness, a thrill that made them simple and clear. "I am the fly," Wire sang in the Roxy: "I am the fly / I am the fly in the ointment." The Frankfurt School critique was rusting boilerplate by 1977, less refuted by history or better ideas than turned into an irritating jingle by having topped too many art-student, student-radical charts in the 1960s: All of social life is organized / From the top down / Through impenetrable hierarchies / To make you into a receptacle / For the culture / That will seduce you into functioning / As a robot in the economy. What was new was the impact of the jingle, its new sound. Now you could name it and claim it. Bits of a theory contrived before you were born rose out of the pavement and hit you in the face as if you'd fallen headfirst onto the concrete. Your face was a totality, in the mirror a representation of the only totality you really knew, and the shock of recognition changed your face—now you walked down the street with a frozen mouth that looked like a death sentence to passersby and felt like a smile to you. Because your face was your totality, and the shock had changed it, the shock changed the street. Once out of the nightclub and onto the pavement, every gray public building came alive with secret messages of aggression, domination, malignancy.

TO MASTER

To master this vision of ugliness, people acted it out. Today, after more than a decade of punk style, when a purple and green Mohawk on the head of a suburban American teenager only begs the question of how early he or she has to get up to fix his or her hair in time for school, it's hard to remember just how ugly the first punks were.

"**T H E P H O N E** never stopped ringing," said fire Capt. Donald Pearson, 32. "People were calling from all over the state. We now understand the term 'media event.'"

Pearson said, "The most memorable part of the week was when we cut the tree through and the bees started coming out. There were 30 or 40 reporters and photographers around and some of them started running."

The fire fighters said [Officer] Racicot had the best description of the killer bees.

"The killer bees are the ones with the leather jackets and the punk hairdos," he said. "You can't miss 'em."

—San Francisco Examiner, 28 July 1985, on the first discovery of "killer bees" in California

They were ugly. There were no mediations. A ten-inch safety pin cutting through a lower lip into a swastika tattooed onto a cheek was not a fashion statement; a fan forcing a finger down his throat, vomiting into his hands, then hurling the spew at the people on stage was spreading disease. An inch-thick nimbus of black mascara suggested death before it suggested anything else. The punks were not just pretty people, like the Slits or bassist Gaye of the Adverts, who made themselves ugly. They were fat, anorexic, pockmarked, acned, stuttering, crippled, scarred, and damaged, and what their new decorations underlined was the failure already engraved in their faces.

The Sex Pistols had somehow permitted them to appear in public as human beings, to parade their afflictions as social facts. "I was waiting for the Communist call," Johnny Rotten sang on his way to the Berlin Wall in "Holidays in the Sun"; from the same western side of the wall, the narrator in Peter Schneider's 1982 novel *The Wall Jumper*, his mind turned inside out by repeated viewings of the ideologically reversed versions of the news offered by East and West Berlin TV, asks the same question punk raised: "Doesn't every career in Western society, whether that of an athlete, investor, artist, or rebel, depend on the assumption that every initiative is one's own, every idea original, every decision completely personal? What would happen to me if I stopped finding fault with myself, as I've been taught to do, and blamed everything on the state?" More than trash bags or torn shirts, punks wore Adorno's morbid rash; they inked or stenciled it over themselves in regular patterns. As Adorno's prepared corpses, more consciously prepared than he could have imagined, they exploded with proofs of vitality—that is, they said what they meant.

In so doing, they turned Adorno's vision of modern life back upon itself: Adorno had not imagined that his corpses might know what they meant to say. Punks were those who now understood themselves as people from whom the news of their not quite successful decease had been withheld for reasons of population policy—as punk defined the no-future, society was going to need a lot of zombie counterpersons, shoppers, bureaucrats, welfare petitioners, a lot of people to stand in lines and man them. The difference was that these people had heard the news.

I WISH

"I wish I could see us," Sex Pistols guitarist Steve Jones said. Maybe that's what Johnny Rotten meant when he said he wanted "more bands like us." He got them—dozens of groups, then hundreds, then thousands, that cut their own singles weeks after forming (or, if one goes by the sound of some of the sides, before forming), put them out on one-shot labels with names like Raw, Frenzy, and Zero, and sold them at shows, independent record stores, through the mail. Most were never meant for the radio; as if in answer to the repression suffered by the Sex Pistols, groups like the Cortinas, the Lurkers, Eater, and Slaughter and the Dogs made music so brutal, haphazard, or obscene that airplay was out of the question. Given the assumption that the normal channels of pop communication were irrelevant, all restrictions on what could go into a record or a performance, on what a record could sound like or what a performance could look like, were forgotten. Males could abjure macho posing or push it to ridiculous extremes; females could ignore the few roles reserved for women in rock—they could ignore roles altogether.

If in wartime only the clandestine press is free ("The only great nation with a completely uncensored press today," A. J. Liebling wrote two months before D-Day, "is France"), then it was the fact that the official pop space was closed to most of punk that allowed punk to create its own space of freedom. Though the best-known bands immediately signed with major record companies, that half-dozen meant nothing to the hundreds and thousands in the pop wilderness: there something like a new pop economy, based less on profit than on subsistence, the will to shock, marginal but intense public response—a pop economy meant to support not careers but hit-and-run raids on the public peace of mind—began to take shape. People cut records not so much on the off-chance that they would hit, but to join in: to say "I'm here" or "I hate you" or "I have a big cock" or "I have no cock." Teenagers discovered the thrill of shouting "FIRE" in a crowded theater—or even in an empty theater.

It was a fad, something to do when you could get your parents' permission to stay out late and change your hairstyle (you didn't tell your parents you had changed your name from Elizabeth Mitchell to Sally Thalidomide). A satire of the time caught the fad as well as anything, matching the heedless typography and illiterate syntax of the fanzines that were spreading the news:

x . . . tell me wolf, how did this whole snuff rock scene start?

wolf frenzy . . . well . . . huh . . . like its difficult to be precise, but I think it was the night the bass player in the noise offed himself. he was really pissed off because hed been getting a really good sound out of his equipment, so he jumped off the top of his bass stack breaking his neck and impaling himself on his tuning pegs.then there was a really spontaneous reaction from the crowd.

x . . . what sort of reaction?

wolf frenzy . . . well . . . you know . . . they all laughed an that.

x . . . what do you think of the so called disease groups like the boils,pus,or superdischarge,who rather than killing themselves outright,infect themselves with deadly diseases and deter deterior det get sicker ever gig until they die.

frenzy . . . well it depends.its and interesting concept and it certainly attracts a hard core of fans.they dont like to miss a gig cos they like to see how the sickness is progressing.some of them will travel hundreds of miles just to watch a finger fall off somebody.but it really depends on the disease,i mean someone with rabies is gonna do a really high energy gig,with lots of leaping about whereas a guy with yellow fevers gonna be just too laid back,like j.j. cale.what interests me more is the sounds coming out of jamaica,you know like natty dead,i dub a snuff,or snuffin in a soundcheck,that sort of thing.

x . . . what do you think of the news that andy williams is reported to be doing a simulated snuff act in his new tv series.

frenzy . . . its just pathetic innit.its just what youd expect from him.but this is one scene they cant package and sell back to the kids who created it because theyre all dead.but were not elitist. wed dearly love to see some of the really big stars like rod stewart and elton john getting snuffed.

x . . . i think most people would.

It was a fad, so people banished the love song: the sleeve of Radio Stars' *Songs for Swinging Lovers* pictured a young couple hanging from a tree. They sang instead about masturbation, jobs, class, cigarettes, traffic lights, fascist dictators, race, the subway. Banishing the love song, people discovered what else there was to sing about. The love song had draped their lives in cheap poetry; maybe now other matters might poeticize their lives. As faddists, punks played with Adorno's negative dialectics, where every yes turns into a no; they straddled their unstable equations. The mother of Sex Pistols drummer Paul Cook coined the name Johnny Rotten in honor of the singer's green teeth; singing about advertisements, deodorants, fake identities, supermarkets, an overweight half-caste teenager with braces on her teeth changed herself from Marion Elliot into Poly Styrene and called her band X-ray Spex after the glasses she liked to wear. "Anti-art was the start," she roared in her one-note voice; an interviewer asked her what she was about. "I like to consume," she said, "because if you don't, it consumes you." No one knew what that meant, or if "Poly Styrene" was good or bad, irony or embrace, an attack on better living through chemistry or a claim that Poly liked to wear it.

That was punk: a load of old ideas sensationalized into new feelings almost instantly turned into new clichés, but set forth with such momentum that the whole blew up its equations day by day. For every fake novelty, there was a real one. For every third-hand pose, there was a fourth-hand pose that turned into a real motive.

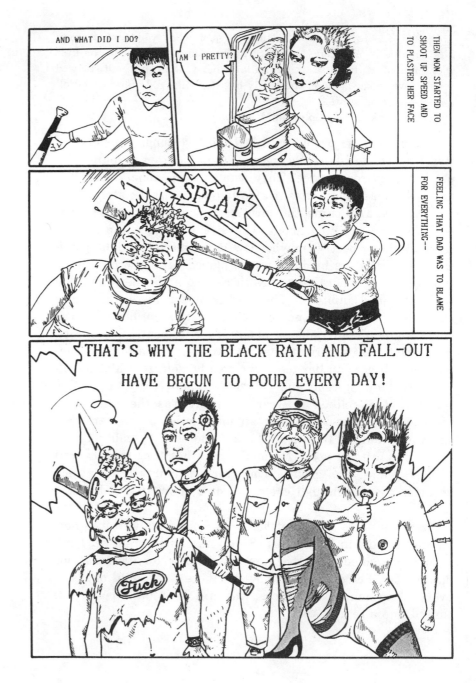

Reading right to left, another version of the punk story, 1986

THE SHOCK

The shock of punk is no longer in its thuggery, misogyny, racism, homophobia, its yearning for final solutions to questions it barely asked, in negation's empowerment of every fraud and swindle. "The punk stance," Lester Bangs wrote in 1979, is "riddled with self-hate, which is always reflexive, and any time you conclude that life stinks and the human race mostly amounts to a pile of shit, you've got the perfect breeding ground for fascism." There was a time in London in 1977 when Jack the Ripper was the ultimate punk, and everything from thuggery to death camps was part of the moment, Eater's frothing "Get Raped" seemingly as true as the Buzzcocks' sly equation of shopping and dating in "Breakdown," all these things briefly legitimized by an irruption affirming itself through the embrace of whatever was officially scorned and stigmatized by society at large.

Today, so many years later, the shock of punk is that every good punk record can still sound like the greatest thing you've ever heard. "A Boring Life," "One Chord Wonders," X-ray Spex's "Oh Bondage Up Yours!," the Sex Pistols' singles, the Clash's "Complete Control"—the power in these bits of plastic, the tension between the desire that fuels them and the fatalism waiting to block each beat, the laughter and surprise in the voices, the confidence of the music, all these things are shocking now because, in its two or three minutes, each is absolute. You can't place one record above the other, not while you're listening; each one is the end of the world, the creation of the world, complete in itself. Every good punk record made in London in 1976 or 1977 can convince you that it's the greatest thing you've ever heard because it can convince you that you never have to hear anything else as long as you live—each record seems to say everything there is to say. For as long as the sound lasts, no other sound, not even a memory of any other music, can penetrate.

As John Peel said, it was like the 1950s, when surprise after surprise came off the radio—but with a difference. If the singers who made fifteen thousand doo-wop records were amateurs, the musicians who backed them were professionals; if they had no idea what social facts the records might dissolve, they knew which chords came next. The punks who made records in 1977 didn't know what chords came next—and they hurled themselves at social facts. The sense that a social fact could be addressed by a broken chord produced music that changed one's sense of what music could be, and thus changed one's sense of the social fact: it could be destroyed. That was what was new: there was no sense of the end of the world in 1950s rock 'n' roll.

There is a feeling in the best punk 45s that what must be said must be said very fast, because the energy required to say what must be said, and the will to say it, can't be sustained. That energy is going to disappear, that will is going to shatter—the idea will go back in the ground, the audience will get up, put on their coats, and go home. Like its rhythm, the punk voice was always unnatural: speeded up past personality into anonymity, pinched, reduced, artificial. It called attention to its own artificiality for more than one reason: as a rejection of mainstream pop humanism in favor of resentment and dread; as a reflection of the fear of not being understood. But the voice was unnatural most of all out of its fear of losing the chance to speak—a chance, every good punk singer understood, that was not only certain to vanish, but might not even be deserved.

The sense of risk one can hear in punk is a distrust of the punk moment itself. It is the will to say everything cut with the suspicion that to say everything may be worth nothing. No one knew where the chance came from, and no one knew what would come of it—save that it couldn't last. Rock 'n' roll had barely said its name in the 1950s when Danny and the Juniors announced that "Rock and Roll Is Here to Stay"; there was no such song in punk. Punk wasn't here to stay. Punk was not an opportunity to exploit, no matter how many commercial plots Malcolm McLaren hatched, no matter how many one-time Sex Pistols fans went on to international New Wave

"ANYTHING THAT'S new takes a while before it gets disseminated across the country. You get the J. C. Penney versions of fashions of what the style leaders are wearing. There's an interesting premise in all of this, in the youth world, you take the lunatic fringe, the avant-garde, the style leaders, the nuts. And if you are careful enough to determine what they come up with that's a legitimate trend, then you'll be able to figure out eventually what the people in the middle, I don't mean necessarily geographically, but in the case of our country it is pretty much the middle, will be doing in the next number of months."

—Dick Clark, in Lester Bangs, "Screwing the System with Dick Clark," Creem, November 1973

fame and success. "New Wave" was a code word not for punk without shock, but for punk without meaning. Punk was not a musical genre; it was a moment in time that took shape as a language anticipating its own destruction, and thus sometimes seeking it, seeking the statement of what could be said with neither words nor chords. It was not history. It was a chance to create ephemeral events that would serve as judgments on whatever came next, events that would judge all that followed wanting—that, too, was the meaning of no-future.

MUCH HAS

Much has been made of punk's antecedents in Chuck Berry; in the Kinks and the Who; in the American garage bands; in the Velvet Underground, the Stooges, the New York Dolls; in such British precursors as David Bowie, Roxy Music, Mott the Hoople; in the arty, ironic New York scene that emerged in 1974—especially as exemplified by the Ramones. "Beat on the brat / With a baseball bat"—what could be more punk than that? Not stopping there—and that is where the Ramones stopped for years. Yes, the Sex Pistols encored with the Stooges' "No Fun," as sons they killed their father-Dolls with "New York," Velvets covers were a punk touchstone, but this is just arithmetic. If what is interesting about punk is something other than its function as a musical genre, there is no point in treating it as one.

As algebra, one could as easily say that punk came from two lines in "Tale in Hard Time," a song Richard Thompson wrote in 1968 for Fairport Convention, a mostly quiet, reflective British folk-rock group: "Take the sun from my heart / Let me learn to despise." Whether or not a single punk ever heard those words is irrelevant, as irrelevant as whether or not a single punk ever read a word by the writers whose adventures make up most of the story of this book. The best of them played those words out. Drawing whatever truth Thompson's plea held out of their own history, their own blind inheritance, the first punks used his plea as a bet. The likely result was that one would pass through the future not as a survivor, but as a ruin: a shabby old man in the rain. The odds were implicit in the event—and in 1985, in Los Angeles, with "punk" still the only new story rock 'n' roll had to tell, a band called God and the State, formed two years before, defunct about the same time, would sum up the story with its sole, posthumous record, a collection of demos called *Ruins: The Complete Works of God and the State.*

Here it was: the punk pottery shard. The notes to the disc told the reader that the band members had come together in a certain place and time, and then separated—scattered all over the globe. Whoever was left in L.A. to put out the album wrote on the sleeve: "The record was produced in ten hours, for $200. There are a lot of jokes in the songs; but some listeners don't think they're funny, and others don't even think they're jokes, rather symptoms of spiritual decay. There is an intended message of hope, of finding power in yourself against domination and power's corruption; but some find the songs as cynical and as glib as the clever people they occasionally denounce." And that may be the best possible description of punk's would-be secret society, save for these words from Jean-Pierre Gorin's film *Routine Pleasures,* which is about a model railroad club: "We are all like bit players in a Preston Sturges movie, ready to testify in front of a small-town jury in terms whose relevance would escape anyone but ourselves."

IN WINTERLAND

In Winterland on 14 January 1978, punk was no secret society. When the crowd was faced with a band that was already legend, with the thing itself, "punk" became a representation several times removed. One had heard that, in the U.K., audiences "gobbed"—spit—at punk performers; in San Francisco the Sex Pistols were greeted with a curtain of gob. One had heard that, in the U.K., there was violence at punk shows (the storied event told of a woman losing an eye to a shattered beer glass; Sid Vicious was said to be responsible, though he denied it, but not that he had beaten a journalist with a chain); in San Francisco a man in a football helmet butted his way through the crowd, smashed a paraplegic out of his wheelchair, and was himself beaten to the floor. Hadn't Johnny Rotten said he wanted to destroy passersby? It was, at this point, an act: a collective attempt to prove that the physical representation of an aesthetic representation could produce reality, or at least real blood.

NOT FOR LONG

Not for long; with the Sex Pistols on stage, everything changed. Slumping like Quasimodo under heavy air, Johnny Rotten cut through the curiosity of the crowd with a twist of his neck. He hung onto the microphone stand like a man caught in a wind tunnel; ice, paper cups, coins, books, hats, and shoes flew by him as if sucked up by a vacuum. He complained about the quality of the "presents"; a perfectly rolled umbrella landed at his feet. "That'll do," he said.

Sid Vicious was there to bait the crowd; two fans climbed onto the stage and bloodied his nose. A representation of a representation, even streaked with his own gore, his arm bandaged from a self-inflicted gouging, he was, in a strange way, hardly there at all: this was actually not happening. For decades, pulp rock novels had ended with a scene out of *The Golden Bough*, with the ritual devouring of the star by his followers, and Sid Vicious was begging for it, for the absolute confirmation that he was a star. A few feet away, Johnny Rotten was eating the expectations the crowd had brought with it.

Paul Cook was hidden behind his drums. Steve Jones sounded like he was playing a guitar factory, not a guitar; it was inconceivable there were only three instruments on stage. The stage was full of ghosts; song by song, Johnny Rotten ground his teeth down to points.

I CAN COMPARE

I can compare the sensation this performance produced only to
Five Million Years to Earth, a film made in England in 1967
under the title *Quatermass and the Pit.*

The time and place is Swinging London, where the reconstruction of a subway station has revealed a large, oblong,
metal object: a spaceship, as any moviegoer could tell the cops
and bureaucrats who can't. Near the object are the fossilized
remains of apemen; within it are the perfectly preserved
corpses of human-sized insects. The scientist Quatermass is
called in.

Putting the pieces together, he determines that, five million
years before, Martians—the insects—faced with the extinction
of life on their own planet, sent a small band of scientists to
earth. Their goal is to implant the Martian essence in an alien
life form (the gimmick is a nice anticipation of the theory of
the selfish gene): to find a home for the soul of the Martian
race.

The Martians, Quatermass slowly learns, were by nature
genocidal: the death of their planet is their own work. Indeed
it is their masterpiece, and so to maintain themselves on earth
they must destroy it. The Martian scientists select the most
promising earth creatures—australopithecines, which emerged
perhaps eight million years ago, and which most paleoanthro-
pologists consider directly ancestral to our own genus—and,
through genetic surgery, set a small group on the road to pla-
netary dominance. Endowed with the Martian traits of cogni-
tion and bloodlust (the latter notion, in 1967, a nod to the
fashionable human-origin theories of Robert Ardrey), the
chosen australopithecines follow their coded path to Homo sa-
piens and inherit the earth. Once the new species has achieved
the technology necessary to dominate nature, destiny will be
manifested in its destruction.

But the graft is not perfect; the contradiction between earth
and Martian genes is never fully absorbed. Though there is no
consciousness of the intervention, there is a phylogenetic mem-

ory. Freud believed that modern people in some fashion remember, as actual events, the parricides he thought established human society, and unconsciously preserve that memory in otherwise inexplicably persistent myths and rituals; in *Moses and Monotheism* he argued that, hundreds of years after the fact, the Israelites carried a memory of their forebears' murder of a first Moses, even though in oral and written traditions the event was completely suppressed. In *Five Million Years to Earth* the argument is that modern people remember step-parents who, with infinite patience, set out to kill their progeny—and the idea explains why, with their all-powerful science, the Martians did not simply wipe out life on earth as they found it. They meant to perpetuate themselves on earth by making its history—by coding its end in its beginning. A passion for prophecy, it seems, is also a Martian trait: they loved drama as much as death.

For Quatermass, all sorts of phenomena that as a scientist he has dismissed as relics of an irrational past take on a new meaning. Poring through books on ritual and myth, he begins to understand that along with its domination of nature, its march toward mastery and abundance, the new species has produced irreducible images of a primordial displacement. They are attempts to cast the alien out; to abstract the implanted traits from the body, to reify them into demonism. But there is a contradiction here too: it is only the alien intelligence that permits the species to engage in a process as complex as reification—a sort of fetishization of alienation, where human properties are transferred to things that human beings have themselves produced, things that then operate autonomously, finally turning human beings into things—and reification cuts a two-way street. Once expelled, once removed into a representation of the demonic, the alien presence casts a spell. Quatermass discovers that not only did the Martians put their name on the site of the subway station where their remains were found (frantic research reveals that its address, "Hobb's Lane," once meant "Devil's Haunt"), thus making it, in medieval times, a cursed place, they have, in the shape of the part-human, part-horned-animal figure of "The Sorcerer," inscribed their image on the wall of the Cro-Magnon sanctuary of Trois Frères, thus making it, in paleolithic times, a place of worship. "The Sorcerer" echoes across fifteen thousand years into an otherwise inexplicable Christian prayer: "The Lord is in this place, how dreadful is this place." Human history begins to make sense, but it is no longer human.

The disturbance in the subway station calls up the dormant Martian presence. The spaceship begins to vibrate, and the energy released by the vibrations creates a vacuum. The vacuum sucks up sleeping genes, which create a repulsive, beckoning image: a glowing, horned devil, overshadowing London, the Martian Antichrist.

Across five million years, genetic drift is not uniform. By the twentieth century, some people are coded for destruction; some carry only a few broken alien messages. Some respond to the Martian image; some do not. For those who do, the ancient codes become language, and memories of the original Martian genocide course to the surface. For those who do not respond, language dissolves. Humanity is split into two species; there is anarchy in London. Men and women surge through the streets smashing all those they recognize as alien: all who carry less of the Martian essence than they do. The Martian image turns red. Hobbes's state of nature was "the war of all against all"; this is it, and it is lurid beyond belief.

More human than Martian, Quatermass lives to see the demonic image vanquished and the Martian genes put back to sleep—but not before a comrade, more human than Quatermass, who can stand to gaze into the face of the image as Quatermass cannot, has been exploded in the attack. The image is pure phylogenetic energy; guiding a steel crane straight into it, Quatermass' comrade negates the image with mass—a neat Einsteinian twist.

Quatermass' assistant, more Martian than he, returns to his side as if awakened from a dream; minutes before, she was squeezing blood out of his neck. In a long, silent shot, the movie ends—and because there is no freeze frame, no automatic irony, the movie doesn't seem to end at all. Quatermass and his assistant are seen in the wreckage of London; he leans on a ruined wall. Everything he has seen is in his eyes, and he is trying to forget what he has seen, but the shot—it goes on and on—doesn't last long enough for his assistant's eyes to focus.

Now it is plain that *Five Million Years to Earth* is a 1960s version of 1950s atomic-bomb-mutation films; an exculpatory allegory of Nazism and the Blitz; a quick and easy update of the gnostic heresy in which the world is split between equally empowered Good and Evil gods; a bid to make fast money off whatever dislocations might be circulating in modern society at any given time. It doesn't play like that. It is progressively horrifying—especially at 2 A.M., when it is most readily seen on television; when, as Nietzsche wrote, "man permits himself to be lied to . . . when he dreams, and his moral sense never even tries to prevent this"; when there is no one with whom one might dominate the film. Quatermass' victory is the victory of rational certainty over irrational doubt; the doubt in his face at the end is not doubt that he has won, but doubt that he wanted to. Perhaps it is no accident that, on occasion, the Late Show has cut the last twenty minutes: cut the anarchy, offering only the mystery, its formal solution, and then the film's last shot, which no longer carries any meaning.

THAT WAS HOW

That was how I felt when Johnny Rotten sang "Anarchy in the U.K.," "Bodies," "No Feelings," "No Fun." When he finished that last number, his last performance as a member of the Sex Pistols, when he threw it all back on the crowd—which was, to him, no more than a representation of a representation, five thousand living symbols of Scott McKenzie's 1967 Love Generation hit, "San Francisco (Be Sure to Wear Flowers in Your Hair)," symbols of mindlessly benevolent hippies who knew nothing of negation—when he said, leaving the stage, carefully gathering up any objects of value, "Ever get the feeling you've been cheated?," that was how I felt.

At Altamont in 1969, as the Rolling Stones played and a man was stabbed and kicked to death in the midst of the crowd in front of the stage, I had felt only loathing and distance; the peace symbols people flashed were almost as ugly as the violence itself. They affirmed nothing but the primacy of symbolization; the same people who raised those symbols also snarled and pushed for a patch of ground. I wasn't implicated for a second, and I contemplated the degradation of it all. At Winterland people pushed, but not, it seemed, with anger or fear, but with delight, almost as a greeting—if André Breton's old "simplest surrealist act," firing a pistol into a crowd of strangers, or ramming through it in a football helmet, can be called a greeting. Halfway through the show, what had begun in the crowd as an act was turning into a new way of walking.

Over the next years this moment took many forms. In punk clubs in Los Angeles, then throughout the United States and around the world, it would be stylized into slam dancing and pit diving. It would shape a glossary in which the passive neologisms of 1970s human-potential and self-improvement therapies ("Thank you for sharing your anger with me") were translated back into active English ("Fuck off and die"). In convoluted ways, it would help define the spirit of the riots that swept the U.K. in the summer of 1981. More proximately, in contempt of all authority, it would lead to an immense increase in littering. It would permit thuggishness and scapegoating to be glamorized as self-expression (in the 1983 film *Suburbia*, a skinhead in an L.A. punk club approaches a woman dressed in a glitzy party dress. "I'd like to fuck your brains out," he says, "but you don't look like you got any." She tries to push him away; he rips her clothes off and leaves her to the crowd), and it would inspire Gudrun Thompson's "Manners for Muggings," which appeared in a San Francisco punk tabloid called *Damage*. Illustrating her demand for a new etiquette with photos of herself beating up the hulking Stannous Fluoride, her boyfriend, Thompson wrote:

The eyes are the most vulnerable points in the body. The best way to attack the eyes are with the fingers or thumbs. Stiffen your fingers, part them slightly, and drive them THROUGH your attacker's eyes. Drive your finger THROUGH HIS HEAD . . . Never believe a promise that you will not be harmed if you cooperate. Once gaining control over your life for even a few minutes, your attacker may decide to exterminate you. He is not considering you as a human being with a right to exist—don't consider him one. DESTROY HIM before he destroys you.

Never feel sorry for someone who attacks you or feel you asked for it. Anyone who dares to threaten your safety and well being DESERVES TO DIE.

I pushed, too. Walking the aisles of Winterland as the Sex Pistols played, I felt a confidence and a lust that were altogether new. Thirty-two years had not taught me what I learned that night: when you're pushed, push back; when a shove negates your existence, negate the shove. I felt distant from nothing, superior to nothing. I also felt a crazy malevolence, a wish to smash people to the ground, and my eyes went to the ground, where I saw small children (what sort of parents would bring little kids to a place like this, I wondered, thinking of my own at home), and thought of smashing them.

Reviewing the concert for a magazine, I mentioned none of this. Days later, it seemed unreal. Seeing Johnny Rotten on stage, I was sure I would never see his like again, and so far I have been right.

. . . .

AFRIKA BAMBAATAA: "Who wants to be / A president or king?"

JOHN LYDON: "ME!"

—"World Destruction," Time Zone, 1984

. . . .

IMMEDIATELY AFTER

Immediately after the last show of the Sex Pistols' only American tour, Johnny Rotten reclaimed his given name, John Lydon. In May 1534 John of Leyden, a Dutch heretic also known as Jan Bockelson, was proclaimed king of the German town of Münster, the New Jerusalem was, thus, proclaimed king of the whole world.

Earlier in the year, a group of radical Anabaptists—one of many new Protestant sects bent on replacing decadent church rituals with a literal practice of the Gospels—had seized control of Münster. At first they simply forced the town council to pass a bill legalizing "liberty of conscience"—that is, legalizing heresy, an unthinkable act even in the heyday of the Reformation. The Anabaptists quickly drove out the Lutheran majority, repopulated the town with like-minded neighbors, and, under the leadership of a baker named Jan Matthys, established a theocracy. By March, Norman Cohn wrote in 1957 in *The Pursuit of the Millennium* (a book that, published in France as *Fanatiques de l'apocalypse*, the situationists would carefully plunder), Münster was purified: refounded as a community of the Children of God, bound by love to live without sin.

All property was expropriated. Money was abolished. The doors of all houses were made to be left open day and night. In a great bonfire, all books save the Bible were destroyed. "The poorest amongst us," read a Münster pamphlet meant to subvert the countryside, "who used to be despised as 'beggars,' now go about dressed as finely as the highest and most distinguished." "All things were to be in common," John of Leyden said later. "There was to be no private property and nobody was to do any more work, but simply trust in God." In every instance the new commandments were enforced with the threat of execution.

Outside the walls of the city, Anabaptism—bits of which survive today in certain Pentecostal creeds—was itself made a capital offense; hundreds, perhaps thousands, were tortured and put to death. The local bishop organized an army of mercenaries and laid siege to Münster; in a divinely ordained sortie against the bishop's forces, Jan Matthys was killed and John of Leyden took his place.

He ran through the town naked, then was silent for three days. During that time God revealed a new order. Matthys' social revolution was suddenly exposed as abstract; John of Leyden was to take the revolution to the smallest details of everyday life, where death was to be the only sanction against any sin: murder, theft, avarice, quarrelling, the insubordination of children, the naysaying of wives.

Polygamy was mandated. It was made a capital crime for women of childbearing age to remain unmarried, or for new wives gathered under one man's roof to differ. The streets were given new names, and John of Leyden chose the names of newborns. Spectacles were staged: great dinners, followed by beheadings. Black masses were held in the cathedral, gutted long before.

Still under siege, though carrying out a fierce defense that kept supply lines open, the citizens of Münster lived on rations; John of Leyden feasted, and dressed in gold and silk. The Brethren of the Free Spirit, who since the early thirteenth century had spread the social heresies of "all things in common" and "never work" across Europe, had believed that for those truly free in spirit, no crime was a crime and no sin was a sin—indeed, God's grace was to be found in the practice of the worst "sins," for it was only so that one could prove one was incapable of stain. John of Leyden told his city that he was permitted luxury and indulgence because he "was dead to the world and the flesh"—and that, soon, so would be all.

In January 1535 the bishop regrouped his forces and blockaded the town. By April every animal, the last rat and mouse, had been eaten; then grass, then moss, then shoes and whitewash, and finally human bodies. John of Leyden announced that as the Bible promised God would turn the cobblestones to bread; people tried to eat them. Cursed with eternal damnation, doubters were permitted to leave; able-bodied men were immediately killed by the bishop's troops. Women, children, and old men, as if infected with plague, were left between the battlements and the walls of the city to starve. Begging for death, howling, they crawled on their hands and knees scrabbling for roots; they ate dirt. Resistance to John of Leyden grew within Münster, and he carried out the executions himself. The corpses were cut into pieces, and the pieces were nailed up on posts.

In June 1535 the city was betrayed and taken; except for John of Leyden and two confederates, all of the men were exterminated. "At the Bishop's command," Cohn writes, John of Leyden "was for some time led about on a chain and exhibited like a performing bear." In January 1536 he and his two living followers were returned to Münster, where they "were publicly tortured to death with red-hot irons. Throughout their agony the ex-king uttered no sound and made no movement. After the execution the three bodies were suspended from a church-tower in the middle of the town, in cages which are still to be seen there today."

So much for one true Christ, for one true Antichrist. And to root motives in a mere coincidence of names is specious—but serendipity is where you find it. John Lydon was raised a Catholic; when in 1980 two born-again Christian rock critics (one of whom later took to the Christian airwaves to denounce rock 'n' roll as the devil's music) asked him if he suffered remorse for his blasphemies, Lydon said he did, and disavowed nothing. Nik Cohn, one of the first rock critics, is Norman Cohn's son; in 1968, in *Pop from the Beginning*, the first good book on the subject, he disavowed all claims on meaning the form might make, affirming instead a pure, sensual anarchy, summed up in the watchword of Little Richard (who by the Sex Pistols' time made his living as an evangelist denouncing rock 'n' roll as the devil's music): A WOP BOP A LOO BOP, A LOP BAM BOOM.

Nik Cohn was likely not interested in the possibility that Little Richard's glossolalia could be traced back thousands of years to gnostic chants that moved through time until they became the sort of prayers offered by mystics like John of Leyden, after which they found their way into Pentecostal churches, where Little Richard learned the language of "Tutti Frutti." Nik Cohn may not have been interested in the possibility that a version of this story, as told by his father, produced the money he would use to buy Little Richard records. Cohn was taking Little Richard's syllables as an assault on meaning as such, as a means to a perfect liberation from it; he

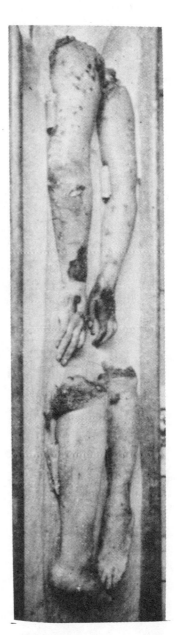

Münstermash

was arguing that anyone who believed differently, who believed that rock 'n' roll could support concepts more complex than yes or no, or tell stories more intricate than "I want" or "Leave me alone," would be destroyed by the form itself—punished for betraying it. You might get a hit, he said, and then take the response to the sound you made as proof you had something to say, but it isn't true. Rock 'n' roll has nothing to say, only a divine noise to make—and anyone who believed otherwise would end up as a shabby old man with a tin whistle, standing in the rain trying to make himself heard, to get someone to listen, to get one more hit.

Of course, Cohn said—claiming rock 'n' roll as the music that creates the moment and thus supersedes it—so would everybody else. Leaving the supermarket one day, I saw four black men in their fifties harmonizing doo wops from "Earth Angel" as they loaded crates into a van, and the thought struck me: were they, once, the Penguins? What else would the Penguins be doing, thirty years after their one hit? It didn't matter; when the sound had maintained itself, not as a memory but as a self-renewing moment, for three decades, it didn't make any difference. These are the shabby old men with their tin whistles, and so is anyone who can hear them.

BY THE TIME

By the time John Lydon reaffirmed his blasphemies the Sex Pistols' explosion was a memory—they had long since exploded, but the pieces were still squirming. In a San Francisco nightclub, a Berlin band called Eisenstürzende Neubauten (Collapsing New Buildings), best known for its lp *Strategies Against Architecture*, turns industrial tools on industrial materials against a backdrop of gothic synthesizer tones; that's the show. "Whatever it was," says the local newspaper critic, usually not sympathetic to such stunts, "it wasn't boring." Also on the bill is action sculptor Mark Pauline, who first attracted local attention with his clandestine redesign of commercial billboards, whose Survival Research Laboratories now constructs infernal Rube Goldberg machines out of metal and animal corpses to a soundtrack of old Crystals records and new releases from the female Zurich punk group Liliput, and who is famous, to the degree that he is famous, for blowing off most of one hand while experimenting with one of his devices (later toes were removed from his feet and attached to his ruined hand as surrogate fingers).

The *New York Times* runs an announcement:

Language and noise will be featured during the first two "Poets at the Public" programs this year. Tomorrow, writers who explore the limits of language and who are called "language" writers will read from their recent works . . . The "noise music" movement, a product of the downtown art community, will be represented by the Sonic Youth Band and by David Rosenbloom's Experimental Chorus and Orchestra, which will present the premiere of a section of Mr. Rosenbloom's "Departure." "Departure" takes its text from the second-century Gnostic Gospel of Thomas.

A mainstream "Rock of the '80s" station plays "Institutionalized," a blithering punk rant by a Southern California band called Suicidal Tendencies—plays it, within the newly successful format of coldly romantic synthesizer ballads and novelty records, as another novelty record. It is a "novelty record," an oddity, because by now it is presumed that "punk" is an oddity, a sterile anomaly. The record is arresting, but it has been arrested: contextualized as a novelty in the rock of the 1980s, it has been denied the chance to make its own context, to connect to anything outside of itself.

A teenager lies in his bed, thinking. His mother comes in: What's the matter with you? Nothing, Mom—could you get me a Pepsi? You're on drugs, I knew it! No, Mom, I'm not on drugs—could I have a Pepsi? Your father and I have been talking about this, and we've decided that you should go to a place where you can get the help that you need . . . . . As the band rumbles behind him, the teenager begins each verse in ordinary, modulated English, talking, not singing, but he ends each verse with each word impossibly speeded up, not by electronics but by breath control, a wail dense and scrambled beyond language, though not beyond rhythm: somehow the band keeps pace.

A twist of the dial away from "Institutionalized," an Adult Oriented Radio station plays Billy Joel's clumsy, lovely "The Longest Time," an acapella tribute to the doo-wop revival, rooted in the vocal music of the early 1950s, in the Five Satins' "In the Still of the Nite" and the Penguins' "Earth Angel," which was staged in New York and New Jersey in 1964 as a protest against the Beatle-era "British Invasion." Twenty years after that little-noticed event, "The Longest Time" is the first acapella recording to become a national hit. The video of the song shows forty-year-old businessmen—overweight, in three-piece suits, silver in their hair—turning into their slim, blue-jeaned, duck-tailed high-school selves, harmonizing in the boys' room, patronizing a black janitor, then turning back into businessmen, strutting their high school corridors as if they were still free men. These old men are not shabby; they are not even old. Youth goes on forever, says the video, going back to the beginning of time, which here dates to the beginning of rock 'n' roll: "They can't take that away from me." Nothing has changed, and nothing ever will.

In one of the countless paradoxes of his performance, Johnny Rotten announced what was taken as a youth revolt while denying the status of youth itself: as an antichrist, he claimed all of social life as his terrain. Now, within the pop milieu, the symbol factory, it is as if he had never been born. It is the year of Michael Jackson, a long year—a year, it was possible to believe as it unfolded, that would never end.

It began on 16 May 1983, with the airing of a television special celebrating the twenty-fifth anniversary of Motown Records. As the eleven-year-old lead singer of the Jackson 5, brothers who combined the teenage yearning of Frankie Lymon with the willful dynamics of Sly and the Family Stone, Michael Jackson had made his first, epochal hits for Motown in 1969 and 1970; now he was back, to pay tribute, to join hands. Lithe, beautiful, grown up but still a child, an Afro-

American with surgically produced Caucasian features, androgynous, a changeling, communicating menace with the dip of a shoulder, comfort with a smile, singing a song from his new album, *Thriller*, stepping forward but somehow seeming to glide backward at the same time, walking the television stage not as if he owned it, not as if it was built for him, but as if his very presence had called it into being, he shocked the nation.

A sparkling, brilliantly constructed version of pop music, *Thriller* sold ten, then twenty, then thirty, then forty million copies. As singles, song after song from *Thriller* entered the top ten. A video of the title tune, made at a cost of $500,000 and priced at $30, sold 750,000 copies. Closeted in his parents' home, keeping company only with family, pets, and mannequins, refusing all interviews, a self-made specter, Michael Jackson became the most intensely famous person in the world.

MICHAEL JACKSON

Michael Jackson stands in the White House Rose Garden with President Ronald Reagan to receive an award for allowing his *Thriller* hit "Beat It" to be made into an anti-drunk-driving TV commercial. On newscasts covering the event, a bit of the commercial is shown: a skeletal hand grasps the hand of one still living. The suggestion of Michelangelo's Sistine Chapel ceiling, where Adam touches the hand of God, is inescapable; so is the feeling that Michael Jackson is becoming a kind of god. The newscasts cut back to the Rose Garden: "Isn't this a thriller," says the president. Previously, for $5.5 million dollars, Jackson had allowed his great *Thriller* hit "Billie Jean" to be turned into a Pepsi commercial.

For television there are in fact two commercials, and both are to be weighted with satisfying intimations of hubris, of tragedy. In the first, young black breakdancers are seen slippin' and slidin' over city streets; Jackson and his brothers ap-

. . . .

WHAT ARE THEY *now? Do pop stars change their opinions? We compare some past and present quotes.*

Johnny Rotten, 1977: "If I was 'appy no one would like me." Today: Paints in isolation. Quote: "It all went horribly wrong. I burned up all my hate."

—The Assassin, *Liverpool fanzine, September 1977*

. . . .

pear, and the dancers halt in awe. Led by a tiny pre-teen virtuoso, they bounce back, and affirm their authenticity as folk
dancers against—no, with: the commercial is saying that in
America anyone can grow up to be Michael Jackson—the authenticity of the star as star. Soon it would be announced that
the tiny virtuoso had broken his neck breakdancing, and had
died.

As with the rumor that Annette Funicello lost an arm while
waving to a fan from a bus, the story wasn't true: radio stations and newspapers that carried obituaries ran corrections.
But it was only a warmup. During the filming of a second
Pepsi commercial, in which Jackson descended a stage to join
his brothers in praise of the drink, explosions of light heralded
his presence, and he was burned. The resulting publicity was
so productive, for both Pepsi and Jackson, that some were sure
the accident had been faked. The day before the official debut
of the commercials, on the 1984 Grammy Awards telecast—
where the advertisements, which were themselves advertised,
were presented to the public like new records, like art statements—TV news shows, still featuring daily medical bulletins
on Jackson's condition, used parts of the commercials as news
footage. Jackson appeared to collect eight Grammys; as he
stepped forward to accept the last, he removed his dark
glasses.

All of this took place in what situationist Guy Debord had
called "the heaven of the spectacle." "I am nothing and I
should be everything," a young Karl Marx had written, defin-
ing the revolutionary impulse. "The spectacle," as Debord developed the concept through the 1950s and 1960s, was at once
the kidnapping of that impulse and its prison. It was a wonderful prison, where all of life was staged as a permanent
show—a show, Debord wrote, where "everything that was directly lived has moved away into a representation," a beautiful
work of art. The only problem was absolute: "in the case
where the self is merely represented and ideally presented,"
ran a quote from Hegel on the first page of *La société du spectacle*, a book of critical theory Debord published in 1967,

"there it is not actual: where it is by proxy, it *is not.*"

"The spectacle," Debord said, was "*capital* accumulated until it becomes an image." A never-ending accumulation of spectacles—advertisements, entertainments, traffic, skyscrapers, political campaigns, department stores, sports events, newscasts, art tours, foreign wars, space launchings—made a modern world, a world in which all communication flowed in one direction, from the powerful to the powerless. One could not respond, or talk back, or intervene, but one did not want to. In the spectacle, passivity was simultaneously the means and the end of a great hidden project, a project of social control. On the terms of its particular form of hegemony the spectacle naturally produced not actors but spectators: modern men and women, the citizens of the most advanced societies on earth, who were thrilled to watch whatever it was they were given to watch.

As Debord drew the picture, these people were members of democratic societies: democracies of false desire. One could not intervene, but one did not want to, because as a mechanism of social control the spectacle dramatized an inner spectacle of participation, of choice. In the home, one chose between television programs; in the city, one chose between the countless variations of each product on the market. Like a piece of avant-garde performance art, the spectacle dramatized an ideology of freedom.

I am nothing and you are everything, the performance artist says to her audience. She leaves the stage, descends into the paying crowd, seals her mouth with tape, takes off her clothes. "Do what you will with me," she mimes—she is turning herself into an object, empowering the members of the audience, discarding all the authority of the artist, and yet somehow that authority is retained. The naturally active artist imitates the natural passivity of the crowd: she lies on her back with her legs open, inviting the audience to fuck her, to set her on fire, to try to get her to talk, to piss on her, to ignore her, to argue and then to come to blows over what you or I or we should do next. All of these things have actually happened at avant-garde performances. But if where the self "is by proxy, it *is not*," these things have also actually not happened, because it is only the artist's dispensation that has permitted the anonymous people in the crowd to seem to act. At the artist's withdrawal of that dispensation (nothing so crude as "STOP!", rather an assistant announcing, "The performance is over"), the counterfeit actors immediately return to their seats. They once again become spectators, and feel comfortable: like themselves.

Like TV fans with a satellite dish, who imagine that they create their own entertainment out of an infinity of channels, the members of the audience feel as if they have intervened in the spectacle of the artist's performance, but they have not; they have played by the artist's rules, where such putative intangibles as chance, risk, and violence were fixed from the start. The only true intervention would be for someone to step out of the crowd and shout, "No, no, *I* am now the artist, you must do what *I* tell you to do, you must play *my* game, which is . . ." Then the rest of the crowd, and the original artist, would be faced with a real choice, a choice containing all the intangibles of epistemology, aesthetics, politics, social life. It would be as if one of the fans who traditionally jumps from the stands during a World Series game then joined the contest, and got everyone playing a new game; as if a mad scientist with a crate of Aladdin's lamps set up a table in Macy's and by her very presence destroyed the value of every other available commodity—but, as with the intervention of the audience member claiming to be the artist, such things have never actually happened.

SO DID

So did the spectacle work on the most prosaic levels of everyday life, but Debord meant much more. As a theater the spectacle was also a church, "the material reconstruction of the religious illusion." Modern mastery, the domination of nature by technology, the potential abolition of the domain of necessity in the modern society of abundance, had not "dispelled the religious clouds where men had placed their own powers, detached from themselves; it has only anchored them to an earthly base."

This earthly base was modern capitalism, an economic mode of being that by the 1950s had expanded far beyond the mere production of obvious necessities and luxuries; having satisfied the needs of the body, capitalism as spectacle turned to the desires of the soul. It turned upon individual men and women, seized their subjective emotions and experiences, changed those once evanescent phenomena into objective, replicable commodities, placed them on the market, set their prices, and sold them back to those who had, once, brought emotions and experiences out of themselves—to people who, as prisoners of the spectacle, could now find such things only on the market.

It was these special commodities—items whose objective form served as a disguise for their subjective content (the suit that wore status, the lp that played identity)—which rose into the heaven of the spectacle. Here a miracle as strange as that claimed by any religion was repeated again and again, every day. What was, once, yourself, was now presented as an unreachable but irresistibly alluring image of what, in this best of all possible worlds, you could be.

In such a world, one finally consumed no ordinary sort of thing, but oneself—which, now removed into the material reconstruction of the religious illusion, where you had placed your own powers detached from yourself, was experienced as other: as a thing. Marxists located alienation in the workplace, where what the worker produced was taken from him. Debord believed that material abundance and technical mastery had for the first time in history permitted all people to consciously produce themselves, but in place of that radical freedom he found only its image, the spectacle, in which every act was alienated from itself. Here what one was was taken away. This was the modern world; to the degree that the real field of freedom had expanded, so had the epistemology, the aesthetics, the politics, and the social life of control.

In August 1980 the union Solidarity emerged out of the Lenin Shipyards in Gdansk, Poland. As an idea and a fact of freedom, Solidarity soon spread across the country, from factories to farms, from clerks to intellectuals, infecting even the armed forces and the bureaucracy of the Soviet client state that had ruled Poland since 1944. "What we find in the people's democracies," Polish emigré Czeslaw Milosz wrote in 1953 in *The Captive Mind*, "is a conscious mass play . . . After long acquaintance with his role, a man grows into it so closely that he can no longer differentiate his true self from the self he simulates, so that even the most intimate of individuals speak to each other in Party slogans. To identify one's self with the role one is obliged to play brings relief and permits a relaxation of one's vigilance." But if everyday life in Communist Poland was a play, then Solidarity, the clandestine Polish publisher Czeslaw Bielecki wrote in an essay smuggled out of prison in 1985, was "antitheater." For the first time, countless men and women spoke in public, for themselves, and were listened to; they acted, and found themselves changed into new men and women, unwilling to go on as before. Against Solidarity's affirmation of the right of all Polish citizens to reinvent their own society, the ruling clique was purged, replaced by a government promising reforms unthinkable only months earlier; suddenly almost anything seemed possible. Despite the threat of Soviet intervention, an air of good feeling rose out of the new milieu of danger and desire—and on the night of 16 December 1980, once more in Gdansk, the leaders of Solidarity, the new government, and the Catholic Church gathered with 150,000 new citizens to seal the moment.

The occasion was the dedication of a monument to the martyrs of December 1970: striking workers massacred by government troops. Until the birth of Solidarity those men had been excluded from the official history of their society, their names mentioned only in secret; now their names were read out by a movie star, and in three steel crosses, each 140 feet high, they were made to symbolize their society. "For those who watched the ceremony, it was all incredible, improbable," Neal Ascherson wrote in *The Polish August*. "It was a moment in which one realized how much had taken place in Poland, and how rapidly." And yet, he said, for

all its splendour, there was something alienating about the ceremony at Gdansk. Andrzej Wajda, the most famous film-maker in Eastern Europe, produced and directed it, with all its use of lighting, of sound, of music, of the solo human voice. It was, indeed, a spectacle: the ordinary people who had brought all these things about by asserting their right to be subjects as well as objects of history now stood in darkness and watched the show as if they were watching a film. Once they intervened: when Tadeusz Fiszbach, the Gdansk Party secretary, spoke of Poland's liberation in 1944 by the Red Army, a soft breeze of whistles ran across the crowd. But for the rest they were passive.

Debord had been there long before, with words that were meant to describe the performance of a commute or a night of lovemaking as precisely as they anticipated such a broken public event as Gdansk on 16 December 1980. "The alienation of the spectator to the profit of the contemplated object"—one's idealized self, or any piece of it—"can be summed up thusly," he wrote in 1967: "the more he contemplates, the less he lives; the more he accepts recognizing himself in the dominant images of need, the less he understands his own existence and his own desires. The externality of the spectacle in relation to the active man appears in the fact that his gestures are no longer his own, but those of another, who represents them to him," and that "another" was the spectacle personified, the star of social life, be it Lech Walesa, the leader of Solidarity, or the martyrs of 1970, or Jesus Christ, or the face on the billboard as one made one's commute, the face of the idealized self in one's mind as one made love. As such the idealized self was always immediately present, always just out of reach. As a perversion of freedom it was, like any perversion, erotic; as alienation it carried the frisson of having just missed the brass ring, a sensation that always brought one back for more. If at bottom revolution was rooted in the desire to create one's own life, a wish so deep and voracious its realization demanded the creation of a new society, then the spectacle took that wish into itself, and returned it as the wish to accept one's life as it already existed, as it existed in the constantly renewing utopia of the spectacle.

SPECTACLE

"Spectacle" had become a fashionable critical commonplace by the early 1980s. It was a vague term, devoid of ideas. It sim-ply meant that the image of a thing superseded the thing it-self. Critics used the cliché not to think, or to imagine, but to complain: to complain that people seemed to believe that through Rambo movies the U.S.A. could win the Vietnam War backward, that consumers were being seduced by advertise-ments instead of choosing rationally among products, that citi-zens were voting for actors rather than issues. This was the theater, but Debord had insisted on the church: the spectacle was not merely advertising, or television, it was a world. "The spectacle is not a collection of images," he wrote, dismissing in advance the obvious social critiques that would follow his book, "but a social relationship among people, mediated by im-ages."

It was a social world in which to be nothing was to be everything, and in which to be everything was to be nothing. "Sadat was a hero of the electronic revolution," Mohamed Hei-kal wrote in *Autumn of Fury: The Assassination of Sadat*, "but also its victim. When his face was no longer to be seen on the television screen, it was as if the eleven years of his rule had vanished with a switch of the control knob." The contradiction was a tautology, and the tautology was the prison: the specta-cle defined reality in the modern world, and that definition de-fined unreality. When everything that was directly lived had moved away into a representation, there was no real life, yet no other life seemed real. The victory of the spectacle was that nothing seemed real until it had appeared in the spectacle, even if in the moment of its appearance it would lose whatever reality it held. "Every notion fixed in this way is ultimately based in its passage into its opposite," Debord wrote. "The true is a moment of the false." *Thrilly right*

Debord had trumpeted "the spectacle" as a monster, a horror movie, a Godzilla of alienation. Twenty years after he set down his theory of modern society, its premises sound both familiar and weird, plain and paranoid, obvious and occult—and this is what it felt like to be part of the world of Michael Jackson in 1984. It was to be loosed from your moorings, to feel simultaneously humiliated and excited, to respond to the claim that even "the true is a moment of the false" with a shrug: "Well, why not? What else can you show me?" The spectacle produced its own opposition, and swallowed it: to reject one spectacle was to demand another.

What happened in the year of Michael Jackson? For the first few million who bought *Thriller*, form and content, subjectivity and objectivity, self and other, commodity and consumer, were one. Those few million bought a record they liked. Then *Thriller* became an image—an image, in the milieu of modern capitalism, in the heaven of the spectacle, of the good: an irresistible image of self-realization and public conquest. After that, form superseded content, which did not mean that Jackson's message was lost in *Thriller*'s gloss—it meant that neither form nor content remained tied to the record itself. The content was no longer the sound of the music, and the form was no longer the manner in which the music was produced or functioned as genre. The content was now one's response to the social event of *Thriller*, the form the mechanics of the event.

To Debord, the society of the spectacle was modern society itself, in no way natural, an interested construction but nonetheless implacably complete: "reality rises up within the spectacle, and the spectacle is real." As it emerged out of the pop milieu, the symbol factory, one could see *Thriller* as a spectacle of the spectacle, a mediation between the pop spectacle and the greater spectacle that, *Thriller* seemed to prove, was social life. The Sex Pistols had forced people to choose—in the beginning, for or against the Sex Pistols, then, should one enter Johnny Rotten's performances, to say yes or no to God and the state, work and leisure, the performer and oneself. The triumph of Michael Jackson was to allow people not to choose. *Thriller* enforced its own reality principle: it was there, part of every commute, a serenade to every errand, a referent to every purchase, a fact of every life. You didn't have to like it. You only had to acknowledge it—but somehow, in the year of Michael Jackson, to acknowledge it was to like it.

IN 1982

In 1982 Elizabeth Taylor filed suit to stop the airing of an unauthorized TV movie about her life. "I am my own industry," she said. "I am my own commodity." A hundred and fifteen years before, Karl Marx anticipated this bizarre invocation in "The Fetishism of the Commodity and Its Secret," the most bizarrely titled section of *Capital*. He wrote:

A commodity appears at first sight an extremely obvious, trivial thing. But its analysis brings out that it is a very strange thing, abounding in metaphysical subtleties and theological niceties . . . It is absolutely clear that, by his activity, man changes the forms of the materials of nature in such a way as to make them useful to him. The form of wood, for instance, is altered if a table is made out of it. Nevertheless the table continues to be wood, an ordinary, sensuous thing. But as soon as it emerges as a commodity, it changes into a thing which transcends sensuousness. It not only stands with its feet on the ground, but, in relation to all other commodities, it stands on its head, and evolves out of its wooden brain grotesque ideas, far more wonderful than if it were to begin dancing of its own free will.

This is pure poetry, but the mystical echoes were not there for color. Marx's allusion was to the Spiritualists, who in his time clasped hands around tables from Boston to Paris to Petrograd, waiting for the spirits of departed loved ones to make their presence known, to shake the tables, to make the tables dance. The Spiritualists had nothing to do with commodities, but the commodity had everything to do with magic—a magic in which the technical notion of transformation yielded to the metaphysical subtleties and theological niceties of transubstantiation. Still, if it is possible that in 1867 Marx could have foreseen a post-industrial Taylorism, it is hard to believe he would have been ready for Jacksonism.

The commodity was the agent of reification: Jackson's built its own heaven, and everyone reached for it. It was wonderful, in that year of Michael Jackson, just to get up in the morning, open the paper, and follow the dance: to discover that a clandestine Michael Jackson cult had formed within the Jehovah's Witnesses (which, as everyone knew, counted Jackson as a devotee, and which, one was informed, was based on a belief in the return of the Archangel Michael); to learn that a teenager, his parents having refused him the money to correct his face so that it might more closely resemble Michael Jackson's, had killed himself; or to read that American companies operating in Mexico "have begun to subsidize food and transportation and to pay workers above the Mexican minimum wage of $4.80 a day. One company is considering giving watches to workers with good attendance and longevity records. Another is giving out Michael Jackson albums." But these were only teasers. Suddenly it was time to make the specter flesh: time for a tour, at $30 a head.

Now the news was hard, and the newsbreaks never stopped: Jackson's father and brothers, left behind so long before, forcing him to go before a public he had preferred not to meet; various would-be promoters fighting for the right to meet the Jacksons' demand for a $40 million guarantee; the suspense over which cities would be visited and which passed over; and, finally, the stipulation that whoever wished to attend a Jacksons concert would be required to purchase, by mail order, no less than four tickets, for $120, with no assurance that the order would result in entry, since ten orders were expected for every available ticket, meaning that, while those who lost would eventually have their money refunded (minus a service charge), it would in the meantime be held and invested in

AN ILLINOIS woman has filed a $150 million paternity suit against pop star Michael Jackson, claiming that he is the father of her three children, she said yesterday.

"Michael is the father, Michael got me pregnant and I want Michael to pay for it," Billie Jean Jackson, 39, said by telephone from a friend's home in Hanover Park, a Chicago suburb . . .

The Illinois Department of Children and Family Services took custody of the children in 1985, charging the mother with lack of supervision. The children live in New York with the mother's relatives.

Department officials refused to comment on the case, but sources said Billie Jean Jackson, who legally changed her name from Lavon Powlis, has made previous claims that other famous personalities fathered her children. None had resulted in a paternity suit, however.

—San Francisco Chronicle, 20 August 1987

three-month notes, with all accumulated interest reverting to the Jacksons. This was real life: dollars and cents. It was also a version of what Ulrike Meinhof called Konsumterror—the terrorism of consumption, the fear of not being able to get what is on the market, the agony of being last in line, or of lacking the money to join the line: to be a part of social life. All over the country, people became happily afraid of tickets they could not afford to buy, of tickets they might not be able to buy even if they could afford them, of tickets that would seal them as everything or nothing, of tickets that, as the humiliating, exciting process began, were not even on sale.

By 6 July 1984, when the Jacksons played the first show of their "Victory" tour, in Kansas City, Missouri—thirty years and a day after Elvis Presley made his first record in Memphis, Tennessee—Jacksonism had produced a system of commodification so complete that whatever and whoever was admitted to it instantly became a new commodity. People were no longer consuming commodities as such things are conventionally understood (records, videos, posters, books, magazines, key rings, earrings necklaces pins buttons wigs voice-alteration devices Pepsis t-shirts underwear hats scarves gloves jackets—and why were there no jeans called Billie Jeans?); they were consuming their own gestures of consumption. That is, they were consuming not a Tayloristic Michael Jackson, or any licensed facsimile, but themselves. Riding a Möbius strip of pure capitalism, that was the transubstantiation.

Jacksonism produced the image of a pop explosion, an event in which pop music crosses political, economic, geographic, and racial barriers; in which a new world is suggested, where new performances can momentarily supersede the hegemonic divisions of social life. Part and parcel of such an event is an avalanche of organized publicity, but also an epidemic of grassroots rumor mongering, a sense of everyday novelty so strong that the past seems irrelevant and the future already present. In all these ways, Jacksonism counted. Michael Jackson occupied the center of American cultural life: no other black artist had ever come close.

But a pop explosion not only links those otherwise separated by class, place, color, and money; it also divides. Confronted with performers as appealing and disturbing as Elvis Presley, the Beatles, or the Sex Pistols, with people who raise the possibility of living in a new way, some respond and some don't—and this, if only for a moment, becomes a primary social fact. It became clear that Michael Jackson's explosion was of a new kind.

It was the first pop explosion not to be judged by the subjective quality of the response it provoked, but to be measured by the number of objective commercial exchanges it elicited. Thus Michael Jackson was absolutely correct when he announced, at the height of his year, that his greatest achievement was a Guinness Book of World Records award certifying that *Thriller* had generated more top-ten singles (seven) than any other lp—and not, as might have been expected, "to have given people a new way of walking and a new way of talking," or "to have proven that music is a universal language," or even "to have demonstrated that with God's help your dreams can come true." To say such things would have suggested that in a pop explosion what is at stake is value: that such an event offers as its most powerful aesthetic and social gift the inescapable feeling that the fate of the world rests on how a given performance might turn out. And this was not what was happening. The pop explosions of Elvis, the Beatles, and the Sex Pistols had assaulted or subverted social barriers; *Thriller* crossed over them, like kudzu. Since *Thriller* never broke those barriers, but only made them briefly invisible, in Kansas City they once again became undeniable.

Michael Jackson's most committed fans were black boys and girls under fifteen; in the past, he and his brothers played to audiences that were almost all black. Kansas City is 30 percent black, and as a city it looks integrated: in any given public place, both clientele and service personnel are black and white. In Kansas City's Arrowhead Stadium, secured for a performance by the best-known black family in the world, the waiting crowd was almost all white. Following the logic of the commodity, which goes where the money is, which will take you there whether you want to go or not, the imperatives of Jacksonism—its insistence on exchange as a mechanism for the production of value, its $30 ticket price, in $120 blocks of four—did not divide the audience of the Jacksonist pop explosion from those who chose not to be part of it; those imperatives divided those who did choose to be part of it from each other. The poor, who could come up with the money to buy a copy of *Thriller*, were out. Some of the poor went without food, clothes, or medical care to raise the $120—for many, more than a month's rent—but, given the mail-order system, which allowed those arranging the concerts to select fans by zip code, they were off the map. The Jacksonist pop explosion was official, which meant not simply that it was validated by the president of the United States. It was brought forth as a version of the official social reality, generated from Washington as ideology, and from Madison Avenue as language—an ideological language, in 1984, of political division and social exclusion, a glamorization of the new American fact that if you weren't on top, you didn't exist. "Winning," read a Nestlé ad featuring an Olympic-style medal cast in chocolate, "is everything." "We have one and only one ambition," said Lee Iacocca for Chrysler. "To be the best. What else is there?" Thus the Victory tour—which originally boasted a more apocalyptic title: "Final Victory."

IT DIDN'T WORK

It didn't work. Days before the first show, LaDonna Jones, an eleven-year-old black girl from Lewisville, Texas, wrote an open letter to Michael Jackson in care of her local newspaper, and the letter was reprinted across the country. It wasn't fair, she said. That was all it took. It was all over. The tour managers sent LaDonna Jones free tickets, but it was too late. Hidden in a uniform that likely weighed as much as he did (dark glasses, military jacket, pants above the ankles, laceless shoes, the uniform that in the Jacksonist explosion produced not the imitators who followed Elvis, the Beatles, and the Sex Pistols, imitators who found themselves forming groups to find out what it was they had to say, but only impersonators, young men emerging from hired limousines or rushing stages to be greeted by those who knew they were fakes with screams appropriate to the real thing), Jackson fought against the fable of the Emperor's New Clothes, denouncing his own ticket scheme, promising to give money away, but no one ever beats a fable.

Given what it was supposed to be, the tour was dead. The show itself was dead from the first night: a stiff, impersonal, over-rehearsed supper club act blown up with lasers and sonic booms, which drew polite applause from people who had whooped as they passed through the turnstiles. In Kansas City the commodity stood on its head once again: Michael Jackson, who began his year as a dancer, turned into a piece of wood.

As the tour went on, some shows failed even to sell out; some were canceled for lack of interest. When all bills were in, the promoter had lost $18 million. On the terms established by the glare leading up to that first show, the tour went on in darkness—not in secret, but in oblivion; on the terms of the heaven of the spectacle, in hell. It ended months later, in the rain, in Los Angeles, unnoticed save for those who were there, who themselves went unnoticed by Michael Jackson and his brothers, who repeated their gestures and their patter lick for lick and line for line from Kansas City, as if nothing had happened, as if they had never been anywhere, as if everywhere was nowhere.

There were echoes; the long year was not quite over. If no longer a god, Michael Jackson remained a celebrity. In an act of celebrity noblesse oblige, along with Lionel Richie he wrote "We Are the World," an anthem meant to raise money for African famine relief, and the song was, in its way, a masterpiece; recorded by a massed choir of pop superstars, it bypassed its putative objects, the starving Africans, and returned to those who made it. They were the world. They held out their hands: the record completed a circuit that erased all differences between performers and spectators, objectifying both in the face of objective good. With *Thriller* you could join social life simply by acknowledging it; here, through the simple act of buying the record, you could become part of the world. As the record played, the Africans ceased to starve. "As God has shown us," Jackson and Richie wrote, not likely thinking of John of Leyden, "by turning stones to bread."

Long after the Victory tour faded, "You're a Whole New Generation," the radio version of Jackson's "Billie Jean" Pepsi commercial, remained on the air. A song about anxiety and guilt, dazzlingly produced, voices flying through discrete layers of sound, "Billie Jean" was the most seductive record Michael Jackson had ever made; at first, his willingness to immediately transform it into an advertising jingle seemed like a slap in the face to everyone who loved it. But months later, when the constant airplay bought for the commercial allowed it not just to replace but almost to erase the original, one could hear "You're a Whole New Generation" as a new piece of music. It was tougher: the rhythm was harsh, the production not elliptical but direct, Jackson's voice not pleading or confused but fierce. When he sang the line, "That choice is up to you," dramatizing the consumer's option of Pepsi versus Coke, he made it sound like a moral choice. Altogether he communicated wholeness where "Billie Jean" had broken into fragments, anger instead of restraint, certainty in place of doubt. That only made the buried, surely slip-of-the-tongue message all the more unsettling. "You're a whole new generation," Jackson sang as the fade began, "you're lovin' what they do . . ." Wait, wait—who was this "they"?

ONE NEGATION

One negation of spectacle is panic, people thrown back on themselves: the "kind of nervousness you've had to experience in order to comprehend it. Somebody only has to yell one loud word on the street and the crowds scatter through the doors of houses. It's a run for your life. At that very moment, machine-gun fire can erupt from some hidden crack, or a hand grenade is dropped from a roof and its fragments tear open your guts. The street is jammed with merchants—it's a street fair, the kind you usually see only in the country or at folk festivals. The fellows selling sausages, who have to carry hot tin boxes, can only get through the doorways awkwardly, pushing hard. They laugh, but they're driven by the fear of death. The machine-gun fire can rattle down the street at any moment and bring all excitement to an end. The atmosphere of a great event hovers over the city . . ."

The city is Berlin, January 1919, in the midst of the Spartacist rising, though it could be San Francisco, January 1978, in Winterland, as Johnny Rotten sings "Bodies"—that's the feeling. The description is by Richard Huelsenbeck, from his 1920 pamphlet *Deutschland muss untergehen!* (Germany Must Fall), subtitled "Memoirs of an old dadaist revolutionary," though Huelsenbeck was not yet thirty. His friend George Grosz provided the illustrations: cartoons of the three pillars of the German ruling class—priest, businessman, militarist—rendered as monstrous cretins. "In those days, we were all 'Dadaists,'" Grosz wrote in 1946 in *A Little Yes and a Big No*, his autobiography—even before dada he Americanized his given name out of hatred for Germany, but now, as an emigré, a new American trying to accept a society that seemed to have no language for the loathing that drove his work, he wanted to put it all behind him, to put quotes around the word, which, if it "meant anything at all, meant seething discontent, dissatisfaction and cynicism. Defeat and political ferment always give rise to that sort of movement. In a different age we might easily have been flagellants."

On stage, railing obscenities on a woman who's thrown her aborted fetus into a gutter ("*She* don't want a baby that looks like that!"), then on himself, the father ("*I* don't want a baby that looks like that!"), then becoming the fetus, crying back from the slime ("MUMMY!"), finally dissolving his tale into curses so driven they can refer back only to themselves ("Fuck this and fuck that fuck it all and fuck the brat"—it is appalling, a tidal wave of filth rises out of the gutter with the sound, you can't get out of the way), Johnny Rotten is a flagellant—all of the flagellants' hatred of the body is in his throat. "I drew and painted from a spirit of contradiction," Grosz wrote, "and I tried by means of my work to show the world that it is hideous, sick and dishonest," but Johnny Rotten is not trying: this is actually happening. And for all of his cool distance, Huelsenbeck too has a corpse in his mouth.

In late October 1918 the world war collapsed on Germany; sailors mutinied. Days later, the November revolution broke out across the country, and the war government of Kaiser Wilhelm abdicated. Spontaneously organized, self-legitimating councils of workers, soldiers, intellectuals, and professional revolutionaries filled the suddenly empty public space. People who before had only muttered secret curses now asked questions, said their names out loud, left the crowd for the front of the room, said strange things. To some, it looked as if the councils were ready to begin everything from the beginning—it looked that way especially in hindsight, after the councils were pushed aside by the legal-fiction government of social-democrat Friedrich Ebert, which set out to administer all possibility backward. Thus on 5 January 1919 Spartacist leaders Karl Liebknecht and Rosa Luxemburg, communists to the libertarian left of Lenin, called for a new revolt to save the November revolution from history; it lasted six days.

The rising was to Huelsenbeck precisely what, in rented halls in the spring and summer of 1918, he and his cronies in the Berlin Dada Club—Grosz, Walter Mehring, Johannes Baader, John Heartfield, Raoul Hausmann—had prophesied in microcosm. "WONDER OF WONDERS!" read one of their broadsides: "The Dadaist world can be realized in a single moment!" They signed it "Rhythms International." Garbling already incomprehensible poetry with crazy gestures, singing ridiculous songs three at a time over pure noise, hurling abuse at the paying crowds, dissolving the ideologies of left and right into glossolalia, they tried to make the crowds strike back, to make the stopped clock strike twelve, to prove that time was up. Prancing on their stage, Huelsenbeck and Hausmann with monocles clamped into their left eye sockets, Grosz's face covered with white pancake makeup, they tried to live out an old, orphaned metaphor as if it were not a metaphor at all. "The criticism" that deals with conditions in Germany, twenty-five-year-old Karl Marx wrote in 1843–44, in "Contribution to a Critique of Hegel's Philosophy of Right,"

is involved in a *hand-to-hand fight*, and in such fights it does not matter what the opponent's rank is, or whether he is noble or *interesting*: what matters is to *hit* him. The important thing is not to permit the German a single moment of self-deception or resignation. The actual burden must be made even more burdensome by creating an awareness of it. The humiliation must be increased by making it public . . . these petrified conditions must be made to dance by having their own tune sung to them! The people must be put in *terror* of themselves in order to give them *courage*.

That was the manifesto of Berlin dada. In 1920, looking back to the Spartacist revolt, Huelsenbeck saw those nights on stage in rented halls, where the Dance of Petrified Conditions was first orchestrated to the hit lieder "Their Own Tune": "For the first time in history," he wrote in another 1920 pamphlet, *En avant dada*, "the conclusion has been drawn from the question: 'What is German culture?' (Answer: Shit.) And this culture is attacked with all the instruments of satire, bluff, irony, and finally violence. And in a great common action." It was a connection no one else could see: out of dada, revolution. Huelsenbeck set down his memories as if the outcome were still in doubt:

The atmosphere of a great event hovers over the city. You can see it: some only become human if death is breathing down their necks. They know how to primitively express their most primitive needs only when death brushes their sleeves. Then it is a joy to be alive. The bourgeois pig, who through the whole four years of murder cared only for his belly, can no longer escape the situation. He stands on his sturdy legs in the middle of hell. And hell is frenzied: it is a desire for life. Life is torture, life is fear, hatred, and vulgarity. Never has it been more so. Thus let life be praised. Through their nervousness, these people almost always turn into precious beasts. Their eyes, which always lodged in their sockets like pebbles, become attentive and active. They sense, darkly, that something is happening—something is happening outside their narrow, so-called God-given private family circle. On the corners, in the streets, everywhere a free space appears, they hack away at each other with poisonous speeches. A crowd quickly gathers around each dialogue. Here, dear reader, dramas are enacted. We find ourselves in Homeric times.

"Against an idea, even a false one," Huelsenbeck wrote in *Germany Must Fall,* "all weapons are powerless"—no matter that the Spartacist rising was crushed, Liebknecht and Luxemburg assassinated, their bodies dumped like garbage. "Even a false one": that idea was the essence of dada, and inside Winterland, where the performance was staged to give the lie to itself, that idea seemed the essence of the Sex Pistols. "FUCKING BLOODY MESS!" Johnny Rotten screamed at the fetus, then as the fetus, then as the Elephant Man—"I'm not an animal!"—it didn't matter what you thought. The song wasn't about abortion; it was an irresistible moment of torture, fear, hatred, and vulgarity. You went into the body, and the body was torn to pieces.

BELSEN WAS A GAS

"Belsen Was a Gas" was the only tune the Sex Pistols played at Winterland that had not appeared on record—that the crowd didn't know. It was a crude, cheesy, stupid number, thought up, it is said, by Sid Vicious, the crudest, cheesiest, stupidest member of the band. It was altogether lacking in the poetry of "Anarchy," "Bodies," "Pretty Vacant": a piece of shit. The audience locked into the song; something kicked up the crowd's ability and its need to shout back the chorus the second time it was played, and "Belsen Was a Gas" didn't even have a real chorus. As earlier people threw objects they had brought into the hall at the stage, now they threw back pieces of what was being thrown at them.

Stymied, perhaps in their attempt to see some history in "Holidays in the Sun," here the Sex Pistols had turned to writing it, starting on 15 April 1945, when Belsen gave the British troops who liberated the murder camp their first good look at the Nazi fact. In a way, then, the Winterland audience had indeed heard "Belsen Was a Gas" before: seemingly affirming nothing but its own vulgarity ("Belsen was a gas, I heard the other day / In the open graves where the Jews all lay)," the song was a musical version of the punk swastika, a motif first popularized, in his pre-Pistols days, by Sid Vicious. In England (and, through newspaper and TV features, in the United States), the ubiquity of the symbol had by 1978 forged a media identification between punk and resurgent British Nazis. The swastika painted on clothes, carved into schoolroom desks, carved into arms—how different was it, really, from the National Front campaign to purify the U.K. of its colored populations, Jamaicans, Pakistanis, Indians, the backwash of Empire? How far, really, was punk from the 1970s rehabilitation of Sir Oswald Mosley, head of the British Union of Fascists in the 1930s, who in his glory days led riots in London's Jewish neighborhoods? As for years in the U.K., colored people were beaten on the streets, and some were killed, but in a context of a new sensationalism, a new seriousness. It was a hot topic until 1979, when the Tory party shifted from noblesse oblige to class war, and Margaret Thatcher, the new prime minister, buried the National Front by coopting much of its program. After that, as in the early punk years, colored people were beaten and killed—more, as it happened—but with the context altered once again: with the hard facts smoothed into a context of legitimacy, the facts were no longer news. A punk parading down King's Road with "SID LIVES" and a swastika stenciled on his black leather jacket caused no panic; he was a tourist attraction.

The punk swastika was a convoluted symbol: a nascent subcultural celebration of the purest racism; a demand for the re-

"The body of Rosa Luxemburg, dragged from a canal in March 1919"

—*King Mob Echo*, April 1968

placement of business as usual with excitement. It meant (to take Nik Cohn's definition of the impulse behind all postwar British pop subcultures—the Teddy Boys of the 1950s, the Mods and Rockers of the 1960s, the Skinheads of the early 1970s), "My dad's a square, I hate him, I hate you too, I'll smash your face in," or diversion of that impulse into public business: I hate them too, let's smash their faces in. It was a touch of the old épater la bourgeoisie. It meant, history books to the contrary, that fascism had won the Second World War: that contemporary Britain was a welfare-state parody of fascism, where people had no freedom to make their own lives—where, worse, no one had the desire. And it meant that negation is the act that would make it self-evident to everyone that the world is not as it seems—but only when the act is so implicitly complete it leaves open the possibility that the world may be nothing, that nihilism as well as creation may occupy the suddenly cleared ground.

Nazi crime was final crime, a buried wish made flesh and turned into smoke, the most complete wish ever given voice—a voice that in 1978, the year the Sex Pistols played their final concert, Guy Debord traced back to the twelfth century, to "the secret the Old Man of the Mountain"—Rashid al-Din Sinan, leader of the Assassins, millenarian terrorists of the Levant—"surrendered, it is said, only in his last hour, and then only to the most faithful of his fanatical disciples: 'Nothing is true; everything is permitted.'"

Debord was not talking about Nazis. He was narrating a film on his own life, looking back a quarter-century over his years as the tribune of the Lettrist International, then of the Situationist International, groups little enough known in their own time and now barely remembered. He was staking his claim on history: "Thus was set forth the best-made program for the absolute subversion of the whole of social life: classes and specializations, work and entertainment, the commodity and city planning, all were to be dashed to pieces. And such a program contained no promise other than that of an autonomy without rules and without restraint. Today these perspectives are part of the fabric of life—and there is combat for and against them everywhere. But when we first set out, they could hardly have seemed more chimerical—if the reality of modern capitalism had not been more chimerical still." "Nothing is true; everything is permitted," Debord was explaining, was simply the watchword the young men who formed the LI in 1952 had taken as their passkey into the realm of "play and public life."

On Debord's screen one saw merely habitués of Saint-Germain-des-Prés cafes, sitting at tables, playing guitars, and then Lacenaire, the "literary bandit" executed in Paris in 1836: Lacenaire as played by Marcel Herrand in Debord's favorite movie, Marcel Carné's 1945 *Les Enfants du paradis*. Dashing and sinister, Lacenaire turns to his rival, the Count, and to the Count's retinue of toadies: "It takes all kinds to make a world . . . or unmake it." "Quite good," sneers one of the Count's men. "Only a pun, but quite good."

The last words of the Old Man of the Mountain too were only a pun, a play on words, an intimation of the absolute reversals hiding in everyday language, in everyday life—it was because Debord had learned that language that he heard his ideas in everyone's mind. And just as Debord's ancient motto contained all the possibilities of nihilism, possibilities that included creation, so too did the palindromic title of his film: "the ancient phrase which comes completely back upon itself, which was constructed letter by letter like a labyrinth one can never leave, in a manner that so perfectly marries the form and content of perdition: *In girum imus nocte et consumimur igni*. We turn in a circle in the night and we are consumed by the fire."

ALL THE FEELING

All the feeling of that line was in "Belsen Was a Gas": not in the words, or in the arrangement, not even in the rhythm, but in the sound, in the way the whole echoed back on itself. That

. . . .

WHAT THE NAZIS
*did, Arendt said, was something
new: they altered the limits of
human action. In doing so, the
Nazis provided humanity with
more than a burden—the need
to comprehend their actions—
they also provided a legacy: "It
is in the very nature of things
human that every act that has
once made its appearance and
has been recorded in the history
of mankind stays with mankind
as a potentiality long after its
actuality has become a thing of
the past . . . Once a specific
crime has appeared for the first
time, its reappearance is more
likely than its initial emergence
could ever have been."*

*—blind fragment in collage of
text and photographs,
Londons Outrage!* no. 1,
*London fanzine, December
1976*

. . . .

night in Winterland, it was as if this straightforward performance, established by means of ordinary equipment (microphones, amplifiers, speakers), had been transformed by onstage aural flashbacks, flash forwards, freeze frames, split screens, matched dissolves, metronomic tracking shots: all the technology of displacement. The echoes were patent, physical. Photographs and film documentaries, the commonplace evidence of Belsenism, came into view.

Everyone has seen some of this evidence, and everyone, for mnemonic reasons as unique as fingerprints, retains a few specific fragments—fragments of an individual response not swallowed up by the ideology of the fact itself. I remember visiting the Dachau extermination camp in Germany in 1961, before it was cleaned up and fitted with audiovisual displays, when the ovens looked as if they had been warm the year before—still that memory, like most of the commonplace evidence, is just genre, iconography. The victims, whoever they were, had no individuality for me, even though I was taken to the place by a man whose parents had been killed there, even though my ancestors had lived and worked just miles away. The victims were part of the pit, or interred soul-wise in some official memorial complete with meditation chapel. But in two photographs I know—"Nazi Execution of Two Russian Partisans," taken by a Nazi photographer, and "U.S. Senator Alben W. Barkley of Kentucky, Chairman of the House–Senate Committee on War Crimes, Buchenwald, near Weimar, Germany, April 24, 1945," taken by a U.S. Army photographer—the sense of individuality is overwhelming, and from opposed directions.

"Nazi Execution" is impossibly expressive: Lewis Hine goes to hell. A girl, a teenager, has been hung. Her dead face communicates the motives that caused her to risk death and the motives of those who have just killed her: the Nazi officers who, in the photo, are visible, people whose task it was to exterminate just this sort of expressiveness. The girl's face says more than those of most living camera subjects. As she dangles in the air, one of the officers fits a noose around the neck of a boy, perhaps the same age as the girl, perhaps much younger. You make up a story to match his face. His face says: "We were comrades, but I never thought I would be made to watch her die; I never thought I would be made to witness my own death; but so be it." Looking at the picture, you are made aware of this image as a doubling of human possibility, as a doubled version of what it means to be human; you are made aware of an event that, one day, actually happened. Two people, specific within the species, were deprived of life in a particular way. Genre and iconography explode; the ideology of the fact cannot contain the moment.

In "Buchenwald, April 24, 1945," Senator Alben Barkley stands before a cordwood pile of corpses. To us today, familiar with such images as Barkley in 1945 was not, what we see first is genre, the pit, which we easily turn into iconography, "The Holocaust." But one must look at Barkley. The corpses are naked; he is heavily clothed in vest, suit, overcoat, hat, shoes. He stares at the corpses; the dignity in his face is bottomless. He is not dignified—the word immediately suggests pose, knowledge, distance, authority. This man, the photograph says, has struggled to understand what he has been made to look at, to understand something all of his experience of contemporary life and all of his reading of history have not prepared him to understand, and he has succeeded. The dignity in his face is not his own, and it is not that of the power he represents. In a moment of unpredictable comradeship and humility, Barkley has taken the dignity of which the people upon whom he gazes were robbed into his own face. If I were to die in this way, his face says, I would want someone to look upon me in this way. "We don't mind!" Johnny Rotten screamed in "Belsen Was a Gas." "Kill someone, be someone! Be a man, kill yourself! Please someone! We don't mind!"

He seemed near to coming loose from his own skin. As in other moments on the same stage on the same night, as in so many moments on the singles the Sex Pistols put out over the previous year, he seemed not to know what he was saying. He seemed not to be himself, whoever that was; once more he was less singing a song than being sung by it. Nothing existed but an objective, historical iconography, the common coin of any crowd called together anywhere in the West, where Nazi iconography, the spectacle of the Nazi fact, still served to diminish the exterminations of the present and to shroud the exterminations of the past, where Nazi iconography functioned not as history but as its most grandiose anomaly, the exception that proved the rule that all was for the best in this best of all possible worlds (it was hard to think, with the song pounding on your head, and impossible not to)—nothing existed but that, that and an objectification of this treasured iconography by a disembodied but still subjective voice, which dissolved iconography as surely as Alben Barkley's face. Johnny Rotten did not seem to be commenting on an historical event, but rather to be quoting from an as-yet-unmade movie:

[In 1985, in *Shoah*, a documentary film on the Nazi exterminations, director Claude Lanzmann interviews historian Raul Hilberg on the agencies responsible for transporting Jews to concentration camps.] "It was the same bureau that dealt with any kind of normal passenger?" "Absolutely. Just the official travel bureau. Mittel Europäisch Reisebüro would ship people to the gas chambers or they will ship vacationers to their favorite resort, and that was basically the same office and the same operation, the same procedure, the same billing . . . With children under ten going at half-fare and children under four going free." "Excuse me, the children under four who were shipped to the extermination camps, the children under four . . ." ". . . went free."

Or reading from an as-yet-unprinted news item:

(UPS, 11 Sept 1980—Salisbury, England)

A former army sergeant thinks he has come up with the ideal British vacation—three days in an imitation Nazi prison camp.

"They'll have a horrible time and love every minute of it, or I'll want to know the reason why," said Bob Acraman, 41.

Having taken over a former army camp on the bleak Salisbury plain, he is inviting vacationers to spend $72 for three November days behind barbed wire, guarded by gun-carrying guards in German uniforms and watchtowers around the perimeter.

Acraman promises "a nice line in psychological interrogation" for vacationers who try to escape.

"There'll be plenty of fog, rain and frost for our 2 a.m. searches," he said.

"The food will be first-class prison nosh—thin soup and stale bread. And there'll be no fires in the huts."

Acraman claims demand for his vacation is heavy.

"There are plenty of crazy people around like me who love being locked up and made to suffer behind barbed wire," he said.

Of course, Johnny Rotten couldn't predict the future; he could only insist that it was contained by the past. That was the meaning of no-future. After "Belsen Was a Gas," "Holidays in the Sun" was still to come that night in Winterland, and Johnny Rotten had no way of knowing, had he been born in another time and another place, that he could have ridden to Belsen for free, or that had he been willing to wait, he could have seen a new Belsen without ever leaving England. Or is that exactly what he meant?

On stage, all one saw was an ugly, unlikely youth declaring that his time as a pop star had come to an end: you could see it happen, hear him deciding to quit. "Ah, it's awful," he said in the middle of "No Fun," his last song as a member of the Sex Pistols, even his loathing leaving him: "It's no good." The disgust that the band had been built to talk about had finally, so quickly, overtaken the one whose job it was to talk about it. The show had gone far enough. All one saw was a failure; all one saw was a medium. The hall shook: it shook like a seance table in nineteenth-century Boston, Paris, or Petrograd, when the devotees sat waiting, ready for the dead to come knocking on the horizontal doors. The show had gone as far as a show can go.

A BARITONE

"A baritone came on, to a round of applause. He had a fine voice and the most funereal aspect imaginable. You would have guessed him to have been in bygone days a *représentant du peuple*, a member of the Montagne, a 'thinker' who prided himself on his looks . . . If this baritone were to figure in the troubles which await us, I for one would not be surprised." So wrote the conservative journalist Louis Veuillot, four years before those troubles, in the form of the Paris Commune of 1871, arrived to match his prophecy. Seance tables weren't the only thing shaking in Paris in 1867.

As cited by T. J. Clark in *The Painting of Modern Life*, Veuillot was describing a performer in the Alcazar, a "café-concert": the warmup act for Thérésa, the singer all Paris came to hear. She was stocky, unlovely, and powerful; the texts of her songs were carefully monitored by the government censor, but he couldn't control her voice or her gestures—the way, Clark says, she won her battles "*against* the standardized melodies, the footling lyrics, the cynical production values, the farrago of violence and souped-up emotion." This was a matter of lifting a hand in the right place at the right time, of turning a phrase, and as Howard Hampton once said of the concerts Bob Dylan put on in 1966, Thérésa had the knack of turning a casual aside into a condemnation of the whole social order: the "audience," Clark writes, "lived for the moment when the band struck up 'La Canaille' [The Rabble] and the singer invited them to join in the chorus of 'J'en suis! J'en suis!' [I'm part of it]."

The Alcazar was a big hall, where drinks were served to thousands. The new petite bourgeoisie, the clerks who filled most of it, would in their workday or domestic lives have taken "rabble" for the crude class insult it would have been. Here they embraced it, out of longing for the proletarian or peasant past they were escaping, out of hatred for the real, propertied bourgeoisie they longed to emulate. Here, in the new domain of regular entertainments and organized leisure, they had a privileged space to dissipate their yearnings and their rage, or to focus them. So Veuillot's anonymous baritone (who along with twenty thousand others was in June 1871 in the extermination of the Commune put up against a wall and shot) (or who had already left town) raises an interesting question: is the cabaret a place where the spirit of negation is born, or is it where that spirit goes to die?

"There was a revolution round the corner," Clark writes, "made by baritones or not." And around the next corner was the trashcan of history. The Commune emerged on 18 March 1871, when Adolphe Thiers's one-month-old conservative parliamentary regime, brought to power by Emperor Louis-Napoleon's surrender in the Franco-Prussian War, fled Paris in the face of the Prussian advance and the desertion of government troops. For the next months almost every radical idea of the previous hundred years was dug out of the ground and put into some sort of practice. Private people once again became citizens, interested in everything, because when everything seemed possible, everything was interesting. "I will never forget those delightful moments of deliverance," one man said. "I came down from my upper chamber in the Latin Quarter to join that immense open-air club which filled the boulevards from one end of Paris to the other. Everyone talked about public affairs; all merely personal preoccupations were forgotten; no more thought of buying and selling; all felt ready, body and soul, to advance towards the future."

To many then and now the Commune was not a revolution at all, but an anarchist parody of what had begun as an old-fashioned bourgeois rejection of ossified authority. If it was a revolution it was certainly queer: "the greatest festival of the 19th century," Guy Debord, Attila Kotányi, and Raoul Vaneigem wrote for the situationists in "On the Commune" in 1962. They were constructing a philosophy of leisure ("Underlying the events of that spring of 1871 one can see the insurgents' feeling that they had become the masters of their own history, not so much on the level of 'governmental' politics as on the level of their everyday life"), of modern leisure as medieval baccanale: as masters of their own history the communards abolished ordinary time. The Lord of Misrule, joke king of the ancient overnight saturnalia, executed the day after, had somehow seized history and declared that misrule would last forever. It was as if, instead of stumbling home drunk and getting up the next day to stand at the counter, Thérésa's fans had poured out of the Alcazar and into the streets, and there changed the world beyond the power of memory to recall what it had been like the day before. "That was the dance that everybody forgot," rockabilly singer Butch Hancock once said of Elvis Presley's first appearance on the Ed Sullivan Show in 1956. "It was the dance that was so strong it took an entire civilization to forget it. And ten seconds to remember it."

A memory of a change in the structures that governed work, family, and leisure—a dissolution of those structures, those separations—was what the Paris Commune left to those few who wanted to remember it. The Commune made the organs of direct democracy that appeared in later revolutionary moments—the Petrograd soviets of 1905 and 1917, the Berlin Räte of 1918, the anarchist collectives in Barcelona in 1936, the Hungarian councils of 1956, perhaps the Free Speech Movement in Berkeley in 1964, the assemblies and occupations in France in May '68, the Solidarity unions in Poland in 1980—seem bureaucratic. The situationists wrote:

The official organizers of the Commune were incompetent (if measured against Marx and Lenin, or even Blanqui). But the various so-called irresponsible acts of that movement are precisely what is needed for the continuation of the revolutionary movement in our own time (even if circumstances restricted almost all of those acts to a purely destructive level—the most famous example being the revolutionary who, when a suspect bourgeois insisted that he had never had anything to do with politics, replied: "That's exactly why I'm going to kill you").

Stevedores, it is said, spread philosophy like gossip; clerks wrestled with absolutes ("That's exactly why I'm going to kill you"). The Commune may have had as much in common with John of Leyden's Münster as with any certified modern revolution—Georges Clemenceau, in 1871 mayor of Montmartre, thought so. It can hardly be an accident that the most convincing rejection of the Commune remains Guy Endore's 1933 horror potboiler, *The Werewolf of Paris*: as a dramatization of freedom, the Commune was also a riot of the social unconscious. As it uncovered every wish for life, it uncovered a wish for death, which contained a wish for the death of the Commune itself. With Bismarck's troops and the whole of the French army massed outside Paris, the Communards never had a chance, and they knew it. Many were willing to die because, after a taste of freedom that could be measured only by the inadequacies of the surprises of the previous day, they found themselves unwilling to settle for anything less, to live as they had lived only one day earlier, much less to return to the freedom of a choice between whatever commodities others had put up for sale, a choice between a Sunday in the park or on the river: so goes the legend invented after the fact. In that sense the Commune was not a seizure of history but a gift to it, or a curse on it, a standard against which the future would be judged: a moment to be worshipped or damned.

AS THE CENTURY

As the century turned, the Commune dropped down into a footnote to the Second Empire, or floated free as an anarchist myth. It began to seem perfect, every failure absorbed into looming possibility: a work of art. In some ways that is just what it was.

The greatest and most prophetic work of art of the nineteenth century was Baron Haussmann's redesign of Paris. In the 1850s and 1860s he cut the city up and put it back together. He straightened labyrinthine alleys, ran huge boulevards through the city like rivers (it was a joke that when he got done with the streets he would straighten the Seine), broke up the old craft districts, separated residences from workplaces, workplaces from places of leisure, neighborhoods from markets, class from class.

It is a truism that Haussmann's boulevards were built to facilitate the circulation of troops, to make the barricades of the revolution of 1848 an impossibility. It is less obvious, but far more wonderful, that Haussmann changed a collection of self-contained villages into a grid for the circulation of autonomous commodities, a transit system to accommodate the new desire of capital to move, to parade. It was art—but, as the avant-garde would boast of itself from that time to this as it attempted to catch up with Haussmann, not art for art's sake. Writing in 1985, Charles Newman caught the dynamic: "a good case can be made for capitalist consumer culture as the Avant-Garde of our time. As Gerald Graff puts it, 'advanced capitalism needs to destroy all vestiges of tradition, all orthodox ideologies, all continuous and stable forms of reality in order to stimulate higher levels of consumption.' Crisis becomes not a revolutionary but the ultimate capitalist metaphor." But in truth capitalism left the essence of the old (hierarchy, separation, alienation) altogether in place, and raised instead a screen of continuous change, a show in which everything that was new was old as soon as it was pictured, and thus could be replaced by something even more falsely new—or so it looked to Guy Debord, who in *The Society of the Spectacle* reached for the dynamic in uglier, harsher terms; who tried to bring the story back down to earth.

Whereas in the primitive phase of capitalist accumulation, "political economy sees in the *proletarian* only the *worker*," who must receive the minimum compensation indispensable for the maintenance of his labor power, and never sees the proletarian "in his leisure and humanity," this ruling class perspective is reversed as soon as the production of commodities reaches a level of abundance which requires a surplus of collaboration from the worker. The worker, suddenly redeemed from the total contempt which is plainly shown to him by all the forms of the organization and supervision of production, now finds himself, every day, outside of production, and in the guise of a consumer; with zealous politeness, he is, seemingly, treated as an adult. At this point, the *humanism of the commodity* takes charge of the worker's "leisure and humanity," because now political economy can and must dominate these spheres *as* political economy.

In other words, by Haussmann's time capitalism had reached a point of critical mass. It had become so effective, and so voracious, that in order to maintain itself, which meant to extend itself, it had to grant the worker, in primitive capitalist times only a hammer or a nail, a degree of autonomy, so that the worker might swell the market for the commodity, the audience for the spectacle. The worker had to be granted a measure of surplus value, of free income and free time—otherwise capitalism would overreach itself and collapse. The secret of the fetishism of the commodity was that the commodity could talk, it could seem human, it could turn human beings into things. For the reifications contained in that secret to take their place in the human psyche, everyone had to learn how to listen—to hear what, in *Sister Carrie*, Theodore Dreiser had made his heroine hear.

When she came within earshot of their pleading, desire in her bent a willing ear. Ah, ah! The voice of the so-called inanimate. Who shall translate for us the language of the stones?

"My dear," said the lace collar she secured from Partridge's, "I fit you beautifully; don't give me up."

"Ah such little feet," said the leather of the soft new shoes, "how effectively I cover them; what a pity they should ever want my aid."

You are nothing unless you have everything: that was modernity. Modernity was the shifting of the leverage point of capitalism from production to consumption, from necessity to wish. It was a difficult project: all desires had to be reduced to those that could be put on the market, and thus desires were reduced to needs and experienced as such. As the situationists would argue, the modern capitalist project required the channeling of the potentially untrammeled desire in every human heart into a housekeeping of practical need, and the reduction of possibility into what they named "survival," the reduction of life to "economic imperatives"—here, the buying of what you buy not because you subjectively desire it, but because it has been objectively proven that you cannot live without it. Listen, with the benefit of nearly a century, as Carrie couldn't listen in her own moment: her new shoes imagine her in jeopardy, and suggest that they can rescue her, or, should she prove her-

Greeting card, 1984

self unworthy, that they might not. What is at stake is not her own desire, but her ability to breathe. A certain transubstantiation, swollen with theological subtleties and metaphysical niceties, is taking place: in this story, power belongs wholly to the commodity.

It was in this sense that the situationists, like Harold Rosenberg and the Frankfurt School critics, liked to speak of the paradox of the "proletarianization of the world." They meant that when political economy dominates life, it turns everyone, the worker who has been made over into a consumer, the bourgeois who already was one, into a sort of proletarian, a mute object in the face of the talking thing: the "humanism of the commodity" means that the commodity becomes human as the human being becomes a commodity. But where others saw only hardening concrete, as a band of self-consciously modern revolutionaries the situationists thought they glimpsed a crack. They had come together—less than a dozen people, representing such spectral combines (aesthetic cults at the most, one-person art movements at the least) as "l'Internationale lettriste," "il Movimento internazionale per una bauhaus immaginista," and "Arte nuclare," holding their first, tentative conference in Alba, Italy, in 1956—in the belief that they could find that crack, map it, pry it open until the old world disappeared into its hole. Their hunch was that abundance, banality, and boredom were modernisms not only as levers of bland tyranny, but as opportunities to discover new desires— desires that a truly modern "International" might identify, publicize with all the weapons of satire, bluff, irony, and finally violence, and then stand ready to guide into a great common action, an irruption of negation, into a new world. "Proletarianization," the tyranny itself, was itself the crack: when almost all were proletarians, almost all were potential revolutionaries.

As theorists, the situationists tried to see themselves as victims, no less proletarianized than anyone else. They tried to lift the weight of the world onto their shoulders, and then to feel out every way in which that weight was crushing them.

Self-consciously superior only to the mindlessness of the condition they were forced to endure along with everyone else, they tried to refuse both the comforts of the past and of the grave. Melancholy and nostalgia are the wheels on which Rosenberg and the Frankfurt School turned their phrases; the situationists fought against both with every word, trying to banish sorrow for fury. As victims, they sought empowerment—and you can still feel it, the aggression and arrogance Malcolm McLaren tried to tell Peter Urban about, an empowerment that sometimes seems to turn into palpable fact, as infectious as a disease, in every good word the situationists wrote.

As revolutionaries, the situationists were gamblers—in their everyday lives, poker players, pinball players—and they placed their bet for a different world on the most subtle modernism in capitalist hegemony: the admission of subjectivity into the objectifying market. The commodity was king, but like the king who after generations of inbreeding ends his line as a mutant, the commodity was also a freak: it could talk, but it was stupid. The commodity could seduce, but it was also blind. It could bend Carrie's ear, but it could not tell Carrie from you or me; in the world of the spectacle, all cats were gray in the dark, and it was always dark. Sooner or later Carrie would figure this out; resentment and rage would well up in a new desire to speak for herself, to make herself heard: I have everything and I am nothing; I am nothing and I should be everything. The situationist project was to make it sooner, before it was too late—before Carrie was ready for the rocking chair.

Objectivity, as Vaneigem defined it for the situationists, meant "I love that girl because she is beautiful"; subjectivity meant "That girl is beautiful because I love her." If the central human faculty is the ability to consciously want more than one can have, then emerging from it is the ability of each person to want something different from everyone else. Capitalism knew that, which is why every product appeared in endless variation. But each variant said the same thing, and, ultimately, no one hears the speech of the commodity in precisely the same way. In this discontinuity is the possibility that the refusal of one person to hear what everyone else hears can lead to the refusal of countless people to listen at all, and that is why a letter from an eleven-year-old girl broke the Möbius strip of Michael Jackson's Victory tour. Rock 'n' roll, which began as perhaps the purest example of laissez-faire capitalism ever known—"I am nothing and I should be everything," said Sam Phillips as he founded Sun Records in Memphis in 1952, Syd Nathan as he founded King in Cincinnati in 1944, Don Robey as he founded Peacock in Houston in 1949 (maybe they said "I should have everything," but the commodities they sold surely said "I should be everything")—was a game of subjectivity in the objective marketplace. No matter how deeply buried, that rhythm could not be killed, and so the chickens came home to roost.

Modern capitalism was a tricky project: dangerous. Free income and free time might provoke desires the market could never satisfy, and those desires might contain a wish to go off the market. In the early and mid-1950s, laissez-faire rock 'n' roll capitalism was so marginal that for all rational purposes it was off the market—and yet the desires it was able to excavate were to prove so powerful that the marginal anomaly soon enough invaded the market, made its own market, which by Michael Jackson's time could be found at the heart of social life.

LaDonna Jones played out a fable, but one need not go back that far: her solitary intervention was a version of the mass intervention that today we call "the sixties." "The '60s' is merely the name we give to a disruption of late-capitalist ideological and political hegemony," wrote the leftist editors of a 1984 anthology on the period, "to a disruption of the bourgeois dream of unproblematic production, of everyday life as the bureaucratic society of controlled consumption." The sixties were first of all fast times, boom times; as in Haussmann's era, capitalism almost overreached itself. Too many people had too much of everything that was on the market, and so they had the leisure to think about what else they might want.

A decade after the formal end of the sixties, there would remain in the West a guilty memory of its incomplete disruptions, a fear of its unsatisfied chaos. As Debord said in 1978, demands for liberation and pleasure, all fragmented but still seeking the free field of autonomy and solidarity, were by then part of the fabric of life, and there was combat for and against them everywhere. But joined by then to an economy that seemed to be collapsing in all directions at once, the fear of chaos would double. Trumpeted like a horror movie by those seeking power, on the part of the voting majorities fear mandated a radical solution: a leap back over modernity, a return to a pre-modern economy, to the economic terrorism of the Thatcherist and Reaganist regimes.

The chaos of the sixties had come directly from the loosed spheres of "leisure and humanity," the domination of which Debord had identified as central to both the continuation of capitalism as power and its continuation as hegemony. To a crucial degree, the speech of the commodity had been interrupted. The difference between the 1960s and the 1980s, Bob Dylan said in response to a question about the supposed "revival of the '60s spirit" in such 1985 events as "We Are the World" and Bob Geldof's Live Aid famine-relief concert, was that before "There were people trying to stop the show anyway they could . . . Then, you didn't know which end the trouble was coming from. And it could come at any time." Political economy had indeed failed to dominate the spheres of leisure and humanity, to dominate them "*as* political economy," and so those spheres had to be forcibly restricted. The problem with the sixties was that people had come to take their leisure and humanity as rights; the Thatcherist and Reaganist project was to turn those things back into privileges. "The Tory solution to Britain's economic recession," Simon Frith wrote in 1984, when that recession was almost a decade into its history, when unemployment in the U.K. had climbed from the scandalous one million that elected the Tories to more than three million, "is a new version of the 19th century's two nations. Growth is now supposed to come from the leisure goods industries. The new jobs will be low skilled and low paid; the non-affluent will service the affluent; the new working class will work on other people's leisure." He could also have said that, in Margaret Thatcher's new U.K., which since 1979 had served as a harbinger of Ronald Reagan's U.S.A., failed mass strikes and riots in the poverty ghettos were not only costs of this new economy, but linchpins: social and economic exclusion organized as spectacle. "You could be next," said the commodity that others could not afford to buy to those who could: "keep your nose clean."

It was as if Thatcher and Reagan had adopted a keynote of situationist theory: abundance is dangerous to power, and privation, if carefully managed, is safe. A mammoth debt encourages fear, which is never revolutionary; a high level of unemployment ensures a ready pool of strike breakers, translates the curse of a bad job into a blessing. "The transformation of the family man from a responsible member of society, interested in all public affairs," Hannah Arendt wrote in 1945 in "Organized Guilt and Universal Responsibility,"

to a "bourgeois" concerned only with his private existence and knowing no civic virtue, is an international modern phenomenon . . . Each time society, through unemployment, frustrates the small man in his normal functioning and normal self-respect, it trains him for that last stage in which he will willingly undertake any function, even that of hangman.

Arendt told a story: an SS member is recognized as a high-school classmate by a Jew upon the latter's release from Buchenwald. The Jew stares at his former friend, and the SS man says: "You must understand, I have five years of unemployment behind me. They can do anything they want with me."

To be sure, the rhetoric of the new rulers was both forgotten and ultra-modern, crude and dreamily paradoxical. Commentators spoke with awe at the way Thatcher and Reagan denounced the hedonistic anarchy of the sixties as a moral wasteland responsible for economic disaster while simultaneously celebrating untrammeled capitalism as a personal quest for autonomy, self-realization, adventure, fulfillment, possibility, imagination, risk, and desire, literally taking fragments of May '68 slogans into their mouths; the key words were adventure and risk. When an ever-growing number of families found their survival in question, "survival" ceased to function as an ideology, for an ideology is dominant to the degree that it falsifies, to the degree that it can float free of all real-world referents: both Thatcher and Reagan promised everything to anyone with the grace to leave the damned behind. At the same time, they spoke of the continuity that should have been. As against the interruptions of the sixties, Reagan said early in his presidency, "We must mobilize every asset we have—spiritual, moral, educational, economic and military—in a crusade for national renewal. We must restore to their place of honor the bedrock values handed down by families to serve as society's compass." That was the rhetoric; working from a speech in which Reagan amended the Declaration of Independence to read "born free" rather than "created equal," the political critic Walter Karp deciphered a reality so weird that almost no one understood it.

The republic's historic assertion that "all men are created equal," which Lincoln regarded as a stumbling block to tyranny, is also a stumbling block to National Renewal. That we are created equal has never meant that Americans were supposed to live alike. What it does mean, what it has always meant, is that the citizens of this republic cannot be treated in law and by government as mere social and economic functions. Yet this is exactly how the Reaganites propose to treat the citizens of the commonwealth. The administration intends to bestow wealth upon the wealthy because it is their function to invest in productive enterprises. The administration intends to impoverish the poor because it is their function to perform menial services and not be a drag on investors.

To release capitalism from its republican bondage is what National Renewal is all about. It is about nothing else . . . As a matter of course, the Reaganites hope to turn public education into class education by financing a middle-class exodus from the common schools. When they become schools for a class and not for the commonality, the American republic will have lost the only instrument capable of turning a mass of future jobholders into a plurality of citizens. The common schools of the republic are one of capitalism's fetters, and so of course they must be broken.

Karp was not writing in some obscure radical journal printed in smudged ink on cheap paper; he was writing in *Harper's*. Nevertheless he wrote with the maddened patience of one who knows the only words that can say what he means have been robbed of their meaning, turned inside out, discredited, then reempowered, passed into their opposites, and this was only 1981—in five years or so, what Karp was saying would sound really crazy, even though by then the facts to prove his case would be on the record. Digging deep into the back pages of the newspaper, you could learn that Terrel Bell, Reagan's secretary of education from 1981 through 1984, had written an article in which he told of "constant battles against a well-organized network of the far right—identifiable by their Adam Smith neckties—who [Bell said] 'enjoyed . . . extraordinary privileges and automatic forgiveness from the White House' . . . Bell says their ultimate goal was the destruction of public education and its replacement by a market-place system of private schools run by entrepreneurs."

In 1986 this sounded even more paranoid than Karp's entrail readings had in 1981. Pretty strange, you said as you read the item—especially that bit about the "Adam Smith neckties"—wonder who thought that one up? Sort of a "human-interest story," like (scanning the paper) the two-headed baby in Peru ("The bishop declared that the baby contains two separate souls") or pingpong-ball-sized UFOs in Brazil ("Fighter pilots pursued the phenomena until their aircraft ran out of fuel"). Karp knew none of this as he wrote—not the neckties, the baby, or the pingpong balls—but he pressed on as if he knew this was the context his words would find. "The Reaganites do not even care about the so-called free market, which is merely one of their confidence games," he said, now almost ranting, shouting, what the Reaganites really cared about, he said, was this: they want capitalism in America to become what Karl Marx thought it would be by nature—the transcendent force and the measure of all things, the power that reduces free politics to trifling, the citizen to a "worker," the public realm to "the state," the state to an instrument of repression protecting capitalism from the menace of liberty and equality, with which it grew up as Cain grew up with Abel . . . Marx's description of capitalist society is the Reaganite prescription for America. That is the meaning of National Renewal.

BUT THAT

But that was later. In the meantime, Haussmann's project went forward. Paris became new; so did Parisians. The separations between work, family, and leisure forced by the new map of the city were internalized by the newly atomized, autonomous individuals of the new Paris—after all, the whole notion of "individualism" was a modernism, a function of one's subjective choice of what to do with free income and free time. The Commune was a comma in Haussmann's sentence; he had won. Paris became a city of symbols, power, and desire. Social life was like a lottery: if everyone has a chance to buy a ticket, everyone has a chance to win, and since only one out of a million can win, the separation of the one from the million, of each from everyone, is complete. As commodities spun through their circuits, each person became, in fantasy, a ruler: the Commodifier. You could see it in the streets. It was as if Haussmann had answered Marx's "All that is solid melts into air"—Marx's awestruck judgment, in 1848, from *The Communist Manifesto*, on the transcendent force of capitalism, on capitalism as the measure of all things—with a Hobbesian boast: Ecce homo!

Behold man! It was Haussmann's genius to open his invented city to the countryside, to ring the new city with parks and marinas. Work and domestic life had been severed, creating new markets for each; a new sector of enticing, seductive, organized leisure made a third separation, a separation that at once assuaged the dislocations of wage labor and domesticity, and provided a new market of its own. Against the inevitable alienations of capitalism (the language of my work cannot be translated into the language of my home; my work and my family turn my leisure into nervous babble), Haussmann set an autonomy of pleasure. A stroll in the park, a Sunday on the riverbank—as spectacles, such things represented free money, free time: freedom. More than that: the trees, the water, the flowers, the grass, they all said that Haussmann's new city was not an interested construction but a natural fact. The language of the stones did not have to be translated; it was plain to all. If Haussmann had extended the division of labor into a division of life, he had also blessed it.

Haussmann's work was what we call today urban renewal, city planning, gentrification, "urbanism"—"a rather neglected branch of criminology," the situationists' two-man Bureau of Unitary Urbanism wrote in 1961. "Urbanism doesn't exist; it is only an 'ideology,' in Marx's sense of the word"—a consensual limit on discourse about the real and the possible. It was an agreement about what constituted the language of the stones—in this case, architecture—and as an ideology, the agreement made everything outside itself seem unnatural. As consent it was a social compact, and as a social compact it was "blackmail by utility . . . Modern capitalism dissuades people from criticizing architecture with the simple argument that people need a roof over their heads, just as television is accepted on the grounds that people need information and entertainment. People are made to overlook the obvious fact that this information, this entertainment, and this kind of dwelling place are not made for them, but without them and against them. The whole of urban planning can be understood only as a society's field of publicity-propaganda—that is" (as Bob Geldof tried to say a quarter-century later), "as the organization of participation in something in which it is impossible to participate."

The hallmark of any ideology is its invisibility as such: this is why, in 1986, a Reaganist fact could be less believable than its prophecy five years before. There were protests against Haussmann in his time; by the situationists' time, his Paris was no longer a new city, but the only city: the model for modernity, the visible fact of modern life. If its ideology was invisible, how to fight it, how to begin speaking a new language, not of stones but of human beings? The "criticism of architecture" was a locus of what the situationists called "revolution," and the situationists were vague: they spoke of "the coordination of artistic and scientific means of denunciation," then of "situationist bases" for "an experimental life," "acting as bridgeheads for an assault . . . fueled by all the tensions of daily life, on the manipulation of cities and their inhabitants." They were clearest when they sounded most desperate: "We must spread skepticism toward those bleak, brightly colored kindergartens, the new dormitory cities of both East and West. Only a mass awakening will pose the question of a conscious construction of the urban milieu."

Like all revolutionaries stranded in a present without revolution, the situationists looked back. It was the Paris Commune that represented *"the only realization of a revolutionary urbanism to date—attacking on the spot the petrified signs of the dominant organization of life, understanding social space in political terms, refusing to accept the innocence of any monument."* As always with the situationists, one has to slow down: what do monuments have to do with revolution? Debord, in *The Society of the Spectacle*:

The first phase of the domination of the economy over social life brought into the definition of all human realization the obvious degradation of *being* into *having*. The present phase of the total occupation of social life by the accumulated results of the economy leads to a generalized sliding of *having* into *appearing*, from which all actual "having" must draw its immediate prestige and its ultimate function. Simultaneously, all individual reality has become social reality, directly dependent on social power, and shaped by it. It is allowed to appear only to the extent that it is *not*.

Nothing that actually happens becomes real until it is represented in the spectacle that is social life—after which it becomes unreal, and passes into its opposite. As a revolutionary, Debord was a mathematician: insisting on the spectacle's transformation of all things into their opposites, he spoke of a "reversible connecting factor" in modern society, the very thing that made modern society modern, the principle of negation growing within the structures of domination. This was the location of the revolutionary impulse on the new terrain of the spectacle, of social life as symbolism. If a monument was a symbol, the spectacle concentrated on a single point, then a demolition of symbols was the surest way to reveal the invisible terrain on which people actually lived.

The Communards, the situationists wrote with regret in "On the Commune," did not destroy all symbols of the division of life. They refused to seize the National Bank. Repulsed by a battery of artists, they fell back from an attempt to burn Notre-Dame to the ground. But if the Communards did not forever erase the divisions of faith, work, family, and leisure—if they did not establish a world in which faith would be brought down to earth, work made pleasurable, family life suffused with the fervor of work, or dissolve all three into leisure—which, the situationists thought, could and should replace faith, work, and family with the free creation of situations, a new use of leisure, a true leisure, a festival wherein material survival, supposedly the provenance of work, and the continuation of the species, supposedly the provenance of family, and faith, supposedly the provenance of the religious illusion, would be natural by-products of each individual's everyday rediscovery of his or her own life in play (what do I want to do today?)—if the Communards did not do that, they did at least pull down the Vendôme Column.

One-hundred-and-forty-four feet tall, four feet taller than the Gdansk crosses, it was a symbol of the first Napoleon: of military glory, the territorial expansion of life as it already was, of domination celebrated as freedom. On 16 May 1871, on the motion of the painter Gustave Courbet, it was toppled onto a bed of straw and manure. To Haussmann's "Ecce homo!" the Communards offered Shelley's "Ozymandias." The act was re-imagined just short of a century later by Gerard Van der Leun:

Tonight, to the consternation of the duly delegated authorities, an unkempt mob of anarchists clad in body paint and fright wigs stormed the Houses of Parliament following their frenzied participation in the Intergalactic Sonic Sit-In at the Royal Albert Hall. After laying siege to the speaker's podium, they used their cigarette lighters to fuse the works of Big Ben into a bronze statue of Smokey Robinson.

So do anarchist myths float free and, occasionally, touch down.

IN 1967

In 1967, a year before French students and workers reenacted the Paris Commune in the uprising of May '68, about the time Gerard Van der Leun was contriving his fantasy, situationist notions about revolution were patent nonsense. "The situationists," Henri Lefebvre wrote then,

propose not a concrete utopia, but an abstraction. Do they really believe that one fine day, or one decisive evening, people will look at each other and say, "Enough! To hell with work, to hell with boredom! Let's put an end to it!"—and that everyone will then step into the eternal Festival and the creation of situations?

—Thérésa says, "let me hear you say *yeah!*"—

If this happened once, at the dawn of 18 March 1871, this combination of circumstances will not occur again.

The agreement, between an eminent sixty-six-year-old sociologist and young extremists drunk on their own theories, was as complete as the breach: the agreement that the Commune had been a rejection of "boredom" in favor of "festival." Those words were not part of conventional critical discourse; they were part of a discourse that, once, Lefebvre and the situationists had invented together.

In the aftermath of the Second World War, Lefebvre was the chief theorist of the French Communist Party, which many

Poster advertising publication
of *I.S.* no. 11, October 1967,
words by Raoul Vaneigem,
drawings by Gérard Joannès

thought was on the verge of taking power. Perhaps the leading Marxist philosopher in France, he was a scientist with a tenure more valuable than any university could guarantee. But over the next decade he turned away from Marxist scientism, arguing that to change the world one had to think about changing life. Instead of examining institutions and classes, structures of economic production and social control, one had to think about "moments"—moments of love, hate, poetry, frustration, action, surrender, delight, humiliation, justice, cruelty, resignation, surprise, disgust, resentment, self-loathing, pity, fury, peace of mind—those tiny epiphanies, Lefebvre said, in which the absolute possibilities and temporal limits of anyone's existence were revealed. The richness or poverty of any social formation could be judged only on the terms of these evanescences; they passed out of consciousness as if they had never been, but in their instants they contained the whole of life. Once, perhaps in the Middle Ages, every moment had been part of a visible totality, just as the language of religion was part of the language of work. In the modern world, where God was dead and the division of labor divided every sector of life from every other, each moment was separate, and none had a language. Still—what if one took a moment as a passageway to totality? What if one based one's life on the wish to affirm the moment of love, or negate the moment of resignation?

This was abstract, aesthetic; the frame of Lefebvre's postwar thought was even more so. Moments, he said, appeared on a mysterious, unmapped territory he called "la vie quotidienne," everyday life, a mode of being defined most readily in the negative: "Whatever remains after one has eliminated all specialized activities." This was not life on the job so much as life on the commute—more than that, the fantasy life provoked by the dullness of the commute or the job. It was not one's role as a wife so much as those small times when one's role was somehow absent, and, for a few seconds, one reinvented oneself out of nothing society recognized as real. Everyday life was a realm of repetition, pettiness, depression; of boredom, mutely

SAME THINGS DAY AFTER DAY TUBE–WORK–DINNER–WORK–TUBE–ARMCHAIR–T.V.–SLEEP–TUBE–WORK HOW MUCH MORE CAN YOU TAKE ONE IN FIVE CRACKS UP

—graffiti in Notting Hill, London, early 1970s, as reproduced in Londons Outrage *no. 2, February 1977*

interrupted by seemingly meaningless desires for heroism, adventure, escape, revenge—freedom.

Lefebvre's critics denied that save as a catalogue of any era's tools and toilets ("Where the Greek woman heated stones, we simply turn on our gas range"), everyday life existed at all; speaking in 1961 at a conference convened by Lefebvre, Guy Debord called it "the measure of all things." He was speaking by means of a tape recorder, "in order to seize the simplest opportunity to break with the appearance of pseudo-collaboration." Dramatizing the habitual submission of the listener to the presence of the lecturer, or the confusion produced by the lecturer's absence, he meant to "demonstrate, by a slight alteration of the usual procedures, that everyday life is right here." The "intervention" was marginal, trivial— but it was in the realm of the marginal and the trivial that any critique of everyday life, and therefore any critique of social reality, began. Against the shining progress of technology and commerce, Lefebvre said, everyday life was "a backward sector" in the modern world—"a colonized sector," Debord said—an affective Third World in the heart of the First. But this was a foreign country where everyone actually lived.

Everyday life, as Lefebvre conceived it—first in *Introduction à la critique de la vie quotidienne* in 1947, then in many books over the next twenty years—was a milieu as unsatisfied as it was silent, as silent as it was ubiquitous: it was implicit in his work that outside of novels, poetry, and music—outside of art—moments no more had a language in the Soviet Union than they did in France. But if those moments could be given a language, a political language, they could form the basis for entirely new demands on the social order. What if one said no to boredom, and demanded surprise, not for a moment, but as a social formation?

This was not Marxism. Marx would have understood it: Lefebvre's theories were rooted in Marx's romantic 1844 *Economic and Philosophical Manuscripts*, which in the late 1920s Lefebvre had translated and published. He bid the Party to pursue them; he was turned aside. The Soviet administrators of the canon deemed these early studies of alienation vaporous juvenilia, suppressed them, and Lefebvre went along, making his reputation in 1939 with *Le Matérialisme dialectique*. That was science. The theory of moments was heresy or, worse, babble; by 1958 it would lead to Lefebvre's expulsion from the Party. But by then he had found other readers.

"The theory of moments converged with research on the creation of ambiance, of situations," he told an interviewer in 1975: Lefebvre was back in 1957, 1958, when he was a Communist in name only and a situationist lacking only the name. "The idea of escaping from the combination of elements of the past—of repetition—was an idea that was at once poetic, subversive, and audacious. It already implied that this was a project with a difference. It isn't easy to invent new pleasures, or new ways of making love . . . a utopian idea—but not really—since, effectively, we lived, we created a new situation, that of exhuberance in friendship, that of the subversive or revolutionary microsociety in the very heart of a society which, moreover, ignores it."

It was, Lefebvre said of his relationship with the new situationists, a "love story." He spoke of "laying aside all mistrust, all ambition, all schemes . . . In an atmosphere of passionate oneness we would talk far into the night . . . We drank, sometimes there were other stimulants, and these nights had an earnestness, an affection—it was more than communication, it was a communion." "Moments constructed as 'situations' can be considered moments of rupture, of acceleration, *revolutions in individual everyday life*," the situationists wrote in 1960. Soon Lefebvre and Debord, traveling together through France, contrived the idea of the Commune as "festival." "And then," Lefebvre said, "naturally, without warning, times changed, love changed." The situationists published their "On the Commune"; then Lefebvre published his "The Meaning of the Commune"; the situationists attacked it as base plagiarism; and Lefebvre would scorn the abstractions he had passed onto them. "I miss the friendship," he said in 1975. "I don't give a damn." He went back and forth, as if he would never get over

it. "I hardly read their attacks. Why attach any importance to it? The important thing is the period of effervescence, of discovery, of friendship, of something irretrievable; once it's lost, it can't be replaced."

The Commune, Lefebvre and Debord decided, created a city free of planning, a field of moments, visible and loud, the antithesis of planning: a city that was reduced to zero and then reinvented every day. That was the agreement. The breach, by 1967, after Lefebvre and the situationists had not spoken for years, was that Lefebvre thought utopia was only art, and the situationists thought art on the level of utopia was life itself. "Realized art" was a situationist catchphrase; what it meant was "realized life."

SOME BLAMED

Some blamed the Commune on art. "The minister of Public Instruction," T. J. Clark says, "was quite clear in 1872 that 'the orgy of songs produced during [the Commune]' was partly to blame for the Communards' depravity"—their trashing of the laws of the church, the workplace, the family. Thus the minister made the dead Commune "reason for reimposing censorship on the café-concert in an effort to prevent such things from occurring again."

In the 1860s, when the Commune was only the paranoid dream of Louis Veuillot, some of those who heard Thérésa thought they heard a call to revolution. She was Poly Styrene: if this ugly fat woman could demand complete freedom, so could anyone. If she could lose and find herself in the rabble, so could you. "I'm part of it!" Complete freedom meant—no one knew. It was most readily defined in the negative: not this gap between the heaven promised in the new advertisements and the everyday satisfactions I can buy. Not this sense that when I leave my work for my family, and bring my family to a Sunday in the park, my leisure feels like work. Not this mad conviction that I'm a stranger in my own home town, that at

work I feel like a machine, that in the park I feel like an advertisement, that at home I feel like a tourist. Why doesn't my life match Thérésa's demands on me? "People believed Thérésa posed some sort of threat to the propertied order, and certainly the empire appeared to agree with them," Clark writes. Though she was invited to sing for the empress, the authorities "policed her every line and phrase" and "made no secret of the fact that they considered the café-concert a public nuisance."

A public nuisance is a triviality. Officials who shut them down—be they those who monitored Thérésa, those who in 1956 permitted Elvis Presley to perform but without moving any part of his body, or those who banned Sex Pistols shows—generally give voice less to real fears than to a lust for free publicity. Still, Elvis Presley and the Sex Pistols changed the patterns of everyday life—raised its stakes—all over the world. If what they did led to no official revolutions, it made life all over the world more interesting, and life continues to be more interesting than it would have been had they never appeared. In a book about movements in culture that raised no monuments, about movements that barely left a trace—movements that cannot be refuted by "Ozymandias" because they were ephemeral from beginning to end—making life more interesting is the only standard of judgment that can justify the pages they can fill.

THERESA'S

Thérésa's performances, captured in the paintings, journalism, and police reports of her time, can be seen as incipient pop culture: not the timeless folk-culture-of-the-people, and not the commodified culture-for-the-people organized by the leisure sector of the capitalist market, but something in between. As Michael Jackson proved, neither nostalgia for the folk community nor the constant movement of the market can contain pop culture, though the market provides access to pop culture—the

audience's access to the artist, the artist's access to the audience—and nostalgia, as a sense of what can be lost, powers it. Pop culture is a product—a show, a spectacle, a channeling of suppressed wishes into marketable form—and it is an impulse—a production of suppressed wishes that once released can call their own tune. In other words, Clark's:

producing the popular is a risky business. What begins as a process of control and containment is too often liable to end in mob rule. That is the case because the "popular" is not simply a commodity made from dead, obedient materials—here a phrase, there a value—waiting to be worked over and decently represented. It is something done with actual violence to resistant forms of life; and those forms survive in Thérésa's chorus and the audience she appeals to; they are always capable of recapturing the apparatus of production. In producing the popular, bourgeois society produces its opposite [the rabble], and for the most part it manages to make that opposite into an image—one withdrawn or provided at opportune moments. Yet the image itself . . . is inimical to everything the bourgeoisie most believes in, and its effects cannot be calculated as accurately as that class would wish. There is always the chance that a line or a phrase will be used by the singer to enforce fleetingly the kind of attention—the kind of collective vehemence—that Veuillot and the censor fear.

IN 1967

In 1967 the SI's "On the Commune" were rich words to T. J. Clark, in 1984 Professor of Fine Art at Harvard University and author of *The Painting of Modern Life: Paris in the Art of Manet and His Followers*. In 1966, Clark joined the Situationist International; he was one of only seventy men and women, and only six from the U.K., to take the name in the fifteen years the group existed.

Unlike earlier books Clark wrote on art and politics, *The Painting of Modern Life* was explicitly situationist. He based much of it on the notion of spectacle—unlike most of those who were using the concept in 1984, he credited its theorist. "If once or twice," Clark said, "my use of the word carries a faint whiff of Debord's chiliastic serenity, I shall be satisfied." Clark and Debord had been comrades once; excluded—expelled—from the group in 1967, Clark had not spoken to Debord for almost twenty years. Still, his book was a continuation of the work of a group that had effectively ceased to exist after the success and failure of May '68, an event in which the group's theories and prophecies were at once realized and dashed. Clark's book was, as a fragment, a recovering of ideas twenty years gone, and yet as a work of history about a time a hundred and twenty years gone the distance of its subject often seemed merely formal. There was in the book a quiet sense of a trouble that could come at any time, as if the Sex Pistols had had their effect on Clark, as the SI had on the Sex Pistols. Transposed as a negative, Clark's judgments on the popular, on the popular artist, on the possibilities inherent in the performance of an 1860s cafe singer, can be read as a version of the ambitions that the Sex Pistols began taking into London nightclubs in late 1975. And then they are not only judgments: they are also a version of what actually happened.

Such a version of what actually happened can advance the cabaret as a place where the conviction that "I am nothing and I should be everything" takes shape—as a place where revolution is born. As a member of a society where the values I was raised to believe in, values that, as I learned to make my own choices, I came to cherish, are every day insulted, mocked, and scorned, and on the part of those in power are every day progressively destroyed (checking the day's mail: a congressman, "serving," he says, "under the authority of the Lord Jesus Christ," calls for the defeat of another on the grounds that the latter "has voted against the traditional American values which have helped build this country into the evangelistic arm it has become . . . Send another Christian to Congress")—as such a person, I am filled with despair and disgust, I am filled with murderous fantasies, whenever I permit myself to stop and think for more than a few minutes at a time. I suppose I am drawn to the performing space because I imagine that there I might find my own kind of insult, mockery, and scorn, because there I might find my murderous fantasies dramatized and affirmed. But I am also drawn to it because as a laboratory of change it seems as good as any other; because I have found out that what is said there is sometimes said with more clarity and more mystery than what is said anywhere else; because I know that one can leave a nightclub with the feeling that nothing can ever be the same. But as I move off to a long look at those things that were, for a short time now long past, brought to bear in a few performances, performances played out on small stages or in the pages of obscure publications, it is worth attending to a version of the performing space as a place where revolution goes to die, where its spirit, to use a favorite situationist word, is "recuperated": where the shout of what should be is absorbed into the spectacle of what is, where the impossible demand is brought back into the fold of expectation and result, where the disease of collective vehemence is cured; where "revolution" means a moment in which people say no, enter into festival, are then in one way or another pushed out of history, their moment dropped down into a footnote, or left to float free as an anarchist myth.

In February 1920, little more than a year after the November revolution of 1918, the Spartacist rising of 5 January 1919, and the murder ten days later of Karl Liebknecht and Rosa Luxemburg, revolution reappeared in Berlin with Max Reinhardt's staging of *Danton*, a play by Romain Rolland. The critic Kurt Tucholsky left the theater and wrote a poem, "Danton's Death":

> Act Three was great in Reinhardt's
>   play—
> Six hundred extras milling.
> Listen to what the critics say!
> All Berlin finds it thrilling.
>   But in the whole affair I see
>   A parable, if you ask me.

"Revolution!" the People howls and cries
"Freedom, that's what we're needing!"
We've needed it for centuries—
our arteries are bleeding.

The stage is shaking. The audience
rock.

The whole thing is over by nine
o'clock.

VERSION TWO . . . .

A SECRET HISTORY OF A TIME THAT PASSED

FACES

Johnny Rotten,
1977

Emmy Hennings,
Munich, 1913

Hugo Ball,
Zurich, 1916

Richard Huelsenbeck,
Berlin, 1920

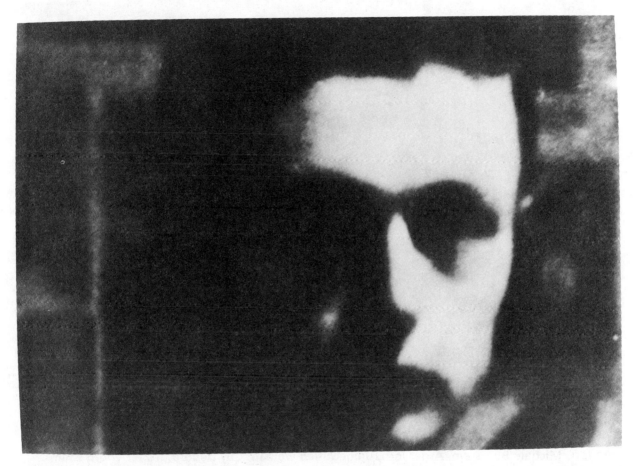

Ivan Chtcheglov, about 1954, from Guy Debord's film *In girum imus nocte et consumimur igni*, 1978

From left, Michèle Bernstein, Asger Jorn, unidentified woman, Guy Debord, from Debord's film
Sur le passage de quelques personnes à travers une assez courte unité de temps, 1959

Punk, London,
late 1970s

Saint-Just at sixteen

LEGENDS OF FREEDOM

In December 1957, Guy-Ernest Debord, born in Paris on 28 December 1931, produced a book he called *Mémoires*. He didn't write it. He cut scores of paragraphs, sentences, phrases, or sometimes single words out of books, magazines, and newspapers; these he scattered and smeared across some fifty pages that his friend Asger Jorn, a Danish painter, crossed and splattered with colored lines, blotches, spots, and drips. Here and there were photographs, advertisements, plans of buildings and cities, cartoons, comic-strip panels, reproductions of woodcuts and engravings, these too scavenged from libraries and newsstands, each piece as mute, all as estranged from any informing context, the whole as much like glossolalia, as the spectral text.

At first the book seemed entirely a conceit—precious. In fact it told a very specific story, and carried an affirmation that it was the only story worth telling: the book was bound in heavy sandpaper, so that when placed on a shelf it would destroy other books.

The story had to be pieced together, and then, as one followed up its clues, deciphered according to where it had come from and where it meant to go. Made out of detritus so apparently random in its organization it communicated as detritus—the book was a history of the first year of the Lettrist International, a shifting group of young people living in Paris, as they were from June 1952 to September 1953—ex-students, ex-poets, ex-filmmakers, now lollards, runaways, drunks—who had banded together under one-line manifestos: "The art of the future will be the overthrow of situations, or nothing," "The new generation will leave nothing to chance," "We'll never get out of this alive." It was the secret history of a time that had passed—"without leaving a trace," said the next to last page.

But *Mémoires* was also made to fix the origins of the Situationist International, the far more visible group Debord, Jorn, and other European artists had formed in July 1957, their founding paper opening with the words "First of all we think the world must be changed"; as a memoir Debord's book was also a prophecy. To follow its story, one needed information Debord withheld—even the words "l'Internationale lettriste," which never appeared. But one also needed the ability to imagine a reinvented world: not merely a "provisional microsociety," as the LI had liked to call itself, but a new, "situationist" civilization, shared by millions, finally covering the globe.

In this new world, the disconnected, seemingly meaningless words and pictures of *Mémoires* would make sense. They would make sense, first, as noise, a cacophony ripping up the syntax of social life—the syntax, as Debord put it in *The Society of the Spectacle*, of "the existing order's uninterrupted discourse about itself." As the noise grew, those words and pictures would begin to link up—as graffiti on countless walls, shouts coming out of thousands of mouths, even as familiar streets and buildings one suddenly saw as if never before—and then, with the old syntax broken, these things would make a second kind of sense. They would be experienced not as things at all, but as possibilities: elements of what Debord called "constructed situations."

These would be "moments of life concretely, deliberately, and freely created," each one "composed of gestures contained in a transitory decor," the gestures the "product of the decor and of themselves," in turn producing "other forms of decor, and other gestures." Each situation would be an "ambient milieu" for a "game of events"; each would change its setting, and allow itself to be changed by it. The city would no longer be experienced as a scrim of commodities and power; it would be felt as a field of "psychogeography," and this would be an epistemology of everyday time and space, allowing one to understand, and transform, "the specific effects of the geographical environment, consciously organized or not, on the emotions and behavior of individuals."

 1793

Chanson des Gardes Suisses

Notre vie est un voyage
Dans l'hiver et dans la Nuit,
Nous cherchons notre passage
Dans le Ciel où rien ne luit

Sous l'influence de l'alcool

Elle restait debout, torturant sa lèvre inférieure

un réseau de souvenirs, d'obses-
sions, de pensées vagues, de ré-
flexions, d'appréhensions

la jeunesse trouve la révolte en elle-même,
quand elle ne la trouve pas près d'elle

Les seins que rien ne dissimule   l'odeur de la marihuana

Now the city would move like a map you were drawing; now you would begin to live your life like a book you were writing. Called forth by a street or a building, an ensemble of gestures might imply that a different street had to be found, that a building could be redesigned by the gestures performed within it, that new gestures had to be made, even that an unknown city had to be built or an old one overthrown. "One night, as evening fell," Raoul Vaneigem wrote in *The Revolution of Everyday Life*,

my friends and I wandered into the Palais de Justice in Brussels. The building is a monstrosity, crushing the poor quarters beneath it and standing guard over the fashionable Avenue Louise—out of which, someday, we will make a breathtakingly beautiful wasteland. As we drifted through the labyrinth of corridors, staircases, and suite after suite of rooms, we discussed what could be done to make the place habitable; for a time we occupied the enemy's territory; through the power of our imagination we transformed the thieves' den into a fantastic funfair, into a sunny pleasure dome, where the most amazing adventures would, for the first time, be really lived.

This was a daydream, Vaneigem cheerfully admitted—but "daydreaming subverts the world." When this free field was finally opened by the noise of the exploding syntax, when the fall of the dictionary left all words lying in the streets, when men and women rushed to pick them up and make pictures out of them, such daydreams would find themselves empowered, turning into catalysts for new passions, new acts, new events: situations, "made to be lived by their creators," a whole new way of being in the world. These situations would make a third kind of sense: they would seem sui generis, unencumbered by the baggage of any past, opening always into other situations, and into the new kind of history it would be theirs to make. And this would be a history not of great men, or of the monuments they had left behind, but a history of moments: the sort of moments everyone once passed through without consciousness and that, now, everyone would consciously create.

As Debord told the tale in *Mémoires*, this story was itself sui generis. Earlier variants were present in his pages—from the

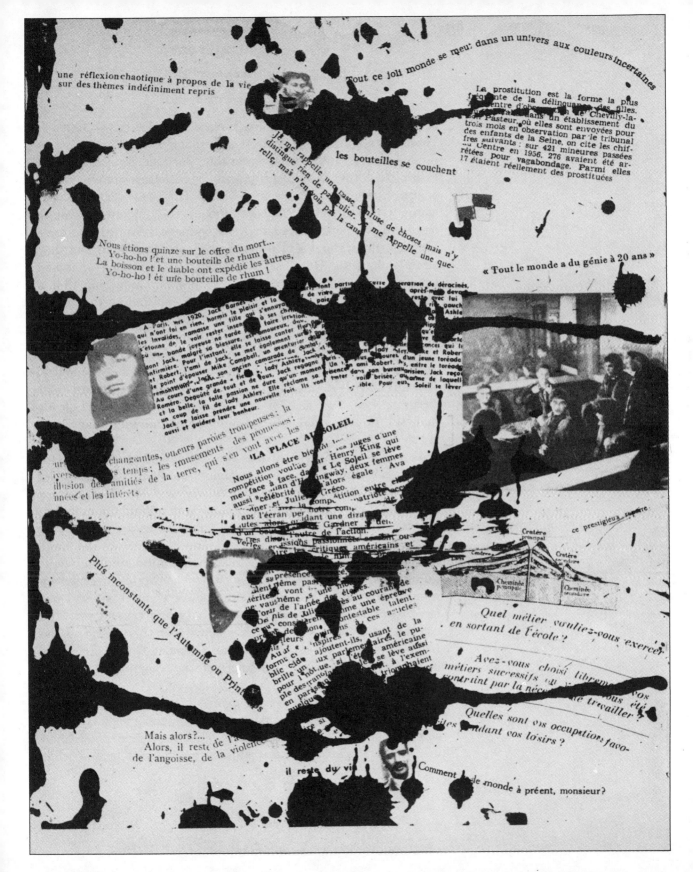

surrealists' discovery of urban "magnetic fields" in the 1920s to Thomas de Quincey's wanderings through London in the early nineteenth century, back even to the "Carte de Tendre" (Map of Feeling) of the seventeenth-century précieuses—but as blind baggage, which means "sealed book." That was what the past ought to be, *Mémoires* said: would be, if the unidentified young men and women pictured in Debord's pages, framed by Jorn's blazing colors, could someday supersede dead time. Or had they already done it? Here, as if for the first time, the unnamed band moving from 1952 through 1953 was discovering that a world of permanent novelty could exist, and finding the means to start it up. These means were two: the "dérive," a drift down city streets in search of signs of attraction or repulsion, and "détournement," the theft of aesthetic artifacts from their contexts and their diversion into contexts of one's own devise. *Mémoires*, with its meandering crossings and stolen words and pictures, was a version of both—just as both were art forms that, the LI believed, could not produce art but only a new kind of life.

As the half-century turned, the delinquent intellectuals of the LI saw the culture and commerce of the West as exiled Frankfurt School critics Theodor Adorno and Max Horkheimer had seen it at the end of the Second World War: a single system of suffocation and domination, "uniform as a whole and in every part." As a benign match for the Stalinism of the East, capitalism completed a double reflection, which reduced everything outside itself to a nullity. With the world governed by what Harold Rosenberg called "the power trance," art was put forward as the last redoubt of creativity and critical will, the note sounded with echoes of Thermopylae or the Charge of the Light Brigade: "What can fifty do," Clement Greenberg wrote in 1947 of the New York abstract painters, "against a hundred and forty million?"

Such a cry sounds hysterical today, if it didn't then; the rest of the United States was not against Greenberg's fifty, it ignored them, and it had its reasons. The members of the LI had theirs. They had found their affinity in art, in a love of what

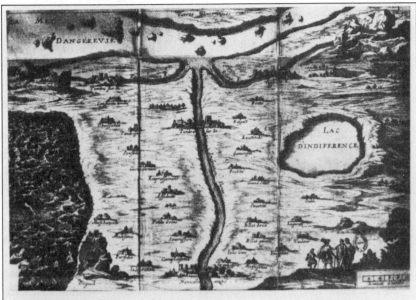

Carte du pays de Tendre, 1656.

Illustrations from "Unitary Urbanism at the End of the 1950s," *I.S.* no. 3, December 1959

Une zone expérimentale pour la dérive. Le centre d'Amsterdam, qui sera systématiquement exploré par des équipes situationnistes en avril-mai 1960.

art promised and a hatred for where those promises stopped, for the separate and privileged realm society reserved for beautiful, impotent dreams—but even the beauty, they thought, had been a lie for thirty years, before any of them were born. Somewhere between 1915 and 1925 art burned itself out in a war against its own limits, in a struggle to escape its redoubt, its museum, its amusement park, its zoo; since then there had been no art, only "imitations of ruins" in a "dismal yet profitable carnival, where each cliché had its disciples, each regression its admirers, every remake its fans." The LI's dreams of a reinvented world came from art, but the group was sure that, in its time, to make art was to lose its time; to claim an image or a line as one's own, as a unique and eternal mark on the wall of a history written in advance, would be to perpetuate a fraud on the history the group meant to make. It would be to buy into myths of blessed genius and divine inspiration, to lend one's hands to a system of individual hierarchy and social control; with God dead and art standing in his stead, it would be to maintain a religious illusion, fittingly trapped in the most magical of commodities. It would be to hold up heaven in a frame instead of pointing to it in the sky like a priest—and what was the difference? To make art would be to betray the common, buried wishes art once spoke for, but to practice détournement—to write new speech balloons for newspaper comic strips, or for that matter old masters, to insist simultaneously on a "devaluation" of art and its "reinvestment" in a new kind of social speech, a "communication containing its own criticism," a technique that could not mystify because its very form was a demystification—and to pursue the dérive—to give yourself up to the promises of the city, and then to find them wanting—to drift through the city, allowing its signs to divert, to "detourn," your steps, and then to divert those signs yourself, forcing them to give up routes that never existed before—there would be no end to it. It would be to begin to live a truly modern way of life, made out of pavement and pictures, words and weather: a way of life anyone could understand and anyone could use.

"Their underlying philosophy," Christopher Gray wrote of the LI in *Leaving the 20th Century*, "was one of experiment and *play*"—but play with all of culture, and the city itself as the field. Why not? "Seek for food and clothing first, then the Kingdom of God shall be added to you," Hegel said; it was time for the kingdom, past time. "Suffice it to say that in our view the premises for revolution, on the cultural as well as on the strictly political level, are not only ripe, they have begun to rot," Debord and Gil J Wolman wrote for the LI in 1956. To the LI, what Hannah Arendt called the social question—hunger, the necessity of the body driving back the will to found freedom, a force that left every revolution promising the Kingdom of God defeated or travestied, short even of food and clothing—had, at least potentially, been solved. As the LI read the signs of postwar technics and abundance, as it read the ads, from now on anyone suffering privation would be a victim not of necessity but of a power trance, a trance that could be broken. Modern poverty was a poverty of passion, rooted in the predictability of a world society rich enough to manage both space and time—so the group dismissed capitalism as an empty present, socialism as a future equipped to change only the past, and spoke instead of building "castles of adventure." Walking the streets until they were too drunk to know which corner to turn, they tried to drive themselves into delirium, in order to emerge with a message of seduction: thus in 1953 Ivan Chtcheglov, nineteen, wrote a "Formula for a New Urbanism," and called on his comrades to create their first city, "the intellectual capital of the world," a sort of Fourierist Las Vegas, a surrealist Disneyland, an amusement park where people would actually live, a ville de tendre with districts and gardens corresponding "to the whole spectrum of feelings one encounters *by chance* in everyday life," constructed realms of romance, confusion, utility, tragedy, history, terror, happiness, death, a city where "the principal activity of the inhabitants" would be "the CONTINUOUS DÉRIVE," a drift through a landscape of "buildings charged with evocative power, symbolic edifices representing emotions, forces, and events from the past, the present, and the future. A rational extension of bygone religious systems, fairy tales, and above all of psychoanalysis into architectural expression becomes more urgent every day, as all the sparks of passion disappear," Chtcheglov said—but in the city he imagined, "Everyone will live in his own cathedral. There will be rooms more conducive to visions than any drug, and houses where it will be impossible not to fall in love."

Addressing himself only to the others in the LI, and for that matter writing under a pseudonym, "Gilles Ivain," Chtcheglov was contriving a secret for his friends to share; at the same time he was writing a manifesto to change the world. "A mental disease has swept the planet," he pronounced: "banalization . . . this state of affairs, arising out of a struggle against poverty, has overshot its ultimate goal—the liberation of man from material cares—and has become an obsessive image hanging over the present. Offered the choice of love or a garbage disposal, young people of all countries have chosen the garbage disposal." To choose the garbage disposal was to embrace reification, to become a garbage disposal. But to choose love was to escape the prison of the alienated self, and so Chtcheglov's lover, dreaming in his own cathedral, was not an isolate, not a babbling cripple hiding in his private Notre-Dame, but a citizen of a new world, ready to speak. He might say what the lover in Paul Auster's 1986 mystery *The Locked Room* says: "By belonging to Sophie, I began to feel as though I belonged to everyone else as well. My true place in the world, it turned out, was somewhere beyond myself, and if that place was inside me, it was also unlocatable. This was the tiny hole between self and not-self, and for the first time in my life I saw this nowhere as the exact center of the world." This is utopia, and utopia means "nowhere," but within the LI all obvious absurdities and impossibilities were shrugged off (who says you have to choose between love and a garbage disposal?); the LI's project was the rational extension of the fairy tale. That utopia, the exact center of the world, was where the LI meant to live.

"Ultimately," Gray wrote, "all that was involved was the simplest thing in the world: wanting to make your dreams come true. And its enemies were equally simple: sterile subjective fantasy on the one hand and, on the other, its objective counterpart: the world of art." Someday one would confront the final enemy, the existing order; the first battle, as Alexander Trocchi wrote in London in 1964, trying to recapture his days as a member of the LI, was "to attack the 'enemy' at his base, within ourselves." Thus the aesthetes of the LI forbid themselves to make art—and in the same spirit they forbid themselves to work. As a provisional microsociety, they meant to live out the future in the present—in a future-present where the tools of mastery already in place in the most advanced societies would sooner or later make work redundant and leisure unlimited. This was the material base on which they floated their vision of a world of constructed situations; drifting through Paris, they looked for that world, and for their next meal.

The LI believed that by replacing work and entertainment with the dérive, art with détournement, and the productive social roles still enforced by a society living in the past-present with a "role of pure consumption"—the consumption, the LI meant, of "its time"—it could "reinvent everything each day." Reinvent everything, or lose everything—as Debord said in 1972 (when the LI, in its day a group known mostly to itself, was an experiment Debord could imagine only he remembered), "Time frightens . . . it is made of qualitative jumps, irreversible choices, occasions which will never return."

That was the burden assumed by those who committed themselves to a life of permanent novelty. Each day the members of the LI would walk the streets not as prisoners of wages and prices, not as employees, shoppers, or tourists, but as travelers in a labyrinth revealed by their wish to find it. Each day they would case the spectacles of art and advertising, news and history, pillage bits and pieces, and make them speak in new tongues, in a counterlanguage, in every instance leaving a small hole in the great spectacle of social life, at least as it governed the group's own space and time. Playing a "game of freedom"—a "systematic questioning," Debord said, "of all the diversions and works of a society, a total critique of its idea of happiness"—the LI would become "the masters and possessors of their own lives."

It was in fact a desperate search, in a utopia that contained its own contradiction, product of a wish that at once went beyond art and found itself returned to it: "When freedom is practiced in a closed circle," Debord wrote in 1959, looking back on the LI in his film *Sur le passage de quelques personnes à travers une assez courte unité de temps* (On the Passage of a Few People Through a Rather Brief Moment in Time), "it fades into a dream, becomes a mere representation of itself." What looked like freedom might be no more than parole, Wolman wrote bitterly to the rest of the group in early 1953, after they rejected Debord's plan for an attack on a girls' reform school: "of course you dream at night if you can always sleep but life threatens there are cops at every turn and by the signs of the bistros the girls your age are scarred by youth." It was a cruel search: "What was missing," Debord said, "was felt as irretrievable. The extreme uncertainties of subsisting without working made excesses necessary and breaks definitive." One after another, those who gathered around Debord were tossed out or dropped away. "Suicide carried off many," he said in 1978, in his film *In girum imus nocte et consumimur igni*, then quoting *Mémoires* as it had quoted *Treasure Island*: "'Drink and the devil took care of the rest.'" But from ·1952 to 1957, as long as the LI lasted, others always took their place. You can see them, the International fully present around a single table, as the idea was set forth once again: revolution begins in a wish for right, which is a wish for justice, which is a wish for harmony, which is a wish for beauty. We cannot live without beauty, but art can no longer provide it. Art is the lie we are no longer living, and it is the trick, the false promise of beauty, the compensation for the destruction of harmony and right, that keeps everyone else from living. As a trick art must be suppressed, and as a promise it must be *realized*—and that is the key to revolution. Art must be superseded, and we, who have suppressed art

"Never Work"

"Preliminary Program to the Situationist Movement"—"This inscription, on a wall of the rue de Seine, can be traced back to the first months of 1953 (an adjacent inscription, inspired by more traditional politics, allows virtually complete accuracy in dating the graffiti in question: calling for a demonstration against General Ridgway, it cannot be later than May 1952). The inscription reproduced above seems to us one of the most important relics ever unearthed on the site of Saint-Germain-des-Prés: a testament to the particular way of life that tried to assert itself there." *I.S.* no. 8, January 1963

in our own space and time, can make it happen. The new beauty can only be a beauty of *situation*, which is to say provisional, and *lived* . . .

The Situationist International was founded on the conviction that this closed circle could be opened: that this new world, at first the private, almost abstract discovery of a separate few, could be explored, explained, publicized, and glamorized, until the demand for it would become overwhelming. Overwhelming, and common, as the situationists linked that demand to the inchoate manifestations of refusal and revolt they were sighting all over the planet—manifestations, they were certain, of an unfathomed dissatisfaction with the quality of life in modern society, scattered bits of a negation of its idea of happiness. They had a plan: drawing the finest talent from across Europe, then from around the globe, the SI would devote itself simultaneously to "the ruthless criticism of all that exists" (Marx, 1843) and to "bringing to light forgotten desires, and creating entirely new ones" (Chtcheglov, 1953)—and then, the SI said in June 1958, in the first number of its journal *Internationale situationniste*, "we will wreck this world." "Everyone must search for what he loves, for what attracts him," they wrote then. On the way to the discovery of what you loved, you would find everything you hated, everything that blocked the way to what you loved. To walk down that street would be to find yourself on a terrain where the smallest obstacle demanded a total contestation of the existing order.

In the beginning this walk would take place as if on a battlefield in a war no one else understood was being fought. That was the burden passed to readers of "The Decline and Fall of the Spectacle-Commodity Economy," the SI's virulent pamphlet on the riots in the black ghetto of Watts, California, in August 1965, a maelstrom that left more than thirty dead—and "the first rebellion in history," the SI said with delight, pressing the dispute between love and the garbage disposal, "to justify itself with the argument that there was no air conditioning during a heatwave." To most, it made no sense that when the far more impoverished blacks of Harlem and Newark were silent, the relatively comfortable blacks of Los Angeles were burning and looting, many with pride and joy. To the situationists, citing the boast of one Bobbi Hollon, a young Watts sociologist who swore "never to wash off the blood that splashed on her sandals during the rioting," it made perfect sense. "Comfort," they wrote, "will never be comfortable enough for those who seek what is not on the market."

The SI was a group of critics; tipping back in their cafe chairs as others acted, they did not apologize. As Debord said years later, "Where there was fire, we carried gasoline." "Theoretical criticism of modern society, in its most advanced forms, and criticism in acts of the same society already co-exist," the SI said of Watts: "still separated, but both equally advancing towards the same realities, both talking about the same thing. These two critiques explain each other; neither is explicable without the other. Our theories of 'survival' and of 'spectacle' are illuminated and verified by actions which [today seem] incomprehensible . . . One day, these actions will in turn be illuminated by this theory."

"The Decline and Fall of the Spectacle-Commodity Economy" was meant to be part of the event it analyzed. It was written in

CRITIQUE DE L'URBANISME (Supermarket à Los Angeles, août 1965).

Illustration from "The Decline and Fall of the Spectacle-Commodity Economy," *I.S.* no. 10, March 1966

Paris in French, but translated into English and distributed in America before it appeared in Europe. The question the SI was raising would have been familiar to some in the U.S.A. in 1965: "How," the situationists asked, in language little different from that of the 1962 Port Huron Statement, the founding paper of Students for a Democratic Society, "do people make history, starting from conditions pre-established to dissuade them from intervening in it?" But the answer the situationists gave might as well have come from Mars: "Looting is the *natural* response to the society of abundance—the society not of natural and human abundance, but of the abundance only of commodities . . . The looting of the Watts district was the most direct realization of the distorted principle, 'To each according to his false needs' . . . [but] real desires began to find expression in festival, in the *potlatch* of destruction . . . For the first time it is not poverty but material abundance that must be dominated." This was delirious, and also seductive: seductive because it was telling. It was, the SI thought, the battlefield, and from June 1958 to September 1969 the pages of *Internationale situationniste* plotted its frontiers.

The situationists tried to see themselves as they saw the people of Watts: confronted with "the reality of a capitalism and a technology that render the individual powerless, except if he is a thief or a terrorist" (words written in 1987 by Stanley Hoffmann, distinguished professor of history, but in 1965 unthinkable outside small circles of fanatics). Thus they practiced intellectual terrorism, and inseparable from that practice was the theft of intellectual property. As a field guide, the pages of their journal were also a laboratory, a testing ground for the SI's experiments with the counterlanguage, with détournement—which the situationists meant to move from new speech balloons on comic strips to a critique so magically true it would turn the words of its enemies back on themselves, forcing new speech even out of the mouths of the guardians of good and right. Like the dérive, this was the aesthetic occupation of enemy territory, a raid launched to seize the familiar and turn it into the other, a war waged on a field of action without bound-

"As the SI says, it's a far, far better thing to be a whore like me than the wife of a fascist like Constantine." Detourned photo of Christine Keeler by situationist J. V. Martin, upon the marriage of Princess Anne-Marie of Denmark to King Constantine II of Greece. *I.S.* no. 9, August 1964

aries and without rules; when in 1962 the SI discovered that one Wolfgang Neuss, a Berlin actor, had "perpetrated a most suggestive act of sabotage . . . by taking an ad in the paper *Der Abend*, giving away the identity of a killer in a television detective serial that had been keeping the public in suspense for weeks," the group gleefully placed the tiny event on the same plane as it would the Watts riots. Making meaning—or unmaking it—went hand in hand with making history. Détournement was a politics of subversive quotation, of cutting the vocal cords of every empowered speaker, social symbols yanked through the looking glass, misappropriated words and pictures diverted into familiar scripts and blowing them up. "Ultimately," Debord and Wolman had said in 1956, "any sign"—any street, advertisement, painting, text, any representation of a society's idea of happiness—"is susceptible to conversion into something else, even its opposite."

What if you could really make it happen? The spectacle was itself a work of art, an economy of false needs elevated into a tableau of frozen desires, true desires reduced to a cartoon of twitching needs. Spreading the bad paper of détournement until it began to turn up everywhere, the SI would devalue the currency of the spectacle, and the result would be a fatal inflation. Then a penny could be a fortune. The détournement of the right sign, in the right place at the right time, could spark a mass reversal of perspective. The one-way communication of the spectacle reduced all other speech to babble, but now the spectacle would fall back on itself; it would sound like babble, and everyone would see through it. The reversible connecting factor would be grasped, the string would be pulled, the tables would be turned, every yes would become a no, every truth would dissolve in doubt, and everything would change. Then the SI, having styled itself "an obscure conspiracy of unlimited demands," "a general staff *that does not want troops*," would realize its dream of a New Jerusalem by disappearing into it: into a riot of social glossolalia, where the "freedom to say everything" would be inseparable from "the freedom to do everything." "*We will only organize the detonation*," the SI

Detourned comics, U.S., 1986

promised in 1963. "The free explosion must escape us and any other control forever." And then *Mémoires* could be happily forgotten, as if it had never been. As a memoir that was also a prophecy, the book would have situated itself in advance as an artifact that, once realized, would remain as unknown as it would have proven itself fecund: the secret history of a time to come.

IT WAS

It was, it turned out, a sort of map to a territory that had ceased to exist, an account of adventures that had taken place there. "There was, then, on the left bank of the river—one cannot dip one's foot twice in the same river, or touch a perishable substance twice in the same state—a neighborhood where the negative held court." So Debord said to his camera in 1978, when the time to come had passed. "There," he wrote a year later, "in 1952, in Paris, four or five unworthy people decided to search for the supercession of art." He did not explain what this meant, or rather he explained in a distant way, putting quotes around another phrase one could have found floating in *Mémoires*: "The supercession of art is the 'Northwest Passage' of the geography of real life, so often sought for more than a century, a search beginning especially in self-destroying modern poetry."

Debord was not, a quarter-century after the four or five had begun their search for transcendence, talking about poetry, not as one usually understands the word; he was talking about "social revolution," a complete transformation of life as people actually lived it, every day. He was talking about what he had glimpsed in the insurrection of May '68—a happenstance, he was now arguing, a month of noise, whose prefiguration could be seen in the interrupted narratives and fragmented representations of *Mémoires*, all transposed back into the vanished daily life of the four or five, the provisional microsociety. Recapturing the language of that self-destroying modern poetry,

not to write it but to live it out and set it loose in the world—
that, Debord was saying, was what the LI had been about.
"Finishing off art; declaring in the heart of a cathedral that
God was dead; plotting to blow up the Eiffel Tower—such were
the scandals occasionally offered up by those whose way of life
was the real scandal." "The domain we mean to replace and
fulfill is poetry," the SI said in 1958; the revolution the SI
wanted was going to "realize" poetry, and "realizing poetry
means nothing less than simultaneously and inseparably creating events and their languages." This was the future, and
also the past, the whole world: "the moment of true poetry
brings all the unsettled debts of history back into play."

"The situationists want to *forget* about the past," they said
as they began, but they never did; the past was a treasure
chest, now the lock, now the treasure. Michèle Bernstein was
a member of the LI and the SI almost from the beginning to
almost the end; in 1983 she sat in her airy living room in England and explained. "Everyone is the son of many fathers,"
she said. "There was the father we hated, which was surrealism. And there was the father we loved, which was dada. We
were the children of both." They were "enfants perdus," Debord often said, lost children, and so they claimed any fathers
in whose faces they could recognize their own: the surrealists,
the dadaists, the failed revolutionaries of the first third of the
twentieth century, the Communards, the young Karl Marx,
Saint-Just, medieval heretics—and all, as Debord and the others began talking in the 1950s, were moribund, forgotten,
memories and rumors, manqué, maudit. All were, at best, legends—to the LI and the SI, part of a legend of freedom.

Moved forward through the 1950s and 1960s by Debord's
groups, given new names and a new shape, this was finally a
legend almost too old to understand, let alone explain: a legend, Debord would helplessly, pathetically say in 1979, of "an
Athens, a Florence, from which no one will be excluded, reaching to all the corners of the earth"—once again, as never before. Back, back, to a new Athens, a new Florence—and there,
as Richard Huelsenbeck prophesied backward in Berlin in

1920, crowds would gather around every dialogue, dramas would be enacted in every street, and we would find ourselves in Homeric times. There, then, as Edmund Wilson prophesied forward in Paris in 1922, we would discover for what drama our setting was the setting. Poetry would be realized: Lautréamont's call, made in 1870, for a poetry "made by all." We would feel the will to speak; discover what it was we wanted to say; say it; be understood; win a response. All at once we would create events and their languages, and live in permanence within that paradise. "We have to multiply poetic subjects and objects," Debord wrote in 1957, in the founding paper of the SI, "and we have to organize games of these poetic objects among these poetic subjects. This is our entire program, which is essentially transitory. Our situations will be ephemeral, without a future: passageways."

At its limit, those words are the legend of freedom: the promise that one's words and acts will float free forever. Those words are themselves poetry; they can stay right where they are, in perfect balance, or they can lead anywhere, a motionless cause. In pursuit of a motionless cause—an idea of transformation so abstract it could hold its shape until the world was ready to be changed by it—the LI and the SI tried to act out a legend of freedom, and at the most that is all they are now. Always, no matter how incisive their ruthless critiques of whatever existed, there was that element of abstraction: an element that gave those critiques (whether applied by the LI to Guatemala in 1954 or by the SI to Watts in 1965 or France in May 1968) a bewitching, negative power, the hint of an event and a language to come, which still keeps the story the groups tried to tell alive. As I tell the story, it all begins, and must be judged against, what once happened in a nightclub and was returned to another—just as what happened in those nightclubs must be judged against what for certain moments was taken out of nightclubs, written on walls, shouted, played out in buildings and streets that were suddenly seen as never before. From one perspective the line is easy to draw, just a line—for example, the LI's 1953 graffiti "NEVER WORK," which

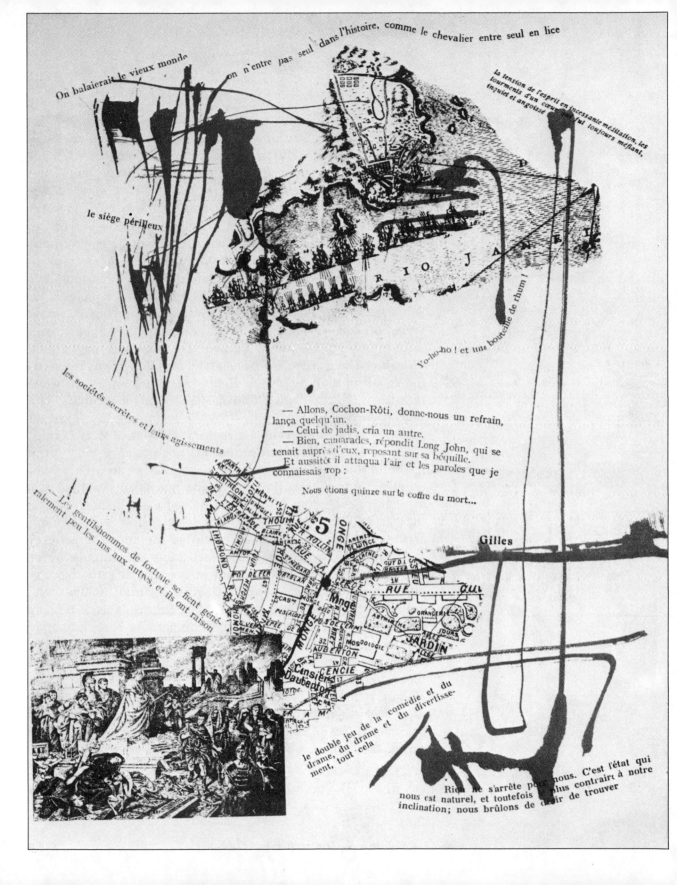

On balaierait le vieux monde

on n'entre pas seul dans l'histoire, comme le chevalier entre seul en lice

la tension de l'esprit en incessante méditation, les tourments d'un cœur inquiet et angoissé ne fut toujours méfiant,

le siège périlleux

RIO JANE...

Yo-ho-ho ! et une bouteille de rhum !

les sociétés secrètes et leurs agissements

— Allons, Cochon-Rôti, donne-nous un refrain, lança quelqu'un.
— Celui de jadis, cria un autre.
— Bien, camarades, répondit Long John, qui se tenait auprès d'eux, reposant sur sa béquille.
Et aussitôt il attaqua l'air et les paroles que je connaissais trop :

Nous étions quinze sur le coffre du mort...

— Les gentilshommes de fortune se fient géné-ralement peu les uns aux autres, et ils ont raison

Gilles

le double jeu de la comédie et du drame, du drame et du divertisse-ment, tout cela

Rien ne s'arrête pour nous. C'est l'état qui nous est naturel, et toutefois plus contraire à notre inclination; nous brûlons de désir de trouver

reappeared as May '68 graffiti, and was rewritten in 1977 for the Sex Pistols' "Seventeen": "We don't work / I just feed / That's all I need." But that connection—a one-line LI manifesto, as featured in one-time situationist Christopher Gray's *Leaving the 20th Century: The Incomplete Work of the Situationist International* and passed down by Gray's friends Malcolm McLaren and Jamie Reid to Johnny Rotten—is tradition as arithmetic. To find its story one has to disrupt the continuities of a tradition, even the discontinuities of a smoky, subterranean tradition, with a certain simultaneity. For example: if in pursuit of a negation of their society's idea of happiness the Sex Pistols found themselves drawn again and again to the verge of dada glossolalia, into the realm of self-destroying modern poetry, *Mémoires* reached the same spot on purpose; though the convergence was no accident, neither was it exactly the result of a transference. Henri Lefebvre's words are worth recalling: "To the degree that modernity has a meaning, it is this: it carries within itself, from the beginning, a radical negation—Dada, this event which took place in a Zurich cafe." Lefebvre was making an argument, not posing a riddle; this negation, he was saying, had persisted, not as an art tradition canalized into an invulnerable future, but as an unsettled debt of history, extending into an unresolved past. It didn't matter that as Lefebvre spoke in 1975 the Sex Pistols were forming, or that neither could ever acknowledge the other, as Lefebvre and Debord once acknowledged each other as comrades in an attempt to make a revolution out of everyday life: the Sex Pistols, taking the stage as an instinctive cultural impulse, with unknown roots in *Mémoires*, a studied cultural thesis, brought the debt back into play. As they brought it back into play, they increased it—and then, as soon as they consented to disappear from history, the debt according to its terms made them, too, a legend of freedom.

That bad paper is the only currency in this tale: lost children seek their fathers, and fathers seek their lost children, but nobody really looks like anybody else. So all, fixed on the wrong faces, pass each other by: this is the drift of secret history, a history that remains secret even to those who make it, especially to those who make it. In the Sex Pistols' hands, and in the hands of those who turned up in their wake, all this appeared as a blind groping toward a new story, driven by the instinctive dada suspicion that ordinary language could not tell it. In Debord's book, which presented itself as a groping, yet so carefully arranged that a lightly constructed page could have the same effect as a violent pause in a piece of music, it was a conscious attempt to use dada language to tell the story that language had passed down to him: a story, and a language, that contained the most abstract and ephemeral legend of freedom he knew.

It was a legend, Debord might have thought as he cut and pasted in 1957, that was part of a past, and part of a future, he had helped make. He had lived it; whatever dada had been, now, from page to page in *Mémoires*, it was something else. Once, the legend had it, it was an experiment in self-destroying modern poetry. Now it was the struggle of a small band, moved by the notion that the language of self-destroying modern poetry was a key to social revolution, to raise fragments of experience ("The evening, Barbara" "our talk is full of booze" "Lights, shadows, figures," one could pick out as *Mémoires* began) to the level of the book's epigraph. "Let the dead bury the dead, and mourn them," Debord quoted Marx, Marx writing in 1843 to his friend Arnold Ruge, just as Marx began by quoting Matthew, who was quoting Jesus, Marx then following with words Debord now made his own: "Our kind will be the first to blaze a trail into a new life."

THE ART OF YESTERDAY'S CRASH

Believe it or not: once a man became famous by reciting poetry that had no meaning. It's easy to believe; on this show, nothing is strange. The viewer sees a bit of film, a reenactment: two men dance hunched over on a shallow stage, peeping and chirping, while a third plays piano. Their movements are cramped; it's boring. A man in a stiff costume with a high, striped toque on his head is brought out (the costume overwhelms his whole body, he can't move, he has to be carried onto the stage and plopped down like a big prop); he reads out disconnected syllables in a heavy, lugubrious voice. This is boring too. It doesn't make sense when volleys of fruit hurled by the unseen audience splatter the poet; it's not worth it. The dancers come back and tote the man off the stage.

Once, the viewer is told, this was a hit. You believe it. Chef Klinmahon throws food in the air to season it; he's a hit. Freud used to hypnotize his patients; he's still a hit. Hostess Marie Osmond lies on a red couch that has been trucked all over the U.S.A. to be photographed for an art book; it's a hit, she's not a hit, she's divorced, and as an overpublicized exponent of traditional values she's not supposed to be, but maybe some of the couch will rub off. The only problem is the space shuttle: no doubt when the program first aired, happy-go-lucky footage of astronauts floating strawberries in zero gravity and trying to catch them in their mouths was funny. Now, not too long after one space shuttle has blown up, blown up seven astronauts and whatever they had in their mouths along with them, it's not funny. This is hard to believe; this is the sort of tasteless juxtaposition TV exists to avoid.

The formal juxtaposition of the evening's items—suggesting identifications between art and science, alchemy and house-

7 11 13 RIPLEY'S BELIEVE IT OR NOT! (CC); 60 min. Included: hypnotism in medical science; Hugo Ball's "sound poetry"; the five-year photographic journey of a red couch across America; Chef Klinmahon from Thailand; the space shuttle. (Repeat)

—TV Guide, *17 April 1986*

work, occultism and militarism, or a general vice versa—is a TV version of what, when the man in the costume was brought onto the stage, was called dada. Along with the attempt to reduce all forms to zero, the juxtaposition of seemingly unrelated phenomena was the basic tactic of twentieth-century modernist art. The idea was that, to the degree aesthetic categories could be proven false, social barriers could be revealed as constructed illusions, and the world could be changed. Things are not as they seem: that was the message then, and that is the message now. The difference—so goes the legend of the 1910s and 1920s, when artists across Europe created new worlds on paper and canvas (worlds so violently new that, gazing at them today, one can read the official history of the century as little more than a desperate retreat from these terrifyingly obvious utopias, from the new worlds implicit in any El Lissitzky construction, any Man Ray photograph, any De Stijl design)—is that then the message was shocking, and now it is not even a message.

WHAT GOOD

"What good is thinking, writing or acting," Henri Lefebvre wrote in 1973, "if one's only achievement is to continue that long line of failures, self-destructions and fatal spells lasting from Jude the Obscure to Antonin Artaud?" What good indeed? "Are we to step out of history," a college student named Steve Strauss wrote in 1967 in a paper I graded, "to join hands with eternal wastrels, fops, and dandies?" It's easier said than done.

Leaving the road most taken we might step out and join Lefebvre's long line almost anywhere: step into the champ libre, the freie strasse, most often the imaginary terrain of a parallel history—once the realm of heretics, alchemists, esoterics, since the French Revolution the domain of political conspiracies and aesthetic "avant-gardes," perhaps little more than a place for naysayers to claim a position ahead of history while fighting a

Work by El Lissitzky in use as a propaganda board at a factory, Vitebsk, USSR, 1919

rear-guard action against it, against the Industrial Revolution, the middle class, the "bourgeoisie," "mass man," "mass society" (in a phrase, modern democracy)—a parallel history powered by the plain wish to break out of the story most told and most often condemned to travel with it like the bird on the rhinoceros, the naysayer's wish circling back, finally, to meet no New Man, no new world, but only what little is left of the desire that set off the journey in the first place. "He could be found at the Livraria Catilina," novelist Mario Vargas Llosa wrote of his character Gallileo Gall, revolutionary manqué of *The War of the End of the World* (he was a veteran of the Commune, washed up in Brazil at the end of the century),

in the shade of the palm tree of the Mirador of the Sorrowful, or in the sailors' taverns of the lower town, explaining to anyone with whom he struck up a conversation that all virtues are compatible if reason rather than faith is the axis of life, that not God but Satan— the first rebel—is the true prince of freedom, and that once the old order was destroyed through revolutionary action, the new society, free and just, would flower spontaneously. Although there were some who listened to him, in general people did not appear to pay much attention to him.

Born in 1901 in Hagetmau, southwest France, Lefebvre first joined the line he would later curse in Paris, in the 1920s—the heyday of surrealism.

We are certainly barbarians, since a certain form of civilization disgusts us . . . Categorically we need freedom, but a freedom based in our deepest spiritual needs, in the most severe and human desires of our flesh . . . The stereotyped gestures, acts, and lies of Europe have run their disgusting circle. Spinoza, Kant, Blake, Hegel, Schelling, Proudhon, Marx, Stirner, Baudelaire, Lautréamont, Rimbaud, Nietzsche—this list alone is the beginning of your downfall.

So read "Revolution, First and Forever!," a surrealist manifesto Lefebvre signed in 1925. This was the line of fatal spells (no less an attempt to cast one); Lefebvre soon left it, following the surrealists into the French Communist Party, and embarked on his great career as a Marxist social theorist.

MY FIRST

"My first article in the review *Philosophies*," Lefebvre said in 1975, looking back to 1924, "[was a] portrait of Dada. It brought me a lasting friendship with Tristan Tzara . . . I had written, 'Dada smashes the world, but the pieces are fine' . . . Each time I ran into Tristan Tzara, he'd say to me: 'So? You're picking up the pieces! Do you plan to put them back together?' I always answered: 'No—I'm going to finish smashing them.'"

Lefebvre had written a review of Tzara's *7 manifestes dada*; the tone was snotty. Yes, Lefebvre had said, he preferred dada to surrealism, which "only bets small change"—literary reputations. Against the careerist pretensions of André Breton and his group, easily satisfied by scandal for scandal's sake, by the applause or catcalls of tout le monde, dada at least reached for an absolute: "the end of the world." But it was a puerile absolute, "solely the spirit-that-says-no," "vainly proclaiming the sovereignty of the instant," a "pseudo-sorcery": "As Dada moves to escape all definitions, its negation defines itself all too powerfully as its own negation." As philosophy dada was a slipknot, your basic Sophistry 1-A: everything I say is a lie.

Only twenty-three in 1924, Lefebvre already had one foot in history to balance the other in the long line of fatal spells. Fast on his feet, he wrote like an old man, smiling over the enthusiasms of his yet-to-vanish youth, ready for serious business: what is to be done? But in 1975, half a century on from *Philosophies*, looking back at his long-gone callow self, he sounded like a twenty-three-year-old: "No, I'm going to finish smashing them." In 1967 he had written even odder lines, leaping out of a sober argument on technics and domination: "Modern art, literature, culture, were they not, one wartime day, blown up—simply because in the right place, at the right time, a young man set down a paradoxically potent little explosion, two redundant syllables, 'Da-da'?" Those syllables were the pieces Lefebvre once promised to finish smashing. Now he held them in his mouth as if they were pieces of the philosopher's stone. What was the old man talking about?

HE WAS

He was talking about the Cabaret Voltaire, launched in Zurich on 5 February 1916, in the midst of the First World War, abandoned five months after that. Its founders were Hugo Ball, twenty-nine, obscure German dramaturgist, poet, lapsed-Catholic mystic, Nietzsche acolyte, and future TV personality, and Emmy Hennings, thirty-one, German chanteuse. They were joined by an Alsatian artist named Hans (Jean) Arp; Tristan Tzara, a Romanian poet; his countryman Marcel Janco, a painter; and Richard Huelsenbeck, a German poet and, when he got around to it, medical student. Formerly the cabaret had been a bar called the Holländische Meierei, run by one Jan Ephriam, in his younger days a sailor; today it is the Teen 'n' Twenty disco. At the foot of the Spiegelgasse, in the old quarter, the city of Zurich has put up a plaque: under the chiseled word "DADAISMUS" someone has scratched "Ne passera pas"—"Dada will stand."

It was a precious nightclub in which the artist's promise to reveal the meaning of life was turned into a vaudeville show where all the acts appeared at the same time. "Dada has been mixed up with an art movement," Huelsenbeck said a few wars later in 1971, "though it has nothing to present as an art movement if you think of Cubism, of Impressionism or whatever, these are all problems of form, of color, of something that is shown or devised or has the aim of being a work of art; now this we didn't have at all. We had practically nothing except what we were."

"The Cabaret Voltaire was a six-piece band," Hans Richter wrote in 1964. "Each played his instrument, i.e., himself." A young German painter, Richter arrived in Zurich in August 1916 after being wounded at the front; the Cabaret Voltaire was already there-were-giants-in-the-earth. Richter had missed it. Arp reports from the scene:

On the stage of a gaudy, motley, overcrowded tavern are several weird and peculiar figures representing Tzara, Janco, Ball, Huelsenbeck, Madame Hennings, and your humble servant. Total pandemonium. The people around us are shouting, laughing, and gesticulating. Our replies are sighs of love, volleys of hiccups, poems, moos, and the miaowing of medieval *Bruitists*. Tzara is wiggling his behind like the belly of an Oriental dancer. Janco is playing an invisible violin and bowing and scraping. Madame Hennings, with a Madonna face, is doing the splits. Huelsenbeck is banging away nonstop at the great drum, with Ball accompanying him on the piano, pale as a chalky ghost.

A year later all this was allegory, naming imitations and analogues all over the West. In New York, Arthur Cravan, Man Ray, and Marcel Duchamp took the tag; in Paris, André Breton, Louis Aragon, Paul Eluard, Francis Picabia, and a dozen more. A urinal was exhibited as the embodiment of the beautiful, the true, and the good, as art; a moustache and an obscene anagram were drawn on a postcard of the *Mona Lisa*. Such acts had effects; some people paid attention, some were irritated, and some were thrilled. Dada was received as nonsense with a straight face, or maybe vice versa, well-dressed young men in good cafes placing "KICK ME" stickers on the rumps of their working-class waiters, a privileged retort to the moral dilemmas posed by the world war ("Let's party"), a joke finally settling into encyclopedias: "A complex international movement, Dada was essentially an attack on both artistic and political traditions. Its early performances were designed to outrage the conventional, but all manifestations had in common anti-social behavior, nihilism and a desire to shock . . ."

Thanks mostly to Tzara, a tireless promoter, the papers were full of it. "Up to October 15," he wrote in 1919, "8590 articles on dadaism." No one has ever checked the figure, which he probably made up, but he was probably right. Still, this had nothing to do with what happened in the Cabaret Voltaire, and it was not what Lefebvre was talking about. The entry in *The Timetables of History* isn't far off, though: "1916. Visual Arts. Dadaist cult in Zurich."

DADA WAS

Dada was a legend of freedom only after the fact; in the act it was a gnostic myth of the twentieth century.

It was a secret history not only of the Great War but of all the I-have-a-rendezvous-with-death poetry written to extract meaning from the war—on dada terms, to justify it. François Truffaut's *Jules and Jim* is a version—with Jules and Jim, conventional bohemians, rational and passionate in their ways, both real people on the screen, and Jeanne Moreau's Catherine, her face first glimpsed in a field of abandoned statues, dada: junk, unreal but irresistible, the fatal spell.

Much has been written about the Cabaret Voltaire as a protest against the war; the dadaists wrote a lot of it. Arp in 1948:

The Cabaret Voltaire,
Zurich, 1986

. . . disgusted by the butchery of World War I, we devoted ourselves to the Fine Arts. Despite the remote booming of artillery we sang, painted, pasted, and wrote poetry with all our might and main. We were seeking an elementary art to cure man of the frenzy of the times and a new order to restore the balance between heaven and hell. This art rapidly became a subject of general disapproval. It was not surprising to us that the "bandits" were unable to understand us. In their puerile megalomania and power-madness, they demanded that art itself must serve to brutalize mankind.

In other words, instead of war for war's sake, or art for war's sake, or even war for art's sake, art for art's sake, or anyway art for the good of humanity. Such notions might have made the papers in 1916, but they were hardly the stuff of legend, let alone myth: rather, old-fashioned romanticism or knee-jerk bohemianism. Writing in 1920, Huelsenbeck had a different idea—or a different voice:

We had all left our countries as a result of the war . . . We were agreed that the war had been contrived by the various governments for the most autocratic, sordid and materialistic reasons; we Germans were familiar with the book *J'accuse*, and even without it we would have had little confidence in the decency of the German Kaiser and his generals. Ball was a conscientious objector, and I had escaped by the skin of my teeth from the pursuit of the police myrmidons who, for their so-called patriotic reasons, were massing men in the trenches of Northern France and giving them shells to eat. None of us had much appreciation for the kind of courage it takes to get shot for the idea of a nation which is at best a cartel of pelt merchants and profiteers in leather, at worst a cultural association of psychopaths who, like the Germans, marched off with a volume of Goethe in their knapsacks, to skewer Frenchmen and Russians on their bayonets.

That last sentence is pure dada, or at least the sort of dada this book pursues: a voice of teeth ground down to points, more suited to manifestos and hit singles than to poems, a near-absolute loathing of one's time and place, the note held until disgust turns into glee. But as dada, that voice surfaced only in Berlin, in 1918 and for a year or two after. It was not the kind of dada one could have found in the Cabaret Voltaire, which this book also pursues. There, in 1916, an experiment was performed in which the language by which the war was justified was destroyed. In the story dada told, this destruction was a necessary preliminary to the discovery of a language so plain the very act of speaking it would grind one's teeth down to points.

A DISCIPLE

A disciple of Kandinsky—and a follower of Thomas Müntzer, Bakunin, and Kropotkin—Hugo Ball was always torn between defilement of authority and abasement before it. Experimenting with narcotics in 1915, he wrote in his diary: "I can imagine a time when I will seek obedience as much as I have tasted disobedience: to the full." He reached for a private megalomania to set against the public megalomania of the epoch: "I could not live without the conviction that my own personal fate is an abbreviated version of the fate of the whole nation"—by which, as a good German philosopher, he meant the fate of the whole world.

Well before Ball opened the Cabaret Voltaire, he wrote a dirty poem about the Virgin Mary, "Der Henker" (The Hangman). He wanted to fuck her, he said. But that was also before he began his diary, in which he testified that this was nothing.

I once used to carry a skull with me from city to city; I had found it in an old chapel. They had been digging up graves and had exposed hundred-year-old skeletons. They wrote the dead person's name and birthplace on the top of the skull. They painted the cheekbones with roses and forget-me-nots. The *caput mortuum* that I carried with me for years was the head of a girl who had died in 1811 at the age of twenty-two. I was in fact madly in love with the hundred-and-thirty-three-year old girl and could hardly bear to part from her . . . This living head here

(Emmy Hennings, from 1913 Ball's mistress, after 1920 his wife, after 1927 his widow)

reminds me of that dead one. When I look at the girl, I want to take some paint and paint flowers on her hollow cheeks.

Certain passages from Ball's diary appear in almost every history of dada; this one never does.

BALL

Ball defined the terms of the Cabaret Voltaire in advance. On 25 November 1915 he wrote:

People who live rashly and precipitately easily lose control over their impressions and are prey to unconscious emotions and motives. The activity of any art (painting, writing, composing) will do them good, provided that they do not pursue any purpose in their subjects, but follow the course of a free, unfettered imagination. The independent process of fantasy never fails to bring to light again those things that have crossed the threshold of consciousness without analysis. In an age like ours, when people are assaulted daily by the most monstrous things without being able to keep account of their impressions, aesthetic production becomes a prescribed course. But all living art will be irrational, primitive, and complex; it will speak a secret language and leave behind documents not of edification but of paradox.

Seven decades on, this translates easily—but as with Arp and Huelsenbeck on dada as protest, one has to pare away the conventional to find the element around which the story turns. First off there is borrowed Freudianism—art as psychoanalysis, art as cure, plus enlightened solipsism versus brainwashed mass society. The embrace of the irrational and primitive is just 1915 cafe talk: a blurb for expressionism and cubism, a leap on the band-wagon of Filippo Marinetti's then-hot futurism, a ride leading straight to Breton's surrealism. But Ball's last words—"it will speak a secret language and leave behind documents not of edification but of paradox"—remain strange. This was what Lefebvre would respond to. It was the heart of the vaudeville show, a reach for the gnostic myth; everyone who made it felt it.

They were never masters of the paradox, but simply messengers—or, as the years went on, victims. For the rest of their lives (save for Ball, the members of the Cabaret Voltaire sextet lived a long time) they returned again and again to their few days in the Zurich bar. They tried to understand what happened to them. They never got over it.

THIS IS

This is the best evidence—the only real evidence—that something actually happened in Zurich in the spring of 1916, something the art-history version of dada can only cover up.

From the beginning it was commonplace to hear punk described as dada. Here are the lines that got me interested, written by Isabelle Anscombe in 1978: "Punk must be willing to reject itself as it becomes established, to be open to change and to forgo the profits. It is a mode of anarchy as much as the Dadaist 'Cabaret Voltaire' at the end of the First World War, and how many people are particularly familiar with that?" A lot of people, it turned out: Andrew Czezowski, who ran the Roxy, told reporters it was "a sort of new Cabaret Voltaire." Plenty of punks had done time in that traditional spawning ground of U.K. rock bands, the state-run art school.

Punk made the dailies as "dole-queue rock"; it made the monthlies as "another art-school demo."

Still, Anscombe was working on an idea, and opposed to literary references ideas about punk and dada were almost nonexistent as she wrote. In London or New York in the late 1970s dada meant what it meant in Paris and New York at the end of the First World War: a not-quite-naked prank, a jape clothed in the barest g-string of aesthetic authority, a Bronx cheer in three-part harmony, Tzara's affirmation of the right "to piss and shit in different colors." It meant Arthur Cravan getting up to deliver a lecture and dropping his pants, a young John Lennon urinating from a Hamburg balcony onto a passing line of nuns ("Let's baptize 'em"), the Sex Pistols saying "fuck" on TV. Dada meant a charming gratuitous act amenable to some future art-historical homage—as opposed to the uncharming simplest-surrealist-act, Breton's man shooting blindly into a crowd, which, since no surrealist ever did anything of the kind, devolves into this sort of dada, into a literary reference, where it meets Zed, a punk gang leader played by Bob Goldthwait in the 1985 film *Police Academy 2: Their First Assignment.*

In his mid-twenties, but seemingly superannuated—fat, balding, sweating, drooling—Zed heads thugs signed as punks by their multicolored hair and studded leather, by 1985 the diffused and floating signs of London 1976. They terrorize a neighborhood for lack of anything else to do with it. Zed is so full of rage he can barely talk: you can feel his vocal cords breaking up every time he opens his mouth.

He's a cuddly anarchist, blithering but lovable. When he tells the mayor "I-VOTED-FOR-YOU!" while his gang trashes her community-outreach street fair, when he says "THANK-YOU-VERY-MUCH-YOU'VE-GOTTA-LOTTA-NICE-BARGAINS-HERE!" after they've unloaded a supermarket, there's not a hint of sarcasm—on some level, he's completely sincere. He wants the mayor to drop dead of shock; he also wants her to like him. "Be reasonable," a cop begs him. "I-HATE-REASONABLE!" he screams; you feel for him. He's just a boy who can't say yes;

any art critic could pin him as dada, just as in 1965 every art critic pinned Andy Warhol as "neo-dada." "Dada is a tomato," said one Paris dada manifesto. "To wear a tomato in your lapel is to be a dadaist," said another. Textbook dada in a phrase: absurd negation that wants no consequences. Unless it's the kind Zed's antics produced: in *Police Academy 3* he became a cop himself.

IN THE LATE

In the late 1970s punk-as-dada did not even mean this much. It meant the history-in-nutshell parallels always needed to explain something new, or explain it away: wasn't there a British band that called itself "Cabaret Voltaire"? Didn't Talking Heads set a Hugo Ball sound poem to music on their third lp? Every book on dada told the story of Kurt Schwitters combing his Hanover streets for cigarette butts and discarded concert tickets to stick into his collages; the formal dada theory that art could be made out of anything matched the formal punk theory that anyone could make art ("Here are three chords," read the famous notes to a diagram in *Sniffin' Glue*, the first U.K. punk fanzine—"now form a band"). "The Dadaist logic of sucking in all the trivia, the rubbish and the cast-offs of the world and then stamping a new meaning on the assemblage," ran a typical gloss on Tzara's recipe for dada poetry (cut words out of a newspaper, shake in a bag, paste at random on a page), "was there both in punk's music and sartorial regime." It was true: there were punk songs about cigarette butts, and a '77 London punk jacket could look like a 1918 Berlin dada collage. Why, though? And so what? Why form a band?

Historical validation turns every no into a yes if the no can be footnoted, just as those who are always happier to announce the death of something than be present at its birth have mastered the knack of turning a casual aside into an embrace of the whole social order. Yes, the safety pin Jamie Reid put through H.R.H.'s lips in his "God Save the Queen" graphic harked back even more loudly to Duchamp's defaced *Mona Lisa* than to the May '68 Atelier populaire poster—but Johnny Rotten had not said the word "dada" since he was two.

No one tried to use dada to find the limits of punk, or vice versa: to start a conversation between the past and the present, to wonder just how it is that an idea jumps a sixty-year gap, or burrows under it. Instead there was a setup. The dada aesthetic went into the books as "anti-art"; punk was "anti-rock." The basic dada act was understood to be the performer's attack on the audience; punks swore and spit from the stage. Like punk, except for a few favored saints dada refused all ancestors: "I'm not even interested in knowing if anyone existed before me," Tzara announced, quoting Descartes. You could find the footnotes in the songs: "Anti-art was the start," as Poly Styrene sang.

The parallel was obviously correct; as a fan, I didn't know what to make of it. I had books by Ball and Huelsenbeck on my shelves, picked up on remainder years before, but I hadn't read them. In art-history surveys one learned far more about the proto-surrealist Parisian dada spinoff than its putative Zurich progenitor, and surrealism was what the historians really wanted to talk about.

The parallel broke down when you put the art of the one against the other, if you weighed punk singles against dada paintings and poems. "I couldn't believe it when I first heard it," a friend said of X-ray Spex's "Oh Bondage Up Yours!" "It was so *funny*." It was funny and scary: you heard Poly Styrene's Shirley Temple voice ("Some people say that little girls should be seen and not heard / But I say—") turn into a raw-meat social chugalug ("OH BONDAGE UP YOURS!"). The opening parodied anyone's expectations, and the follow-up ruined them; Lora Logic kicked off her saxophone solo as if she were kicking down a door, which was exactly what she was doing. Irony was never so exciting as in the Buzzcocks' "Boredom" ("Scene here pretty hum-*drum*," Howard Devoto snapped, as if the notion had just occurred to him). Forget history: the sound of the record was so edgy it simply had to be new. The Adverts'

"Gary Gilmore's Eyes" was a pure punk notion—what if Gary Gilmore had donated his eyes to an eye bank and you got them?—too pure to be anything else.

Compared to this, Zurich art works were tame. I ran the single number of the May 1916 review *Cabaret Voltaire* on microfilm, and there was one explosion: "L'amiral cherche une maison à louer," the transcript of a German-English-French/ Huelsenbeck-Janco-Tzara simultaneous poem as performed in the cabaret (easy to imagine on stage, fabulous to read, dragged down by Tzara's laborious "Note pour les bourgeois," where he explained that the point was to translate cubism into verse). But the layout was sober, the New Man dressed up in the old man's best suit. The result was pious, a sort of avant-garde mass.

Whatever happened in Zurich in the spring of 1916—no tape recordings, no videos, no live lps on the Ephriam label equivalent to *The Roxy London WC 2*—it wasn't in the archives, and whatever happened, most ran from it. With the cabaret a dead letter, in 1917 Ball, Janco, Tzara, and followers like Hans Richter set up the Galerie Dada, offering poetry readings, lectures, and revivals of last year's hits to women's clubs and package tours. "We have surmounted the barbarisms of the cabaret," Ball wrote. Simon Frith visited an Australian punk club in 1979, and all he saw were rules and manners; he measured it against 1976, so long before, when people "didn't know what would happen next." In the Galerie Dada, Ball and the rest knew what would happen: nothing. They restaged the number with the big costume; if TV had existed they would have been on it.

Except for Huelsenbeck, who frothed at the mouth, no one liked to talk about this very much. Soon enough, Ball and Hennings went back to the church. Tzara and Arp attached themselves to Breton and became famous. Janco too came to Paris; disgusted by what he saw as the surrealists' attempt to put the dada spirit "in their pockets," he went back to Romania and slipped into obscurity. Ultimately Huelsenbeck became a distinguished New York psychoanalyst, changing his name to Charles R. Hulbeck both to Americanize it and to kill his dada past. In the Cabaret Voltaire Arp was twenty-eight, Huelsenbeck twenty-four, Tzara turned twenty, Janco twenty-one: as old men they had every right to dismiss their Spiegelgasse hijinks as juvenilia, but they didn't. They tried to—with dada gone in the 1920s they disavowed it almost with the fervor of 1930s Communists damning the god that failed. But it didn't work.

THE CABARET

The Cabaret Voltaire crept back and trivialized all their works and days. It dissolved them, just as on stage in the Meierei they had dissolved the past. As the dadaists got older, faced death, thought about their legacies, the syndrome worsened. They were humble in their megalomania. They spoke of dada in terms so abstract and contradictory no one could really understand them. If punk was like dada then there was something in punk no one had glimpsed—even though the old dadaists were now like pop stars condemned to roll their greatest hit up the hill of the crowd for all eternity, carrying the curse of having been in the right place at the right time, a blessing that comes to no one more than once.

Describing the scene on stage, Arp wasn't reporting—I said he was just to give the scene more punch. In truth he was writing in 1948, past sixty, working from a reproduction of Janco's lost 1916 painting *Cabaret Voltaire*, using it as flesh for memory: Janco's Emmy Hennings was not doing the splits. At the same time, Huelsenbeck and Tzara were entering the thirty-second year of their fight over the authorship of the word "dada": *I was the "young man" Henri Lefebvre will speak of after I am dead!*, Tzara might have said. *No, I was,* Huelsenbeck might have replied, *and I won't be! Top that!* In early 1984 Janco was eighty-eight. On 5 February 1916 he and his brother Jules had appeared along with Tzara in response to an

announcement Ball placed in the papers; along with the rest
on the first night he hung paintings and tacked posters on the
walls of Jan Ephriam's bar. Now, sixty-eight years later, in
Ein Hod, Israel, the artists' colony he had founded in 1953, he
was trying to recreate the Cabaret Voltaire, under the same
name: new versions of discoveries he'd faked in the Galerie
Dada when at twenty-one he had already gone as far as he
would ever go.

"Poems read simultaneously in different languages," said the
Jerusalem *Post*; of course it was pathetic. At the crest the
stone always rolls to the bottom, and only one tied to it by
curse can move it up an inch. Janco sat square in his chair
with a bouquet in his hands and a beret on his head. Everyone
else who had been there was dead. "How would the dadaists
respond to the reconstruction of their acts?" a reporter asked
Steve Solomons, director of the Ein Hod Cabaret Voltaire.
"They'd say it was absolutely ridiculous," he said—but as a
dadaist everything he said was a lie. Janco didn't think it was
ridiculous—or, if he did, he had nothing more or less ridiculous to offer. In the midst of the permanent Arab-Israeli war,
with inflation rising by the day and Orthodox rabbis marshal-
ing the full power of the state for the enforcement of rules so
arbitrary they read like the stipulations of one of the fanatical
dada manifestos Huelsenbeck offered to Berlin in 1918, Janco's
message was "Back to chaos." "Artists can communicate better
than politicians," he said. He was talking about communication between certain Israelis and certain Palestinians, or Syri-
ans, Lebanese, whoever might notice—weren't there some who
had more in common with him, or what he stood for, than he
or they had in common with the official cultures supposedly
their own?

Janco was working against the clock. A new time, a new
place, who knew what might happen? He died on 21 April
1984, before he could explain, but if he had lived another lifetime he would not have been able to explain, which is not to
say that some who heard him might not have understood.

IN ZURICH

In Zurich the Cabaret Voltaire was an immediate hit. Fifty was full; it was full every night. First there were students, who drank and smoked and tore up the room; then burghers, the reviled "bourgeoisie," the curious; then finally, as with the Roxy in 1977, Japanese tourists. There were so many regulars almost nobody paid, a version of the old punk joke: how many punks does it take to screw in a lightbulb? One to hold the ladder, one to turn the bulb, and fifty on the guest list.

On stage there was—on the first night—a reading from the works of patron saint Voltaire. There followed a balalaika orchestra, cover versions of Mallarmé, Nostradamus, Kandinsky, Apollinaire, Turgenev, Chekhov, and Christian Morgenstern's ten-year-old sound-poem hits, evergreens like "Under the Bridges of Paris," the Parisian cabaret ballads of Aristide Bruant as sung by Hennings (in "St. Lazare" she was a whore dying of syphilis contracted in prison), readings by Arp from Alfred Jarry's *Ubu Roi*, plays actually staged, bits of Verlaine, Rimbaud, Baudelaire, futurist manifestos, exhibitions of paintings by Arp, Janco, and cabaret habitué Giacometti, plus mime, rants, crude jokes, shaggy dog stories.

The program notes don't suggest the building sense of possibility Ball recorded. February 26: "Everyone has been seized by an indefinable intoxication. The little cabaret is about to come apart at the seams and is getting to be a playground for crazy emotions." March 2: "It is a race with the expectations of the audience." March 14: "As long as the whole city is not enchanted, the cabaret has failed." A race with the expectations of the audience is a definition of punk at its best: did anyone in the Roxy feel the same? Uncertain about what to do next, Ball and the others held a meeting and decided on an evening of Russian folk songs. Why was it so hard to get over?

From Tzara's 1920 "Zurich Chronicle" to Ball's diary, published in 1927 as *Die Flucht aus der Zeit* (Flight Out of Time), from Arp's 1948 "Dadaland" to Huelsenbeck's 1957 *Mit Witz, Licht und Grütze* (With Wit, Light, and Brains), published in

English in 1974 as *Memoirs of a Dada Drummer*, from Hennings' hagiographies of Ball to Janco's last interview, the dadaists set down the story. Historians have been trying to pull good dates out of them ever since. The dadaists played out the reggae aphorism that there are no truths, only versions; each claimed to have been in the right place at the right time and refused in every instance to say exactly where or when it was. "The libraries should be burned, and only the things that everyone knows by heart would survive," Ball wrote after the cabaret closed. "A great era of the legend would begin." "We have forgotten minor things," Huelsenbeck said. He more than any of them truly didn't care about history, that the cabaret was running concurrently with the Battle of Verdun—or he didn't care about the kind of history Verdun could make. Rationalism, the Enlightenment, had produced a charnel house; the classicist heritage that Huelsenbeck and the rest were born to pass on had turned on them, and so on stage they performed an ancient myth of destruction and creation. As they looked back, they realized it had been no protest against the times but an odd acceptance: wiping the slate clean brought them to life but they expected nothing from the future. The surrealists expected everything: that is why every surrealist document is extant, why every surrealist occasion can be dated with perfect precision; if the dadaists were fools the surrealists were accountants.

When the surrealists looked back, they looked back with certainty, whether it was the certainty of the Stalinism some of them once embraced, or of the textbook citations all of them had won. The dadaists looked back with puzzlement—except for Huelsenbeck, who looked back as if it had all been obvious, inadequate, a rehearsal for a day that never came. Everywhere in the memoirs of the dadaists there is special pleading, legend tending, feuding, threats of legal action over trademark violation or misappropriation of funds, but nowhere is there a fixed point, a line, an ideology of what it was all for. Instead they asked what happened—queerly, they fell back before their own memories. *We stood on the stage and recited a simul-*

. . . .

*. . . **THIS PLAY HAS** not been staged for the theatergoers at all, but for others who unfortunately can't make it. And besides, what else is there to put on?*

—Peter Schneider, The Wall Jumper, *1983*

. . . .

taneous poem, Tzara, Janco, and I, in French, English, and German. (Of course I speak English today—a German accent pulls them in, but the check had better be in dollars!—but not about dada, when I speak about dada I only speak in German, that was the dada language, perhaps I mean the pre-language, it's the best I can do to keep the story straight.) "Every body is doing it, doing it, doing it," Janco recited, and the world turned upside down. In 1954 Elvis Presley sang "Everybody's doin' it, doin' it, doin' it" (well, you know he sang "That's all right, mama, that's all right with me," but what's the difference, it was all in the rhythm), and the same thing happened again. (Or 1948, the Orioles' "It's Too Soon to Know," I have the original It's-a-Natural 78 right here, I play it for my patients when they ask me how long this is going to take, same thing again, I mean before, as Arp said, "Only imbeciles and Spanish professors care about dates," time is a bourgeois construction, to turn an hour into fifty minutes is to be a dadaist.) All it was was my "umbah-umbah," it was just Negergedichte, the big beat—"Jes' grew," Ishmael Reed called it in Mumbo Jumbo, *that wonderful book about ragtime he published just before I died, every body is doing it, doing it, doing it—do you understand? If you do, write Dr. Charles R. Hulbeck, 88 Central Park West, New York, New York. Thank you very much.*

Reading the testimony of the Cabaret Voltaire cut-ups one finds only Série noire: "The Seventeenth Murder" in Dashiell Hammett's *Red Harvest*, the dead chauffeur in Raymond Chandler's *The Big Sleep*, Frank and Cora fornicating in the dirt next to her husband's corpse in James Cain's *The Postman Always Rings Twice*, Sheriff Nick Corey's chiliastic serenity in Jim Thompson's *Pop. 1280*. If dada was a locked-room mystery the door was open and there wasn't even a body—just blood on the bed, a four-letter word scrawled on the wall, and a hundred-and-thirty-three-year-old skull in the closet. Like the private eye in William Hjortsberg's *Falling Angel*, as detectives the dadaists were their own culprits, forced to work simply for the sake of the story. "We killed a quarter of a century, we killed several centuries for the sake of what is to come," Huelsenbeck wrote. "You can call it what you like." At the climax there was no chance to assemble everyone in the drawing room, because Ball and Hennings had gone back to the church, Arp and Tzara were out of town, Huelsenbeck had changed his name, and letters to Janco came back no such number, no such zone. Anyway it would be decades before any of them could even name the victim: what they wanted.

BACK IN

Back in Zurich in the first month of the cabaret there was as yet neither corpse nor story. For that matter there was no dada; the word had yet to be discovered.

It meant "hobby horse" in French; in German it was a dismissal, "Goodbye," "Be seeing you," "Get off my back." In Romanian, "Of course." In Italian, "wet nurse"; in Swabian slang, "sex-crazed moron"; in English, "father," and "get ready"—a fanfare. Deep in the Indo-European substratum it meant both yes and no: it was a magic word.

Tzara decided on it one morning in a cafe, his only affidavit from Arp, who swore he was present with his twelve children while wearing a bread roll in his nose—solid dada evidence Huelsenbeck countered most effectively by outliving Tzara. "When Ball and I discovered Dadaism," he wrote in 1927, putting it all behind him for the first time,

we were unaware of our errand. Ball had just eaten a bowl of noodle soup and I had just thrown the last drunken students out of the Cabaret Voltaire when Ball said, "*Da . . . da* [There, there], don't you see where it all leads!" . . . In this moment—it was an historic moment—the responsibility of a mission was given to me, which until now I have not dared to shake off. I grasped Dadaism.

"When I came across the word 'dada,'" Ball wrote on 18 June 1921, "I was called upon twice by Dionysius." He meant not Bacchus (Dionysus) but someone far more esoteric: a Greek converted by St. Paul in the first century. It was a mystical code, "D.A.–D.A."—a doubling, John Elderfield writes in his introduction to *Flight Out of Time*, "of the initials of Dionysius the Areopagite, one of the three saints who were to form the subject of [Ball's 1923] book *Byzantinisches Christenum*. This, however, is most likely Ball's hindsight . . ." You can almost hear Elderfield muffling his scream.

Dada history is a writer's dream: choosing among versions, one has to make the story up. Following accounts of how in March (or April) 1916, Huelsenbeck, looking for a name to give a there-and-gone Cabaret Voltaire canary (*Shall we call her Divina de la Nuit? Sally Hot Jazz? Irene Dogmatic?*), chanced upon the word in an open dictionary (German? French? English? Romanian?) and immediately realized it would blow modern art, literature, and culture to pieces, one can imagine him edging into a pharmacy the next day to buy a pack of contraceptives, only to come face to face with "DADA SHAMPOO," fine product of Bergmann & Co., on sale at Bahnhofstrasse 51 since 1913. *Oh shit*, Huelsenbeck must have said—or, *Of course! Dada shampoo! The universal cleansing agent!*

IN APRIL

In April 1916 Ball and Huelsenbeck talked long into the night about art as an end in itself. If the growing dissonance of the cabaret was driven by a contempt for what the world outside called art, even hatred for it, that was because Ball and Huelsenbeck were beginning to recognize the conventions of art as merely the most glittering reflection of the conventions of social life, of all that made the war possible, that kept it going as they spoke. Art turned hell into heaven—that was why the war could be fought for "art's sake," for the "German way of life," or for that matter the French way of life, or the English way of life, the Russian way of life, the Austro-Hungarian way of life, not to mention the Bosno-Herzegovian way of life (coming up late but fast, the American way of life), the redundancy cancelling not only each claim but the language used to make it. They were beginning to see art as a trick: to see the freie strasse, the champ libre, the free space, as an asylum. If they opened the cabaret each night as a war against a million bayonets sticking out of a million standard-issue volumes of Goethe, that was because art had fooled humanity, had fooled them, into thinking the world was better than it was; because on art's heavenly scales a single copy of *Faust* outweighed the million men who died that it might stay in print; because art diverted the human desire to remake the world into the lunatic's therapy of making poems, paintings, ashtrays. Give them to relatives visiting on Sundays, put them in a museum—wasn't it all the same?

The conclusions Ball and Huelsenbeck were reaching didn't destroy the impulse that drew them to art. That impulse could not be rooted out: it was the impulse to change the world. When Ball wrote that for "people assaulted daily by the most monstrous things without being able to keep account of their impressions, aesthetic production becomes a prescribed course," he meant that in times when each day creates its own nihilism, meaning has to be created, made up. Out of what? Out of anything, the dadaists were discovering, as they put the detritus of their civilization on stage and watched it change shape—out of anything, to the point of nothingness. Dada was thrilling because it permitted and then demanded a complete and then conscious abdication of responsibility toward art, then toward the society art represented—by representing, the dadaists were discovering, affirmed. They were about to reach the social atom; they were about to take it apart.

Dada was grace but not for the asking, not by faith and not by works. Grace was up to God, and God was indifferent to the paltry, self-destructing ethical systems humanity had fashioned in imitation of the natural order. Thus the dadaists experienced grace as chance, as a matter of the-right-place-at-the-right-time, a bolt of lightning, a fall in the street. Like a fall in the street, grace came forth disguised in the gestures of

Advertisement, Zurich, 1913

ordinary life; like a bolt of lightning, it came to no one more than once, this moment of change in which the whole world was wiped clean and reborn within the New Man, if only for a moment—that was why they never got over it.

He and Huelsenbeck decided, Ball recorded, that art was "only an occasion," a "method" for locating "the specific rhythm and the buried face of this age"—"its foundation and essence," the "possibility of its being stirred." It was the same notion Guy Debord recast and hardened in 1961, in *Critique de la séparation* (Critique of Separation), a film about the situationists and the world of spectacles they meant to abolish. "Normally," Debord said on the soundtrack, as he made art, a movie, to argue art out of its claims (though like all but one of Debord's movies, this was an exercise in détournement, a film made mostly out of bits of other people's films, trailers, photographs, advertisements, cartoons, graffiti, newsreel footage: on the screen, a pinball machine flashed TILT, then prison guards drove rioting convicts back to their cells), "the things that happen to us, the things that truly involve us and demand our attention, leave us no more than bored and distant spectators. But almost any situation, once it has been transposed artistically, awakens our attention; we want to take part in it, to change it. This is the paradox that must be turned upside down—put back on its feet. This is what must be realized in acts." Given the new worlds that artists had revealed in the first quarter of the century, the situationists thought, nothing had happened since. All that was left was the impulse: that wish to "take part," to "change." Of course, to those for whom Ball's paradox was just a word, "time" went on, "art" went on. Whatever it had been in 1916, in 1961 something called dada still inspired people all over the world, many of whom labored to make art they were happy to hear named "neo-dada"—a fraud on both time and art, one-time Berlin dadaist Raoul Hausmann said, because neo-dada took "sides with the object as a 'thing in itself'—which dada denied."

The will to change the world, Debord was saying in *Critique of Separation*—his critique of the separation of art from the world it meant to change, of every person from every other, of each clenched fist from the person who made it—was found most perfectly in the artistic impulse, which was deflected by the object it produced, which became a commodity, an agent of reification, a thing in itself. "Capitalism grants art a perpetual privileged concession," Debord wrote in 1960,

that of pure creative activity, an alibi for the alienation of all other activities . . . but at the same time, this sphere reserved for "free creative activity" is the only one in which the questions of what we do with life and of communication are posed practically and completely. Here, in art, lies the first locus point of the antagonism between partisans and adversaries of the officially dictated reasons for living. The established meaninglessness and separation [of art] give rise to the general crisis of artistic means, a crisis linked to alternative ways of living, to the demand for a new way of life.

This was the crisis that was beginning to emerge in the Cabaret Voltaire: the realization that art's meaninglessness, its separation from what actually happened, rendered the beautiful, the true, and the good into the ugly, the false, and the evil. The artistic impulse could not be rooted out, but its means had fallen to ruin: in the face of the new machines that were transforming the world—destroying it—paint and canvas were the tools of an enterprise as obsolete as alchemy. Maybe one had to "create directly," as Tzara said—to *live* as a "genius"—but the war made genius effete, its communication a solipsism. As a protest, Huelsenbeck said long after the fact, the cabaret was also a panic: a panic over the realization that whatever artists might have to say, they had no way of saying it, and if they didn't, neither did anyone else. Separate art was an illusion hiding the fact that in the twentieth century poetry, true communication, came out of the barrel of the gun pointed at your head. In 1920 in Berlin, Huelsenbeck cast all doubts aside: art had to be destroyed, he said, because it was a "moral safety valve," a mechanism for the unlimited ability of the human mind to turn its worst fantasies into real-life atrocities, then to turn its worst atrocities into pretty pictures. But this was already hindsight, an attempted murder to cover up what hadn't been; it was only guesswork in the Cabaret Voltaire.

IN THE CABARET

In the cabaret art was staged as a nightly revelation of the buried face—now you see it now you don't, no matter that most were drunk, dancing, seeing nothing, just having a good time—a nightly proof that the paradox the dadaists meant to enact was a paradox, not a proof. It was a way to keep the place full and the bar trade moving ("Tip your waitress!" goes a lost line from Ball's diary), "the ideals of culture and art as a program for a variety show," a race with the expectations of the audience, the audience racing against itself. Night after night, unknown people climbed out of the crowd to speak, to recite poems they had treasured all their lives or made up a few minutes before, to sing old songs, to make fools of themselves, to take part, to change. There were no classics. Voltaire was as contemporary as Apollinaire, the singer named Madame Dada as old as Dionysius the Areopagite, because in the heat of the moment both performers and audience succeeded in losing their memory. As Arp wrote in 1966, the year he died, remembering that even before the cabaret opened he had ripped up one of his pictures in frustration, tossed the pieces in the air, watched in wonder as they fluttered to the floor, and then, seized by the moment, framed the pattern as a fact no less objective than bodies arranged in a trench by a grenade: "Before there was Dada, Dada was there . . ."

Sentimentality had crept in: that portentous dot dot dot. Before dada was there, there was a wish to negate the war and make a name; afterward there was the wish to hold onto it. As artists everybody in the cabaret was a nobody; in Zurich they were famous overnight. Why not the world? Pushed by Tzara, who saw dada capitalized as an art movement, the group issued luxurious, special-limited-edition publications aimed straight at patrons and museums. On vellum it was nothing new; there were countless precedents in prewar Europe for pretentious Nietzschean cafes. But Ball's needs were greater than most: just before offering his boiled shirtfront and his piano skills to Jan Ephriam, he had tried suicide; he and Hennings had slept outdoors; begged, searched for food in garbage cans. His desires were greater: "Only the theater is capable of creating the new society. The backgrounds, colors, words, and sounds have only to be taken from the subconscious and animated to engulf the everyday routine along with its misery." Ball started the cabaret as a way to eat, and, if he got lucky, to change the world.

Along with Ball's need to create there was Hennings' buried urge to destroy. Booked into a Berlin nightclub in 1912, she had pulled a rare review—rare in the annals of pop music, if not for her. One Ravien Siurlai wrote in the radical journal *Die Aktion*:

She stepped onto the cabaret stage, ribboned about the neck, her face waxen. With her cropped yellow hair and the stiffly layered ruffles of her skimpy dark velvet dress, she was separated from all of humanity . . . old and ravaged . . . A woman has infinities, gentlemen, but one need not absolutely confuse the erotic with prostitution . . . Who can stop this girl, who is hysteria herself . . . from swelling to an avalanche? . . . Covered with make-up, hypnotizing with morphine, absinthe, and the bloody flame of the electric "Gloire," a violent distortion of the Gothic, her voice hops over corpses, mocks them, soulfully trilling like a yellow canary.

You can sense Siurlai reaching; you can feel him fall back, finally, into the canary cliché, as if to block his own reach: yes, it was just a show. In the late 1970s dozens of new Siurlais would try to describe attempts to create the same sensations (in San Francisco, the singer for Nôh Mercy comes on stage pregnant, squats, emits a torrent of fake blood, and gives birth to a cow bone; in Los Angeles, a woman strides naked onto the bandstand as Vox Pop plays, collapses into the bass drum, rises, pulls a Tampax from her vagina, and hurls it into the crowd—"grown men, skinheads, turned white and ran away"— that was punk, after the Sex Pistols broke up, after Johnny Rotten had taken the show as far as a show can go). Writers would try to make sense of new versions of Hennings' apparition and fall short even of Siurlai's compromise—which perhaps means that something happened in 1912 that did not happen in punk, or that the dread to which Siurlai gave voice required an innocence that could no longer be felt. In 1912 the war was two years away; along with everyone else in Europe, Siurlai had yet to learn the meaning of a phrase like "hops over corpses," or for that matter the meaning of the word "corpse." Still, like Louis Veuillot faced with Thérésa, Siurlai was reaching for a prophecy—and the moral disorder he saw in Hennings would soon find its analogue all over the West. Ball may have found it in 1914, in a visit to the Belgian front, which changed him from an enlistee into a draft dodger; he surely found it in July 1915, when Marinetti sent him the futurists' latest "Parole in libertà" (Free Speech).

"The image of the human form is gradually disappearing from the painting of these times and all objects appear only in fragments," Ball wrote the next year, with the cabaret in full swing. "This is one more proof of how ugly and worn the human countenance has become, and of how all the objects of our environment have become repulsive to us. The next step is for poetry to decide to do away with language for similar reasons. These are things that have probably never happened before." But Marinetti had provided the clue: in 1915 the words and letters of his manifesto leaped over the page like illiterate diagrams of a song, like proof of a critic's inability to keep up with a new music. "They are just letters of the alphabet on a page," Ball said in amazement; "you can roll up such a poem like a map. The syntax has come apart. The letters are scattered and assembled again in a rough-and-ready way. There is no language anymore . . . it has to be invented all over again. Disintegration right in the innermost process of creation."

It was a perfect theory for Hennings' practice, a perfect summation in advance of the strongest moments of the cabaret that would follow six months later—especially if one reverses the first and last words of Ball's final sentence. The cabaret was named for the author of the greatest of all ironies—"All is for the best in this best of all possible worlds," said Voltaire. "Our sort of *Candide* against the times," Ball said of the Meierei—but for those who knew how to listen, there was no irony at all. Disintegration right in the innermost process of creation, creation right in the innermost process of disintegration—no one, the dadaists least of all, has ever been able to figure out if dada was absolute affirmation or absolute negation, only that the absolute was present, as present as Ball's sentence was reversible. But even though in *Police Academy 2* Zed's gang kidnaps a police captain and sends him back to the stationhouse with his face and clothes painted with lines and curls that are preliterate, almost precognitive signs reaching for letters, the cop returning to the fold as a manifesto-against-his-will in favor of syntax coming apart, calling for language to be invented all over again, or never again, the Zedists rolling him up like a map of their disgust, that wasn't quite it either. All dada histories quote Ball's 1915 line about disintegration and creation; like so much of his diary, it was written to be quoted. But no one quotes the line he wrote next, which does not seem to anticipate dada at all: "It is imperative to write invulnerable sentences."

ACCORDING

According to legend the invulnerable sentence was the antithesis of dada; dada denied there was any such thing. But dada was part of its time, and Ball's politely unquoted line is part of dada. It brings dada all too close to futurism, which in the 1920s would happily make the leap from avant-garde aesthetics into the new world of fascism. It was a small leap, from either direction: Mussolini had himself been a poet, a futurist hanger-on, though perhaps one less attracted to Marinetti's experiments with language than to his celebration of war as the highest form of modern art.

Ball's sentence opens dada to the will to power. It sounds like something that should have been written by Hitler—or Lenin, who in 1916 was living just down the street from the Cabaret Voltaire: his house has a plaque too. He came often, arguing night after night with Janco over the fallacy of ab-

Filippo Marinetti, *parolibero*, 1915

stract art when what had to be created (Lenin pounded the table) were new *facts*—or he came never, not even on Russian
folk-song night, having already decided that art in whatever
form was a moral safety valve: "I can't listen to music too
often," he once said of Beethoven's *Appassionata*. "It affects
your nerves, makes you want to say stupid nice things and
stroke the heads of people who could create such beauty while
living in this vile hell. And now you mustn't stroke anyone's
head—you might get your hand bitten off. You have to hit
them on the head, without any mercy." Invulnerable sentences
are death sentences. "Six million exterminated" is an invulnerable sentence. You can't argue with it. There is a way in
which it is dada.

There was real fear in Siurlai's review of Hennings'
performance. "Hysteria," he wrote; "avalanche," "morphine,"
"bloody," "flame," "violent," "ravaged," "distortion," "corpses,"
"infinities." He was right to be scared. Ball's diaries are a du-
bious record because they make up a treatise on ethics; day by
day, as dada unfolded, he sought justifications for the barbarisms of the night before. But inside the cabaret he and the
others abandoned the need for justifications; then like lovers
seeking a way out of an illicit affair they all of them contrived
endless escapes the next morning, and surrendered again by
sundown. They knew Nietzsche's warning that "Whoever fights
monsters should see to it that in the process he does not become a monster"; as they danced in a circle on the stage, making a fire out of all literature, culture, modern art, they remembered those words like junkies reading the warning on a
bottle of narcotics. They knew they had created a monster, and
they had as much affection for it as Mary Shelley had for hers:
"My little child." Huelsenbeck:

If you have had the miraculous good fortune to be present at the
birth of such a "sensation," you will want to know how it happens
that an empty sound, first intended as a surname for a female singer,
has developed amid grotesque adventures into a name for a rundown
cabaret, then into abstract art, baby-talk and a party of babies at the
breast and finally—well [Huelsenbeck said in 1920], I shall not antic-

ipate. This is exactly the history of Dadaism. Dada came over the Dadaists without their knowing it; it was an immaculate conception, and thereby its profound meaning was revealed to me.

. . . In the hands of the gentlemen in Zurich, Dada grew into a creature which stood head and shoulders above all present; and soon its existence could no longer be arranged with the precision demanded by a businesslike conduct of the Dadaist movement in art. Despite the most impassioned efforts, no one had yet found out exactly what Dada was.

THERE IS

There is a figure who appears in this book again and again. His instincts are basically cruel; his manner is intransigent. He trades in hysteria but is immune to it. He is beyond temptation, because despite his utopian rhetoric satisfaction is the last thing on his mind. He is unutterably seductive, yet he trails bitter comrades behind him like Hansel his breadcrumbs, his only way home through a thicket of apologies he will never make. He is a moralist and a rationalist, but he presents himself as a sociopath; he leaves behind documents not of edification but of paradox. No matter how violent his mark on history, he is doomed to obscurity, which he cultivates as a sign of profundity. Johnny Rotten/John Lydon is one version; Guy Debord is another. Saint-Just was an ancestor, but in my story Richard Huelsenbeck is the prototype. God only knows what he was like as a psychiatrist.

"I still have a clear memory of the evening on which I entered the Cabaret Voltaire," he wrote in 1957.

Hugo was sitting at the piano, playing classical music, Brahms and Bach. Then he switched over to dance music. The drunken students pushed their chairs aside and began spinning around. There were almost no women in the cabaret. It was too wild, too smoky . . .

Hugo had written a poem against war and murderous insanity. Emmy recited it, Hugo accompanied her on the piano, and the audience chimed in, with a growl, murdering the poem.

Huelsenbeck idolized Ball. They met in 1912, in Munich, where Huelsenbeck was studying literature and art and Ball was working in the theater. The next year Huelsenbeck contributed to Ball's magazine *Revolution* as its in-house Paris correspondent (he had at least been to Paris, studying philosophy at the Sorbonne in late 1912; after dada he would become a real-life foreign correspondent for Berlin newspapers, traveling around the world, interviewing Chiang Kai-shek and turning up at the funeral of Sun Yat-sen). When Ball left Munich for Berlin in 1914, Huelsenbeck followed. In the first months of the war they organized readings to honor newly dead poets from both sides; in 1915 they put on an explicitly antiwar, anti-German "Expressionist Evening," offering nonsense verse and "Negro poems" to counter the destruction of Europe. When Ball first abandoned dada in July 1916, Huelsenbeck had a nervous breakdown that lasted almost six months ("punishment for dada hubris," he said). He was in Zurich only because of Ball—and his draft board. He arrived on February 8, 11, or 26, three, six, or twenty-one days after the cabaret opened.

Despite the noise and the crowd, he found it dead. He wanted a big beat, and he was ready to make it: with those "Negro poems," Negergedichte, based on fragments of information about ragtime—based on nothing. Each poem ended with bones-in-the-nose: "umbah-umbah." He read the poems out on stage.

Jan Ephriam took Huelsenbeck aside. He explained that the German medical student's bourgeois primitivisms were hopeless fantasies, not even fakes: the old sailor had spent years with African "Negroes." *Fine*, Huelsenbeck said (well, really he said *Fuck off*, but Ball turned him around)—*give me something authentic*. A few days later Ephriam returned with scribbles: "TRABADYA LA MODJERE MAGAMORE MAGAGERE TRABADJA BONO."

It was, Ball would prove with his celebrated sound poems, the dada language. If words that cannot contain facts can dissolve facts, Ephriam's sounds called up the invulnerable sentence. Huelsenbeck stood on the stage and recited the cabaret owner's blank syllables, then made up his own, refusing in every instance to give up his stupid "umbah-umbah"; the crowd responded in a hundred different ways. He sat behind a big bass drum, pounded it, shouted the new words, then like Jerry Lee Lewis in "Whole Lotta Shakin' Goin' On" whispered them, then roared back. Reciting his poem "The End of the World," he stalked the stage and slashed the air with a riding crop, spitting out his meaningless sounds as if they were apochrypha straight from the lost gnostic *Gospel of Truth*: "poème bruitist performed for the first time by Richard Huelsenbeck Dada," he liked to say, "or, if you prefer, the other way around." It was still a fraud but no one knew: "I secretly went to the University and started studying medicine," he told the audience at the Institute of Contemporary Arts in London in 1971. "I couldn't say it to anybody because they would have thought I was a terrible liar and bourgeois. In the morning he goes to the University and at night he makes *umbah-umbah*." But in Zurich in 1916 neither the dada six nor the crowd could have told "umbah-umbah" from "Hold On, I'm Comin'," and so the dadaists made their rhythm as the crowd clapped off the beat, rushed the stage, grabbed at Huelsenbeck's legs—it didn't matter what language he was speaking, or if he was speaking any language at all. "All art begins with a critique," he said, "with a critique of the self, the self always reflecting society. Our critique began, as all critique begins, with doubt . . . *Doubt became our life*. Doubt and outrage. Our doubt was so deep, finally, that we asked ourselves: Can language express a doubt so deep?"

On stage he kicked back. Fights broke out; he encouraged them. "You are invited to interrupt me any time you want to," he said in London. "I would like you to be a little bit lively such as we were. Now I am approaching the last third of my life," he said at seventy-nine, "and I'm not as lively as I was in 1916 in Zurich at the Spiegelgasse, then I was very lively— I could jump over tables and chairs, beat people up and was beaten up of course too, but there's still a little bit of this spirit left in me . . . Ball in his famous book *Flight Out of Time* describes me there as a young, aggressive, disagreeable person who always attacks the public, who spits at it, and always as his third word says his *umbah-umbah*. It cannot go on this way, something will have to be done about it sooner or later if he does not discontinue that. So we went on."

"A terrible chaos," Huelsenbeck said that night in London. "The meaning of chaos, that's what I'm going to talk about." But he never got around to it.

DISINTEGRATION

"Disintegration right in the innermost process of creation," Ball wrote. "It is imperative to write invulnerable sentences." 15 June 1916:

Huelsenbeck comes to type his latest poems. At every other word he turns his head and says: "Or is that an idea of yours?" I jokingly suggest that we should draw up an alphabetical list of our most frequent constellations and phrases, so that production can proceed without interruption; for I too sit on the window seat trying to resist unfamiliar words and associations; I scribble and look down at the carpenter who is busy making coffins in the yard. To be precise: two-thirds of the wonderfully plaintive words that no human mind can resist come from ancient magical texts. The use of "grammologues," or magical floating words and resonant sounds characterizes the way we both write. Such word-images, when they are successful, are irresistibly and hypnotically engraved on the memory, and they emerge again from the memory with just as little resistance and friction. It has frequently happened that people who visited our evening performances without being prepared for them were so impressed by a single word or phrase that it stayed with them for weeks. Lazy or apathetic people, whose resistance is low, are especially tormented in this way.

So it came up: the blind oath, the severed gesture, the buried curse, the dance it took an entire civilization to forget, and ten seconds to remember. The pieces Lefebvre would promise to finish smashing had been discovered. The momentum was there; the task was to increase it. "Some things assisted us in our efforts," Ball said—"first of all, the special circumstances of these times, which do not allow real talent either to rest or mature and so put its capabilities to the test. Then there was the energy of our group; one member was always trying to surpass the other by intensifying demands and stresses." Janco contributed the masks.

Ball saw them as abstractions of the passions, images that had somehow floated free for more than two thousand years, arriving in a crooked street in Zurich en route from the secret olive groves where the Greeks performed their first plays. At the same time he recognized the masks as absolutely modern: cutups that remained faces, but just barely. With paste and hair and cardboard Janco had taken the noses, eyes, mouths, chins, cheeks, and foreheads of his friends and skewed them, attacked them, practiced unlicensed medicine on them.

To Arp the masks were at once "fetuses and autopsies." Flatly, they took the Cabaret Voltaire draft dodgers to the front. In Germany it was already being rumored there were soldiers so hideously disfigured by the new weapons that they would have to be imprisoned in secret hospitals for the rest of their lives; after the war, photographs were smuggled out to prove it. They are so horrible they look like fakes, photo collages—like the postwar collages of Berlin dadaist Hannah Höch, like her *Fröhliche Dame* (Happy Lady), which looks like a burn victim smiling. But cubism was dismemberment; if war was the highest form of modern art, who could say that a face blown up by a bomb did not reveal character? Ball:

We were all there when Janco arrived with his masks, and everyone immediately put one on. Then something strange happened. Not only did the mask immediately call for a costume, it also demanded a quite definite, passionate gesture, bordering on madness. Although we could not have imagined it five minutes earlier, we were walking around with the most bizarre movements, festooned and draped with impossible objects, each one of us trying to outdo the other . . . The motive power of these masks was irresistibly conveyed to us.

So much for Russian folk-song night.

Tristan Tzara, Zurich, 1917

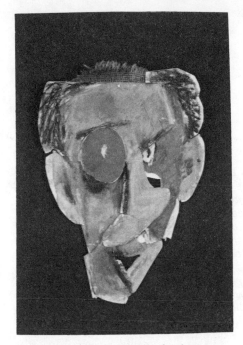

Reconstruction of mask of Tristan
Tzara by Marcel Janco, 1916–17

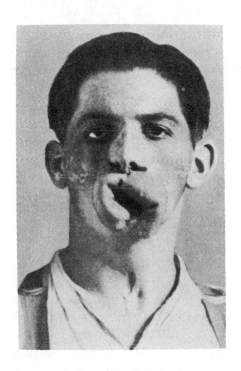

German victim of World War I

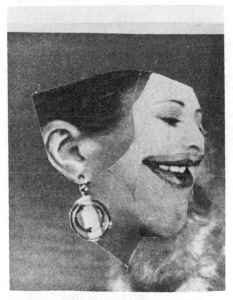

Hannah Höch, *Fröliche Dame*, 1923

THE MASKS

The masks brought forth slow dances, made up on the spot and named after the fact: "Festive Despair," "Nightmare," "Fly-catching." In every case the masks affirmed the existence of a language no one knew how to speak, but which contained the only words capable of forming the only truths worth knowing. Trabadya-la-modjere was turning into the philosopher's stone. The dadaists were going back in time, falling through the stage: "Modern artists," Ball would write in 1917, "are gnostics and practice things that the priests think are long forgotten; perhaps even commit sins that are no longer thought possible." These were the sins to be found in an embrace of an ancient heresy, the belief that certain forms of knowledge, of gnosis, accessible only to a few, could bring one so close to the Godhead that the seeker would drive God out of time as if God had never been; in the early Christian era, even as the church drove the gnostics out of history, the rituals they practiced continued. With their gospels burned and adherence to them punishable by death, some adepts, the historian Benjamin Walker writes, remained familiar

with the reputed occult virtues of sound and the latent potency of sacred names, hermetic formulas and magical invocations . . . The most important of all sounds, they believed, is the phoneme, which is the smallest articulable sound unit . . . There evolved in time the practice of singing each [vowel sound of the Greek alphabet] in a single breath . . . combining the vowels with certain consonants, especially those producing a buzzing or humming sound: Zeeza, Zezo, Zoza, Ozzi, Omazu, Nozama, Amenaz, Arazaz . . . As far as possible these archaic syllables were used in unaltered form, even when their meaning, if they had any, was forgotten.

The dadaists were coming into the knowledge that what had been forgotten could be remembered, even by accident; they were realizing that the language everyone knew how to speak was capable of forming only those truths they didn't want to hear. They didn't know what they wanted to hear, so they

. . . .

. . . *(THERE WERE)*
empty fictions, as if they were sunk in sleep and found themselves in disturbing dreams. Either (there is) a place to which they are fleeing, or without strength they come (from) having chased after others, or they are involved in striking blows, or they are receiving blows themselves, or they have fallen from high places, or they take off into the air though they do not even have wings. Again, sometimes (it is as) if people were murdering them, or they themselves are killing their neighbors, for they have been stained with their blood. When those who are going through all these things wake up, they see nothing, those who were in the midst of all these disturbances, for they are nothing. Such is the way of those who have cast ignorance aside from them like sleep, not esteeming it as anything, nor do they esteem its works as solid things either, but leave them behind like a dream in the night.

—from the gnostic "Gospel of Truth," the Nightmare Parable, c. 150 A.D.

. . . .

made a sound they called "medieval bruitism," "noise with imitative effects," a simultaneous poem, all the acts appearing at the same time, but no longer acts. It meant wails, the bass drum, glissandos, prehistoric harmony, cries of pain and hilarity; if the dadaists did not replace God, they replaced themselves. Huelsenbeck:

The problem of the soul is by nature volcanic. Every movement naturally produces noise. While number, and consequently melody, are symbols presupposing a faculty for abstraction, noise is a direct call to action. Music of whatever nature is harmonious, artistic, an activity of reason—but bruitism is life itself, it cannot be judged like a book, but rather it is a part of our personality, which attacks us, pursues us and tears us to pieces. Bruitism is a way of looking at life which, strange as it may seem at first, compels us to make an absolute decision. There are only bruitists, and others . . . In modern Europe, the same initiative which in America made ragtime a national music led to the convulsion of bruitism.

Here, Huelsenbeck, who at the time—1920—was lecturing to a psychiatrists' convention in the Free City of Danzig (today, Gdansk), where he had set up a practice in 1922, stepped out from behind his lectern, did a few steps of the Eagle Rock, pulled a paper bag over his head, scribbled blindly on it with a grease pen, punched out eye holes, drew a pistol from his jacket, and fired a full clip of blanks at the audience. The half-dozen or so who had seen the act before were primed to applaud.

Ha. Thank you. Bruitism—well, you see. Bruitism is a kind of return to nature. It is the music produced by circuits of atoms—

(at this point a member of Huelsenbeck's claque rose from his chair and fired a pistol filled with blanks at Huelsenbeck, who bit down on a capsule secreted in his mouth, causing fake blood to drip down his chin and over his shirtfront. He grabbed the lectern and continued speaking, bent over and turned away from his listeners) death ceases to be an escape of the soul from earthly misery and becomes a vomiting, screaming, and choking. The Dadaists of the Cabaret Voltaire took over bruitism without suspecting its philosophy— basically they desired its opposite: a calming of the soul, an endless lullaby, art, abstract art. *They wanted the moral safety valve—"Disgusted by the butchery of World War I, we devoted ourselves to the Fine Arts," "Our sort of* Candide *against the times," our sort of four-ply comforter—but dada grew into a creature which stood head and shoulders above all present. Do you understand? We are psychiatrists; we are Germans; we have read Nietzsche; we know that to gaze too long at monsters is to risk becoming one—that's what we get paid for!*

IT ALL

It all came together on 23 June 1916 in the cabaret, unless it was July 14, in a rented hall, when Ball dressed up like a sorcerer in the weird costume, designed by Janco, built out of cardboard by his brother ("It was fun to do it," Jules Janco said in 1984, "and even more fun to undo it!"). On Ball's head was a blue and white striped hat two feet high; his body was covered in an obelisk painted blue. Huge claws replaced his hands. Wings, red on the inside and gold on the outside, went down to his waist; as Ball chanted his sounds, two different poems on reading stands at his sides, he flapped his arms like a bird.

It was a moment of panic: Ball suddenly realized he didn't understand what the costume was demanding of him, didn't recognize the audience, didn't know what his empty words ("blago bung / blago bung / bosso fataka") didn't mean. In his terror, he felt himself drawn back to the cadences of a priest celebrating the mass as he, little Hugo, knelt with his mother and father two decades before; the years rose up, then died. It was a moment of hubris and fear that took Ball straight out of dada, opened the road back to the church, and, eventually, got him on TV.

KARAWANE

jolifanto bambla ô falli bambla

grossiga m'pfa habla horem

égiga goramen

higo bloiko russula huju

hollaka hollala

anlogo bung

blago bung

blago bung

bosso fataka

ü üü ü

schampa wulla wussa olobo

hej tatta gôrem

eschige zunbada

wulubu ssubudu uluw ssubudu

tumba ba- umf

kusagauma

ba - umf

Hugo Ball   dada-kasserolle 1916

(1917)
Hugo Ball

The famous photograph of Hugo Ball dressed as a sorcerer, as used in *Dadaco*, Munich, 1920

BY THE TIME

By the time Huelsenbeck gave his Danzig lecture (it was no lecture, none of the events described ever happened, but the words in roman type are from his 1920 pamphlet *En avant dada*), thanks to the holes punched in his eyes in the Cabaret Voltaire he had seen it all, far more than he ever wanted to see. As time went on he saw it again and again. "The dadaist is a man of reality who loves wine, women and advertising," he said in 1920; soon enough advertising would be dada, dada would be everywhere he looked, dogging his footsteps, and so like the rest he would run from it. The great goal of dissolving all boundaries between art and life would be realized, which meant there was nothing left to do but contemplate the strange way in which the realization of the great goal had not granted everyday life the transformative power of art, but only dissolved art's power and produced nothing to replace it, contemplate that, or talk about the legend, for a fee, those days in Zurich, *I was there*—or remember that before there was dada, there was an ad for Dada Shampoo.

In 1980 Bob Acraman advertised a vacation package at a New Belsen theme park, and a wire service picked up the story. By then the word dada was in the dictionaries, artists from all countries claimed it, there were quarterlies and conferences, archives and revivals, but if dada lived it was in such novelty items buried in the daily papers, weird tales that blew up the frank-exchange-of-views prose of front-page propaganda, or never touched it—Bob Acraman, not Andy Warhol, was the real neo-dadaist, even if on this level too dada was a replica of itself: old news. After all—it was only 1921 when the Basel *News* offered its readers a package tour to the battlefields of Verdun, promising "the quintessence of the horrors of modern warfare," real life as modern art, "unforgettable impressions" of destroyed villages, "enormous cemeteries containing hundreds of thousands of fallen men," and every body was doing it, doing it, doing it, first come first served:

Not only to the French mind is [Verdun] the battlefield *par excellence* on which the enormous struggle between France and Germany was finally decided . . . If the entire war cost France 1,400,000 dead, almost one third of that number fell in the sector of Verdun, which comprises but a few square kilometers. The Germans suffered more than twice the number of casualties there. In this small area, where more than a million men—perhaps a million and a half—bled to death, there is not a square centimeter of soil that was not exploded by grenades. Afterwards the traveler should cover the battlefields of the Argonne Forest, the river Somme, wander through the ruins of Reims, returning via St. Mihiel and the Priest Forest: but everything merely repeats

umbah, umbah—

details which at Verdun combine into an unprecedentedly phenomenal panorama of horror and dread . . . wine and coffee and gratuities included.

The great Vienna critic Karl Kraus was appalled. "I am holding in my hand a document which transcends and seals all the shame of this age and would in itself suffice to assign the currency stew that calls itself mankind a place of honor in a cosmic carrion pit," he wrote. "After the monstrous collapse of the fiction of culture . . . [the age] has nothing left but the naked truth of its condition, so that it has almost reached the point where it is no longer capable of lying." Kraus's first sentence was Huelsenbeck's kind of language, his second, Ball's, but Kraus was not a dadaist; he was simply saying what he meant. Fifty-six years after he wrote, the Sex Pistols would offer him an answer record, "Holidays in the Sun" (Bomb sites! Hitler's Bunker! The Berlin Wall! Wine and coffee and gratuities not included!)—and by what means was it that a line from the Basel *News* to Karl Kraus to excursion rates for Auschwitz cattle cars to the Sex Pistols to Bob Acraman pieced itself together? This is the history the dadaists were fighting and the history they were acting out, all of it appearing on the stage at the same time; to reduce the age and its language to the point where it was no longer capable of lying, even if that meant it would no longer be capable of speaking, had been precisely their goal. Had they been there at the end of the line they would have been in ecstasy, convulsed by the thrill of having been proved right. Then they would have thrown up—but dada would still be laughing. To be a dadaist was to be a man of reality who loved wine, women, and advertising; to have a smile on your lips, a song in your heart, and a skull in your pocket.

BY JANUARY

By January 1917 Huelsenbeck was in Berlin, a dada courier. There he would join with new comrades who were almost as mean as he was: Raoul Hausmann, Walter Mehring, Franz Jung, George Grosz, Johannes Baader, Hannah Höch, John Heartfield, Wieland Herzfelde. After the "health resort" of Zurich, Huelsenbeck exulted, Berlin was real life: "Fear was in everybody's bones." All authority was collapsing, which meant that anything was possible, that anyone could be shot down in any street.

Destruction beckoned. "In 1917 the Germans were beginning to give a great deal of thought to their souls," Huelsenbeck wrote of the last days of the war. "This was only a natural defense on the part of a society that had been harassed, milked dry, and driven to the breaking point . . . A phenomenon familiar in German history was against manifested: Germany will always become a land of poets and thinkers when it begins to understand that it has mismanaged itself as a land of judges and hangmen." Thus came the Omphaloskepsist-Himmelists: the expressionists, who "pulled people gently by the sleeve and led them into the half-light of the Gothic cathedrals, where the street noises die down to a distant murmur and, in accord with the old principle that all cats are gray in the dark, men without exception are fine fellows." Expressionism performed the magic trick of taking Germany inward and heavenward at the same time, so the new Berlin Dada Club countered with magic of its own: the word.

That was all they had: "dada," a thousand times and a thousand different ways, *mene mene tekel upharsin* dropped down into a two-step ("Dada-trott," they named the dance, thoughtfully publishing photos demonstrating exactly how to do it). They trumpeted the word as the great mystery, secreting it in the corners of paintings where people turned into monsters and machines; they left it dripping on walls. Launching the word like a rocket out of their cut-ups and collages, printing it up on handbills, wearing it on sandwich boards and on their clothes, shouting it in the streets or on stage, they claimed it as the most obvious fact. The word became the Modifier, no other word capable of meaning without "dada" attached to it, no other word able to hold its meaning with "dada" riding on its back. Crowds came to hear it happen, to watch the void be conjured up: "Now," Huelsenbeck said, "they were suddenly confronted with people who deliberately severed the process of communication, the causal nexus between payment and ware, between expectation and fulfillment." Hausmann broke the sound poems Huelsenbeck brought from Zurich into letter poems; the dictatorship of the phoneme was overthrown. Even names split and reformed: "groszfield," "hearthaus," "georgemann." The dadaists ruled an invisible empire, so they took titles: "Marschalldada" (Grosz, who cultivated his resemblance to a Prussian Junker), "Monteurdada" (Heartfield, the photomontagist), "Progress-dada" (Herzfelde, a Communist), "Dadasoph" (Hausmann, "the philosopher," the word perhaps taken to mask his Neandertal brow), "Oberdada" (Baader, who thought he ruled the world), "Meisterdada" (Huelsenbeck).

Dada became a game; powered by a loathing so strong at times it was all but undifferentiated, dada became fun. Throwing off all vestiges of aesthetics, philosophy, ethics, dada became what perhaps it had always wanted to be: merely a voice, a sound. The voice battered itself against the walls of honor and decency, looking for limits, finding none. When Huelsenbeck, speaking the dada language of backward and forward so fast not even he knew what he was saying, announced that "We were for the war and Dadaism today is still for war. Life must hurt," there were mutilated veterans in the audience. But on the stage behind him there were no aesthetes like Arp, no careerists like Tzara, no Catholics like Ball to stop the show to ask what it all meant: the momentum was all toward spleen. The most arresting images the group left behind are mouths, Hausmann's or Heartfield's, open, teeth bared, words or letters spewing forth like giant microbes: *We will drown you out.*

Like the extraterrestrial slime in *The Creeping Unknown,* the 1954 film that preceded *Five Million Years to Earth* in the Quatermass series, dada in Berlin began as a speck, and expanded until it swallowed the city; so it went, in the invisible empire. When in 1918 the time came for Huelsenbeck and Hausmann to ask "What is Dadaism and what does it want in Germany?," the answer was self-evident:

Dadaism demands . . .

The introduction of progressive unemployment through comprehensive mechanization of every field of activity. Only by unemployment does it become possible for the individual to achieve certainty as to the truth of life and finally become accustomed to experience . . .

The Central Council demands . . .

Compulsory adherence of all clergymen and teachers to the Dadaist articles of faith . . .

The immediate erection of a state art center, elimination of concepts of property in the new art (expressionism); the concept of property is entirely excluded from the super-individual movement of Dadaism which liberates all mankind;

Introduction of the simultaneist poem as a Communist state prayer;

Establishment of a Dadaist advisory council for the remodeling of life in every city of over 50,000 inhabitants;

Immediate organization of a large scale Dadaist propaganda campaign with 150 circuses for the enlightenment of the proletariat;

Submission of all laws and decrees to the Dadaist central council for approval;

Immediate regulation of all sexual relations according to the views of international Dadaism through establishment of a Dadaist sexual center.

Aber es ist noch etwas anderes, was für diese Bewegung, die von Kurt Hiller

MELIORISMUS

getauft worden ist, bezeichnend bleibt: es ist der Mangel an psychologischer Einsicht. Gegen die Psychologie hat man einen Sturm gelaufen, seitdem man den Kampf gegen den Naturalismus begann. In ihr, die sich die Klarlegung der zartesten seelischen Verhältnisse zur Aufgabe gemacht hat, die das Wachsen der Empfindungen und Gefühle in ihrer Abhängigkeit von den zahllosen Widerwärtigkeiten und Begünstigungen des Lebens mit allen technischen und wissenschaftlichen Mitteln untersucht, wollte man das Abbild einer im kleinlichen klebenden und in den Dingen befangenen Epoche erkennen. Der beseelte und der psychologische Mensch. Der psychologische Mensch, der Realist, der lächerliche Kopierer der Wirklichkeit, ja der feige und dumme Mensch – der beseelte Mensch, das kühne Individium, das die Tiefen des Kosmos mit seinem Geiste ausmißt und an der Schwelle der wunderbaren Dinge sein Inneres erzittern fühlt, in einem Wort, der Bürger und der Dichter. Es war die Wirklichkeit, die man in der Psychologie haßte, das Bild der Erscheinungen, aus dem einem die Fratze der Bosheit entgegensah, von der man sich abwandte, um sie in Wut zu verdammen. Ja, um sie in Wut zu verdammen, aber doch in Momenten, wo die Sonne schien, das Leben auf den Straßen rollte und der Tag schrie, sie geeignet zu finden, verbessert zu werden. Es ist aber so, daß man ohne einen Aufwand von psychologischen Findigkeit mit dieser Welt nicht fertig wird. Du mußt wissen, was Dein Nächster denkt, wenn er Dir nicht gleich in den Arm fallen soll. Du mußt das Lächeln des alten Herrn dort in der Ecke deuten können, ehe er sich als Geheimpolizist legitimiert. Mit allen Mitteln ihrer eigenen Schurkerei mußt Du den Verbrechern begegnen, wenn Du sie ausrotten willst, **als Irrenarzt versenke Dich in die Abgründe des tollsten Wahnsinns.** So kommt es, daß diese Herren Weltverbesserer mit Brillen und Mädchenmuskeln mit dem Geruch ihrer Studierstuben, noch von der Wärme ihres Schlafrocks begleitet, vollkommen scheitern und heute für den Einsichtigen lächerliche Figuren bilden. Mit der Heirat des Häuptlings schloß eine Bewegung ab, die seit ihrem Beginn nichts als traurige Farce gewesen ist, eine durchaus jugendliche und naive Verkennung der der Möglichkeiten etwas zu tun.

Und doch haben die

Melioristen

trotz ihrer kindlichen Ziele etwas gehabt, was sie uns vor dem andern Teile jener Jugend sympathisch macht, die, wie schon angedeutet, mit antiktragischer Geste ihr Haupt verhüllt, die die bestehende Welt haßt, aber nicht wagt, in ihr etwas zu tun – es ist die Aktivität. Einen Schimmer von Aktivität, ein blasses Abbild menschlicher Betätigungslust hatten sich die Melioristen gerettet, und es ist bezeichnend, daß sie dieses Wort mit an die Spitze ihres Programms gestellt haben, weil sie darin etwas gutes ahnten.

Die Aktivität, dieser ungeheure Begriff der Farbe, des Rhytmus und der Geräusche, was haben

jene Schwächlinge damit zu tun, die heute unter dem Begriff des Expressionismus mit Sehnsucht eine bürgerliche Anerkennung erwarten. Das sind diejenigen, die in angeborener Hypokrisie stolz auf ihre Verblendung und auf ihren Mangel an vitalen Voraussetzungen sich eine Philosophie aus ihrer Passivität gemacht haben. Ich spreche von den Menschen, die sich unter einem Namen gesammelt haben und ihn nachträglich mit ihrer Bequemlichkeit füllen, nachdem er für andere ein Hornstoß und ein Signal gewesen war. Die Einsicht, daß der Realismus keine Lösung für das Geschehen der Welt gab, hat mit den Einsichten dieser anämischen nichts mehr zu tun, hier muß Litanei Gebet ersetzen, zurückziehen vor dem Kampf bedeutet hier Innerlichkeit. Die Tatsache, daß man die Natur nicht kopieren darf, die den Initiatoren der Bewegung ein Anstoß zum Handeln war und ein Ruf zur Selbstbesinnung, ist hier eine Rechtfertigung der **Erwartung auf eine gute Pension.**

anlogo bung
anlogo bung
blago bung
blago bung
blago bung

Page from *Dadaco*, Munich, 1920

It sounds familiar because two decades later all Germany would be living it out. Hausmann always thought it was a joke, he said after the Nazis had come and gone; he was never sure about Huelsenbeck. "The significance of this program," Huelsenbeck wrote in 1920, was dada as "no more than an expression of the times," taking "into itself all their knowledge, their breathless tempo, their skepticism, but also their weariness, their despair of a meaning or a 'truth.'" But that wasn't it at all, he said as an old man, speaking to his friend Hans J. Kleinschmidt: he had wanted to change society. "There was a moment in Berlin when I would have accepted the help of the Devil to accomplish it," he remembered, but the devil was otherwise occupied; all Huelsenbeck left behind was a legend, which he carried with him the rest of his life. "NO! NO! NO!," he said in one of his milder Berlin moments. "The highest art will be that which in its conscious content presents the thousandfold problems of the day, the art which has been visibly shattered by the explosions of last week, which is forever trying to collect its limbs after yesterday's crash." Dada was to be the art, and also the explosion, and then another, called up by the art of yesterday's crash. There was to be no end to dada.

Still, all this was hard to get across. In January 1917 Huelsenbeck crossed the border from Switzerland into Germany far more easily than his neighbor Lenin would four months later; for Huelsenbeck, no sealed train was required. The police weren't stupid: for Huelsenbeck there would be no Finland Station. He too returned to revolution, but not to power; the invisible empire aside, he returned, first, to pedantry. When he first spoke publicly in Germany on dada—in a lecture hall, for a fee—he simply recounted the discovery of the philosopher's stone: it was, he said then of the Cabaret Voltaire, a "hexensabbath," a sorcery. "I was the cantor, an almost mythic figure," he said—"with plenty of schmaltz." You know: Ball's "aesthetic production" in the face of what, in those days, passed for total war. A nightclub versus a theme park.

The history of the twentieth century was to be the account

of the creation of reality through its erasure: through killing people, through the extermination of subjective objects, of realized or potential individuals as forests to be cleared. The triumph of this work can be found in the fact that we have neither art nor language to translate it—that when we try to think about those who were exterminated in Europe in the 1910s and 1940s (Hitler, 1939: "Who today remembers the Armenians?") or in the USSR in the 1920s and 1930s, in China in the 1950s, Indonesia in the 1960s, Cambodia in the 1970s (out of the ashes, the New Man), we can't think of those people as such. We can see Alben Barkley, but we can't see what Barkley saw. When Ball wrote of the need to erase everything that had been written, when Tzara said he didn't care if anyone existed before him, when Huelsenbeck chanted "The End of the World," the dadaists fed on this impulse, even as their disgust over its wastes brought them to life.

Dada, like the century, was the right to piss and shit in different colors: white, yellow, black, and red. Repeatedly in the first years of the Nazi regime, the Gestapo came looking for Huelsenbeck (*Is this the residence of Huelsenbeck the dadaist? No*, his wife would answer, *this is the residence of Huelsenbeck the doctor*); safe in the United States, he would never tire of citing the 1936 Nuremberg speech in which Hitler condemned dada as a slime pit as proof of dada's innocent power. But it is not difficult to conclude that Hitler, once part of a bohemian milieu, always a painter, an artist, railed so long and hard against dada because it had touched him, because he felt its pull, just as Ball felt the nihilism in Marinetti's "Parole in libertà," Siurlai the whiff of death in Hennings' "Gloire," Huelsenbeck the thrill of total rule in "What is Dadaism and what does it want in Germany?" Certainly Carl Jung, speaking in London in the same year Hitler spoke in Nuremberg, would not have found it difficult; he knew the pull went in two directions.

A purely personalistic psychology, by reducing everything to personal causes, tries its level best to deny the existence of archetypal motifs and even seeks to destroy them by personal analysis. I consider this a rather dangerous procedure which cannot be justified medically . . . Can we not see how a whole nation is reviving an archaic symbol, yes, even archaic religious forms, and how this mass emotion is influencing and revolutionizing the life of the individual in a catastrophic manner? The man of the past is alive in us today to a degree undreamt of before the war [of 1914–1918], and in the last analysis what is the fate of great nations but a summation of the psychic changes in individuals?

That had been Ball's argument, which could have been Hitler's: "I could not live without the conviction that my own personal fate is an abbreviated version of the fate of the whole nation." It is no matter that, in all his megalomania, Ball would have been horrified by Nazism—which, as a fact of history, Jung went on to weave into a version of the thesis Norman Cohn would set forth in 1957, in *The Pursuit of the Millennium.* Cohn was greeted with incredulity when he argued that the exterminating impulses of the twentieth century could be traced to unsatisfied debts first levied by the heretics and inquisitors of the Middle Ages; to Jung it was obvious.

There is no lunacy people under the domination of an archetype will not fall prey to. If thirty years ago anyone had dared to predict that our psychological development was tending towards a revival of the medieval persecutions of the Jews, that Europe would again tremble before Roman fasces and the tramp of legions, that people would once more give the Roman salute, as two thousand years before, and that instead of the Christian Cross an archaic swastika would lure onward millions ready for death—why, that man would have been hooted at as a mystical fool.

So Jung explained:

There are as many archetypes as there are typical situations in life. Endless repetition has engraved these experiences into our psychic constitution, not in the form of images filled with content, but at first only as *forms without content*, representing merely the possibility of a certain type of perception and action. When a situation occurs which corresponds to a given archetype, that archetype becomes activated and a compulsiveness appears, which, like an instinctual drive, gains its way against all reason and will.

Alben Barkley, Buchenwald, 24 April 1945

This was Jung's account of Nazism. In it was the power principle Debord would grasp: the reversible connecting factor, the idea that the empty repetitions of modern life, of work and spectacle, could be detourned into the creation of situations, into abstract forms that could be infused with unlimited content. But the situationist idea was at bottom a dada idea, and Jung's account of Nazism needs only an excision of its specific examples to serve as an account of what the dadaists sought in the Cabaret Voltaire. Dada was a protest against its time; it was also the bird on the rhinoceros, peeping and chirping, but along for the ride. Dada was a prophecy, but it had no idea what it was prophesying, and its strength was that it didn't care.

Dada was a traffic accident; it was a cult. Dada was a mask, eyes without a face. Dada was a religion, spawn of ancient heresies. Dada was a war, but over souls, not bodies. So are all wars.

FOR SEVENTY

For seventy years dada has been tended like a holy flame. The same lines, the same photographs, have been trotted out again and again. The trick is to catch dada triviality (Russian folksong nights, vellum folios of "The New Poetry") along with dada mystery (the burden of Huelsenbeck's helpless, never-ending exegesis); to catch what has always been obvious and what has always been out of reach. Typically Huelsenbeck, who gained entry into the New York psychoanalytic community by way of a didactic analysis with Karen Horney, put it best: "and so as a doctor I was a success," he wrote in 1969, five years before he died, "and as a dadaist (the thing closest to my heart) I was a failure." The point is not to ask what he meant; that was his business. The point is to ask what it would mean to live with that kind of phantom in your heart.

Strange things happened in the Cabaret Voltaire. The members of the band played themselves, but they also called up a

Frankenstein monster to a hoodoo beat, which played them: a monster mash. Raoul Vaneigem replayed it for the situationists in *The Revolution of Everyday Life*:

Working to cure themselves and their civilization of their discontents—working, in the last analysis, more coherently than Freud himself—the Dadaists built the first laboratory for the revitalization of everyday life. Their activity was far more radical than their theory. Grosz: "The point was to work completely in the dark. We didn't know where we were going." The Dada group was a funnel sucking in all the trivia and rubbish cluttering up the world. Reappearing at the other end, everything was transformed. Though people and things stayed the same they took on completely new meanings. The reversal of perspective began in the magic of the rediscovery of lost experience.

Fixing the precedent for Debord's reversible connecting factor, Vaneigem didn't care what dada had been. Like the dadaists as they tried to say what they'd done, he was trying to find the limits of what their moment could be made to say. Attempting to put into play the central tenet of situationist theory—that the nature of social reality and the means to its transformation were to be found not in the study of power, but in a long, clear look at the seemingly trivial gestures and accents of ordinary experience—Vaneigem was glamorizing what once actually happened, not caring if it had or not. He was writing a how-to manual on revolution in modern society, a revolution to be made with the means available to anyone who at home felt like a tourist; with his glamorization in place, Vaneigem was calling on his readers, whoever they might turn out to be, to act it out. He was contriving a prophecy of May '68, when so many of the lines in his book would be copied onto the walls of Paris, then across France, and then, as the years went on and the words floated free of their source, when the book had been lost in the vagaries of publishing and fashion, around the world. "ACT LOCALLY, THINK GLOBALLY," I can read today on a bumper sticker in my hometown; Vaneigem wrote the words, though the person who bought the sticker will never know it.

Vaneigem wouldn't mind. That was the idea. That was why each number of *Internationale situationniste* opened with an anti-copyright: "Any of the texts published in 'I.S.' may be freely reproduced, translated, or adapted, even without notice of their origin." But if the situationists wanted readers freed from the authority of authors, what Vaneigem found in the Cabaret Voltaire was a father he could love: "amidst this upheaval," he said, was the first realization of Lautréamont's demand for a "poetry made by all." Putting the pieces together, Vaneigem was living up to his patrimony by increasing it: if Huelsenbeck could get up and declaim his corny Negro poems and make the history books, then anyone could make those books irrelevant. Any spot could be a stage, and any stage could be a real terrain: anyone could make history. This was how much experience had been lost, and how much remained to be discovered: under the paving stones, no one knew what treasure might be found. "May '68 was an enormous street theatre with the service personnel on strike waiting for it to happen," Alain Tanner said of *Jonah Who Will Be 25 in the Year 2000*, his 1976 film about people who found themselves in that event and then found themselves cast out of history by its failure. "And much more important than the 'events' are the cast-offs, exactly insofar as this theatre brought out hopes and caused hidden desires to flower which have remained on the surface ever since."

It isn't hard to demonstrate that a few one-time art students purposefully coded a crude version of all this—a subterranean tradition of chimerical events and manifestos written in invisible ink—into the punk milieu in 1976 and 1977. It is less easy to demonstrate that, as a constellation of hidden desires, the time during which those desires remained hidden, and the magic of rediscovering both the desires and the time, all of this was blindly coded in certain rhythmic shifts and turns of phrase, so that each gesture and accent bespoke the negation of an old world and a reach for a new one—but that is why every good punk record can sound like the greatest thing you've ever heard. And that is why the dadaists never got over it: they saw the transformation of the world for a few days in a Zurich bar, and while they glimpsed fragments of that vision for the rest of their lives, they never again saw it whole. "Though people and things stayed the same they took on completely new meanings": as the dadaists walked the clean streets of Zurich the day after the night before, they saw shoppers taking off their clothes, heard clerks saying blago bung instead of thank you very much, felt alleys rising into fire escapes that leaped over buildings which collapsed under the weight of the people pouring up the stairs. The dadaists sensed the power to think anything, to say anything, to do anything—but they kept quiet, talking only among themselves, storing up their doubt, their laughter, and their rage for the night to come, when they would pour it all out, when everything would be thought, said, and done.

That was the legend of freedom. Dada was the notion that in the constructed setting of a temporally enclosed space—in this case, a nightclub—anything could be negated. It was the notion that, there, anything might happen, which meant finally that in the world at large, transposed artistically, anything might happen there, too.

It was not art—not exactly. One can look at Janco's painting *Cabaret Voltaire*: behind the jumping crowd, the frozen dancers on the stage, and the man bent over the piano, the word DADA appears on the wall over the piano player's head. It appears: it does not seem to have been written, painted, put there. On this wall, the word communicates not as a slogan, or even a talisman, but as an emanation—rising out of some primeval memory, the shout of a forgotten voice. That was culture, in the Cabaret Voltaire.

Arp: "We were given the honorary title of 'nihilists.'" All they shared was the conviction that the world they were asked to accept was false. They were gratified by reviews accusing them of turning the legacy of Western civilization into manure; damned for their barbarism, the next night they tried to see how far they could take it. Legs were ripped off tables; they saw legs ripped off bodies. Glasses were smashed; they saw spectacles smashing, eyes lying on the ground. Blood was spilled; they swam in the river. It was a play, staged in competition with another theater. Ball, 16 June 1916: "The slaughter increases, and [people] cling to the prestige of European glory . . . they cannot persuade us to enjoy this rotting pie of human flesh they present to us . . . One day they will have to admit that we reacted very politely." In 1918, in Berlin, that would be Huelsenbeck's argument—his first rebuke to all that had happened in the Cabaret Voltaire, and all that hadn't.

DADA WAS

Dada was nothing more than the theory and practice of the right place at the right time. What was new was the discovery that both could be created: that was the legend of freedom. What was old was the dim apprehension that whatever was created would outstrip its creators forever. That is the tone of every Cabaret Voltaire memoir, a sense of what those who were there didn't see, the specter of a creature that stood head and shoulders above all present—and this, the conviction that there was something in the twentieth century that could never be understood or controlled, was the gnostic myth.

The ultimate justification of social control in the modern world was ancient: human beings were sinners, and that was why there was evil and suffering on earth. Human beings were sinners because Original Sin separated them from God; in that separation was the ubiquity and permanence of sin, its guarantee as the first principle of human life. This was the source of all other separations: patriarchy, authority, hierarchy, the division of humanity into rulers and ruled, owners and workers, the separation of every individual from everyone else, of oneself from oneself. But gnosticism, in its countless forms, over thousands of years, had always denied that any of this was so. There was no necessary separation of human beings from God, the gnostics said, because even as God created human beings, human beings created God, and whoever achieved this knowledge became "not a Christian, but a Christ." The root of evil and suffering was ignorance of this first principle of human life—and such ignorance was the only sin. Most would wallow in it forever, because this was a knowledge that could not be learned but that had to be lived; it could be explored, but never exhausted. And this was the myth that dada had put back into play, the invulnerable sentence: one that could be understood but never explained.

WHEN

When in 1924 Henri Lefebvre dismissed dada as a pseudo-sorcery, solely the spirit that says no, the vain proclamation of the sovereignty of the instant, he knew he was right, but he also knew that he had not been in the right place at the right time. His snottiness was jealousy: only eight years late and he had missed it.

A half-century later, Lefebvre was no longer jealous; Tzara was dead, Ball was dead, Arp was dead, Huelsenbeck was dead, Hennings was dead, and Janco was forgotten. Still, though Lefebvre had indeed picked up the pieces, and put his name on the "Theory of Moments," Lefebvre had yet to forget what he had missed. Reliving the legend in 1975, speaking into a tape recorder for an interviewer, Lefebvre forgot that just two years before he had cursed the legend: the "long line of failures, self-destructions and fatal spells," the line he himself traced from the beginning of his friendship with Tzara to the end of his friendship with Debord. He forgot that in 1925 he signed his name to "Revolution, First and Forever!"—to what, even at the time, he recognized as a careerist imitation. He was a teenager when the dadaists took the stage, and now, as an old man, whose life's work had been the investigation of "modernity," he said so queerly that what was truly modern about modernity, what was actually new, what was really interesting, was not its works—technology, abundance, the welfare state, mass communication, and so on—but the peculiar character of the opposition modernity created against itself: an opposition he still called "Dada."

It was, he was trying to say, a creature still standing head and shoulders above all present. He had seen it; like everyone else who heard the story, he had been there. He was only fifteen, a busboy, nobody knew his name, nobody gave him the time of day, but he felt it. Like anyone else he took the stage of the Teen 'n' Twenty disco. Arms grabbed at his legs as he chanted his "Meaning of the Commune," danced his never-published manifesto "You Will All Be Situationists," pantomimed his *La Matérialisme dialectique*: a shuffle to the left, a shuffle to the right, then collapsing on the boards in his mask and borne into the wings as Ball banged out a Longines Symphonette "Favorite Moment" from the *Appassionata*, as advertised in *TV Guide*. At the end of every phrase Lefebvre shouted "umbah-umbah"; he kicked back. He spit out the pieces he had finished smashing. He killed a quarter of a century, he killed several centuries for the sake of what was to come—or just to see if he could get away with it. That was the faith of the dada religion: "Against an idea, even a false one, all weapons are powerless."

THE CRASH OF YESTERDAY'S ART

In 1974 I was writing about Elvis movies. The films were so shoddy, I thought, they seemed to embody a whole new kind of cinema: the 1960 *G.I. Blues* was my example. "When Elvis strums his acoustic guitar," I said, "an electric solo comes out. When bass and guitar are seen backing him, you hear horns and piano. When he sings, the soundtrack is at least half a verse out of synch . . . Someday, French film critics will discover these pictures and hail them as a unique example of cinéma discrépant. There will be retrospectives at the Cinémathèque, and not long after Elvis movies will be shown on U.S. public television, complete with learned commentary deferring to the French discovery and bemoaning America's inability to appreciate its own culture . . ."

But one can never underestimate the Left Bank—where, in 1951, Isidore Isou launched his "Manifeste du cinéma discrépant," well before anyone heard of Elvis Presley, and thirty years before I heard of Isidore Isou. The manifesto was the rallying cry of his film of that year, *Traité de bave et d'eternité* (Treatise on Slime and Eternity). "Our school," Isou later wrote, "has gone beyond 'synchronism,' and even beyond 'harmonious asynchronism'" (what, apparently, Elvis movies would begin to offer with *G.I. Blues*—*Jailhouse Rock* and other 1950s Presley films were synchronized), "and has revealed total *antisynchronism*, or *discrepant montage*, which breaks the unity of the two 'pillars' of film, the sound and the picture, and presents them in divergence one from the other."

Cinéma discrépant will have its moment in this tale—but first it is necessary to answer a question not often asked outside of France: who was Isidore Isou?

ISIDORE ISOU

Isidore Isou was born in Romania in 1925. He came from a pe-tit-bourgeois Jewish family and he was raised as a prodigy. He read nearly everything, as he would never cease to tell anyone who read him (citing not only the authors he mastered but how many pages of each he chalked up), and at the age of seventeen, on 19 March 1942, he discovered a theory of culture and the meaning of life.

Isou began with a first cause: the motor of social evolution was not the instinct to survive, but the will to create. Creation was the highest form of human activity, and art was its essence; through the act of creation, the artist moved from the slime of unconscious existence to the eternity of history consciously made. By such an act, one became god—for it was only through the conscious creation of the world that God, the first artist, had established his own existence.

Within this circular ensemble of premises there was already a system, a set of rules: the first was that not even God was free from the laws of creation. Creation was never simply a matter of a purely subjective intervention against the slime; creation meant the recognition and the purposeful use of the "mechanics of invention." All aesthetic forms, and the social formations they spoke for—political structures, temporal styles, modes of seemingly natural behavior—moved from a stage of "amplitude" (amplification) to a stage of decomposition. This was the history of human existence, and nothing could stop it; the point was to master it.

In the period of amplification, any new form (impressionist painting, industrial capitalism, bourgeois gentility, short skirts) works as a metaphor for life itself: the new form reaches out to incorporate the world, to transform it. Within the prism of the metaphor, life seems whole and full of meaning; then the new form reaches its limit, begins to decay, and life shrinks. One can see that God was the first victim of this first law of the mechanics of invention. Look at the Bible: out of the slime, paradise; then rot, corruption, the slime, a faint memory of a golden age.

In the inevitable period of decomposition, those forms devised to transform the world turn in upon themselves and implode. The form, once world-historical, becomes its own subject. History stops; action is replaced by an endless series of repetitions. As the form decomposes, symbolically, so does the world—it becomes sterile, inaccessible, worthless, unreal. Any aesthetic form could illustrate the necessity, but the novel will do: we move from Fielding, where a story, a creative account of the world, is in question, to Joyce, where communication itself is in question. The result is the post-Joycean novel, which asks no questions and communicates nothing: it is merely a set of empty gestures, a dead commodity, a thing whose only use value is its exchange value. We move from eternity (Fielding is still read, and, as you read him, you still feel the world changing) to slime (to believe that the present-day novel will be read in a hundred years is not to praise the novel but to condemn the world).

Smashing the faith in genius, the belief that God blessed the artist with special powers and guided his hand toward some transcendent revelation, dada had revealed the process. After dada, all art sat in a compost pile, its mystifications sucked into the methane. There could be no real communication; all words had come loose from their meanings and floated free of their owners. Still, a compost pile was good for something: fertilizer. Along with the preordained stages of amplification and decomposition there was another possibility: that of "ciselant" (chiseling away). This was active, conscious decomposition, and it was the only means to active creation. The true artist, the true god, would position himself as a lever beneath the edifice of art. He would force it toward changes that were, because of inertia and fear, everywhere resisted—changes that the mechanics of invention demanded but that, without the intervention of the nascent god, would never come, at least not while the nascent god was around to enjoy them. That any given form contained within itself the seeds of its own transcendence did not remove the need for intervention; because all forms were human inventions, this fact demanded it. Whatever had been made had to be unmade, and then made new. Civilization, Isou was sure, was mindlessly perpetuating the Last Days; without him, it would live them out forever.

THUS LETTRISM

Thus "lettrism": "the avant-garde of the avant-garde." Isou began with poetry, because as creation was the highest form of human activity, and art the highest form of creation, poetry was the highest form of art.

The amplifying stage of poetry, the seventeen-year-old Isou determined, ended with Victor Hugo. Then Baudelaire destroyed the anecdote in favor of the poetic form; Verlaine destroyed the poetic form in favor of the pure line; Rimbaud destroyed the line in favor of the word; Mallarmé perfected the word and turned it toward sound—and then, heedlessly overreaching the mechanics of invention, Tristan Tzara had destroyed the word in favor of the void: "Dada," Tzara's motto ran, "signifies nothing." Isou corrected him: "nothing" was a stage, not a goal. Yes, the word signified nothing, a roomful of talkers was a roomful of confetti—so Isou would rescue the letter from the word. He would reenact and redirect a stage in the reduction of the word, and the world, to nothing: he would forcibly reduce the word to the letter, the pure sign, seemingly meaningless, in truth endlessly fecund.

He would set the sign loose in the ether. It would float past time, through history, in and out of consciousness, until it had repelled all old meanings—and then, with its charge reversed, it would begin to attract new meanings. The letter would be ready to form a new alphabet and a new language, a language that could say what had never been said, in tones that had never been heard. On the plane of the mechanics of invention, this would mean that once again the creation of the anecdote, the telling of new stories, would be possible. Once stories could be told, they could be lived; because a story was an account of the world, a new world could be created. And because Isou was speaking not only of the history of poetry but of the poetry of

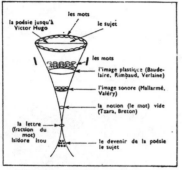

Diagram from Isidore Isou, *Introduction à une nouvelle poésie et une nouvelle musique*, 1947

history—of consciousness, which like memory is of time but not in it—this absolute transformation could happen in a flash. It would be like time travel in a 1940s radio play: "I will be gone for a thousand years," says the scientist to his assistant, "but to you it will seem only like a moment."

Now there is no question that the fanatical symmetry of Isou's system was absolutely teenage—or that, in the mid-1940s, it contained a real challenge to the accepted view of what art was, what it could do, and what it was for. Isou was ready: all that was left was to reach Paris, to him the capital of culture, announce his discovery, and change the world. With the help of local Zionists, he escaped from the Nazis in Romania; in August 1945 he arrived in the City of Light as a twenty-year-old crank.

HE WAS

He was, though, a crank with a sense of history, and a fierce sense of publicity. He wasn't born "Isidore Isou"; he was born Jean-Isidore Goldstein, just as his Romanian-Jewish dada forebear was born Sami Rosenstock. Rosenstock gave himself the exciting new name "Tristan Tzara"; awarding himself a name almost as alliteratively memorable, Isou played Chubby Checker to Tzara's Fats Domino.

That was not all. Isou was sexy—sexy in an androgynous manner far ahead of its time. His lower lip was enormous, enticing; his mouth was all sensuality, all come-on. His dark curls began in an elephant's trunk and ended in a proto-D.A.; in some early 1950s photos he looks amazingly like Tony Curtis, whose internationally right, cuddly-delinquent face would appear on the Hollywood screen about the same time Isou gained his first taste of fame. So I suggested to Michèle Bernstein, as we stood in her living room before Guy Debord's first lettrist metagraphic ("a fancy word for collage"), which featured a torn photo of Isou. "No!" she said. "Elvis Presley!" Isou's field of action may have been high art, his theories penumbratic; physically, instinctively, he was a hound dog.

High culture at the turn of the half-century: Isidore Isou, 1951

Isou's own description of his invasion of Paris—from his 1947 *L'Agrégation d'une nom et d'un messie* (The Making of a Name, the Making of a Messiah)—gives something of the flavor of his monomania. Hitting the city with a suitcase full of manuscripts and a letter of introduction to Jean Paulhan, in 1945 managing editor of the Gallimard publishing house, Isou made straight for the offices of his—he was sure—patron-to-be; it being a Saturday, Paulhan was not in. Putting into effect his principle of "the minimum and the maximum" (derived from the mechanics of amplitude-ciselant: life, like art, had to be taken to extremes), Isou then claimed to be a Romanian journalist and demanded an interview with Gaston Gallimard himself. Once through the door he abandoned the minimum and pressed the maximum, offering his book-length "Introduction à une nouvelle poésie et à une nouvelle musique, de Charles Baudelaire à Isidore Isou." Gallimard agreed to consider it; Paulhan read it and, according to Isou, "expressed interest," though perhaps "acknowledged receipt" pops up between the lines. But no decision was forthcoming—and so, Isou continues, he brought to bear his system of "calculated impatience," retrieved his manuscript, and began taking it to other publishers. This brought no results.

It was only when Isou began to exploit his talent for publicity that he gained a foothold in Paris—and for that he needed disciples. His first was Gabriel Pomerand, whom he met at a canteen for Jewish refugees. Born Pomerans, Pomerand was an indigent, nineteen-year-old devotee of the surrealist saint Lautréamont; after making common cause with Isou he would style himself the "cantor of lettrism" and the "saint of Saint-Germain-des-Prés." Expelled by Isou from the lettrist movement in 1956, he became an opium addict; he killed himself in 1972.

Impressed by the famous authors Isou claimed to have met—André Gide, Jean Cocteau—Pomerand agreed to double the membership of the lettrist crusade. In the dead of night, the two plastered the walls of the Latin Quarter with handbills denouncing socialist-realist and surrealist poets as reactionary enemies of true creation. Nothing happened. They held a reading; few took notice.

Their chance for a coup came—with dada-trumps-dada serendipity—with the 21 January 1946 premiere of Tristan Tzara's play *La Fuit* (Flight), which was to be preceded by a lecture by former surrealist Michel Leiris. Tzara was Isou's hero, the father he had to kill, the false god: the perfect target. Isou and Pomerand rounded up everyone they knew and bought tickets; when Leiris began to expound on dada, with Tzara seated in the audience, they stood up. "We know about dada, M. Leiris—tell us about something new! For example—*lettrism!*" "Dada is dead! Lettrism has taken its place!" Understandably, Leiris had no idea what they were talking about. The cries went on: "Long live lettrism!" "You're kidding! You've never heard of *lettrism?*" A shout came from the back of the room: "Throw the lettrists in the toilet!"

Rattled, Leiris broke off his talk and the play began. Afterward, Pomerand bulled his way onto the stage and demanded that the creator of an epochal breakthrough in the arts, one Isidore Isou, be permitted to explain his theories and recite his letter poems. Isou stepped forward; most of the audience walked out. A few people approached.

Thus did Isou make the papers for the first time—and brilliantly. A front-page article in the left-wing daily *Combat* put Isou into headlines: "THE 'LETTRISTS' SHAKE UP A READING ON TZARA." More publicity and more recruits followed—and on that basis, according to Isou, Gallimard finally offered a contract. According to the word on the street, Gallimard did so because Isou's followers threatened to burn down his offices—but such rumors were merely fuel for the fire. Six months after his arrival in Paris as a nobody, Isou was on his way.

INSISTING

Insisting on the maximum even before his first book appeared, Isou began placing exclusive interviews with luminaries of literary Paris: Gide, François Mauriac, and others. That the conversations were entirely made up displeased the publication in which they ran, so Isou began his own: *La Dictature lettriste* (The Lettrist Dictatorship), there and gone with a single number, but the first of many lettrist reviews.

Today, one has the luxury of taking the title as an effusion of simple puerility, or flat megalomania. In 1946 it was appalling. Every day, the papers were full of stories exposing Frenchmen who collaborated with the Nazis, with reports on unthinkable Nazi crimes and dispatches from the Nuremberg trials; in this context the flaunting of the word "dictatorship" was worse than the punk celebration of the swastika, and it worked on the same levels. Isou's provocation was a way of getting attention; it was an argument that, in the world everyone accepted without questioning, one dictatorship had been replaced by another; it spoke for an authentic flirtation with the fascist abolition of limits. The result was more publicity and more adepts.

Isou produced books on the theater, on himself, on love: the latter was *La Mécanique des femmes* (The Mechanics of Women), which in 1949 made his name a password on the Left Bank. In his preface Isou more or less dared the police to arrest him (the brochure was in essence a sex manual), announcing that he was sure the police would not arrest him—after all, hadn't he already issued a far more subversive manifesto, a call for a "Lettrist Revolution"? The minister of the interior took the bait: he banned the book and had Isou picked up. Hauled before a magistrate, Isou declared that his work made a "useful contribution to the education of youth"; the judge ignored the Socratic jibe and packed Isou off to a state psychiatrist. Meanwhile, *The Mechanics of Women* topped the black-market charts.

After hours at the Tabou—once Boris Vian's jazz band packed up, Sartre, Camus, and Merleau-Ponty had stumbled on home, and Juliet Greco vanished into the night—Pomerand mounted the tables, shook a tambourine, and recited letter poetry. He passed the hat among drunken tourists and turned the proceeds over to the Messiah. In the cafes, more serious work continued. Submitting to the mechanics of invention—and thus, if one divined the rules correctly, making cultural history by definition—the lettrists pushed their post-dada letter poetry into "estheperist" poetry, a poetry of the final element, a proto-language based on linguistic particles "that have no immediate meaning, where each element *exists in so far as it allows one to imagine another element which is either nonexistent or possible*"—a typically mathematical isouienne formula that soon produced extraordinary results. They replaced both visual art and narrative prose with metagraphics (later "hypergraphics"), a neo-hieroglyphics where sentences were interrupted or completed by pictures and vice versa, "thus introducing into alphabetic writing not only the art of painting, but the graphics of all peoples or social categories past and present, as well as the graphics or anti-graphics of every individual imagination." In 1950, with his *Saint ghetto de prêts*, subtitled "grimoire" (book of spells or, alternately, gibberish), Pomerand raised the metagraphic to the level of a cosmic pun. It was a fabulous production: every word was shifted by a picture, every picture subverted by a word, and what the situationists would call "the insubordination of words" was dramatized even in Pomerand's title. With the substitution of the word "prêts" (loans), the neighborhood of Saint-Germain-des-Prés—the lettrist stomping ground, the "protagonist" of the book—became a place where people lived on borrowed time; with the substitution of the word "ghetto," it became a place no one could leave. But as one turns the pages, the neighborhood becomes a labyrinth, where every chance encounter with a word, a picture, a building, or a person seethes with legend and possibility, opening into a secret utopia accessible to anyone capable of recognizing it. "Saint germain des prés is a ghetto," Pomerand began. "Everyone there wears a yellow star over his heart . . . Saint germain des prés is a mirror of heaven."

As the years went on, the lettrists replaced poetry, music, dance, the novel, philosophy, theater, cinema, architecture, photography, theology ("All will be gods—all will be masters"), radio, television, and video with new forms based on the same principles of particle physics that Isou first applied to poetry. They are doing it now, as I write, still in their self-made ghetto—but in postwar Paris the lettrists remained best known for replacing civility with noise. Because Raoul Hausmann had in fact invented letter poetry in Berlin after the First World War (in 1968, past seventy, Hausmann gave a demonstration, growling "OFFEAHBDC/BDQ" through a long speaking tube, then hefting it like a harpoon and highstepping, finally hammering it to the floor: "You don't think I remember this 1918 crap by heart, do you?"), Isou and his followers attacked the originator as a plagiarist—to Hausmann's eternal bafflement and fury, though there survives a wondrous 1946 tape of Hausmann and various lettrists debating the question entirely through imaginary letter languages. It is said that in 1971, as Hausmann lay dying, Isou sent him a weekly letter, each containing only the repetition of a single word: "Ordure, ordure, ordure."

The lettrists attacked Gide ("old bitch," "faggot") and Isou's benefactor Paulhan ("the style of a toad"). André Breton was savaged as a windbag leaking "flabby rage," hysterically attempting to maintain his place in times that had passed him by: "He offers himself, himself and his generation, to every faith, to every hope, to every boutique. One has learned not to be fooled—and there he stands." Existentialism was dismissed as a pallid, vulgarized melange of Nietzsche, Husserl, Heidegger, and Jaspers—a not entirely inaccurate assessment. The culture war was on.

Isou's declaration that his goal was to become god ("but," he noted in 1958, "without renouncing the pleasures of suspicion and skepticism") was not a joke; neither was his claim that anyone else who created a new form could become god as well. Just as dada called up millenarian ghosts, Isou too excavated the gnostic belief that those who gathered around the truth, they and no one else, would become the Gods of Truth, and inherit the earth. "He was the Messiah," says Jean-Paul Curtay (today a doctor and a poet, in the late 1960s a member of Is-

yankee.

Comme ivrogne, je me sens dépaysé, en butant aux becs de gaz, qui me cabossent en usant des dictionnaires de la perfide Albion.

Tous les peaux-rouges portent des croix de guerre au cou.

Ce sont des nœuds-papillons multicolores, ou des papiers tue-mouches qui donnent à Saint germain des prés son air de cimetière minuscule.

Le mandarin du quartier est xxxxxxx xxxxxxx mais c'est aussi son pékinois néologique.

C'est aussi l'homme à la sansonnette

Two pages from Gabriel Pomerand, *Saint ghetto des prêts*, 1950. Comment by Jean-Paul Curtay. "The right page displayed the magic of the mysteriographic transformation of the text, which was printed on the left page in regular words. [It was] a strange hybrid wherein ideograms, rebuses, Hebrew alphabet, cuneforms, and sign language intermingled . . . *croirait* ('would believe') [might be] represented by a cross (*croix*) drawn on the back of a ray (*raie*); *déniche* ('rummage') by faces of dice (*dé*) drawn on the roof and wall of a dog house (*niche*); *chaivre* ('overturn') by a cat (*chat*) whose tail had the form of a phallus (*vit*) and whose behind bore a stave and the note D (*ré*)."

ou's group). "He promised paradise: that the economy would be a horn of plenty, art a continual excitement, life a wonder."

Cold on the page, it is hard to imagine anyone believed it— but in many ways, many did. What matters is not to take Isou's declarations literally—though the more unbalanced among the lettrists, such as Pomerand, swallowed them whole—but to grasp, within a postwar context of social conformity and official artistic entropy ("This is a time," Breton told Isou, "for adding to legends"), the power of Isou's extremist appeals. Isou was not a dadaist; he was a politician. Throughout his early and mid-twenties his great role was to bring out the fanatic in anyone—especially in young people convinced of their own unacknowledged genius. In any time, this means a lot of young people; in Paris in the late 1940s the alternatives to lettrism included hanging out at the Deux Magots in order to learn what brand of cigarettes Simone de Beauvoir smoked. A few years later, Françoise Sagan and J. D. Salinger would offer young people self-pity and narcissism; Isou offered them heroism, comradeship, and, perhaps most important, their names in print. Isou himself, enemy of all conventional discourse, wrote hundreds, then thousands of pages explicating his theories; the productions of his followers, treatises and tracts on every kind of art filled with every kind of graph, chart, and equation, matched the master's scholastic concentration and his cabalistic hermeticism—if not his endurance. But the curls cascading down Isou's smooth forehead were no less inspiring than his words. "Even today," Michèle Bernstein said of the picture of Isou on her wall, "when my nieces come to visit, they always ask the same thing: 'Who's the pop star?'" Isou's visceral message was that the world belonged to the young—if they could make it.

The most casual comparison of lettrism to the exploits of the Cabaret Voltaire or the Berlin Dada Club makes it obvious how unoriginal, academic, and precious Isou's program was. Judged on the level to which he aspired, on the level of aesthetic purity and high art, lettrism was a screaming oxymoron, systematized dada. Judged as news, it was gossip. Judged as history, it was, absent anything better, something to do: if, as Roger Shattuck wrote from Paris in 1948, postwar French culture was a vacant lot and existentialism "a means of clearing the ground," lettrism was merely "a temporary shack." But these were not the only levels on which the small drama of lettrism was played out. A comparison of the first lettrists to those with whom they really shared the postwar terrain reveals an element that makes the story interesting, an element the lettrists cultivated and their true contemporaries ignored. That element was consciousness, and the terrain was still unnamed: pop culture.

POP CULTURE

Pop culture—the folk culture of the modern market, the culture of the instant, at once subsuming past and future and refusing to acknowledge the reality of either—began about 1948, in the United States and Great Britain. There, where the Nazis never arrived, the war years not only regimented society—through conscription, rationing, curfews, and vastly intensified production—they loosened it, breaking up old ties of social life. For a long moment, an entire level of patriarchal hierarchy was stripped away. Like so many soldiers in combat, on the home front some people experienced a sense of purpose, fellowship, and freedom they never knew before and would never know again. Ordinary housewives might not have come up with the words surrealist poet René Char found when, with the occupation of France ending, he confronted what it would mean to leave behind his life as a Resistance partisan—"I shall have to break with the aroma of these essential years, silently repress (not reject) my treasure"—but they would have known what he meant. Photographs of wartime American female factory workers reveal smiles unlike any to be seen in the photojournalism of the years that followed: strong, almost surprised smiles radiating shared purpose, autonomy, and self-worth.

With the war over the women who owned those smiles were returned to a subservient life. The project of the postwar West—which can be read most clearly as a project in Betty Freidan's *The Feminine Mystique*, the history of a propaganda campaign far more sophisticated than the concurrent demonization of communism—was to prove that real life was back, and to restrict the definition of real life to the pleasurable consumption of material goods within a system of male supremacy and corporate hegemony. The new freedoms discovered during the war were cut off from words and cut out of pictures; the most intense and complete days many had lived, at home and away, were turned into an anomaly, and those who could neither get over them nor, according to the new rules, talk about them, were charted as deviant cases. Thus all sorts of anarchic protests against the reorganization of social life appeared out of nowhere: refusals of the affective limits placed on the unlimited material future promised by the managers and promoters of public discourse, a future whose promises were fixed in advance. "How can we live," Char wrote in 1947, "without the unknown before us?"

IN JULY

In July 1948 a bizarre, almost silent record began playing on a black music station in Harlem; soon it spread up and down the East Coast and across the country. It seemed to come out of the ether, not so much carried by the airwaves as floating on them, and no one knew what to make of it, except that it stopped time, and stopped hearts. It was "It's Too Soon to Know," the first record by the Orioles, five black men from Baltimore, led by a twenty-three-year-old truck driver who called himself Sonny Til. The song was written by Deborah Chessler, a young Jewish woman who one night found herself transfixed by a black vocal group called the Vibranaires. She became their manager, had their name changed, offered them her tune, and with them made history—for if the title can be awarded with any certainty, which it probably cannot, this was the very first rock 'n' roll record.

Earlier popular black harmony groups—the 1930s Mills Brothers, the early-1940s Inkspots, the 1947 Ravens—made their music according to the rules of well-ordered rhythms, close ensemble singing, shaped tones, recognizable lyrics. These were white, bourgeois, altogether orderly modes of communication. They suggested definition, suppressed ambiguity, presented the listener with a finished fact—and a finished fact says "all is well" or it says "there's nothing you can do about it." The Orioles' sound reached the listener as the voice of another world; it demanded that you finish the sound, fill in the silences with your own wishes, fears, fantasies. With its falling sighs, its constant hesitations, the sound implied that against every accepted promise, everything was in doubt.

"The only accompaniment," Charlie Gillett says of the Orioles' most distinctive records, "was a guitar played so quietly its only purpose might have been to prevent the group from [coming] to a complete stop. Sonny Til seemed to try to withdraw himself from the situation, refusing to become involved." Framed by high, drifting moans that faded almost before they could be registered, Til's fragile tenor was so emotionally distant, so aurally crepuscular, that it did not sound like singing at all. It was a voice that seemed to treat the forming of a word as a concession, a voice less of someone singing than of someone thinking about the possibility of singing, as if to say, "What would it mean to care?"

The records were constructed, felt through, out of lacunae. Til's always aborted desire to commit himself, his inability to believe that anyone could ever make a commitment to him, made a metaphor for the evasion of any confrontation with any sign of things-as-they-were; he wanted to care, Til's sound said, but he didn't. The feeling was delivered whole, with a passion so plainly repressed it implied not revolt but suicide. When Til sings, lifting every second phrase out of its syntax and almost into onomatopoeia,

Though I'll cry
When she's gone
I won't die
I'll live on
If it's so
It's too soon
Way too soon
To know

you don't believe he'll outlive the song.

The Orioles were in their time but not quite of it. The biggest black record of the late 1940s was "Open the Door, Richard," a broken-beat novelty number, Stepin Fetchit in a tuxedo. It was a top-ten hit for no less than seven artists, both Count Basie and the Three Flames took it to number one in the same month, and one has to stop over that weird fact—impossible since the advent of rock 'n' roll, it speaks for a world in which only a very few songs were heard, in which only a very few conversations were permissible, or comprehensible. But one has to look beyond music to see how strange the Orioles really were.

In the early 1980s, the detritus of late 1940s and early 1950s advertisements was resurrected by a host of American and British collage fanzines (all of them inspired, in one way or another, by the recoding spirit of punk), and what these magazines showed, be they the kitchen-table *Tacky World* or the slickly printed *Stark Fist of Removal*, was so clear, so single-minded, it now looks like an art project commissioned by the CIA. It's not just that every person pictured is white, middle-class, and well-off; black people in post-1960s American TV commercials were white, middle-class, and well-off. It is the sense of confidence that is so unsettling.

The smiles on the faces of the men are easy, unconcerned; the fulfillment of every desire is taken for granted. The smiles on the faces of the women have come a long way from those of the wartime factory workers: they are pursed, determined. There is a hint of resentment beneath the surge toward gratification, unfulfilled desire puts the necessary edge into the ads, constitutes the subliminal hook, and so together the men and women make a world that is both open and closed, a world that cannot be touched. In 1958 *The Family Physician* published an illustrated guide titled "You Can Beat the Atomic Bomb" (note the active verb; twenty years later it would be "You Can Survive"): a couple is fleeing radioactive fallout. They are dressed for a night on the town—in fact they seem to be out on the town, having already heard the news, covering their mouths with handkerchiefs as casually as one might open an umbrella against the rain.

It would be specious to connect the Orioles' quiet refusals to the Bomb—but perhaps not so to connect those refusals to the monochromatic orchestration of confidence that accompanied them. That orchestration did not include the Orioles. In 1948, or for that matter in 1958, downtown hotels in Baltimore would not have admitted them, restaurants would not have served them, and had Sonny Til, with new money in his pocket and his combat medals on his sharkskin suit, persisted in a demand for entrance, the police would have been called and the nigger thrown in jail. Penned in on itself, the black ghetto produced a culture of violence, hedonism, and despair; with the Orioles, Gillett writes, "the harsh, fast life produced a slow, gentle response." Sonny Til became an artist of the reverie, always one step removed, a mole in the ground.

Sonny Til fantasized; he ran his fantasies down. As he fell back and his fantasies slipped out of his grasp, he communicated the notion that the real world could be different from the apparent—that the apparent world, the world of ordered rhythms and distinct words, was not real. There was no confidence; there was only an erotic concentration on loss, hopelessness, and failure. Til imagined what it would mean, what it would feel like, to love, to be loved, to hurt, to be hurt, to say no, to say yes. He could, he said, do none of it—but because he was imagining, he spoke with more purity than real life ever allows. His music was an affirmation, an emotive utopia, where everything could be said; it was a negation, a nowhere, where nothing could be done.

Pop culture at the turn of the half-century: the Orioles, with Deborah Chessler, left, and Sonny Til, right

NEGATION

Negation was accompanied by nihilism—which, once glamorized in the media, was understood by young people eager for new myths as a promise of freedom. In 1947, four thousand motorcyclists invaded the quiet town of Hollister, California, and held a party; the town was partially destroyed. In 1948, four Paris teenagers, "les tragiques de Lagny," joined in an inexplicable scheme involving sexual jealousy, a supposedly imminent Soviet invasion of France, and a nonexistent fortune; three of them held a trial to decide the fate of the one who claimed to have the money, sentenced him to death, and carried out the sentence. In 1958, Charley Starkweather, nineteen, and his girlfriend, Caril Fugate, fourteen, murdered ten people in Nebraska and Wyoming, including Fugate's mother, stepfather, and baby half-sister; among the other victims was a couple about the same age as the killers.

These events and others like them became myths almost before they were acknowledged as events, and within the matrix of the postwar rhythm the incident most immediately and completely mythologized was one of the first to take place. In the fall of 1948, a twenty-four-year-old gunman and triple murderer named Ivanhoe "Rhyging" (Raging) Martin became a hero in Jamaican shantytowns because, advertising himself in the papers with scrawled threats and two-gun photos, trumpeting himself as Alan Ladd and Captain Midnight, he sensed the pop dimension of the nihilist role. On 9 October 1948 he was trapped by police on Lime Cay Beach and shot to death. Featuring a picture of the corpse in the sand, the Kingston *Daily Gleaner* devoted its entire front page to the story.

CRIME DOES NOT PAY
KINGSTON'S SIX WEEKS TERROR IS ENDED! "RHYGING" IS
   DEAD!!
"I SAW HIM SHOT"
THOUSANDS AT THE MORGUE
WHO WAS THIS MAN WITH A PRICE ON HIS HEAD?
ACE COP-SWIMMER JOINS HUNT
DOWN THE CROOKED ROAD TO DOOM

And, bringing it all back home, the inevitable prosaic angle:

LIME CAY, NATURE LOVERS' HAVEN

In time, movies would be made, songs would be written, iconographic books and sociological studies would be produced about all of these occurrences, from Laslo Benedek's 1954 film *The Wild One* to Bruce Springsteen's 1982 tune "Nebraska"; far from being merely trapped in legend, Rhyging's event was the founding crime of postwar Jamaican popular culture, and it was always understood as such. Rhyging was the ghost guiding the hand of every rude boy, the voice of every reggae singer. When Perry Henzell told the story in his 1973 film *The Harder They Come*, bringing it into the present, he made Rhyging the pop star that Ivan Martin wanted to be: this "Rhyging" not only killed people, he cut records, topping the hit parade and the most-wanted list at the same time.

Claude PANCONI   Bernard PETIT

AUX ASSISES DE MELUN

Panconi juge Gide Rimbaud et Baudelaire

avant de s'expliquer sur le meurtre de Guyader

Compte rendu d'audience par Robert COLLIN

UN monstre (sacré) du bimillénaire appelé Claude Panconi, cet enfant du demi-siècle nommé Bernard Petit et surnommé « fils de poulet » par un enfant assassiné : la délégation du Tout-Paris des Lettres, de la scène et du film qui assistait à la première journée du festival judiciaire de Melun, aura trouvé des héros à hauteur de ses vues. Ces meurtriers d'une certaine classe — la première moderne du Cours George-Sand — ont donné leur sentiment à propos de tous nos bons auteurs.

Pour sauver Mac Gee

WASHINGTON, 7 mai. — Plusieurs délégations de blan

Caril Fugate and Charley Starkweather, January 1958

Lagnyites on trial, *Combat*, 8 May 1951

Today these crimes would be a version of everyday news: in their time they communicated as a violation of it. Each briefly marked a moral panic, and an inflation of the moral currency. I sometimes think that to understand why these crimes turned into myths, and why the crimes of the serial or (savor the words) "recreational" and "theme" killers of the 1970s never transcended their numbers, is to understand culture—or the day Elmer Henley Jr. was arrested in Texas for the rape-tor-ture-murder of twenty-seven teenage boys. The TV news hap-pened to run an interview with Juan Corona, who was appeal-ing his conviction of the murder of twenty-five California farmworkers; "Well, Juan," I was sure the interviewer would ask him, "how does it feel to lose the record?" It was barely a fantasy: "I've been reading about Gacy, and he says he killed thirty-three," Henley told his prosecutor while awaiting trial. "If you cut me some slack on the time I can find you some more bodies and get my record back." But then Theodore Bundy reached the forties; Henry Lee Lucas claimed 188 vic-tims, then 600. Inflation outstripped any possibility of mean-ing; the only use value of a murder was its exchange value.

The violations of Rhyging, the motorcycle gangs, the Lagny trio, Starkweather and Fugate were packaged and sold, but they resisted commodification. They were a kind of noise and a kind of silence. They were still sufficiently outside the limits of the public conversation to be received as art statements: as attempts to willfully construct life, or to represent its absence. As mythical assaults they were self-justifying: art for art's sake, which is a form of nihilism. For many, these crimes, in their very muteness—the noise they made, the silence they left behind, the refusal or the inability of the actors to explain themselves—were experienced as a common dream of the post-war period. Some people, following the news, felt they them-selves dreamed these events—which, given the buried, shape-less desires for novelty, adventure, and revenge to which these events gave voice, they did. If they didn't the media dreamed for them—after the fact, but also in advance. Just as Ivan Martin, a.k.a. Alan Ladd, saw himself in American crime movies, Starkweather saw himself in the central mythic story of his era, Nicholas Ray's 1955 film *Rebel Without a Cause*, which dramatized the coming of age of one Jimbo Stark, as played by James Dean. For hours, Starkweather stood before the mirror, combing his hair, arranging his slouch, positioning his cigarette, adjusting his shirt and pants, until he and Dean, Stark and Starkweather, two ordinary midwestern boys, the first already dead, the second knowing he soon would be, were one. It is not hard to believe that, in moments, Starkweather convinced himself that what he wanted to do was no more than what Stark wanted to do—would have done, if Hollywood were more than a fixed game of chicken. Facing the electric chair, Starkweather refused to plead insanity: "but dad i'm not sorry for what i did cause for the first time me and caril had more fun."

THE APPEAL

The appeal of Isou's crusade cannot be understood except as a systematic version of this scattered no: as an attempt to turn emerging negationist and nihilist energies back toward the creation of a new culture. "The great American substitute for social revolution is murder," the political scientist Walter Dean Burnham said at the height of the serial killing fad; Europe had other traditions, among them Lefebvre's long line of fatal spells, in which Isou had found a place. Lettrism was no less bizarre—and thus, to a few, no less seductive or exciting—than the Lagny killing or "It's Too Soon to Know." Like the teenage Lagny murderers, who could not explain themselves, and the Orioles, who refused to explain themselves, Isou began with rules and language; he knew, as the review *La Tour de feu* would put it in 1964, writing about the situationists, that "when the crisis of language and poetry is pushed beyond certain limits it ends up placing the very structure of society in question." For both the lettrists and the situationists, that crisis was the goal; to reach it one had to say things others did

Wanted For Murder

HERE IS THE WANTED MAN—IVAN MARTIN, alias "Rhyging," alias "Ivan Brown,"—Aged, 39. Height, 5 feet, 7 inches; medium build; colour, black; eyes and hair black; several front teeth in upper jaw missing. When last seen was wearing trousers and a light brown check shirt. Will probably be found in possession of a revolver. Any information should be given to C.I.D. Telephone 3834, or to any Police Station. Martin is extremely agile, and dexter, and has the habit of looking both ways over his shoulders at every step or few steps. He was feared for his violence by the other prisoners.

EDWIN CHARLEYS RUMS — FINE OLD JAMAICA

MYERS'S RUM

The Daily Gleaner.

LARGEST CIRCULATION   Price: TWOPENCE

Vol. CXIV. No. 211. — KINGSTON, JAMAICA, THURSDAY, SEPTEMBER 2, 1948.   SIXTEEN PAGES

Police hunt desperado after running gun battle in city's west-end

2 KILLED, 4 SHOT BY ESCAPED CONVICT

Gunman Trapped In Hotel

SHOOTS WAY OUT POLICE CORDON, SLAYS WOMAN

BULLETS from the revolver of an escaped convict took two lives and caused injury to four other persons between Tuesday night and early yesterday morning in West-end Kingston.

Dead were: Detective Corporal Edgar Lewis of the Criminal Investigation Department and Lucilda Tibby Young of 257 Spanish Town Road.

Injured were: Detective H. E. Earle of the C.I.D. Ex-Sergeant Gallimore, of the Jamaica Constabulary, (a brother of the St. Ann M.H.R.), Estella Brown and Iris Bailey, both of 257 Spanish Town Road.

From one of the windows of the General Penitentiary, Ivan Martin, serving five years in the brickyard for burglary and larceny, leaped to freedom one night early in April. All police stations were notified, and the biggest man hunt in Jamaica's police history started.

Martin was quiet. He stayed underground, but somebody talked.

Running Gun Battle

Shortly after 10 o'clock on Tuesday night members of the Criminal Investigation Department attempted to effect the arrest of Martin, otherwise called "Rhyging" or "Ivan Brown." Scene was the Carib Hotel, at Regent Street, Bennett Town. Detective Corporal Lewis and Detective Earle moved in on the wanted man, and revolver shots were exchanged. Martin started as though he was hit, and before they could take cover a bullet struck Detective Corporal Lewis in the chest, and Detective Earle in some other part of his body. Martin was still shooting as they fell to the floor.

According to a Police statement issued yesterday morning, it is believed that the wanted man escaped from the hotel into a block of tenements bounded by Regent Street, Trinity Lane, Blount Street and Dumfries Street. A call for sufficient police was made to form a cordon around the block, but before adequate numbers assembled for the purpose, a running gun battle, reminiscent of Chicago gangster days ensued, and ex-Sergeant Gallimore of the Jamaica Constabulary, who had been called out of his bed in the regular police in the capture of the dangerous convict, was struck by a bullet, and together with Constable Earle and Detective Corporal Lewis, who was then dying, conveyed to the Kingston Public Hospital.

The Police cordon was soon established, and it was believed that the wanted man was still held within the block, as he was then only trapped in cubic-packs, and was without outer clothing and footwear, but owing to the amount of cover provided by the wall-to-wall tenements and the darkness the fugitive escaped, although the Police ring was held until daytime.

The trail of blood, death and violence did not end there. A man named Eric Golden, was marked for death. Ivan Martin, so it is alleged, believed that Golden had "shoaled" on him.

"I'm Going To Get You"

He knocked at the door. Lucilda Tibby Young answered, opened the door. A gun was in the man's hand. He asked for Golden. Golden was not there. Estella Brown dived under the bed. The sight of the gun had unnerved her. The man's face tightened into a snarl. "I can't get him. I'm going to get you," he said. The revolver exploded and Young clutched her hands at her chest.

(Continued on page 2)

Trail Of A Sharp-Shooting Convict's Escape

A MAN ESCAPED from the General Penitentiary through one of the windows, shown (left) above, four months ago. On Tuesday night and early yesterday morning, two Policemen were shot in the Carib Hotel in the picture at right (below), one of whom died in the Kingston Public Hospital, and a woman was killed, and two others injured in the building, down in the picture at right (top). The Bellas press has linked all three incidents together.

AND THESE ARE THE VICTIMS...

DETECTIVE, CORPORAL LEWIS

LUCILDA YOUNG

Berlin Military Heads Meet Again

Secrecy shrouds talks

BERLIN, September 1.—(Reuter).—The four Military Governors of Germany met again today in the Allied Control Authority building to try and solve Berlin's currency problems.

A British official spokesman said: "The same secrecy as characterised the Moscow talks, are being maintained."

Discussions between the commanders had been agreed upon by the Western powers and the Soviet Foreign Minister Molotov in Moscow.

The first meeting of the governors Marshal Vassily Sokolovsky (Russia), General Sir Brian Robertson, (Britain), General Pierre Koenig (France), and General Lucius D. Clay (United States), was held in Berlin, yesterday.

No official communiqué or statistics discussed at this meeting was issued, but it is believed that the chief cabinet was withdrawal of the Western currency from the city, and introduction of the Eastern mark into the Western sectors under Soviet control. The Western powers brought into a Berlin free market today.

New German Constituent Assembly Meets

Premiers Of W. German States Yield Mandates

BONN, September 1 (Reuter)—Dr. Konrad Adenauer, leader of the German Christian Democratic Party, today became first President of the new German Constituent Assembly which met at the historic university city of Bonn to inaugurate the Parliamentary Council of German States.

Adolf Schoenfelder, aged Social Democrat and Provisional President, who elected Vice-President.

Zhdanov Said To Have

MONTREAL, September 1.—(Radio)—these unofficial reports say the Russian march will be introduced to all sectors of Berlin, the Western mark will be withdrawn. One report says the second meeting of the "Big-4" Military Governors may lead to the lifting of the Russian blockade of Berlin. Another report says the blockade will be lifted tomorrow.

Fear Vast Strike Movement May Erupt In France

PARIS, Sept. 1 (AP)—Serious labour trouble threatened to complicate France's political crisis. Sporadic strikes were breaking out all over the country as Premier Robert Schuman struggled to form a new cabinet.

Schuman spent most of the day trying to persuade a reluctant Socialist Party to come into his cabinet.

Marmalade— We Used To Buy It, Now We Sell It

Five thousand cases of marmalade — the first such shipment to be sent from Jamaica—are leaving the island for England tomorrow in the s.s. ArabY, a Royal Mail Lines steamer. Made from Jamaica grown oranges, the history creating cargo was loaded into the holds of the vessel at the Royal Mail pier yesterday.

Making the shipment is the Caribbean Preserving Company, operators of the big canning plant along the Spanish Town Road, and a spokesman for the company made the happy comment to the 'Gleaner' that whereas in the past Jamaica used to import marmalade from England now she instead was exporting the product to the U.K.

At the same time, the spokesman announced that the canning committee of the first-hand distributors of the British Ministry of Food had declared that the Jamaican product (which they had sampled in advance of the shipment) was the finest marmalade that has ever been imported into England.

"This is the beginning of a very big contract," said the spokesman. He also disclosed that the company had also made requests from the Ministry of Food for simple or mango jam. These samples were being flown by air-express through British South American Airways by the earliest opportunity this weekend.

We are also shipping a quantity of grapefruit marmalade and several samples of lime marmalade, added the spokesman. "We hope to build up a new industry and a big one in the export of preserved fruits to the United Kingdom.

SUGGESTION:

'A FEW MORE PENNIES PER COUNT BUNCH'

A suggestion that the leaders of the banana industry should ask Government for a few more pennies per count bunch" out of the banana reserve fund, so as to encourage the greater production of the crop, was thrown out to the Hon. W. A. Bustamante yesterday.

Speaking at his former residence by the Hon. Donald Sangster, acting Director of Agriculture. Mr. Bustamante said he was prepared to support such a request for an increase.

The escape of Ivan Martin, Kingston *Daily Gleaner*, 2 September 1948

not understand, and thus provoke them into doubting the ability of their own language to say anything at all.

The Lagnyites were not lettrists; Claude Panconi, who pulled the trigger, testified at his trial that he "hoped to become a writer," but he scorned the avant-garde, rejecting Rimbaud ("frenzied") and Baudelaire ("morbid") in favor of Stendhal and La Rochefoucauld. Though Isou sometimes spoke of letter-song hits, he never wrote "Théorie des loriots," which today would be fun to read. But like the Orioles and the Lagnyites, lettrism was utterly part of its time and outside of it, socially determined and the product of individual choice, a myth of a creation to be glimpsed in destruction. Unlike its contemporaries, lettrism demanded that one explain oneself, if only in riddles and runes; more than that, it required a willingness to understand just how one's individual choice was determined, and how a tension between determinism and choice could be brought to the point of explosion. Most of all, it required both a sense of history and the faith that one could willfully transcend it.

The group Isou gathered around himself (by 1946, when he was twenty-one, the lettrists numbered more than two dozen) was full of the spirit of youth. It was anarchic and charged with strict codes of private manners, ebullient and full of resentment, ambitious and irresponsible. As opposed to every other youth manifestation of the late 1940s, it had taken on the burden of thought. The group was drenched in theory, in critique, in intellectualism. But it was an intellectualism so severe, so unfinished, and in the real world so completely laughable, that in concert with the ruling passion of every other youth manifestation of the time it was never more than a few steps away from exploding into violence.

THE TENSION

The tension Isou was creating demanded more than poems—it demanded a call to action, and Isou was eager to provide it. In that invisibly convulsive year of 1948 he and his followers covered the Latin Quarter with posters—"12,000,000 YOUTHS WILL TAKE THE STREETS TO MAKE THE LETTRIST REVOLUTION," they read—but few paid any mind. Thus in the next year Isou put posters aside and formulated another theory. What was exceptional—what, in 1949, when there was no such thing as a youth market, when all minds were on social integration and division was what Charley Starkweather was learning in General Math, seemed absurd—was Isou's claim that youth itself was the only possible source of social change.

Isou wrote the first version of his *Traité d'économie nuclaire: le soulèvement de la jeunesse* (Treatise on Nuclear Economy: Youth Uprising) and made an attempt to form a national youth organization (coopting the once-scorned Breton who, according to Isou, sniffed a new constituency for surrealism). This fell flat, but the attendant publicity attracted the man who was to prove Isou's most faithful and energetic disciple: Maurice Lemaitre, born Moise Bismuth, a young journalist for the anarchist paper *Le Monde libertaire* and a Jewish fan of the antisemite Céline. He showed up to do an interview and remained as a convert—a convert in a hurry. Dissatisfied with the paltry few who rallied around Isou's "Youth Uprising," in 1950 Lemaitre started the review *Front de la jeunesse* (Youth Front), meant as the flag of a "mass student union," and published Isou's unsigned "Our Program" in the first number. Radically anticipating Herbert Marcuse, Paul Goodman, and their epigones in the 1960s New Left, Isou produced an analysis of youth as an inevitably revolutionary social sector—revolutionary on its own terms, which meant that the terms of revolution had to be seen in a new way.

Isou's argument was grounded in the notion of insiders and outsiders: "internists" or "co-exchangists," those with something to sell within the market economy and the means to buy what others sold, and "externists," those with nothing to sell and no means to buy. Youth were automatically outsiders: people who could neither freely produce nor consume. But if society was a structure of buying and selling, then the young were not people at all: they were mere "luxury items," "utensils." Since they could not take part in the "circuit of exchange," in real social life, they could only seek out and expend "units of gratuitousness": aimless and consciousless activities (juvenile delinquency), or whatever degraded, trivial commodity compensations they could find (new clothes).

There was an opening in this argument, and Isou dove through it. If economic facts defined youth, then youth could not be defined strictly by age. Rather, "youth" was a concept, and it could be enlarged to include anyone who was excluded from the economy—and anyone who, through volition, or for that matter dissipation, refused to take a preordained place in the social hierarchy. It was only among those who, whatever their age, were not encumbered by the routines of family and wage labor that one could find the source of revolution.

By 1968 this was a cliché, if not a full-fledged ideology. "Our answer," said Robert F. Kennedy as he campaigned for the presidency of the United States, "is to rely on youth—not a time of life but a state of mind, a temper of the will, a quality of the imagination, a predominance of courage over timidity, of the appetite for adventure over the love of ease." In 1950— well before an organized market appeared to capture Isou's units of gratuitousness, before the youthful demand for cultural autonomy was sealed by the *Wild One–Rebel Without a Cause*–rock 'n' roll explosion of signs, before the youth market turned into a shadow electorate—it was pure fantasy, and right on the mark.

TYPICALLY

Typically, the twenty-five-year-old Isou set forth his ideas with heroic logic chopping and unparalleled dash:

Every politician defends the interests of one or another specifically defined "mass," while subjugating to it the surging force which is our youth—and those who manipulate the masses deny the suffering of youth as such. Their argument is this: "While the proletarian or the bourgeois"—the economic agent—"remains definitively within his condition, and finds himself obliged to defend his interests, youth is only a passing, fluctuating state. One is only young for x number of years."

This assertion is false. Neither the proletarian nor the bourgeois remains definitively within his condition. Both die. They leave their place for another: death.

They will only be "proletarian" or "bourgeois" for x number of years.

The young, Isou said, were "slaves, tools . . . the property of others, regardless of class, because they have no real freedom of choice . . . to win real independence they must revolt against their very nonexistence." And this revolt would be open to all:

We will call young any individual, no matter what his age, who does not yet coincide with his function, who acts and struggles to attain the realm of activity he truly desires, who fights to achieve a career in terms of a situation and a form of work other than that which has been planned for him . . . Any reform must begin with the millions of "pre-agents" who collectively comprise the "sickness of society." So long as youth suffers in slavery, or is super-exploited by the seniority system, it will hurl itself into all the warlike follies and all the banalities which are permitted it as a compensation for its own non-existence. Those who know and love their places, whether proletarians or capitalists, are passive, because they don't want to compromise themselves by appearing in the streets. They have goods and children to protect! The young, who have nothing to lose, are the attack—indeed, they are adventure. Let youth cease to serve as a commodity merely to become the consumer of its own elan.

Don't consume your own elan—in slightly different language ("DON'T LET THE CAPITALISTS RIP OFF YOUR CULTURE AND SELL IT BACK TO YOU!"), so said every underground newspaper of the late 1960s. For anyone who lived through those times, to read Isou's statement today is to experience an unnerving displacement: because in 1950 Isou's ideas were completely at odds with any other sociological formulation, because time has made the holes in his ideas so evident, and because displacement is the sensation that inevitably accompanies a confrontation with a first, living version of dead, received ideas.

ONCE IDEAS

Once ideas go into receivership, there is nothing that cannot be done with them. In a few years the youth market caught up with Isou's notion of youth as a class: there was music, movies, clothes, books, even cars only for the young. Youth's consumption of its own elan became a whole new economic sector; then that sector expanded, seizing the notion that youth was a concept, not an age, and generated the values used to sell anything to everybody else. As with Jacksonism, Marx's metaphors were turned inside out: if the proletariat was the motor of history, and youth the new proletariat, a youth free of definition by age was the ever-idling motor of a world bent not on making history but on stopping it.

In 1984 Catherine Deneuve, born 1943, appeared on television to promote Youth Garde, a skin cream. "I've done a lot of living," she said frankly, "and I have nothing to hide." Translated from the franglais, the semiotics of her script did not merely suggest that Youth Garde would "guard" one's youthfulness, that it would "keep one youthful"—rather, Deneuve was saying, youth could not be defined by age. Youth Garde, the blonde film star said (her face still striking, barely slipping around the edges, but squaring), was a spiritual product: not an elixer, but a talisman. Youth Garde, unlike other skin creams, hid nothing—it made what one had done, what one knew, what one was, glow.

The young, Deneuve argued, were those who'd done a lot of living and were ready for more. An inversion far more fabulous than Isou's was taking place: merging experience and anticipation, years of suffering and an unbroken lust for novelty, Deneuve was insisting that in 1984 those over forty represented not a memory of youth but its avant-garde.

Sociology intensified semiotics. As Deneuve read her lines, her generation still made the biggest bulge on the census charts. As it had ruled the glamor principle of the go-go economy of the 1960s, it ruled the supposed scarcity economy of the 1980s. More than that: her generation had acted. It had fought for change: it was the generation of the soixante-hui-tards, the '68ers. Everyone knew that the youth of 1984 were not young at all: they were scared. Faced with a world to accept and a life to surrender, they did nothing but beg for a career in terms of whatever work was planned for them. Deneuve's unspoken subtext could have been written by Adorno: "The hysteric who wanted the miraculous has thus given way to the furiously efficient imbecile who cannot wait for the triumph of doom."

But those imbeciles were not Deneuve's target audience, and there was a message even beneath her subtext. Symbolically if not physiologically, Deneuve and those to whom she spoke were past childbearing (in 1984, her son was a movie star in his own right). Under the banner of Youth Garde she and her generation signified the freedom to indulge untrammeled sexual desire without the wish for children—a wish that made the generations behind her slow and timid, paralyzed by the fear or the fact of families to protect. Deneuve and her comrades were free to act without consequences: to consume directly, for themselves.

Her TV spot was not an advertisement for a product. It was the reification of a market, and of an idea. To be young, Deneuve said, one must be old. If "this too will pass away" is the only absolute truth the human species has produced, "this too will be stood upon its head" is its corollary.

OUR PROGRAM

"Our Program" contained a more immediate contradiction, and it reflected Isou's own inordinate personal ambition: the idea that the real motive force of modern revolt would be the will of the historical actor to "achieve a career in terms of a situation and a form of work other than that which has been planned for him." That the transcendence of such a quandary is generally known as the "American Dream" may have been irrelevant in Europe in 1950, or even in 1968, and it may be irrelevant today. That no other wish could then or now be more easily bought off was not. At its center, Isou's manifesto was not a call for revolution, for a clash between rulers and ruled; if "the millions of pre-agents" comprised "the sickness of society," it was a blueprint for recuperation.

The slipknot was pulled almost immediately. There was one dramatic action: a raid by some thirty Youth Front members on the Auteuil orphanage, a Catholic institution notorious for brutality, and the result was riot, violence, and, for some, jail. But this was little more than a publicity stunt. Soon, again under the rubric "Youth Uprising," with Isou's approval lettrist Marc, O recast the open-ended "Our Program" into what Jean-Louis Brau, a member of Isou's group at the time, would call "a ridiculous boy-scoutism": demands that superior students be permitted to (1) skip grades, (2) leave school early, and (3) receive government grants for creative activities. One can imagine that Isou would have been happy with a seat on the awards committee; even after May '68 he was still propounding the same solutions to the "youth question," thesis for thesis, word for word. As Brau, speaking of the May days, mordantly put it, "The disciples of 'Youth Uprising' were not to be present when, finally, youth rose up."

THE PERFECT

The perfect symmetry of Isou's theories ensured that his new world would be self-limiting. For all the dialectical tension of amplitude and ciselant, it was a world in which the Messiah worked to see his revolutions take place in a controlled space. But theories cannot be kept on paper, and Isou's call for the subversion of everything subvertible and the overthrow of everything overthrowable soon led to consequences he did not anticipate, and could not stop.

It began at the beginning. In 1950 Brau and his fellow lettrist Gil J Wolman invented a new kind of sound poetry, a real sound poetry in no way tied to made-up words or floating letters: Brau's "Instrumentations verbales" and Wolman's "Grands soufflés" (Big Breaths) or "Megapnèumes" (Superinflations). The shift from amplitude to ciselant has been described as the transition from "a giant sigh," where the arts take "in oxygen, sunshine, and other nutrients which are transformed into a rich lifeblood," to a "huge exhalation, the part of the sigh which signifies the consumption of all usable oxygen, expelling carbon dioxide, muscles full of lactic acids and the brain fatigued"; at first, offering elaborate theorems postulating the mechanics of "synthetic death," this is what the Brau-Wolman poetry aimed to realize. Then the two leaped over Isou's rules and made them seem quaint.

They did not return language to its constituent elements. They went back to its purely physical origins. They went out of history, past the inevitable distance of the conscious human being from the natural world—past Hegel's definition of alienation, his definition of what it meant to be human. They knew what Hegel thought; they knew too that Marx had turned Hegel's idea of alienation upside down by socializing it, fixing alienation in the distance of human beings from the world they themselves made, insisting that in the recognition of that distance was the beginning of consciousness, in its refusal the beginning of revolt. As students, Brau and Wolman probably agreed—but from where they stood as poets, revolt somehow preceded consciousness, and superseded it. Posters went up—working from later recordings, one can imagine the scene.

Isou, Lemaître, Pomerand, and the rest recite their scrambled letters. Words are separated from their meanings. The breach between humanity and its invented world is plain, but it is an old story, and it is incomplete: words shatter, but the letters hold their shape. Then Wolman, a twenty-one-year-old with a carefully trimmed moustache, stands on a table. He proceeds to create a pre-phonetic explosion that denies any lexical description. Unknown tongues flow from his mouth—not languages, but the linguistic organs as such, searching the air and slamming the cheeks and teeth.

Sound shoots out of the top of Wolman's head. Hideous

Gil J Wolman, *Ion*, April 1952

noises range the room. He has become a primeval Homo erectus on the verge of discovering speech but he remains unready to recognize it. The two dozen or so people in the Tabou lean forward: Wolman is creating an absence they can feel. The possibility that the human species could have gone on without language is inescapable. Clicks, coughs, grunts, and broken moans reach crescendos and crumble; every nascent rhythm is defeated. Now it is the diaphragm that is speaking, then the nose, then the bowels. Suddenly Wolman seems to form an actual signifier, and panic invades his performance. Like a man trying to catch a fly in his fist, he struggles to hold onto the phonemes, but they escape.

ON ISOU'S TERMS

On Isou's terms—no matter that this poetry suggested that nothing was certain and everything possible—such "ultra-lettrist" experimentation was a sophomoric exaggeration, an infantile disorder: a heedless attempt, Isou wrote in words Phil Spector might have appreciated, to "smash the wall of sound." The mechanics of invention did not allow for it; conscious decomposition could not go so far. One more step, and there would be nothing left but the void, a babble that could never find its way back to language—a call that only madness or suicide could satisfy. Still, though the lettrist movement was not casual—members might be fined, put in purdah, or even expelled for malingering—aesthetic pluralism remained in effect. With heat and without rancor, Isou, Lemaitre, Brau, and Wolman debated the question in issues of the lettrist review *Ur*.

This could be contained. As a public space the Tabou was a secret. The invasion of Notre-Dame by another band of lettrists was a different story.

THE ASSAULT ON NOTRE-DAME

At 11:10 A.M. on 9 April 1950, four young men—one got up from head to foot as a Dominican monk—entered Notre-Dame in Paris. Easter high mass was in progress; there were ten thousand people from all over the world in the cathedral. "The false dominican," as the press called him—Michel Mourre, twenty-two—took advantage of a pause after the credo and mounted the altar. He began to read a sermon written by one of his co-conspirators, Serge Berna, twenty-five.

Today Easter day of the Holy Year
here
under the emblem of Notre-Dame of Paris
I accuse
the universal Catholic Church of the lethal diversion of our living
    strength toward an empty heaven
I accuse
the Catholic Church of swindling
I accuse
the Catholic Church of infecting the world with its funereal morality
of being the running sore on the decomposed body of the West

Verily I say unto you: God is dead
We vomit the agonizing insipidity of your prayers
for your prayers have been the greasy smoke over the battlefields of
    our Europe

Go forth then into the tragic and exalting desert of a world where God
    is dead
and till this earth anew with your bare hands
with your PROUD hands
with your unpraying hands

Today Easter day of the Holy Year
Here under the emblem of Notre-Dame of France
we proclaim the death of the Christ-god, so that Man may live at last.

The cataclysm that followed went beyond anything expected by Mourre and his fellows, who first planned merely to let loose a few red balloons. The organist, warned that a disruption might take place, drowned out Mourre just after he pronounced the magic words "God is dead." The rest of the speech was never delivered: swords drawn, the cathedral's Swiss Guards rushed the conspirators and attempted to kill them. Mourre's comrades took to the altar to shield him—one, Jean Rullier, twenty-five, had his face slashed open. The blasphemers escaped—his habit streaked with Rullier's blood, Mourre gaily blessed the worshippers as he made for the exit—and were captured, rather rescued, by the police: having chased the four to the Seine, the crowd was on the verge of lynching them. An accomplice had a get-away car ready; seeing the mob advancing on the quai, he didn't wait. Marc, O and Gabriel Pomerand, present in the cathedral, slipped away and headed straight for Saint-Germain-des-Prés to spread the news.

THE CONTEXT

The context of this event, which made the papers all over the world and is now forgotten, is no longer obvious. In 1950 religion had been granted a new respect, a new silence in its face. The campaign to get women off the job and back into the kitchen was matched by a campaign to get everyone back to church. The pope—Pius XII, an antisemite whose fascist sympathies were only lightly veiled—was treated by even the secular press as beyond criticism, a dispensation never granted John XXIII, or for that matter John Paul II. The action of the Notre-Dame four would be an outrage today; in its time it was tantamount to murder.

The following day the *New York Times* devoted its first four pages, four full pages, to Easter-around-the-world. The lead stories featured the Fifth Avenue parade and the pope's homily on the social gospel; the "untoward" Notre-Dame incident received the same number of lines as an item from rainy London:

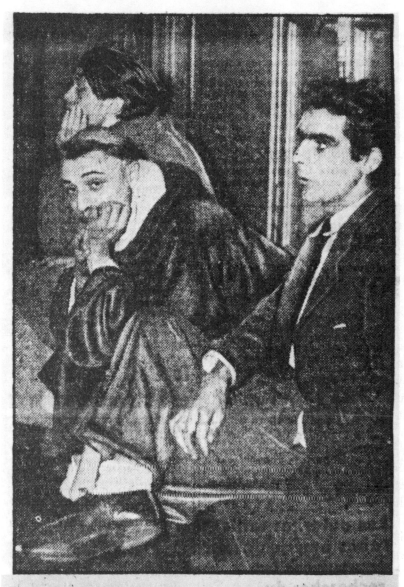

Trois malades?

Trois goujats?

Trois héros?

Cette page est faite pour vous permettre de fixer votre opinion sur le geste de Michel Mourre, 21 ans (faux dominicain), Serge Bernard et Ghislain Desnoyers de Marbais, que l'on voit ici réunis après le « scandale » sur le banc du commissariat du quartier Saint-Gervais.

"Three mental cases?
"Three boors?
"Three heroes?"

Michel Mourre, center, with lettrist poets Ghislain de Marbaix, left, and Serge Berna, in police custody following the Notre-Dame incident, *Combat*, 12 April 1950

In the late morning there was an "Easter Parade," stimulated by an offer of one of London's popular papers of a £50 prize for the best dressed woman seen in Central London. Radio, stage and screen stars braved the weather wearing their best finery.

In Paris Notre-Dame was front-page news in banner headlines. *L'Humanité*, the Communist Party daily, denounced it. In more liberal terms the unaffiliated *Combat* did the same: "One recognizes the right of each person to believe, or not believe, in God. One recognizes as well that farce is necessary, and that, in certain circumstances, even practical jokes are defensible. But . . ." Sticking to its role as the popular forum for the avant-garde, the paper opened its pages to a debate on the matter: led by André Breton, much of surrealist Paris rallied to the defense in letters that ran for days.

The basic tone of these letters was oddly nostalgic. What was odd was the nostalgia for a past that had never quite happened, for great days that had not exactly been lived, for an explosion that never took place. The surrealists joyously claimed patrimony over a great public event, but within that joy was a vacuum of shame over their twenty-year wait in cafes and galleries for bastard children to fulfill their legacy. "It is fitting that the blow should have been struck here, at the very heart of the octopus that is still strangling the universe," Breton wrote of Notre-Dame. "It was there too that, in our youth, I and some of the men who have been and are my traveling companions—Artaud, Crevel, Eluard, Péret, Prévert, Char and many others—sometimes dreamed of striking it." In all his years as a tribune of revolt, had Breton ever yielded up so much surrealist territory, ever conceded that as against an event, even a false one, a dream was just a dream? Mourre "took action," René Char wrote, as if Mourre's crystallization of the surrealist spirit, if that was what it was, suddenly revealed Char's years as a Resistance fighter as no more than a contemplative substitute for a confrontation with real life. Showering apologies, the bad fathers came forth to claim their sons, but the sons did not claim the fathers.

Postcard, 1980s

Of the four "illuminati" (*Combat*), only Mourre was held: the archbishop charged him with impersonating a priest. Dispatched for psychiatric testing, Mourre won *Combat*'s editorial reversal when the court-appointed alienist, one Dr. Robert Micoud, summarized Mourre's "frenzied idealism," "contempt for external perception," "prereflexive cogito," "indifferent ocular-cardiac reflexes," "ortho-sexuality (shamefacedly admitted)," "ability to go straight to the heart of a doctrine" and "to travel in an instant through various epochs," "irritation at the suggestion that Being may have preceded Existence," "ideational fugacity," "surprise attacks by sonorous parachute-drops and nose-diving neologisms," and "exaggerated angular paranoiac logic, in which there is more rigorous narrowness than narrow rigorousness."

This was a masterpiece of French literary criticism. Clinically, it was also accurate—but mixing politics with his prescription, Dr. Micoud blew himself out of the water. Mourre might cause no more trouble in cathedrals, the psychiatrist reported, but short of confinement in an asylum he posed a definite threat to "public tranquility in middle-class districts."

Dr. Micoud had gone too far, a second scandal drowned out the first, and after eleven days in custody Mourre was set free. Three months later he wrote *Malgré le blasphème* (In Spite of Blasphemy), a book so acceptable to the church that the archbishop, the very man from whom Mourre seized the mass, recommended that all church libraries stock it. Once past biographies of Charles Maurras (1868–1952), the charismatic leader of the monarchist, protofascist faction Action française, and of Felicité de Lamennais, a nineteenth-century crusader for religious liberty, Mourre became a hack ecclesiastical encyclopedist; he died, respectable and bygone, in 1977. The Notre-Dame incident, one *Combat* correspondent noted at the height of the furor, was if nothing else "a fine beginning for a literary career."

IN SPITE

In Spite of Blasphemy remains an extraordinary document. "Why," Mourre wrote, "had we not been able to adapt ourselves to the world?"

Armed with their complex-detectors, the psychiatrists could always pin it on our anti-social attitude. It was very strange, however, that there were so many anti-socialites and paranoiacs, very strange that an epidemic of mental diseases had suddenly laid low the whole of French youth. In this world, where we had been looking for life, we had found only wreckage. We could have dreamt, as I had, of the good old days of prosperity or tried to make a pilgrimage through the old institutions which once spread their blessings over the face of the earth; but all we could find were empty structures without a soul, all cracked, crumbling and condemned. Ghosts of splendour, memories of vitality—in spite of ourselves, we had to indulge in a romantic taste for ruins and dead glory.

We would *force* ourselves to keep quiet at the mention of our old dreams, accept the ruins and be happy in them, and become ruins ourselves, self-conscious, self-satisfied ruins. We had reached the point where we systematically went out of our way to find ugliness, evil and error in everything, but for most of us this was undoubtedly only a desperate show of bravado, a mask to conceal our disappointment at not having found truth, beauty and good.

In the tradition that stretches from Augustine's *Confessions* to the sermons of Little Richard ("I was a drug addict! I was a homosexual! I sang for the devil!"), Mourre's nihilist testimony only meant that the worse the sins, the greater the ultimate piety—or, as Raoul Vaneigem would put it, "pissing on the altar is still a way of paying homage to the Church." Always, Mourre explained, he looked for a whole truth, an absolute: God had promised it. Marxism, existentialism, and their like were no more than dessicated versions of God's promise—since without God man is nothing, they were, like all other humanisms, megalomaniacal solipsisms. Because God's promise never left him, Mourre said, he found himself incapable of living out either the abstractions of philosophy or the routines of everyday life: "It was God that I had to kill objectively in order to be free." Announcing the death of God, Mourre felt that death fall back on him, a reeling blow that felt like a kiss: Christ's kiss to the Grand Inquisitor. The circle closed; Mourre had written "the history of a failure," and now it was over. No wonder the archbishop was happy.

From the first day, the papers made the most of the irony that "the false dominican" had, once, actually prepared for the priesthood. That was not the half of it. It had been a seeker's road; on it one could travel in in instant through various epochs. To read *In Spite of Blasphemy* today is to begin in Paris in the 1940s—and then to find yourself in the mid-1960s, when every question was open, then in the early 1970s, when so many one-time questioners desperately surrendered to answers. It is to feel yourself carried forward to London in 1976, when Mourre's "We would become ruins" would have been painted on punk jackets if the grammar hadn't been too fancy and Jamie Reid's Sex Pistols slogan "BELIEVE IN THE RUINS" wasn't already on them, to move backward to May 1968, when "SOON TO BE PICTURESQUE RUINS" spray-painted on the boulevard St. Michel was graffiti advertising a vacation for tourists the new revolution promised would never be born, and then to cross the boulevard St. Germain to the rue de Four, to walk into a cafe called Moineau's, in the early 1950s, when a few people who called themselves the Lettrist International set out to keep the promise Mourre had made and broken. For there was another tradition of the absolute, moving alongside that of sin and redemption: the long line of fatal spells, the tradition of seeking ugliness, evil, and error in everything, the legend of the attempt to turn the mask of disappointment over the absence of truth, beauty, and good into a real face. As with the music of the Sex Pistols, the noise of the dadaists, and the prophecies of the groups that formed around Guy Debord, the road Michel Mourre took to Notre-Dame is itself a version of the story I am telling, just as his event was sketched out in the versions that preceded it and was engraved in the versions that followed it. In the years that brought him to the cathedral, Mourre acted out a secret history of a time to come, a time that would never know his name.

HE WAS

He was born in 1928, into a bourgeois, suburban Paris family; socialist, almost red, but cut with doubt. His father was a municipal architect, dependent on political connections for his commissions. No Mourre, he proudly told his only child, had been baptized for a hundred years, and Michel did not see the inside of a church until he was sixteen. The official family hero was Michel's paternal great-grandfather, a member of the Paris Commune. But when Michel's father was away, Michel's maternal grandmother whispered tales of another ancestor—an aristocrat, she thought, who ended on the guillotine, martyr to the bloodlust of Robespierre and Saint-Just.

Politics dominated the dinner table, all brags and taunts; Michel's mother kept silent. She was crazy. When Michel was eight and the family was on vacation in Brittany, she took him to a narrow wooden bridge overhanging a deep gorge and said that she was going to dash herself to pieces on the rocks below. If Michel loved her he would follow: "We'll punish the lot of them!" Back in Paris, she turned to tarot cards, seance tables, automatic writing: suburban surrealism.

In 1940 she died a long and miserable death from cancer; Michel's father had all but abandoned her for his mistress. As the Nazis approached Paris, the father made ready his escape to the south, convinced that as a socialist he would be immediately put up against a wall and shot. He led Michel up to the attic and there burned twenty years of left-wing newspapers, manifestos, talismans: his pictures of Léon Blum, Popular Front prime minister of France in 1936–37, of La Pasionaria, Communist heroine of the defeated Spanish Republic. He did it, he explained, to protect the family—Michel and his grandmother—who were to be left behind.

To Michel his father was already as dead as his mother. He was a hypocrite. Before the war he parked his car well away from Popular Front meetings, so as to arrive on foot "like the rest of the workers"; following the Communist Party line that with the Hitler-Stalin pact in force "National Socialism was still Socialism," he soon returned to Nazi Paris. He married his mistress; Michel refused to live with them. He went through puberty parentless, under the wing of his hapless grandmother. Sometimes he was shunted off to his Alsatian uncle, who reveled in the Nazi conquest. Why not? The Germans put on good concerts in the parks. They were polite. Life went on.

RIGHT FROM

Right from the start, *In Spite of Blasphemy* is full of real venom: throughout, "I hated" seems its most common claim. The book offered no apologies to the pieties of the postwar period. "[He was] a weak man," Mourre wrote of his father, "who could not understand the need for heroic adventure or the lust for power . . . [he] refused to admit that Fascism was the price he had to pay for Democracy, for the lies of Democrats like himself." La Pasionaria, a Stalinist, might have agreed—but to Michel's father, whose politics were as sentimental as they were convenient, La Pasionaria was an innocent. To Mourre, looking back after Notre-Dame, or even to adolescent Michel, looking forward into oblivion, no one was innocent. As Michel and his grandmother tried desperately to board a train out of Paris, as they were shoved back by the crowd, the boy saw the same people he had seen at his father's Popular Front rallies, and he was sickened.

I think that the memory of those terrified men and women crowding round the Gare de Lyon on the 11th of June 1940, that soulless, spiritless mob which was without hope because it was without a leader, will keep me forever from believing in the fine fairy-tales of Democracy. In my childish heart there occurred a sort of revelation, through which I recognized the necessity for order and the advantages of authority. The god that my father had wanted me to worship was crying for a railway ticket! The masses, the divine masses, were dying of fright because they were leaderless and cursing the freedom that had led them to ruin.

Such rhetoric might have been acceptable after May 1958, after de Gaulle seized power out of the chaos of the Fourth Republic. In 1950, it was obscene.

ABUSED

Abused at school for his shabby clothes and beaten up for his inherited anticlericalism, Michel fought back. Still, he had nowhere to go—and so in early 1944 he found himself caught up in the teenage collaborationist milieu. Fascism was a noble, exciting cause, Mourre wrote: "an amazing adventure was taking place." The amazing adventure consisted mainly of rescuing victims of Allied attacks on the outskirts of Paris, but Michel's group leaders wore attractive uniforms and carried real revolvers. He claimed in retrospect that he might just as well have joined the Resistance. But this was safer.

The Liberation of August 1944 struck Michel as a joke. Everything changed and nothing changed. One form of cowardice was exchanged for another. Jailed for collaboration, Michel attended his first mass: anything was better than the boredom of a prison cell. He heard a message he didn't understand; he was filled with a vague sense of possibility. Released, he was arrested twice more in 1945; finally the charges were purged. "What had I betrayed?" Mourre said. "My country? I could not have betrayed it. I had never belonged to it."

EXPELLED

Expelled from school for his presumptive crimes, sixteen-year-old Michel found a job as a government bureaucrat. He was required to sit in his chair for eight hours and work for one; he spent his time reading newspapers. In Lyons, Charles Maurras was on trial for treason.

Maurras founded Action française in the aftermath of the Dreyfus affair. In 1894 the French officer Alfred Dreyfus, a Jew, was convicted of treason and sent to Devil's Island; thanks in part to Emile Zola's polemic "J'accuse," the documents on which the conviction was based were proven false, and in 1906 Dreyfus was exonerated. The controversy split France. It exposed French antisemitism and official corruption; to many it deprived all hierarchical power of legitimacy. The scandal drew a line through French society, attaching thousands of intellectuals not to country but to values free of any nationalist patrimony; it set the stage for the surrealist revolt. To Maurras, the whole matter proved one thing: French culture was decadent, weak, and bankrupt. And he drew this conclusion not because Dreyfus had been expelled from French society, but because he was welcomed back to it: wearing the badge of the Legion of Honor, the kike traitor walked the streets like an honest man. France no longer existed; Maurras would recreate it.

In fringe newspapers and pamphlets Maurras campaigned for a return of the monarchy, simultaneously calling for a revival of classicism and an end to modern art. Against modernist ambiguity and relativism he demanded the purity of the Greeks; he discovered a "Mediterranean" link between the founders of Western civilization and their now lost and scattered descendants—all those who might read him and understand. It was a marginal movement in the 1910s, 1920s, and 1930s, but it was fierce, seizing every defeat as a promise of final victory; brick by brick, Action française laid the foundation for the French acceptance of Nazism. Conquered by Hitler, Denmark tried to shield its Jews; France vomited them up.

With Hitler dead and Nazis on trial in Nuremberg, Michel was less captured by Maurras' doctrines than seduced by his tone of voice. In the dock, the old man stood on his feet and denounced his accusers. Deaf and condemned, he spoke for hours; he left nothing out. He called for a greater France, a "true France." He asked the youth of France to follow him—to avenge him. He "focused the first beams of order and essential discipline onto my spiritual anarchy," Mourre wrote. "I no longer felt I was on my own. For several months I was as happy as an orphan who suddenly finds he has a mother and father." As he faced the judgment of history, Maurras was a relic. To Michel he was the first promise of youth: no compromise, against all odds.

MICHEL EMBARKED

Michel embarked on his first obsession. Looking over his shoulder, he searched the bookstores for Maurras' banned tracts; in a great coup, he found a twenty-five volume set. With France surrendering to a soulless materialism, to the survivalist mentality of food rationing and the mindless craze for gadgets and conveniences, the now-illegal AF was the new underground, the new resistance; Michel sought it out. Joining secret gatherings in the postwar 1940s, Michel and other acolytes tried to relive the heroic prewar 1930s.

At a royalist meeting, Michel encountered "Jacques," the young man who would become his best friend. For Jacques fascism was merely the least corrupt part of a wholly corrupt modern world: he lived for true salvation, for a Church Militant unafraid of stakes and fires, for the wonders of an epoch close to heaven, innocent of the rationalism that had brought life down to earth. He introduced Michel to the notion of faith: the goal was surrender and the spark was authority, but there was no authority to be found in France. The Spanish Civil War, Jacques told Michel, was the first true crusade in seven hundred years, and France turned away from it. Michel's father burned his picture of La Pasionaria; no matter what the torture, Michel knew Jacques would never disavow Franco.

The two linked up with the far-right but legal Republican Freedom Party. Thrown together with demobilized Free French fighters, former Resistance partisans, self-proclaimed Nietzscheans, would-be poets, petty criminals, unemployed workers, French Nazis, homosexuals, and certifiable lunatics, the whole lumpen petite bourgeoisie of postwar France, Michel and Jacques became RFP goons. Like most of the rest, they were recruited out of Latin Quarter cafes—as, more than three decades later, punks and skinheads would be drawn out of British pubs by agents of the neo-Nazi National Front. Promised travel, free meals, and excitement, the gang disrupted opposition meetings and served as an RFP bodyguard. They learned the techniques of ambush; when leftists arrived at their own cafes, Michel and his comrades rose from the tables and beat them up. What they were trying to kill, Mourre would explain, was the dullness of the peace.

Michel was dispatched across France to convert workers in thrall to Marxist ideology—in thrall, the Marxists said in turn, to the sort of businessmen who were standing as RFP candidates. Listening to the laborers, Michel understood one thing: whoever their masters, he could never free them. For that matter the RFP was going nowhere; one by one, the most admirable of Michel's fellows were heading back to the church. He approached a priest and received instruction; on 14 August 1946 he was baptized.

Nothing happened. He sought a bolt of lightning and gained the right to light a candle. Back in Paris he and Jacques determined to start their own fascist magazine; a government license was required, none could be forthcoming, and so they made common cause with a moribund royalist sheet. Michel floundered; he quit going to mass. He pressed for rigorous narrowness rather than narrow rigorousness, deciding that if lust was the human flaw, Original Sin, for any son of God even marriage was filth. To keep their magazine going, he and Jacques organized lectures on the Left Bank; for a treatise on Socrates, he found himself quoting Nietzsche, stumbled into the arms of Zarathustra, and came face to face with "the fearful, bloody blasphemy: 'God is dead.'"

Today we call such a moment an identity crisis; in those days psychology yielded to politics. For Michel it was a social crisis, world-historical. He had the ability to go straight to the heart of a doctrine, to travel through epochs in an instant. He understood that Original Sin was the beginning of the will; as God's curse it was man's blessing. God offered man salvation along with a Master, but along with damnation Original Sin made every man his own master, master of the kingdom of no. With Michel's ravings, the owners of the royalist magazine began to worry; they accused their editors of fanaticism. "We argued," Mourre wrote,

that the world had a great burning need of fanatics and madmen, men who would sacrifice themselves entirely for a faith, a belief or a creed. Faced with an East transformed by Communism and Communist loyalties and bursting with fresh confidence, our worn-out West was frightened of losing its material and moral riches which it had not even the courage to defend. To counteract Communist faith on earth and Communist ambitions to appropriate the world, it was necessary to establish absolute faith in Eternity, to create fanatics about

Eternity and prove that the craze for Eternity was not yet dead among the people of the West.

They were losing their grip; the kingdom of no turned into the kingdom of yes. Michel reveled in the awful freedoms of Original Sin; Jacques became fixated on Don Quixote. Together they attacked the cafes with rants on the greatness of folly, the folly of greatness, the bottomless pit of sex, the sexless pit of bottomlessness, the splendor of holy martyrs, the marvels of the Inquisition. *Imagine! Once, only yards from where we stand, men and women were burned alive for the glory of God! My friends, the choice is yours to make!*

It was 1947. The young men and women in the cafes smiled and turned away. You saw all kinds on the Left Bank. To Michel everything became clear: "it was not a change in the social system that was needed, but a change in one's inner life." He decided to become a monk.

Being under age, Michel met with his father to get permission; relieved that his son was not about to join the army, he granted it. Michel visited a Dominican monk to profess his wish to surrender his worldly existence to the order; overcome by a sense of unworthiness, he fled. Ultimately, on the advice of his father—shockingly, the old church-hater was himself on the verge of conversion—Michel found his way to the Dominican monastery of Saint-Maximin in Toulouse. There he contrived a remarkable fantasy: someday soon, he would administer his father's first communion. And then he would go forth, herald of a great revival, transforming the "whole world into one vast church," remaining forever unsatisfied until God was "worshipped and glorified at every minute in the life of every man." Within two weeks Michel was back in Paris; on Christmas Day 1947 he enlisted in the army for a three-year hitch.

He was sent to Germany, part of the occupation forces. He became a clerk, no less a joke than his first government job. He learned to despise the Germans, people he once thought fit to rule the world, but now so craven they ate French dirt for a

. . . *IN A SPEECH* last weekend to the general assembly of the Church of Scotland, Thatcher quoted from scripture to demonstrate what she said was a biblical injunction to "work and use our talents to create wealth."

Illustrating her belief that the exercise of "individual responsibility" is more beneficial to society than the collective action of the welfare state, Thatcher noted that Jesus Christ's decision to die for the sins of others was a matter of personal choice.

—San Francisco Chronicle, *26 May 1988*

glass of cheap champagne; he mastered the art of goldbricking. Sitting at his desk, bored and full of hate, he got fat and dreamed of Paris. Two-and-a-half years of nothing to go.

Misery brought illness, which revealed a heart condition. In January 1949 Michel received indefinite leave and a disability pension pending a full discharge. He made straight for the Left Bank and Jacques, but Jacques was in Nice, sunk in decadence and luxuria; on his own, Michel was sickened by the degeneracy of Saint-Germain-des-Prés. Everywhere he looked he saw pederasts and prostitutes. Once more he journeyed to Saint-Maximin, and this time stuck it out. In June he received his habit and began his novitiate.

LIFE

"Life," Mourre wrote, "was no longer 'historical.' At first I was amazed at the contempt for history shown by the Dominicans of Saint-Maximin. History no longer counted for them; it had no more secrets to disclose. *Everything* was already a thing of the past, an accomplished fact, for the ultimate meaning of history had been revealed two thousand years before, when the final triumph of Christ was assured. The historical sufferings of our time never penetrated the walls of the cloisters." To Michel the gift of nothing-new-under-the-sun was absolute freedom, freedom from himself.

The world receded into an impenetrable past, a never-ending present, a preordained future. Spurning all vices, abandoning all possessions, Michel touched peace of mind. Discipline was everywhere; he felt showered with love. In the wonders of obedience and fellowship, he took eternity into his mouth.

The food was generally good. Life became a struggle between grand hopes and petty faults; Michel fought his desires. The novitiate exposed everyone of them.

The fathers lived in perfect harmony; Michel and his fellows had to create it. That was their testing. In brutal meetings every gesture, every word, was scrutinized. Life was broken down into tiny moments; as if ruled by a great magnet, each one was drawn back to a standard of piety no man could match.

The monk would get up and accuse himself of his faults. Then he performed another *venia* [abasement] and remained lying on the floor while one by one the other monks would get up and accuse the penitent: "I accuse Brother G. of failing to keep a modest expression on his face while out walking, and of glancing at people he meets with too much interest!" . . . Or: "I accuse Brother B. of talking to Brother F. who was seeing to his tonsure and of showing too much concern on that score!" . . . Or: "I accuse Brother A. of showing too much pleasure in accusing himself and of performing the gestures of humility in an ostentatious manner!"

To hold his own each new pledge sought a scapegoat; each became one. Michel found his whipping boy; another novice found him. Michel placed one foot in front of the other in fear of what someone else might make of the movement. There was nothing new under the sun, but the world began anew with every instant, and could end there. The world of freedom, Michel decided, was a world of terrorism.

As always, he looked for an escape. He met with the master of the monastery and spoke his mind. *Master, we cannot stay here, cloistered within our walls—there is a world to win! We must go into the world to preach, we must preach like the old Dominicans, in the streets, in the doorways of houses, in the cafes—in nightclubs!* The other novices were country bumpkins and city virgins; Michel had seen it all. He felt free, ready to act. But the rules of Saint-Maximin insisted that he was already acting, with every curl of the lip, every raising of a hand—and that his acts fell short of a very close mark. Tied to eternity, Michel was a nobody.

For that matter he wasn't free—free of himself. Joining Sunday vespers with the nuns of Saint-Maximin, he knelt, gazed upon the Passion, heard the women praying, and got an erection. No one noticed, Michel did not confess at the sessions of autocritique, and so the moment festered. Michel tried to channel his lust for women back into his first lust: books.

There were few. The novitiate library was strictly controlled. Saint-Maximin was a Thomist institution, the purest of the pure; what was acceptable to the Dominicans of Paris was heresy in Toulouse. Of all the authors of Christendom one might read only Aquinas himself, Saint John of the Cross, Catherine of Siena, Saint Theresa of Avila, and "the blessed Suso." Michel read them all, and it is inescapable that he came across what, today, are Suso's most famous words.

HEINRICH SUSO

Heinrich Suso (1300?–1366) is variously described as a disciple of the great German mystic Meister Eckhart and, given the accusations of heresy Eckhart suffered, as a dissenter from his doctrines. Suso's works were two: *Das Büchlein der Wahrheit* (The Little Book of the Truth) and *Das Büchlein der Ewigen Weisheit* (The Little Book of Eternal Wisdom).

He spent twenty-two years as a flagellant; then God told him to throw down his scourge, shake the stones from his shoes, and unclasp the studded belts from his ruined flesh. For seventeen years he wandered through the German province of Swabia as a homeless preacher, begging alms and eating garbage. He was in the realm of a mystical underground: the Brethren of the Free Spirit.

The church administered Europe by means of its monopoly over the meaning of life. The meaning of life was found in the Christian mysteries, which moved back and forth between the two poles of Original Sin, the fact of innate depravity, and the Resurrection, the promise of salvation. Both were principles of authority, for both signified that no one's fate was one's own work. Always containing seeds of antinomianism, mysticism inevitably undermined that authority, but because the church's hegemony rested on mystery, mysticism could not be altogether prohibited. The common will to reach God was too strong, and the church was political before it was anything else. Mysticism was permitted up to a point, and the point was precisely the margin where the absolute authority of the church over an individual's apprehension of the meaning of life could be maintained. This was the epiphany—where, on earth, for a moment, one achieved union with God. In that mini-miracle, which could not last, one glimpsed the reality of salvation; one returned with a tale of the truth that, the church wagered, would only buttress its claim to be beyond history. Thus the church sanctioned the brotherhoods of the Franciscans and the Dominicans; in imitation of Jesus, the brothers set out in the twelfth century to live in poverty, to abjure all finery and clothe themselves in dulled and hooded robes, to feel hunger and thirst, to sleep if necessary outside of roofs and walls, to practice mortification of the flesh: to make the desert in which each man might find his temptation and overcome it. Writ large for the populace to whom the brothers preached, this was the meaning of life in acts. It was a play: a dramatization of God's promise to allow those who were worthy to exchange the misery of human existence for the perfection of heaven.

The Brethren of the Free Spirit were the first "false dominicans." As they walked through the towns of Europe their dress was the same, save for subtle variations meant to alert those who knew the signs: colored patches on the hoods of their habits, a split in the trailing cloth. Like the real Dominicans, they begged—but where the Dominicans did not work because they sought privation, the adepts of the Free Spirit refused to work because they placed themselves above it, convinced that the enjoyment of every luxury was theirs by right. The Dominicans affirmed the base nature they shared with all humanity by incarnating the consequence of sin, which was suffering; at the same time, they affirmed that humanity could be delivered from its nature and changed into a race of angels. Free spirits sought paradise with the claim that only through the affirmation of sin could one negate it.

The partisan of the Free Spirit did not incarnate sin. He—or she, since within the cult complete spiritual power was within the reach of women as well as men—incarnated God. God could not sin; God was perfect; God created men and women; therefore men and women were perfect. What appeared as free will—the practice of sin—was God's will. Searching the Bible for the clues God had left for those capable of recognizing them ("I love him who has a free spirit," Jesus said), the brothers and sisters returned to the pantheistic forests of pre-Christian Europe: "Whatever is, is God." The only question was to know it, the only paradise to live it, the only task to tell it. Thus the Free Spirit set out across Christendom to free humanity from the Antichrist: the Church. Certainly, the world was to be destroyed—but from that fire the Free Spirit and those who understood its message would step forward into a new life.

It was to be a life of eternal pleasure; under torture by the pope's inquisitors, the Free Spirit gave up its wisdom. As collected in Norman Cohn's *The Pursuit of the Millennium*: "He who recognizes that God does all things in him, he shall not sin." "He who attributes to himself anything that he does, and does not attribute it to God, is in ignorance, which is hell . . . Nothing in a man's works is his own." "A man who has a conscience is himself Devil and hell and purgatory, tormenting himself. He who is free in spirit escapes from all these things." "Nothing is sin but what is thought of as sin." "One can be so united with God that whatever one may do one cannot sin." The conclusion followed: "It would be better that the whole world should be destroyed and perish utterly than that a 'free man' should refrain from one act to which his nature moves him." Half a millennium later, Nietzsche, speaking through Zarathustra, exchanged the language of negation for the language of affirmation, but only to give the same claim more force: "What is the greatest experience you can have? It is . . . the hour when you say, 'What matters my happiness? It is poverty and filth and wretched contentment. But my happiness ought to justify existence itself.'"

The goal was to achieve union with God not for the officially sanctioned moment but in permanence. It was a great struggle—it might take years. Once finished it was the opening of one's front door. As the door opened, time became eternity, every momentary lust God's eternal commandment, every transitory desire a first principle of existence. It was the most extreme anarchism ever devised, driven by the incorporation of the single, all-knowing, ever-present God—the most powerful authority ever dreamed up.

THOUGH

Though in some ways as old as Christianity, or even older than that, as an identifiable cult the heresy of the Free Spirit came to light not long after the founding of the orthodox orders. Emerging out of the University of Paris, near what would be known as Saint-Germain-des-Prés, early Free Spirit illuminati were exposed and burned in about 1210. Marguerite Porete, whose *La Mirouer des simples ames* (The Mirror of Simple Souls) is one of a handful of surviving Free Spirit texts not brought forth by torture, was put to the stake in Paris a hundred years later; her book reached England a century after that. The Free Spirit grew in strength and numbers when the Franciscans and the Dominicans began to slide into wealth and bureaucracy, leaving their roads for monasteries; from the mid-thirteenth century the heresy spread across Central Europe and rooted itself there. Traveling under different names, it was never an organized, let alone hierarchical sect, though Free Spirit houses remained in place for generations. If one moves forward to the full-blown revival of the Free Spirit that Norman Cohn identifies in England in the revolutionary 1650s—if one returns to the Ranters, to the sermons and tracts of Abiezer Coppe and Joseph Salmon—the heresy maintained itself whole for more than four hundred years. It was, Cohn writes, "an invisible empire."

The house of the Free Spirit had many mansions. As the adepts believed that sin was a fraud, they believed that property—the result of work, humanity's punishment for Original Sin—was a falsehood. Thus all things were to be held in com-

mon, and work to be understood as hell, which was ignorance—only fools worked. Work was a sin against perfect nature: "Whatever the eye sees and covets," ran a Free Spirit
maxim, "let the hand grasp it." Those who understood this
phrase back to its first principle could steal and kill to realize
it, because all things belonged to them.

If Original Sin was traced to lust, lust had to be pursued in
all of its forms. One destroyed the lie of Original Sin by refut-
ing it in acts. In Erfurt, Germany, in 1367, Robert E. Lerner
says, free spirit Johann Hartmann testified that "he could
have intercourse with his sister or his mother in any place,
even on the altar, and . . . it would be 'more natural' to have
sex with one's sister than with any other woman. Nor would a
young girl lose her virginity after sexual intercourse, but if
she had already been robbed of it she would regain it after
having relations with one free in spirit. Even if a girl had suc-
cessive intercourse with ten men, if the last of them was a free
spirit she would receive her virginity back."

The mansion of the Free Spirit held a labyrinth of corridors
and rooms. If most converts were enticed by the promise that
sin was an illusion, only those who followed the staircases to
the top were capable of understanding what existed to be
understood: that just as a man or a woman could achieve permanent union with God, one could become God. This was not
the petty free will of Original Sin, the freedom to say no that
Michel discovered long before he entered Saint-Maximin, but
something more.

The heresy overreached creation: one could go beyond God.
If God created the world, it was only because a free spirit had
given his or her assent, which could be withdrawn. Beyond
this last door, it was plain not only that one's happiness
should justify existence, it did; that not only should the world
be destroyed if a free spirit refrained from one act to which his
or her nature moved him, it would be.

Anything was possible; the heresy overreached itself. "The
women of Schweidnitz," Cohn writes of one Free Spirit collective, "claimed that their souls had by their own efforts at-

tained a perfection greater than they had possessed when they first emanated from God, and greater than God had ever intended them to possess." To these women, the Holy Trinity was only a horse. They rode it "'as in a saddle.'"

IT REMAINS

It remains the all-time blasphemy; today we recognize only the catchphrase, severed from its history. One could find it in the *Village Voice* in 1984:

All that remained was the irony of severed history: according to the ad, to be a free spirit was to be ready to leave one's work for a moment of pleasure, and Corzealious means "fervent heart."

But the poetic conviction of the Free Spirit remains so fierce that one can almost believe that the little notice was allowed to appear—that time was permitted to continue, that the world was not destroyed—because, in their day, those of the Free Spirit did not refrain from those acts to which their nature moved them. Like the Ranters, they stripped off their clothes and preached naked; if they did not commit incest or murder it was because they wished not to. Naturally their inquisitors made no such distinctions. To the church free spirits were capable and culpable of atrocities beyond description, of ecstasy beyond God's word. According to law, those heretics who refused to renounce their beliefs went to the flames; many laughed. All this Heinrich Suso knew when an apparition of the Free Spirit approached him.

It was about 1330, in Cologne. The cult could not be suppressed; the church was losing control of the mass to enemies who meant not to subvert it but dissolve it. Suso felt himself on the verge of temptation.

"Whence have you come?" Suso asked the spirit.

"I come from nowhere."

"Tell me," Suso said, "what are you?"

"I am not."

"What do you wish?" said the man of God.

"I do not wish."

"This is a miracle!" Suso said. "What is your name?"

"I am called Nameless Wildness."

"Where does your insight lead to?" Suso asked.

"Into untrammeled freedom."

"Tell me," Suso said, "what do you call untrammeled freedom?"

"When a man lives according to all his caprices, without distinguishing between God and himself, and without looking before or after . . ."

KILLING TIME

Killing time in the monastery, Michel would have read these words in *The Little Book of the Truth*. It was everything he wanted, everything he was fighting against. The wedge was in.

MICHEL

Michel drew back. He dreamed of Saint-Germain-des-Prés, where the Free Spirit first loosed its words, where he had lived without work and without money, sleeping on benches, begging meals, peddling ass, conning tourists. How different was it from the vow of poverty he took at Saint-Maximin, and how different was that from the plea of free spirits as they went from door to door hundreds of years before: "Bread, for God's sake"? "They ask for little," a political scientist wrote in 1970 of Left Bank cafe squatters. "They are willing to pay with their health. Violence and self-destruction are forms of existentially necessary penance. Every man is his own Christ." The same words could have served in 1953 or 1871 or 1924 or 1949. "Generation to generation," Nik Cohn wrote in 1969, judging the hippies after reading his father's book, "nothing changes in Bohemia." But in Saint-Maximin, touching the Thomist philosopher's stone, Michel felt his hand freeze.

Everything came to bear on the startling return of his urge to smoke. Against the simple lust for a cigarette, the rules of the monastery lost their force. Michel determined to leave; the fathers refused him. In secret, so as not to disturb the other novices, the fathers finally sent him on his way. It was a ceremony: Michel's tonsure, the fringe of hair around his shaved skull, was removed. Like Frenchwomen who slept with Nazi soldiers, he was exiled among everyone else. With a naked head, exposed to all who saw him as a sinner, a reprobate, a deserter, a freak, he went back to the world. Waiting for his train to Paris, shunned by everyone else on the platform, Michel was filled with regret.

IN PARIS

In Paris the existentialists were already a tourist attraction, the Deux Magots a stop on the tour. Michel slept in the parks and went to mass. Once more he abandoned the church. God dogged him. Michel knew of the Free Spirit and would have lived in its house if he could have found it, but the Free Spirit was gone, so Michel reached again for its mouthpiece, and in Nietzsche he found age-old words: "Nothing is true; everything is permitted." Prowling the side streets of Saint-Germain-des-

Prés, Michel made new friends in the bookstores: Heidegger, Sartre, Camus. They opened up the void; he dove into it.

He panicked. Done with the Dominicans, he made straight for their arch-enemies, the Jesuits; a priest sent him off to teach German at a school in Normandy. Soon, Michel was sure, he would become a Jesuit monk. But he was not allowed to teach; he was forced to drill. God's school was a military academy. He quit and returned to Paris.

These constant, countless reversals: psychiatrists could have been called in, but the pathology was social. As the years went on it became epidemic. In Berkeley in the mid-1960s, I used to wonder at the way friends made the world new each day by cartwheeling down the street, moment to moment exchanging Trotskyism for anarchism for Stalinism for the occult for drugs for religion while professors who in the 1930s were Communists and now were Freudians explained it all. In every case there was a received answer to every question, which meant there were no questions. Everything seemed possible, and the prospect was terrifying—so "nothing is true," one basis for "everything is possible," was exchanged for one truth, whatever it was. Everything was present save a critical spirit, which might have made real the great adventure in doubt that, as Descartes described it, lay behind his "Cogito, ergo sum": his dead slogan. No doubt the mad multiplication of choices by which "the sixties" are known led straight to a surrender of choice in the next decades, a surrender to authoritarian religion, authoritarian politics—for some, freedom from doubt was always the point, peace of mind worth any price. An aide to Senator Jesse Helms, tribune of the American right, could speak of the need to go back beyond Descartes, explaining that inside all the vulgar propaganda of fetus murder and racist nightmare was a true project: the repeal of the Enlightenment, the rebuilding of a world where the affirmation of one's own thoughts was sin, the return of the will to God. Everyone knows history moves in circles; the surprise is how big the circles are.

. . . .

THE DADAIST IS the *freest human being on earth. The ideologist is any man who falls for the fraud perpetrated on him by his own intellect: that an idea, i.e., the symbol of a momentarily perceived reality, can possess absolute reality, or that you can manipulate a collection of notions like a set of dominoes.*

—Richard Huelsenbeck, Dada Almanach, *1920*

. . . .

Michel pressed on. In Paris he found kindred souls: poets, part of a gnostic cult called lettrism, led by a messiah called Isidore Isou. Chafing under the master's yoke but not ready to throw it off, in a blank parody of their sect they formed the Circle des ratés, the Washouts' Club.

I found my place among the disillusioned and embittered failures of Saint-Germain-des-Prés. Like them, I settled down in the cafes on the Boulevard Saint-Germain or the bars of the Rue Jacob and proclaimed that life was pointless and absurd.

Everyone was bored and forcing himself to be bored. Thanks to Camus we had learnt that man is a stranger on earth, has been "dumped" on this "scrap-heap" and forced to live in a world of which he will never be a part. If he tries to participate, he gets lost, "objectivises" himself and disintegrates. And if he does not try, he is still in the wrong, for he is neglecting the responsibilities he has towards everything that exists.

All that was left to affirm was despair, hate, sloth, self-loathing. With that affirmation a whole culture had been built on Roger Shattuck's vacant lot: a cultured sleeping sickness, a slow suicide. As Mourre wrote *In Spite of Blasphemy* with the archbishop looking over his shoulder, it may have seemed only an act, "a mask to conceal our disappointment at not having found the truth, beauty and good." But in the months before Easter 1950, Michel found the words carved into his cafe table, each crossed out: ~~WARHEIT~~, no truth, ~~SCHONHEIT~~, no beauty, ~~GUTIG~~, no good.

Or so I like to imagine—as if, after the Second World War, a few thousand cafe tables had been commandeered out of a Berlin warehouse by French occupation forces and shipped to Paris, fair exchange for art treasures the Nazis had shipped the other way. As if, sometime around 1918, Raoul Hausmann and the rest of the Berlin Dada Club sat around one of those tables. As if, having boiled their knowledge down to words Hausmann would not bother to commit to paper until 1966 ("Dada," he wrote then, "was the issue of an indifferent creator"), they got out their pocket knives and put the logical conclusion into the wood—and in this fantasy, it wouldn't matter that Michel Mourre would never read the words Hausmann finally wrote. Those words were according to the rhythm of the century predestined, its natural language, or its anti-language: as Michel sat sodden in his cafe, Hausmann's words would trap him in a vise. Whatever one man can remember is another man's fate. "An indifferent creator"—setting down the words in 1966, Hausmann was translating all the manifestos he and his comrades launched nearly half a century before, as they fought for the destruction of idols, the destruction of the talismans that said every compromise was made in heaven, "the destruction of the Beautiful, the Good, and the Truth, by the strangeness and intransigence of Dada, the fearless innovator."

In Saint-Germain-des-Prés all that was left of the fearless innovator was a messiah who called himself Isidore Isou; all that was left was the Washouts' Club. There was nothing new under the sun; what was really interesting was that there was no sun.

TASTING NEGATION

Tasting negation, taking it into his mouth, Michel could never swallow it. What he lacked was what Hausmann's words still contain, the fury of an old man still refusing a world still refusing to satisfy him: a final intransigence, the harshness that comes from cutting all ties, the sense carried by the French word "franchise," which means "candor," but also "empowerment." Bound to the stake, Michel would have felt recantation rising in his soul; cut free, he would have yearned for the flames; loose in the labyrinth of Saint-Germain-des-Prés, where couples of all combinations fucked in the courtyards, dope was sold in the doorways, and the future of humanity was decided in the cafes, Michel always kept one hand on the string. Nevertheless he would inspire people more bent on franchise than he ever was—people whose goal in life was to find a way to say a no so strong it would create the will never to take it back. So it was for Guy Debord and Johnny Rotten, neither of whom has ever acknowledged the other, though Malcolm McLaren and Jamie Reid surely gave Johnny Rotten *Leaving the 20th Century* to read, and Debord surely read the papers Johnny Rotten made; even though *Leaving the 20th Century* begins with a fanciful account of Michel Mourre's invasion of Notre-Dame.

The innovator was fearless because it came out of itself. The innovator was first of all intransigent, and it could not be satisfied. But even from beyond the grave precursors demanded fealty, and followers could only affirm negation, make it false, turn it into ideology, reify, trap whoever created it; to be a negationist was to be ready to acknowledge that one did not exist at all. The mysticism of the Free Spirit progressed through its several stages: only the strongest made it to the end, and the end was oblivion, the "annihilation of the soul" that had emanated from God. If one was lucky, after that fire there was a new soul; if one was not, there was nothing. In the fifteenth century the mystic Pico della Mirandola wrote it down: "If by charity we, with His devouring fire, burn for the Workman [God] alone, we shall suddenly burst into flame in the likeness of a seraph." Pico was an enemy of the Free Spirit. But as Robert E. Lerner says, Pico's words "could just as well have been written by Marguerite Porete," the Free Spirit adept burned on the site of Michel Mourre's cafes in 1310—and she could have written James Wolcott's *Village Voice* review of *Never Mind the Bollocks Here's the Sex Pistols*, the band's lp. When the record appeared in late 1977, Wolcott declared himself unsatisfied and looked instead to the Sex Pistols' imminent American tour—the tour that ended in San Francisco, on 14 January 1978, with the self-destruction of the band. "I want to see Johnny Rotten laugh unmockingly," Wolcott wrote. "I want to see him burst into flames."

The most distant sort of Free Spirit inheritor, Johnny Rotten was by some epistemological alchemy being judged on the strictest Free Spirit terms. It was as if his faraway ancestors were present to match his trademark stare, standing in the crowd to throw it back at him—as if his first line, "I am an antichrist," delivered just right, was enough to raise his unacknowledged ancestors from their graves. Unfulfilled desires transmit themselves across the years in unfathomable ways, and all that remain on the surface are bits of symbolic discourse, deaf to their sources and blind to their objects—but those fragments of language, hidden in the oaths and blasphemies of songs like "Anarchy in the U.K." or "God Save the Queen" ("God save history," Rotten sang; "God save your mad parade / Lord God have mercy, all crimes are paid / When there's no future, there cannot be sin"), are a last link to notions that have gone under the ground, into a cultural unconscious. All that remain are wishes without language: all that remains is unmade history, which is to say the possibility of poetry. As the poetry is made, language recovers and finds its target: the history that has been made.

Am I like you?, people asked Huelsenbeck and Hausmann in the 1970s, when the old rebels allowed themselves to be interrogated on their dada past; Debord in the 1960s, when he presided over a small group bent on a revolution beyond the demands of all known revolutionary parties; Johnny Rotten in the 1980s, when the Sex Pistols were a ruin and he was John Lydon. As would-be new rebels, those who asked the question wanted approval, confirmation, sanction: franchise. The answer Huelsenbeck, Hausmann, Debord, and Rotten always gave was that there are several stages in the journey toward annihilation; finally, they always said, negation is sui generis; in plain speech, the answer was always no. Those who asked wrote the bad answer off to arrogance, and there was that, but something more: franchise. You have to do it yourself. "We absolutely refuse disciples," the situationists wrote in August 1964. "We are . . . interested only in setting autonomous people loose in the world." If dada was the issue of an indifferent creator, real dadaists held themselves indifferent to the issue of their creation.

TO MICHEL

To Michel absinthe always left a taste of bile. As he wrote his book in the summer of 1950, Mourre saw the few months that separated him from Saint-Germain-des-Prés as centuries: *Once, people actually lived like that!* He had lived like that—moment to moment, he and his friends had found a way to say no to any question. *Do you have a philosophy of life? Fuck off*—or, *Yes, I have a philosophy of life: "fuck off."* In a store: *May I help you, sir? Fuck off.* In a cafe: *Yes? My good man, the question you have answered is a question I have refrained from asking—fuck off.* Michel set out one last time for Saint-Maximin; in a week he was back with the Washouts. Sometimes they hit Isou's cafe and heckled him. That was the best they could do.

Michel felt life reaching a verge. Confused, he went to Saint-Sulpice Cathedral to confess; he got bromides. It was the beginning of Easter Week; he went to Notre-Dame to hear the word of God and got a lecture on existentialism. "I felt as if I were attending a literary discussion in the Café de Flore," Mourre would write. "The Holy Year was in full swing, and in the papers one could read this sort of advertisement: 'Tour to Rome. Audience and pontifical blessing guaranteed. 14,000 francs inclusive!'" "You don't fault a theme park for not being a cathedral," a reviewer said in 1984 of Steven Spielberg's *Indiana Jones and the Temple of Doom*; to Michel, the cathedral was no less a theme park than Saint-Germain-des-Prés. Cut into one of Michael Jackson's 1984 Pepsi commercials, a line from a giveaway echoed back to Michel's deadend: "Why take a risk when you can take a vacation?" For a price, Michel could become just like the people who stared at him from their buses as he sat in his cafe. God promised him freedom; the church delivered indulgences and package tours.

Picking up the latest issue of *Ecclésia*, Michel chanced on a poem in homage to Saint Maximin; it set him on fire. He had to act.

AT FIRST

At first, Mourre wrote, the assault on Notre-Dame was meant as a prank. Of course he wanted a reaction, but in himself, not in the world. It was his own God he had to kill to be free; he had to destroy the church within himself. But sitting in the Mabillion with Serge Berna, Ghislain de Marbaix, Jean Rullier, and a few more who chickened out at the last minute, another dimension was revealed: this could be a real "cry of revolt." The Washouts could free all mankind. It was midnight; the one cup of coffee that bought the table was coated with ashes and dirt. They rose.

There were forty-eight hours to go. Michel found a costume store and rented a Dominican habit. Almost certainly, he telephoned the cathedral and warned that a disruption was about to take place. He shaved his head, carefully leaving a tonsure. With his friends he crossed the bridge from the Left Bank to the Ile de la Cité. He approached the cathedral. As every year of his life hammered in his head ("I thought," he told the police the next day, "my heart would stop") he entered Notre-Dame. He mounted the altar and seized the mass. Before ten thousand people from all over the world he said that God was dead. Then, as he must have pictured it a hundred times before, the guards drew their swords, rushed forward, and attempted to kill him.

OUTSIDE

"Outside of the revolutionary periods when the masses become poets in action," the situationists wrote in 1963, "small circles of poetic adventure may be the only places where the totality of revolution subsists, as an unrealized but haunting possibility, like the shadow of a missing person." They meant that the impulse to change the world finds its way to absolute demands or it is mute—that when this impulse finds its voice it is heard as poetry or it is not heard at all. In 1950, in the midst of a frozen present—the "malaise du demi-siècle," sociologists were calling it—twenty-year-old Gil J Wolman and teenagers Guy-Ernest Debord, Michèle Bernstein, and Ivan Chtcheglov responded instinctively to the invasion of Notre-Dame and the blasphemies of Mourre and Serge Berna as an outbreak of just such a poetic adventure. It wasn't "poetry in the service of revolution," as the old surrealist slogan had it, but as the situationists would reverse it: "revolution in the service of poetry." The inversion would come from the conviction that revolution meant "realizing poetry"—and that "realizing poetry means nothing less than creating events and their languages."

Notre-Dame was the first event that Debord and the rest took as their own. Though they had yet to meet when it happened, as they came together over the next two years they took it as their founding crime. For them, Notre-Dame made a breach in stopped time, opening a route to "play and public life"; they took it as a sign that as they had heard Mourre, as what they heard made them come alive, others might hear them. It was an event, and they set out to find its language. So quickly disavowed by its actor, the incident gave them a first sense of what Saint-Just might have called "public happiness," and it gave them a first sense of legacy—it gave them, among other fathers, Saint-Just. For the moment of poetic adventure not only opened up the possibility of creating events and their languages. It also brought "all the unsettled debts of history back into play," and in this case there were enough.

THROUGHOUT

Throughout the 1920s the surrealists sought a poetry to destroy the hypnotic symbolism of the church. Luis Buñuel, who as a young man went about Madrid dressed as a priest, risking prison for a private joke, and who in 1930 made the blasphemous film *L'Age d'or*, was first attracted to the surrealists by a photo published in 1926 in the review *La Révolution surréaliste*: "Benjamin Péret Insulting a Priest." Characterized by

Robert Hughes as "one of the world's first documented 'performance' pieces, forerunner of a thousand equally trivial actions that would be recorded on Polaroid or videotape by American artists in the seventies," today the picture is almost impossible to read; a more obvious caption would be "A Priest Giving Benjamin Péret a Dirty Look." All of which only proves that at the right time and place the most marginal poetics—here, an ambiguous photo titled by fiat—can lead somewhere: in this case, to *L'Age d'or*, which still changes lives.

Péret himself was present in 1950 to celebrate Michel Mourre and his comrades in terms more extreme than any other *Combat* correspondent. "I no longer despair of one day seeing the children of Paris imitate the children of Barcelona," he wrote—"those who, in 1936, played in the blazing light of the churches their elders had destroyed." That was one debt: the unfinished anarchist revolution that took place in Catalonia during the Spanish Civil War, defeated first by Stalinists, then by Franco, a defeat that Mourre had once embraced as the last true crusade. As he stood in Notre-Dame he hadn't changed his mind—but to Péret Mourre's act brought Stalin and Franco's victims back to life.

Pumping the story, *Combat* claimed there was no precedent for the assault on Notre-Dame. That the world did not turn upside down with the announcement that God was dead allowed the paper to forget how many of the deepest desires unleashed by the French Revolution had begun in blasphemy—in such unread poems as Saint-Just's "Organt," a 1789 epic of orgy and nun rape—and to forget that in November 1793 revolutionaries seized Notre-Dame, changed its name to the Temple of Reason, built a Mountain in the choir, and cheered as a woman dressed as Liberty led a dance for the death of God. The Communards who tried to torch the place in 1871 were forgotten as well.

Neither *Combat* nor any of its surrealist chorus, Communist or not, noticed that the leading images in the sermon Berna wrote for Mourre came from Marx's "Contribution to the Critique of Hegel's Philosophy of Right." "The criticism of religion is the prerequisite of all criticism," he said:

Man, who has found only the *reflection* of himself in the fantastic reality of heaven, where he sought a superman, will no longer feel disposed to find the mere *appearance* of himself . . . This state and this society produce religion, which is an *inverted consciousness of the world* . . . The abolition of religion as the *illusory* happiness of the people is their demand for their *real* happiness. To call on them to give up their illusions about their condition is to *call on them to give up a condition that requires illusions.* The criticism of religion is therefore in *embryo* the *criticism of that vale of tears* of which religion is the *halo.*

One can of course go back much farther, to the true christs and antichrists of the late Middle Ages: to Thomas Müntzer (hero of an early book by Friedrich Engels), who in 1525 led German peasants to slaughter in their search for the Kingdom of God on earth; to John of Leyden, who briefly found it. "The social revolt of the millenarian peasantry," Debord wrote in *The Society of the Spectacle,*

naturally first of all defines itself as a will to destroy the Church. But millenarianism spreads in the historical world, and not on the terrain of myth. Modern revolutionary expectations are not irrational survivals of the religious passion of millenarianism, as Norman Cohn thought he had demonstrated in *The Pursuit of the Millennium.* On the contrary: it is millenarianism, revolutionary class struggle speaking the language of religion for the last time, which is already a modern revolutionary tendency that as yet lacks *the consciousness that it is solely historical.* The millenarians had to lose because they could not recognize the revolution as their own action.

In more than four hundred years, little had changed; men and women had yet to truly learn that God was dead, that he had never been born, to recognize history as something they could make for themselves—had to make for themselves, if the ledger of history was to be more than a spectacle of "appearance," a book of the dead. Thus did Mourre's words echo back through various epochs—but given the accounting Debord and his comrades would favor, there was a more pressing debt.

On 17 November 1918, unless it was August 16 (unless it was 1917), Berlin dadaist Johannes Baader entered Berlin Cathedral. If it was 17 November 1918, it was ten days after Kurt Eisner proclaimed a soviet republic in Bavaria, nine days after the outbreak of Berlin's November revolution, one day after the convening of the nationwide Räte Kongress: the congress of councils, the autonomous circles of workers, soldiers, and intellectuals now federating to organize a new world out of the ruin of the old. There was shooting in the streets and starvation behind closed doors. For a moment, Germany ceased to exist.

At times limiting himself to an obsession with Joseph Smith, the founder of Mormonism, most often Baader professed to be Jesus Christ, a claim that dada's embarrassed apologists try to smooth away with offerings of irony; there was none. Baader was the sort of borderline psychotic inevitably attracted by negationist movements, and thrust into the forefront of movements that by their nature blur the lines between idealism and nihilism—as George Grosz said of the Berlin dadaists, in another age they might have been flagellants. But Baader was more than that: "a Swabian pietist who journeyed through the countryside as a Dadaist priest" (Huelsenbeck), out of time and forced to create his own context, his own language, he was a clear cultural reincarnation of the Free Spirit adept who was sure that just as he could do nothing without God, God could do nothing without him. In Berlin in 1918 Baader was a lunatic with a chance to change the world. He held the planet in his mouth; the indifferent creator would determine whether he would swallow it or spit it out.

The German government had certified Baader insane. In Huelsenbeck's words, Baader was awarded a "hunting license"; since unlike the rest of the Berlin Dada Club he could not be held accountable for his actions, he could safely do what his comrades only dreamed of. As the Oberdada, he took advantage. In the heart of the cathedral—or from the altar, or on horseback—he announced—depending on which account one chooses to believe:

"DADA WILL SAVE THE WORLD!"
"TO HELL WITH CHRIST!"
"WHO IS CHRIST TO YOU? HE'S JUST LIKE YOU—HE DOESN'T GIVE A DAMN!"
"WE DON'T GIVE A DAMN FOR JESUS CHRIST!"
"YOU'RE THE ONES WHO MOCK CHRIST, YOU DON'T GIVE A DAMN ABOUT HIM!"

Or ultimately:

"CHRIST IS A SAUSAGE!"

Baader followed up with an announcement of "The Death of the Oberdada"—widely reported in the Berlin press, which covered dada provocations assiduously—only to trump it the next day with "The Resurrection of the Oberdada," thus beating out Christ the First by forty-eight hours.

There is an uglier version of this monomania, which for an instant found a field where it appeared not as madness but as culture. Raoul Hausmann, Baader's closest friend, recalled in his memoirs:

I had seen in him a man capable of driving his head through a brick wall in the service of an idea . . . In June of [1917], it became clear to myself, Franz Jung and Baader that the masses needed to be shaken from their stupor . . . I took Baader into the fields of Südende, and said to him: "All this is yours if you do as I tell you. The Bishop of Brunswick has failed to recognize you as Jesus Christ, and you have retaliated by defiling the altar in his church. This is no compensation. From today, you will be President of The Christ Society, Ltd., and recruit members. You must convince everyone that he too can be Christ, if he wants to, on payment of fifty marks to your society. Members of our society will no longer be subject to temporal authority and will be automatically unfit for military service. You will wear a purple robe . . ."

It was, at least from Hausmann's side, a fully conscious recapitulation of the devil's temptation of Christ. There were further plans: a great march through Berlin, where the cathedral would have been not disrupted, but stormed. The march never came off ("Funds were lacking," Hausmann explained; what funds?, the reader wonders). The world was denied the sight of Baader and a thousand others parading through the streets as saviors—or as Dada Death, Grosz's sometime promenade costume, a long black cloak, a huge white death's head mask, a costume that reappeared all over Germany in the 1980s, as students and punks, some explicit about their sources, paraded through the streets in protest against nuclear weapons.

Hausmann wanted to use Baader as a human battering ram. Though his schemes came to little, once in place Baader went his own way. Before catching the dada disease he was a promising architect, though it was not dada that caused his madness—dada simply rationalized it. Born in 1875 and much the oldest of his comrades, he died in 1956, penniless and forgotten, a sometime resident of asylums, an old man occasionally glimpsed on park benches, talking to himself—unlike almost all of the rest, who, living into the 1970s, went on to productive, honored lives after giving up the dada ghost. But though following his appearance in Berlin Cathedral Baader disappeared from history, which is to say from dada surveys and hagiographies, he achieved one more day of glory—almost unrecorded but even more perfectly ambiguous. Hausmann's companion Vera Broido-Cohn told the story a half-century after the fact:

[In about 1930] Hitler was at the beginning of his [final ascendance]. One of the most curious symptoms that showed all was not right with Germany was the extraordinary number of people who thought they were Christ . . . Each one had his apostles and his disciples. They were so numerous that one day they decided to hold a Congress of Christs to find for themselves the true Christ among the imposters. As it was in the summer and in Thüringia

—in the Middle Ages a center of radical heresy, especially of the Free Spirit, and a focal point of religious mania ever since—

the Christs seemed to sprout like mushrooms. The meeting was organized in a large meadow near a town, and Baader did a fantastic thing.

Time, 30 November 1981

George Grosz as Dada Death,
Berlin, 1918

George Grosz, untitled
collage, c. 1950

As he was [then] a journalist, Lufthansa had offered him a pass which enabled him to make whatever trip he wanted, free, if he went to an important rally in Germany. He called the company and asked them if he could be brought to Thüringia and set down in the middle of the meadow. It was accepted.

All of the people at the rally stood up and formed an enormous circle. Each Christ went to the middle, and behind him came all of his supporters. The spectators pushed from behind and then all eyes went up to see Baader descending from the sky. He landed, then went away. They saw his face, and were rendered speechless.

This was a convolution of farce, satire, practical joke, insanity, faith, alienation, and revolt; a convolution of the personal, the historical, the religious, the cultural, and the political that cannot be untangled. Baader's appearance in Berlin Cathedral was the same. Because it could never be factored, which is why it could never be reported, the latter event found its place in almost every dada chronicle, and chroniclers gave it no more thought than they would have to any other meaningless prank. Decades later it was a good story. There is no reason to think that Michel Mourre or Serge Berna knew what Baader did, any more than there is reason to think that Baader, sitting on his park bench in 1950, read the news of what they did and then laughed, or cursed, or stared blankly through the pages without understanding a word. But Baader had charged history with a debt: the debt of the unsatisfied act. If the Notre-Dame four did not come close to settling it they surely brought it back into play—the debt, and all the history that came with it.

DADA WAS

Dada was defined by its refusal to make predictions and by its refusal to be surprised. "Dada," read a 1919 manifesto credited to Huelsenbeck, Hausmann, and Baader, "is the only savings bank that pays interest in eternity." "Invest in Dada!"

dada is the secret black market . . . dada is not subordinate to the sovereignty of the inter-allied economic commission. Even the

Deutsche Tageszeitung lives and dies with dada. If you wish to obey this summons, then go at night between 11 and 2 o'clock to the spot in the Siegesallee between Joachim the Lazy and Otto the Milksop and ask the policeman where the secret dada depot is. Then take a one-hundred-mark bill and paste it on the golden H of Hindenburg and shout three times, the first time piano, the second forte, and the third fortissimo: dada. Then the Kaiser (who does not, as claimed for tactical reasons, live in Amerongen but between Hindenburg's feet) will climb through a trapdoor out of a secret passageway with an audible dada, dada, dada and give you our receipt. Be sure that "W.II" is followed not by "I.R." but by "dada." I.R. will not be honored by the savings bank. In addition you can transfer your balance to dada at any branch office of the Deutsche Bank, the Dresden Bank, the Darmstadter Bank and the Discountocompany. These four banks are called the "D" or dada-banks and the emperor of China and the emperor of Japan and the new emperor Koltschak of Russia have their court-dada in every bank (they used to be called "Goldschitter," but now they are called "dada"; one is standing on the left corner tower of Notre-Dame).

Dada floated high-risk bonds on the cheap. The price went up with the dada version of the word on the street, the exemplary act, but the bonds were odds on to be bad paper the next day. Dada paid off on the reversible connecting factor: all or nothing. You could get in on the action for a penny; to get out you had to pay in kind. You might come in out of contempt for history—then you'd fall in love with the idea that you could make it, because history had assumed a debt that had never been paid—because, save in apparently trivial, vanishing moments, the debt had been forgotten, and even the chits had been lost.

The chits had been signed by God. They said that, failing to make good on the promise of the Garden of Eden, of the Kingdom of God on earth, he would give men and women all his fixed assets: all the beasts of the field, all the birds of the air. The catch was that men and women were to be unfixed; as masters of creation they could never be masters of themselves. In the logic of those who understood Notre-Dame not as a momentary scandal but as a breach in stopped time, this meant that God was simply a debtor with a good lawyer: Jesus Christ, Esq.

Those chits not lost had been burned along with those who tried to redeem them. The gnostic revelation that God could be fully manifest in human beings, that human beings could be god, that earth could be heaven, that heaven could be fully manifest on earth, was driven underground. But there this revelation was placed under so much pressure that when it surfaced it could, to some, carry the power to transform a gesture into a sign, a joke into a bomb.

The power principle of the Brethren of the Free Spirit had never been completely suppressed. In the Middle Ages, it was the idea that the authority of the church could be collapsed by an intensification of the mysticism the church carried within itself. In the modern world, it was the idea that a tiny group like the Lettrist International could collapse secular authority by intensifying the mysticism secretly contained in the secular realm—a mysticism, now imprinted in commodities and representations, in money and in art, that had been taken over from the church. In the early 1950s, this was the freedom to prove that society was only a construct and fate only a swindle, that a new world was no less likely than the old—that, given the right weather, the right light, the right words, the right actors, the right theater, all of social life, every institution and habit, might fall to ruin as swiftly and as finally as any empire celebrated in the history books.

The Brethren of the Free Spirit, Norman Cohn wrote in the book the situationists knew as *Fanatiques de l'apocalypse,*

Johannes Baader, about 1919

were not social revolutionaries and did not find their followers amongst the turbulent masses of the urban poor. They were in fact gnostics bent on their own individual salvation; but the gnosis at which they arrived was a quasi-mystical anarchism—an affirmation of freedom so reckless and unqualified that it amounted to a total denial of every kind of restraint and limitation. These people could be regarded as remote precursors of Bakunin and of Nietzsche—or rather of that bohemian intelligentsia which during the last half-century has been living from ideas once expressed by Bakunin and Nietzsche in their wilder moments. But extreme individualists of that kind can easily turn into social revolutionaries—and effective ones at that—if a potential revolutionary situation arises.

In October 1967, in *Internationale situationniste* no. 11, one could have found a blind quote from Cohn under a photo of a ratty storefront, the photo purposely miscaptioned "ALLEGED MEETING PLACE OF THE INTERNATIONAL SITUATIONISTS IN PARIS":

It is characteristic of this kind of movement that its aims and premises are boundless . . . Whatever their individual histories, collectively these people formed a recognizable social stratum—a frustrated and rather low-grade intelligentsia . . . And what followed then was the formation of a group of a peculiar kind

—"a true prototype," Cohn had continued, in a line the situationists did not quote, "of a modern totalitarian party"—

a restlessly dynamic and utterly ruthless group which, obsessed by the apocalyptic phantasy and filled with the conviction of its own infallibility, set itself infinitely above the rest of humanity and recognized no claims save that of its own supposed mission . . . A boundless, millennial promise made with boundless, prophet-like conviction to a number of rootless and desperate men in the midst of a society where traditional norms and relationships are disintegrating—here, it would seem, lay the source of that peculiar subterranean fanaticism . . .

The situationists were practicing détournement: all cultural production is held in common, there is no separation between authors and readers, and no sources are cited, because all ideas float free. The situationists were practicing irony, because irony is always a component of détournement. But their irony was of a peculiar kind; it simultaneously alerted the reader to the fact that the situationists understood the ludicrousness of their apocalyptic fantasy, and confirmed that they meant every stolen word. It was this long-cold cauldron under which Isou's theories and the action of the Notre-Dame four had once again lit a fire.

THE ATTACK ON CHARLIE CHAPLIN

Isou himself was not involved in the Notre-Dame brouhaha. He was busy attracting disciples, repelling enemies, organizing Youth Uprising, and, by the by, decomposing the movies.

In the year after Notre-Dame, Isou made his first film, his *Treatise on Slime and Eternity*. During the course of a Left Bank love story of almost unbelievable pretentiousness (not to say length—the movie ran four-and-a-half hours), he both pronounced and demonstrated the manifesto of cinéma discrépant, mixing up his images and his soundtrack, negating the filmic aspect of the film with torn and scratched celluloid, intentional flickering, and passages of blank screen. "I believe first of all that the cinema is too rich," he proclaimed. "It is obese. I announce the *destruction of the cinema*, the first apocalyptic sign of rupture in this fat organism we call film." The imperatives of the minimum and the maximum naturally led Isou and his group from the altars of their austere Parisian meeting rooms to the fleshpots of Babylon—to the 1951 Cannes Film Festival, where they disrupted one gathering after another in a crusade to get Isou's movie shown.

When the attempt was first made, Isou did not show himself. The act of creation made one god; Isou, it was announced, made his film in six days, and thus on the seventh day, purportedly the day the lettrists presented the work, he rested. Post-Cannes screenings of the *Treatise* in Paris advertised an astonishing cast, including actor Jean-Louis Barrault and cineaste Jean Cocteau, neither of whom had anything to do with it. For the time being, Isou settled for dedicating his work to the masters of classic film (D. W. Griffith, Erich von Stroheim, Abel Gance, etc.), thus placing himself in their company.

Soon enough, the lettrists caused enough trouble to win Isou a screening—restricted, at the last minute, to an audition of his soundtrack. The *Combat* critic was aghast, though he allowed that "between Eve and Isidore there is still a place for true cinema" (Joseph L. Mankiewicz's *All About Eve* won the Cannes Special Jury Prize). Critic Maurice Schérer (later better known as director Eric Rohmer) rallied with a rather apologetic defense in *Cahiers du cinéma*, which caused even a young Jean-Luc Godard to blanch. Through the graces of Cocteau, the festival actually awarded Isou the "Prix de l'Avant-Garde"—which was contrived on the spot.

THE CANNES ACTION

The Cannes action attracted Guy-Ernest Debord, then nineteen, who joined the lettrist group; he soon fell in with Wolman, Berna, Jean-Louis Brau, and Ghislain de Marbaix. In April 1952 he published an elaborate, provisional scenario for a first film in *Ion*, a thick, one-issue lettrist journal devoted to the cinema—which, since Isou had announced its destruction, was thus ripe for renewal.

Ion is an interesting document—though less for its assembly of tracts and scripts than for the photos of the contributors. Isou, who leads off with "Aesthetics of the Cinema," appears in his proto-Elvis posture, complete with flowered tie, boyish face, and aged eyes; Wolman is a dandified Jewish intellectual; Marc, O, the editor (under the name Marc-Gilbert Guillaumin—the lettrists were constantly changing their names, or their spellings, accenting, or pairings, as Debord finally did in about 1960, dropping the "-Ernest"), is a heroic young-man-with-a-movie-camera; sound poet François Dufrêne strikes a bathing-beauty pose on a high rock wall; there are two smiling, clean-cut young women; then there are those who made their portraits into acts.

Serge Berna contributed an essay called "Down to the Bone"; he looks ready to stare his way down to it. Within a thick, smooth-skinned, utterly expressionless face, his eyes are preternaturally empty. It is a prophetic face: the face of the generic 1950s mass killer. It is nothing one would see on the front pages a few years later (Charley Starkweather always leered); it is the face that appeared in everyone's bad dreams, the face of a man who didn't know what he wanted but knew how to get it, a face so blank its only cinematic equivalent is the hockey mask Jason wears in the *Friday the 13th* movies. In its way Berna's portrait says more about the motives behind the Notre-Dame incident than anything in the incident itself. Silent, it calls up the most threatening of all Free Spirit maxims: "The perfect man is the motionless Cause." And, the picture asks, the ruined man? "When you look into the abyss, the abyss also looks into you," Nietzsche said, and then this is what you look like.

Gabriel Pomerand sits in front of a wall painted in triangles filled with lines; his face is streaked to match the backdrop. He is part shaman, part alchemist, part living metagraphic. Like the sounds Wolman brought forth from his body, there was something impossibly old about the paint on Pomerand's face. The lettrists liked to use their clothes for letter poetry, painting their coats, trousers, and ties with new alphabets, so this might have been a small jump, except that there were no letters on Pomerand's face: what he had drawn on himself was more like the blind instinct to communicate, to symbolize, to make a mark. If one goes back to the oldest known symbolic representation, a bone engraving found in a Middle Paleolithic level in the Pech de l'Azé cave in the Dordogne, the markings, dated to about 150,000 B.C., plainly speak the same language Pomerand was using—and body painting is older still, a million years older.

Face-streaking in modern art can be dated at least to the futurists; it has been spreading ever since. In 1968 the lettrist poet Roberto Altman appeared in public with his face obliterated by letters drawn in heavy dark ink, strokes so broad and brutal they looked less like the irreducible constituent ele-

Serge Berna, *Ion*, April 1952

ments of language than some horrible new disease; in 1980, in tiny subterranean Los Angeles punk clubs, Darby Crash of the Germs, who killed himself later in the year, caught it. He went beyond the punk gesture of handing the microphone to the crowd, beyond the punk star's self-abasing demystification of the barrier between performer and spectator; by his time that was already a cliché. Lying on his back with his shirt stripped off, he proffered a magic marker, and let members of the audience write on his body. They made graffiti that in the act came forth as more of a violation than any act of punk self-mutilation, than the sadism of any paying customer approaching a naked performance artist.

The violation took place in the cracks of one's knowledge of how performance, or any art, is supposed to work. If you pay to see others believe in themselves, as Kim Gordon wrote, as you put your money down you might not quite know that, but you would know that the performer embodies subjectivity, and thus turns those who watch into objects, or dissolves the objectified selves spectators have brought to the performance. But Darby Crash was doing something much more confusing. It was as if he had wired his body for sound, wired it such a way that the circuits made audible noise out of the scrawls on his skin, as if, when he passed the magic marker, which might have been the microphone, into the crowd, the voices of others came out of his mouth—or as if, when he took the marker, the microphone, back, he heard his voice coming out of other mouths. Or was it that, lying on the stage, he destroyed the commodified subjectivity of the performer and became an absolute object, no theoretical objectification, but a thing? You could write on it with no more compunction than you would bring to a wall—FUCK YOU GERRI LOVES TONY THE CRITICISM OF RELIG—until the marker went dry.

One can return to Pomerand's face and look in vain for a sign of surprise. Altman's disease, Darby Crash's violation— Pomerand's eyes are focused tightly enough to see it all coming, as if he meant his face to bring forth just this future. As

Gabriel Pomerand, *Ion*,
April 1952

with Wolman's noise, Pomerand's face was an affirmation of a poetry beyond the ability of language to contain it; as a negation of ordinary language it was a negation of ordinary life. Marx's poetry was word-magic; his constant inversion of the genitive ("To call on them to give up their illusions about their condition is *to call on them to give up a condition that requires illusions*") was his rhythm, his new way of talking. In microcosm it was also the reversible connecting factor: the "insurrectional style," Debord called it as he took it as his own ("even the true is a moment of the false"). Magic: as a negation of ordinary life the style was an affirmation that the words used to describe that life could reveal the tune one had to call to make life dance. If lettrism did not excavate this phenomenon its negation of all extant forms of communication cleared the ground for it; the suggestion was almost present that if it was poetry that brought the unsettled debts of history back into play, unsettled debts of history brought forth poetry. The longer one looks at Pomerand's portrait, the more unstable it becomes; this is why.

Even keeping company with Pomerand and Berna, Debord's portrait stands out—perhaps because it is more obvious, easier to read, less shocking, not shocking at all, but no less demanding. Made on "purposefully damaged film"—a technique borrowed from Isou's movie—the picture looks like a relic, something scavenged out of the attic of a dead relative. As an argument, the mottled photo was clear: for Debord, "lettrism" is already a memory.

The shot frames Debord against a wall from head to knees. He poses tieless, his head cocked to one side, hands jammed into his pockets. Inside the cracks and spots of the film stock the posture is completely up to date, the essence of postwar cool. One sees a disturbingly casual, confident, smug, seductive young man who promises love or violence, or both, a man who seems to be judging whoever might be judging him. He doesn't have Berna's horror or Pomerand's mystery; what he has, the shot says, is a future. But it was Wolman's film that had already caused trouble.

Wolman's 1951 *L'Anticoncept* combined a seemingly endless "autochronistic" (opposed narrative) script, a lovely motto ("The days of the poets are finished / Today I sleep"), and a visual content entirely restricted to black-framed white spheres. ("Everything round is Wolman," ran a second, punning motto.) The movie had its debut on 11 February 1952 at the Avant-Garde Film Club in the Musée de l'Homme in Paris, projected on a helium-filled balloon anchored to the floor with a leash.

The government censor, apparently convinced that anything so obscure necessarily carried subversive messages—the lettrists would have naturally agreed—banned the work. Its only hope was a guerrilla screening at Cannes: recognition from the festival might force the censor to back down. The campaign to get it shown did not repeat the triumph of the previous year; though eleven lettrists were arrested for disturbing the peace, *Le Figaro* dismissed the troublemakers as indistinguishable from autograph hounds. Three decades later *L'Anticoncept* was shown with honor as part of the "Paris-Paris" exhibition at the Pompidou—an edifice that by then dominated what was left of Wolman's Marais neighborhood. Debord's film, as it was ultimately presented, took place on another level.

In *Ion*, in a preface to his filmscript—a preface modestly titled "Prolegomena to Any Future Cinema"—Debord described his then-imaginary movie as a superseding not only of conventional cinema but of *cinéma discrépant* itself, which according to the mechanics of invention could not be superseded, since it was the breaking down of film into its constituent elements. "All this belongs to an era which is finished," Debord said, "and which no longer interests me." He expressed regret that he "lacked the leisure to create a work that would be less than eternal," a work that would endure no longer than the impulse behind it; the making of a real moment, he was saying, was the hardest work of all. Given the script that followed, this was wildly unconvincing. Split down the page between descriptions of soundtrack and images, Debord's scenario pitted liter-

Guy-Ernest Debord, *Ion*, April 1952

ary references against intended footage of riots, colonialist military maneuvers, Left Bank hanging-out, and a fair number of shots of Debord himself. There were a few isouienne blank spots and a lot of letter poetry. Stripped of its lettrist conventions, it was a twenty-year-old's funeral oration on lost youth; the tone was misty and received. ("I have destroyed the cinema," Debord said, quaintly returning to the simplest surrealist act, "because it was easier than shooting passersby.") Various surrealist icons and suicides were trotted out and put through their paces. "You know," said the narrator as the script ended, handing reviewers a tagline, "none of this matters." Within the lettrist milieu, or twentieth-century bohemia as such, it was really nothing new.

Debord's claim that his film—*Hurlements en faveur de Sade* (Howls for de Sade)—represented a superseding of cinéma discrépant paid off when the film was finally made and finally screened. It contained no images at all.

IT WAS

It was first unspooled at the Musée de l'Homme, on 30 June 1952; the plug was pulled after twenty minutes. Several members of the lettrist group quit in protest over Isou's endorsement of the atrocity. A second screening, three months later, made it to the end thanks mostly to a guard of radical lettrists. In London, where *Hurlements* was first presented in 1957, at the Institute of Contemporary Arts, the program carried a warning: "OUTRAGE? The film . . . caused riots when shown in Paris. The Institute is screening this film in the belief that members should be given a chance to make up their own minds about it, though the Institute wishes to be understood that it cannot be held responsible for the indignation of members who attend." The ICA couldn't have sold more tickets with a sex film starring Princess Margaret.

The art historian Guy Atkins describes a 1960 ICA screening:

When the lights went up there was an immediate babble of protest. People stood around and some made angry speeches. One man threatened to resign from the ICA unless the money for his ticket was refunded. Another complained that he and his wife had come all the way from Wimbeldon and had paid for a babysitter, because neither of them wanted to miss the film. These protests were so odd that it was as if Guy Debord himself were present, in his role of Mephistopheles, hypnotizing these ordinary English people into making fools of themselves.

Atkins went on:

The noise from the lecture room was so loud that it reached the next audience, queueing on the stairs for the second house. Those who had just seen the film came out of the auditorium and tried to persuade their friends on the stairs to go home, instead of wasting their time and money. But the atmosphere was so charged with excitement that this well-intentioned advice had the opposite effect. The newcomers were all the more anxious to see the film, since nobody imagined that the show would be a complete blank!

Afterwards one realized that Debord's use of emptiness and silence had played on the nerves of the spectators, finally causing them to let out "howls in favor of de Sade."

The slightest familiarity with the history of the avant-garde makes it obvious that nothing is easier than the provocation of a riot by a putative art statement. (When *Hurlements* ran at the Musée de l'Homme, there was some real violence and destruction.) All you have to do is lead an audience to expect one thing and give it something else—or, as Alfred Jarry proved in Paris in 1896, opening the first performance of *Ubu Roi* with the only formally disguised obscenity "Merdre" (Shittr, more or less), that you violate a taboo everyone can recognize as such. By 1952 audiences no less than artists had long since learned the game—and Debord began from that premise.

The format of his full-length movie was a black screen when the soundtrack was silent, a white screen when there was dialogue between the five speakers: Wolman, Debord, Berna, one Barbara Rosenthal, and Isou, all of whom read their lines in monotone. The film presented fragments of the lettrist milieu and surrounded them with the detritus of the dominant world the lettrists meant to replace; its real subject matter was Debord's first attempt to claim a set of metaphors through which he might identify a new terrain and place himself upon it. He chased his themes in a disconnected fashion—but what little there was to hear (twenty minutes of sound out of eighty minutes of celluloid) was hardly the random verbiage described by those few who have written about the film. In its way, *Hurlements* was as shaped as anything from Hollywood.

It begins with a few minutes of white screen/dialogue:

Berna: Article 115. When a person has ceased to appear at his residence or domicile, and when after four years no information has been received concerning said person, interested parties may lodge an appeal with the local court in order to make such absence known.

Wolman: Love is only valid in a pre-revolutionary period.

Debord: You're lying—no one loves you! Art begins, grows, and fades because dissatisfied men transcend the world of official expression and the displays of its poverty.

Rosenthal: Say, did you sleep with Françoise?

Isou declaims on the death of the cinema; Berna jokes about the Youth Front attack on the Auteuil orphanage. There is a key line from Wolman that Isou must have missed ("And their revolts were turning into acts of conformity"); blind quotes from John Ford's *Rio Grande* and from Saint-Just ("Happiness is a new idea in Europe"). Topping Isou's implied self-insertion into the cinematic pantheon, there is a rundown of film history highlights, from 1902, the year of Georges Méliès *A Trip to the Moon*, through 1931, noted as the year of both Charlie Chaplin's *City Lights* and the "birth of Guy-Ernest Debord," then a leap over two decades of posited dead time to Isou's *Treatise*, Wolman's *L'Anticoncept*, and *Hurlements* itself. And there is the line around which the rest of Debord's life would turn—"The art of the future will be the overthrow of situations, or nothing"—followed by an anticlimax from Berna—"In the cafes of Saint-Germain-des-Prés!"

The soundtrack stopped and the screen turned black. After

two minutes the screen turned white and the dialogue resumed. The sequencing continued, the alternating passages varying in length, the dialogue becoming more disassociated. New motifs appeared: sexual frenzy, the suicide of a twelve-year-old radio actress, the suicide of surrealist hero Jacques Vaché, the suicide of dada hero Arthur Cravan, the presumed suicide of Jack the Ripper, a summation of the theme ("The perfection of suicide is in equivocation"), and a nice homage to the assault on Notre-Dame ("More than one cathedral was built in memory of Serge Berna").

There was a buried reference to the low-life heroes of *Les Enfants du paradis*—those who, by the end of the picture, have become celebrated actors, celebrated courtesans, or celebrated criminals. It was as well a celebration of the five speakers in *Hurlements*: "They'll be famous someday—you'll see!" There were overblown tributes to the terrible sensitivity of youth, cut with passages of real lyricism, borrowed from Joyce; then a fine pun that deflated every easy embrace of suicide: "We were ready to make every bridge jump—but the bridges got their own back." Cued by the opening reading from "Article 115," there was more from the French Civil Code: regulations on insanity and on a builder's responsibility to his client, the latter perhaps to bring in the number of the statute: 1793, the year the revolution, with Saint-Just leading the prosecution, sent Louis XVI to the guillotine. The intermittent dialogue was a groping toward a critique of the ruling morality—Isou's no less than that of society at large—and it presented itself as a groping.

Because *Hurlements* is a conceptual piece, one might treat it conceptually. For that matter I have no alternative. Debord published versions of his final scenario in 1955, 1964, and 1978; today the film itself is impossible to see. I can only work from my own reaction to seeing *Hurlements* on the page.

One can imagine an audience, at first utterly thrown by blankness, but attuned to Left Bank scandale pour la scandale, quickly becoming accustomed—art-socialized—to the new rules perpetrated by the film. Imagining yourself part of the audience, you can imagine soon looking forward to the shifts from black screen/silence to white screen/dialogue, or even vice versa. You can imagine relaxing, accepting this supposedly unacceptable anti-show, this absolute "decomposition of the cinema," this "displacement of the values of creation toward the spectator" (Debord, in his "Prolegomena"). But as you grasp the form of the negation, grasp that form as such is a negation of negation, an affirmation that creation is possible, the world begins to reform—to comfortably reform.

An hour into the thing, you'd expect at least another tidbit of conversation, another aphorism, another quote to please those in the know and mystify any stray tourists; maybe, you might think, at the end there will even be a picture. If the purpose of lettrism, as Debord and Wolman summed it up in 1955, was to cause a "fatal inflation in the arts," then this was truly ultra-lettrism: here a single image, of what it would not matter, would carry more force than all the mushroom-cloud shots closing avant-garde films all over the world in 1952. A penny would truly be a fortune; the dada bank would make the audience rich beyond its dreams. In this setting, the final self-portrait Debord wrote into the *Ion* version of *Hurlements* would be the second coming of Christ.

So you can picture an audience giving into the event, recognizing the film's prescriptions and abiding by its orders—certainly, as I read the final script after a year of reading various accounts of this movie-without-images, that was my imagined response I caught on; it all began to seem reasonable. That was the reaction Debord wanted—and so, after more than fifty minutes of shifting white screen into black, talk into silence, he pulled the string. "We are living like lost children, our adventures incomplete," Debord said on the soundtrack. Enfants perdus: the audience would have known that he was referring to the lettrists and to the Auteuil orphans; that he was using French military slang for soldiers sent on almost suicidal reconnaissance missions; that he was parodying then-current sociological jargon for postwar French youth. And the audience would have known that Debord was most of all calling up the "enfants perdus" of Marcel Carné's 1942 film *Les Visiteurs du soir* (The Night Visitors), Gilles and Dominique, young emissaries of the devil sent to destroy love on earth, destroyers seduced by earthly love; the audience would have known that in *Les Visiteurs du soir* the devil is meant to represent Hitler, and that there was no way Debord did not know it. The film would have reached a moment of obviousness, confusion, suspension: "Nous vivons en enfants perdus nos aventures incomplètes." There followed fully twenty-four minutes of silence, during which the screen remained black. Then, on those rare occasions when audiences or house managers allowed the work to reach its conclusion, the film ran out.

NOW EVEN

Now even allowing that it might have been lack of money or mere laziness that led Debord to scrap the images and much of the soundtrack of his *Ion* scenario, one can perhaps conjure up Debord's state of mind as he finally contrived his movie. After convincing an audience that it could accept an acceptable version of nothing, he would insist on the real thing.

John Cage's silent *4' 33"*, introduced the same year as *Hurlements*, was a concept—and the audience was given a performer to watch, a man sitting at a piano he did not play. Debord's film was both less (on the terms of decomposition, every additional minute was a geometric reduction) and more (seventy-five minutes more). Of course it was also a joke, like *The Best of Marcel Marceao*, an lp released in 1971 on the MGM/Gone-If label by Mike Curb (in 1978 elected lieutenant governor of California, and, for a time, seriously discussed as a Republican candidate for the presidency), which featured two sides of "Silence: 19 min., applause: 1 min." To experience *Hurlements* might have been boring beyond description: a provocation staged in the most sterile environment, not even worth fighting over. You could pull the plug or you could leave. To read Debord's final script so many years later—to read it as an argument, as a manifesto, as a before-the-fact event taking place in the mind of its creator—can be a pure shock, a pure thrill.

The manifesto had its obvious clauses. The blank screen suggested that art was a trick; that any real movie one might pay money to see was full of nothing; that the lettrists were invisible to the dominant society, living in its shadows, working in the dark—that no matter how incomprehensible the lettrists' words and unwords might be to anyone else, the blackness accompanying their silence meant that they alone had a claim on their time. But the center of *Hurlements*, and the key to its aesthetics, was its assembly of references and metaphors: *Les Enfants du paradis*, Saint-Just, the Notre-Dame scandal, *Les Visiteurs du soir*, "enfants perdus," and the odd exclamation that the art of the future would have nothing to do with the decomposition of the cinema or anything else—that art, and the future, would be a question of "situations."

"I was there—up in the balcony with Guy, with the bags of flour," Michèle Bernstein said in 1983, thirty-one years after the first complete screening of Debord's film: the 13 October 1952 show at the Latin Quarter Film Club. "Below us were all the people we knew—and Isidore Isou, and Marc, O, who'd broken with Isou, and who we'd broken with. Before the film Serge Berna came on stage and delivered a wonderful speech on the cinema—pretending to be a professor. The flour was of course to drop on the people below. And in those days I had a voice—a voice that could break glass. I don't know where it went—if it's smoking or drinking. It wasn't a scream: just a sound I could make. I was to 'howl' when people began to make noise, when they began to complain—I was to make a greater noise. And I did.

"I can't remember if Guy and I even stayed to the finish— you know the last twenty minutes are silence, nothing. But I do know that Serge Berna tried to keep people from leaving. 'Don't go!' he said. 'At the end there's something really dirty!'"

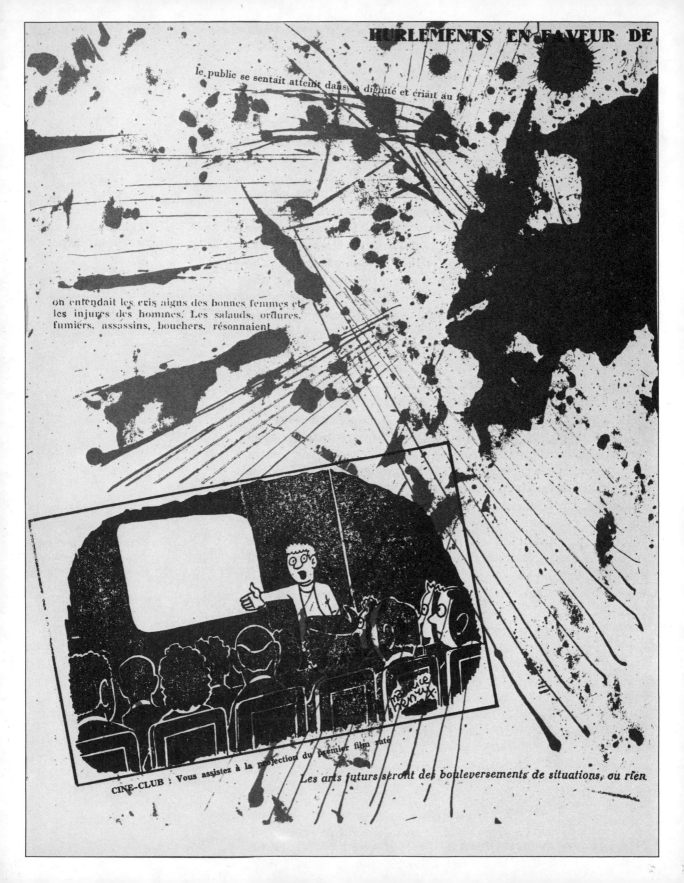

HURLEMENTS

Hurlements opened a route to a break with Isou, though not because the master, faced with defections over the film, disavowed his participation. In 1979 he published *Contre le cinéma situationiste, néo-nazi* (Against Neo-Nazi Situationist Cinema), a pamphlet on *Hurlements* and Debord's later films so splenetic that Isou was unable to bring himself to mention Debord by name; in 1952 Isou welcomed *Hurlements* into the lettrist canon. With screenings of his unmovie Debord "created situations"—and those incidents, riot and outrage, separating a few from a few more, suggested that if the creation of situations could replace art as everyone understood it, then the creation of situations could replace life as everyone accepted it. Dada was a marriage of prank and negation, so was *Hurlements*— what if one went further? What if, out of art, one created something that could not be returned to art—something that was not a representation of what was or should be, but an event in itself, seeking a moment, and a new language to talk about it? What if one created something that would simply go on creating of its own accord, a set of wishes translated by gestures, an ensemble of desires whose force fields would level all museums, habits, routines, all everyday walk and talk, until every moment had to be a new work of art, or nothing?

This was not "lettrism." In July 1952, just after the first, abortive screening of *Hurlements*, Wolman and Debord, two certified artistes maudits, one banned by the government, the other by the public, formed a secret tendency within Isou's movement: the "Lettrist International." Without quite knowing that they were about to move into their own territory, they looked for a further breach; a few months later they found it.

THE OCCASION

The occasion was the arrival in Paris of Charlie Chaplin, on tour to promote his new film, *Limelight*. Upon his departure from the United States (and on the eve of a presidential elec-

◀Page on the first screenings of *Hurlements en faveur de Sade* from Guy-Ernest Debord, *Mémoires*, 1959

tion during which Richard Nixon, the Republican candidate for vice-president, was accusing the sitting Democratic administration of being soft on communism), Chaplin had been officially cited by the attorney general as a subversive, and barred from reentering the country. Days after, Chaplin was received by the newly-crowned Elizabeth II at the Court of Saint James, where as a British subject he performed the requisite bow. England welcomed him home; on the next leg of the tour, Europe opened its arms. In Paris the newspapers were beside themselves; "Charlot" was front-page day after day. Chaplin was accepted into the Legion of Honor. He granted a round of interviews; on 29 October 1952 he held a final press conference in Paris, at the Ritz, and the Lettrist International announced its existence to the world.

As the crowd outside the hotel chanted without cease for Charlot while Debord and Berna tried to block the doors, Wolman and Brau broke through police barriers, shouting curses and scattering leaflets. The leaflets read:

NO MORE FLAT FEET

Sub-Mack Sennett director, sub-Max Linder actor, Stavisky of the tears of unwed mothers and the little orphans of Auteuil, you are Chaplin, emotional blackmailer, master-singer of misfortune.

The cameraman needed his Delly. It's only to him that you've given your works, and your good works: your charities.

Because you've identified yourself with the weak and the oppressed, to attack you has been to attack the weak and the oppressed—but in the shadow of your rattan cane some could already see the nightstick of a cop.

You are "he-who-turns-the-other-cheek"—the other cheek of the buttock—but for us, the young and beautiful, the only answer to suffering is revolution.

We don't buy the "absurd persecutions" that make you out as a victim, you flat-footed Max de Veuzit. In France the Immigration Service calls itself the Advertising Agency. The sort of press conference you gave at Cherbourg could offer no more than a piece of tripe. You have nothing to fear from the success of *Limelight*.

Go to sleep, you fascist insect. Rake in the dough. Make it with high society (we loved it when you crawled on your stomach in front of little Elizabeth). Have a quick death: we promise you a first-class funeral.

We pray that your latest film will truly be your last.

The fires of the klieg lights have melted the makeup of the so-called brilliant mime—and exposed the sinister and compromised old man.

Go home, Mister Chaplin.

The Lettrist International:

SERGE BERNA   JEAN-L. BRAU

GUY-ERNEST DEBORD   GIL J WOLMAN

There was an argument here: the notion that Chaplin's sentimental art, the art of *City Lights*, any art, was "emotional blackmail"—a diversion of one's living strength toward an empty heaven, where everything was true and nothing was possible. The argument did not exactly make the papers. *Combat* identified the anti-Chaplin hooligans as "lettrists"; along with Pomerand and Lemaitre, Isou thus disassociated himself from the action, though in the mildest terms. In a letter to *Combat*, Isou noted the "excessive hysteria" that had greeted Chaplin, but rested his case with the argument that Chaplin's creative work in the cinema rendered him inviolate: a god was a god. Isou did not denounce his four disciples; he merely joined in "the homage everyone has rendered to Chaplin."

Debord and the others were not about to yield their opportunity. For the first time, they occupied the terrain of public life, and they were happy there. From Belgium, where they had gone to screen Isou's *Treatise*, they wrote to *Combat*:

Following our intervention against the press conference held by Chaplin at the Ritz, and the bits and pieces of the tract "No More Flat Feet" reproduced in the newspapers—a tract which, alone, took a stand against this artist—Isou and his submissive, graying followers have published a note disapproving of our actions (in this specific circumstance) in *Combat*. We have appreciated the significance of Chaplin's work *in its own time*—but we know that today novelty lies elsewhere, and that "truths which are no longer interesting turn into lies" (Isou).

The members of the Lettrist International staked out their ground:

"Those who no longer stand close to the edge," 1987

We believe that the most urgent expression of freedom is the destruction of idols, especially when they claim to represent freedom. The provocative tone of our leaflet was a reaction against a unanimous and servile enthusiasm. The fact that certain lettrists, and Isou himself, have chosen to disclaim us is proof of the incomprehension which always did, and still does, separate extremists from those who no longer stand close to the edge, and separates us from those who have relinquished "the bitterness of their youth" and "smile" upon established glories—and separates *those over twenty from those under thirty*. We claim sole responsibility for a text we alone have signed. We ourselves disclaim no one. Indignation leaves us utterly indifferent. To be reactionary is not a matter of degree.

We abandon our detractors to the anonymous crowd of the easily offended.

Ignoring the law mandating a right of reply for disputes aired in the press, no doubt because of the ephemerality of the whole affair once Chaplin took his leave of France, *Combat* did not publish the statement. The anti-Chaplin "intervention" was swallowed in the publicity of its moment: two days' gossip in Saint-Germain-des-Prés. At most it was a small-time replay of the Notre-Dame affair, on the trickier terrain of popular culture. It did not have the same effect: neither Marx nor anyone else had ever suggested that the criticism of popular culture was the prerequisite of all criticism. The new members of the Lettrist International swiftly vanished into their own lives, into their own unformed activities, into the obscurity affirmed in *Hurlements en faveur de Sade*. They did not share Isou's taste for publicity—and they would not really emerge for almost six years, when the first number of *Internationale situationniste* appeared across Western Europe. "YOUNG GUYS, YOUNG GIRLS," read its last page, facing a photo of Brigitte Bardot supine on horseback, raising her breasts into the air,

Talent wanted for getting out of this and playing
No special qualifications
Whether you're beautiful or you're bright
History could be on your side
WITH THE SITUATIONISTS
No telephone. Write or turn up:
32, rue de la Montagne-Geneviève, Paris, 5e.

LIPSTICK TRACES (ON A CIGARETTE)

Early in 1953 a teenager named Jean-Michel Mension turned himself into a living poster and paraded through the streets of Saint-Germain-des-Prés with cryptic slogans scrawled up and down his pants. Ed van der Elsken, a young Dutch photographer, stopped the boy and posed him with one Fred, a thug. Today you can just make out the inscriptions: "L'INTERNATIONALE LETTRISTE NE PASSERA PAS" on Mension's right leg, bits of an advertisement for *Hurlements en faveur de Sade* on his left ("film dynamique," and something about "lots of girls"). A few days later, Mension and Fred got drunk, streaked their hair with peroxide, and stumbled through the quarter slapping female shoppers and picking fights with businessmen. They were beaten to the pavement, where the police found them and took them to jail.

About the same time, new graffiti began to appear on the walls of the neighborhood:

> LET US LIVE
> THE ETHER IS FOR SALE FOR NOTHING
> LONG LIVE THE EPHEMERAL
> FREE THE PASSIONS
> NEVER WORK

New, my eye, anyone on the Left Bank might have said—it was old-time surrealism, and a crude imitation at that. But the crudity was the point. The surrealists had first launched such slogans in the 1920s, when revolution seemed inevitable; in the early 1950s, when revolution seemed impossible, the words were barely language at all. They made an inversion. The poor phrases were so primitively surrealist they were pre-surrealist. They said that surrealism had never happened, that everything remained to be invented from the beginning. "All those who attempt to situate themselves *after* surrealism," read the first article in the first number of *Internationale situationniste*, June 1958, "once again discover questions which *predate* it." In the Cabaret Voltaire, as Raoul Vaneigem would tell the story in *The Revolution of Everyday Life*, nothing, not the war, not the way you placed your beer glass on the table, stayed the same: "Everything was transformed." That was the situation the Lettrist International set out to construct, but not in a cabaret; thus it began with living posters beating up people in the street. "The only modern phenomena comparable to Dada are the most savage outbreaks of juvenile delinquency," Vaneigem said. He thought the role of the Situationist International was to apply "the violence of the delinquents on the plane of ideas." The Lettrist International began by applying its ideas on the plane of delinquency. Running down the street in slogans, taking aim at the unconscious agents of the spectacle-commodity economy—it must have seemed like an idea at the time.

THE LI

The LI did have an idea: ". . . A New Idea in Europe," it titled a manifesto on 3 August 1954, reaching back for the phrase Saint-Just coined as he reported to the Convention of the Revolution on 13 vêntose, Year II—3 March 1794. "Happiness is a new idea in Europe," said Saint-Just; "Leisure," said Michèle-I. Bernstein, André-Frank Conord, Mohamed Dahou, Guy-Ernest Debord, Jacques Fillon, Véra, and Gil J Wolman in the seventh number of the LI bulletin *Potlatch*, "is the real revolutionary question."

In any case, economic prohibitions and their moral corollaries will soon be completely destroyed and superseded. The organization of leisure—the organization of the freedom of a multitude *a little less* driven to continuous work—is already a necessity for capitalist states just as it is for their marxist successors. Everywhere, one is limited to the obligatory degradation of stadiums or television programs.

It is above all for this reason that we must denounce the immoral condition imposed upon us: this state of poverty.

Having spent a few years *doing nothing*, in the common sense of the term, we can speak of our social attitude as avant-garde—because in a society still provisionally based in production, we have sought to devote ourselves seriously only to leisure.

If this question is not openly posed before the collapse of current economic development, change will be no more than a bad joke. The new society which once again takes up the goals of the old society, without having recognized and imposed a new desire—that is the truly utopian tendency of socialism.

Only one task seems to us worth considering: the perfecting of a complete divertissement.

More than one to whom adventures happen, the adventurer is one who makes them happen.

The construction of situations will be the continuous realization of a great game, a game the players have chosen to play: a shifting of settings and conflicts to kill off the characters in a tragedy in twenty-four hours. But time to live will no longer be lacking.

Such a synthesis will have to bring together a critique of behavior, a compelling town planning, a mastery of ambiances and relationships. We know the first principles . . .

The LI's theory of anti-economics was followed on the page by "The Best News of the Week," a regular *Potlatch* feature:

Washington, D.C., July 29 (A.P.): In a speech delivered to a religious convention, Mr. Richard Nixon, the vice-president of the United States, declared that he believed those who imagined "a full bowl of rice" could prevent the people of Asia from turning toward communism were "gravely deluding themselves."

"Economic well-being is important," continued the vice-president, "but to claim that we can win the people of Asia to our side simply by raising their standard of living is a lie and a slander. This is a proud people, with a great record behind them."

Thus did Richard Nixon add his voice to the growing Lettrist International chorus.

ARMED

Armed with its theory, the LI had a practice. Writing to Jean-Louis Brau in the spring of 1953, Wolman summed it up:

Where were we when you left? Joël has been out of jail for some time: parole. Freedom too for Jean-Michel and Fred (in for speeding—under the influence, of course). Little Eliane came out last week after a dramatic arrest in a maid's room somewhere in Vincennes. She was with Joël and Jean-Michel (need I say they were drunk), who refused to open the door for the police, who called in reinforcements. In the confusion, they lost the LI seal. Linda not yet tried—Sarah still in jail, but her sister, sixteen-and-a-half, took her place. There have been more arrests, for drugs, for who knows what—it's getting boring. Then there is G.-E., who spent ten days in a sanitarium where his parents sent him after he tried to asphyxiate himself. He's back now. Serge will get out of jail May 12. The day before yesterday I threw up in Moineau's. The latest amusement in the quarter is to spend the night in the catacombs (another one of Joël's bright ideas) . . .

This, the members of the LI tried to convince themselves, was a rehearsal for the revolution they had promised each other to make: the supercession of art and the end of work, a shifting of settings and conflicts that would kill off the characters in a tragedy and bring real people to life—the first revolution, the LI told itself, consciously based not in a critique of suffering in the dominant society but in a "total critique of its idea of happiness," a critique in acts, a new performance of everyday life. Happiness was still a new idea in Europe, one-hundred-and-sixty years after Saint-Just heard himself condemned as a traitor to the revolution—after he, voice of the New Man, stood silent as he was driven overnight from the Committee of Public Safety to the guillotine. Since then all official revolutions had rested their case not on happiness but on justice, and on that rock they had broken to pieces or turned to stone. But weren't all true revolutionaries driven by the desire for happiness—as Ivan Chtcheglov said for the LI in his "Formula for a New Urbanism," by a lust for a world in which it would be impossible not to fall in love? They had been embarrassed to admit it; those few instances in which they did admit it were expunged from the official record. What matters my happiness, against a multitude crying for food and clothing? It matters not, said the owners of the revolutionary tradi-

Jean-Michel Mension and Fred, 1953, by Ed van der Elsken

tion. Taking up residence in "the catacombs of visible culture," the LI stumbled on a notion that went back to the Free Spirit: "My happiness ought to justify existence itself." So did the opposed first principles of justice and happiness turn into one; that, the LI thought, was what Saint-Just was talking about.

Born in 1767, executed in 1794, Louis-Antoine de Saint-Just was the prophet of the Republic of Virtue: of a virtue, dormant in every human heart, suppressed and twisted by the masters of the old world, which had to be drawn out of each new citizen—or enforced. Recognizing a new desire for happiness, for a moment Saint-Just had the power to impose it: the words with which he followed "a new idea in Europe" were "I propose to you the following decree." He spoke on the stage of world history, one foot in Paris and the other in Sparta. He spoke to Lycurgus and Thucydides, to Lenin and Pol Pot, and he knew they would hear what he said. The LI spoke in a bar that sold franchise and solace along with beer and wine—"Cafe Megalomania," the Berlin dadaists had called their version of the place. There the LI tried to recapture Saint-Just's tone of voice, and it was hard to catch, austere and ecstatic, furious and still, the tone of the cryptic slogan: "The mind is a sophist who leads virtue to the scaffold." You could puzzle that out for days, or you could look at Saint-Just's face, at busts and engravings, but like the young man himself when his time was up, they said nothing. If one portrait was cold, all hard cheekbones and hooded eyes, the next was soft, the cheeks full and smooth, the eyes innocent. "To tell the truth, the only reason one fights is for what one loves," said the philosopher of the Terror. "Fighting for everyone else is only the consequence."

The LI, Eliane Brau wrote in 1968 (as Eliane Papai, she was the "Little Eliane" of Wolman's letter), was "autoterrorist." The group demanded that one practice terrorism on oneself—"a self-educational process," Raoul Hausmann said of the psychology of the Berlin Dada Club, "in which routine and conventions have to be ruthlessly wiped out." The LI worked hardest to maintain the conviction that nothing was more important, and so every person found unworthy of the game was excluded from it; Saint-Just, in whose ideal society banishment was to be the ultimate sanction, would have approved. Officially, the first to be removed were Isidore Isou, Gabriel Pomerand, and Maurice Lemaitre, who had never been present (claiming rights to the words "lettrist" and "lettrism" after the Chaplin incident, the LI incorporated the founders only to expel them as traitors to their own ideas)—and then, in the year between Wolman's letter to Brau and ". . . A New Idea in Europe," Brau himself ("militarist," read the second number of *Potlatch*), Serge Berna ("lack of intellectual rigor"), the emblazoned Mension ("merely decorative"), and even the visionary Chtcheglov ("mythomania, delirium, lack of revolutionary consciousness"). "It's pointless to hark back to the dead," Wolman wrote to seal the LI's first execution list. As in certain fundamentalist sects, those who remained within the group were never to speak to any who had been shut out, or even of them. But Debord did, in 1978, in his film *In girum imus nocte et consumimur igni*, matching a picture of Chtcheglov to a blind quotation from *Julius Caesar*. Debord read it on the soundtrack: "'How many times, through the ages, will the sublime drama we are creating be performed in unknown tongues, before an audience which is yet to be!'"

The years had burdened the words with irony, but they still held real wonder; tracing the theme, Debord put a comic-strip panel on the screen. "THE KNIGHTS OF PRINCE VALIANT IN SEARCH OF ADVENTURES," read the title: "HE ADVANCES NEAR THE MYSTERIOUS GLEAM WHICH LIGHTS UP THE PLACE WHERE NOTHING HUMAN HAS EVER BEEN FOUND." Then Chtcheglov reappeared, and Debord spoke for himself: "It is said that merely by subjecting life and the city to his gaze, he changed them. In one year, he discovered the subjects of vengeance for a century." That discovery was the LI's drama, Debord was saying, and those subjects of vengeance its legacy.

It is this expressive contradiction—between nihilist acts so puerile as to cut themselves off from any philosophical justification, and a voice so classically sentimental it could ennoble the most puerile act; between a found ancestry carrying seeds of totalitarianism and mass murder, and a will to a negation containing "no promise other than that of an autonomy without rules and without restraint" (Debord, *In girum*)—that defined the Lettrist International. In a conversation that moves from the Cabaret Voltaire to the Sex Pistols, the LI is a culmination of the first side of the story and a source of the second. More vitally, the LI frames the possibility that each actor might speak the language of every other.

In this story, the LI is ground-zero, a vessel both empty and full. The LI had a seal, which represented history—and which, before it was lost in a drunken moment, the group meant to apply to what philosophy it might derive from joy rides and nights spent in underground tombs. At the same time, the LI damned all those who believed in "leaving traces," and it left few enough: in five years, less than three dozen skimpy news-letters, a clutch of fugitive essays, various renderings of détournement, some telephone-pole stickers, a slogan scratched on a wall. One can add a small pile of memoirs: Debord's sandpaper-covered collage book, his films *On the Passage of a Few People Through a Rather Brief Moment in Time* (1959) and *In girum*, and Michèle Bernstein's novels, *Tous les chevaux du roi* (All the King's Horses, 1960) and *La Nuit* (1961)—queer memoirs, because while each cast back to the LI for subject or setting, none ever mentioned it.

In a way that is fitting, because it truly was a void the band had meant to conjure up. The LI's unlikely project was to "do nothing" and yet maintain itself; thus its most tangible accomplishment was to persist from 1952 to 1957, when those few who were left (those who, as Bernstein put it in 1983, had somehow refrained from placing "their wine glasses on the table in a bourgeois manner") joined with others, working artists older and far more notable than the lollard intellectuals of the LI, to form the Situationist International.

As an organization that from 1958 to 1969 made unique public sense of great public events, and with the revolt of May '68 even shaped them, the SI dwarfs the LI, even if the LI holds a deeper story: the fable behind the tale the SI told as fact. There was an absolutism in the LI the primitivism of the group conceals, but this is why Debord justified the LI's dissolution into the impressive new federation with an argument titled "One Step Back." "What we did can be put on the table; what we did was what we wrote," Bernstein says of the SI; still, the violent glamor of what the SI wrote, its spectacular authority, conceals the primitivism of the SI itself. Because the SI worked to make its critique public while ensuring that its authors remained obscure—because its members (sometimes as many as twenty, sometimes, as in early 1968, less than a dozen) found a tone that let them speak as tribunes of an invisible empire—the group became mythical almost before it began, and remained spectral even in its most public moments; this is why its history, whether recorded in punk fanzines or academic journals, is full of myth, of accounts of "street theater" and symbolic Ürsprunges, of public pranks on the level of the intervention in Notre-Dame. As attributed to the SI, the events are fictions—but they were also real, made first in miniature and in secret by the LI, and then on stages of world history (albeit stages built in a day and taken down almost as quickly) by the SI's readers, its fans, or its inheritors. That is because the spirit of such events, the LI's wish for them not as interventions but as foundings, went into what the situationists wrote. And that spirit—as a totality, altogether absent in any other voice of the time—was at once enraged and playful, critical and willful, desperate and happy: "Ours is the best effort so far to *get out* of the 20th century."

BEGINNING

Beginning in 1957, the Situationist International was dimly perceived as a pan-European association of megalomaniacal aesthetes and fanatical cranks, despised on the left and ignored by everyone else. Then in 1966, with the takeover of the student union at the huge University of Strasbourg by a cabal of situationist fans (who used the union's $500,000 budget to

. . . .

WRITING THAT made me feel cheerier. There is no better antidote for the terrible feeling of powerlessness which clutches modern man by the throat than a vigorous exercise of the imagination. It is the allurements of the imagination which has allowed all those ragtag guerrilla movements of the last thirty years to succeed, that and the will to endure for the sake of the future. It is only the lack of the latter that has prevented me from accomplishing great things in my own right.

—*Guy Vanderhaeghe,* My Present Age, *1985*

. . . .

spread situationist propaganda all over the world), and in 1968, with the May days, the SI became famous as the "occult International" behind the explosion President de Gaulle blamed on a few people who "delight in negation," though he never explained how it was that a few people could have brought his government to the verge of dissolution. A few people, as de Gaulle said, "in revolt against modern society, against consumer society, against technological society, whether communist in the East or capitalist in the West"—it was true enough. "The merit of the situationists," the SI wrote in September 1969, in *I.S.* no. 12, the last number of its journal, "was simply to have pointed out the new focuses of revolt in modern society"—a revolt against that society's idea of happiness, against the ideology of survival, a revolt against a world where every rise in the standard of living meant a rise in "the standard of boredom," a world whose language was so impoverished by its own falsity that the smallest refusal could become a no everyone understood. "If many people *did* what we *wrote*," the situationists wrote one last time, "it was because we wrote the negative we had lived, and that had been lived by so many others before us." But if the negative the situationists wrote was a sort of hidden treasure of modern life ("another, evil Grail," Debord said in *In girum*), the LI had drawn the maps.

The SI began with a "declaration of war against the old society"—in *I.S.* no. 1 culture was declared a walking corpse, politics a sideshow, philosophy a list of shibboleths, economics a hoax, art worthy only of pillage, statutory rights a renunciation, freedom of the press a consensual limit on discourse about the real and the possible. Made by writers from half a dozen countries, the attack was intricate and whole, keyed to the news of the day, dancing with theory, and illustrated with shots of models and bathing beauties. With every issue of the magazine, about one a year in runs of a few thousand copies, each number soberly printed and gleaming with a different metal-board jacket (*I.S.* no. 1 was gold, no. 12, purple), the attack spread. With a kind of resistant complicity, as if people who once were rational shoppers had become mad social scientists, the situationists decoded advertisements from the press, the cinemas, metro stations; then they made negative images out of "publicity-propaganda" photos of Haussmannized cities and citizens, until a shot of tens of thousands of Chinese performing a card trick that produced the gigantic face of Mao Tse-tung needed only the caption "Portrait of Alienation" to turn back on itself. They embarked on what they called "the correction of the past," which meant the reconstruction of a new history out of forgotten utopian experiments and massacred rebellions, until soon enough the momentary revolutionary councils of Hungary 1956 or Berlin 1918 could seem like all the politics the future would need and next year's election already a dead letter. Scabrous insults ("bidet scraping" can't be topped, except perhaps by "coagulated undertaker's mute") took on a life of their own, as did a sort of philosophical delirium, the pursuit of a heretical, affective Marxism that did not so much disguise an irreducible lust for destruction as intensify and glamorize it. Situationist writing was a form of criticism, and it was a form of noise, directed with equal force against "all forms of social and political organization in the West and the East" and all those "trying to change them" (*Le Monde*, 1966): rulers, bureaucrats, technocrats, union leaders, welfare theorists, city planners, Leninists, artists, professors ("M. Georges Lapassade," read almost a full page of *I.S.* no. 9, August 1964, "est un con"), students, capitalists, entertainers, royalty, Castroites, provos, surrealists, neo-dadaists, anarchists, the South Vietnamese government, its American masters, the North Vietnamese government, architects, existentialists, priests, and excluded situationists. Then detourned comic strips sent the SI's voice out of the mouths of characters from *Terry and the Pirates* and *True Romance*, as if real people actually cared about the commodification of love and the reinvention of revolution; collections of newspaper clippings organized around situationist notions of leisure, religion, technology, mental illness, ordinary language, and violence (the extraordinary "The World of Which We Speak," *I.S.* no. 9) bound power to a chair with its own lies, blinded it with its own images, and forced it to confess its terrible schemes: *We have* ways *of making you talk* . . .

The critique carried a sense of drama, of suspense. If once the claim that even King Kong and the Loch Ness monster were "collective projections of the monstrous total State" (Adorno, 1945) carried a note of dementia, now it all fit: as one read the situationists, the Godzilla of the spectacle rose up to freeze all potential subjects of history into objects, to reduce the energy of alienation to the stupor of reification, and then—

Then one might read about the symbolism of President John F. Kennedy's fallout-shelter program, in "The Geopolitics of Hibernation," about the salubrity of the Watts riots, in "The Decline and Fall of the Spectacle-Commodity Economy," about Mao's cultural revolution as the latest trick of the Red Queen, in "The Explosion Point of Ideology in China," or about the genius of an actor's sabotage of a TV whodunit, in "The Bad Days Will End," and suddenly it could seem as if all social facts were constructed illusions, that none was immune to the urgency of the SI's language, that no private wish was separate from its call for a new world. But no matter how sophisticated or voracious the SI's critique became, in every moment of crisis or opportunity, whenever the critique was taken off the table and put into play, it almost automatically devolved back into the primitivism of the Lettrist International. And that was a spirit best caught by Debord, in 1953, the year he tried to asphyxiate himself, and the year Chtcheglov wrote his "Formula for a New Urbanism": "Oblivion is our ruling passion."

That meant opening oneself to a disgust so deep it might black out all routes of escape save madness or suicide—the dead end of an antiworld where the refusal of work and art guaranteed only self-loathing and solipsism. It also meant: we want to act; we don't care what comes of our actions; this is our idea of happiness, a good way to live. Transposed into the negative, "Oblivion is our ruling passion" was an affirmation of absolute subjectivity; a version of Chtcheglov's "Everyone will live in his own cathedral," of Saint-Just's "The only reason one fights is for what one loves," of fighting for everyone else as the only way to make a city where one could find what one loved, or find out what that was—to make a city where one could discover for what drama one's setting was the setting. Debord's call to oblivion was the LI's gold. In the SI, it would fuse with Saint-Just's call to action, promising the solitary a festival: "Our ideas are in everyone's mind."

That was how the disgust of a few, even the refusal of one, could bring a government to the verge of dissolution—at the least, it was the conclusion de Gaulle could not afford to draw. As an attempt to reveal all the contradictions of the geopolitical and the world-historical, to find the string of the reversible connecting factor and then pull it, the work of the SI could always be boiled down to crude slogans, to "I TAKE MY DESIRES FOR REALITY BECAUSE I BELIEVE IN THE REALITY OF MY DESIRES," to "I want to destroy passersby." But the slogans were also cryptic, hinting at untold stories, carrying a whole way of being in the world in a phrase, and in the drama the SI wrote, the cryptic slogan, the legacy of the LI, was itself the reversible connecting factor: like LaDonna Jones's letter to Michael Jackson, simply the right graffiti on the right wall, at the right time, in the right place. "[Our] work is not destined for the Louvre," the LI wrote in *Potlatch* no. 19, 29 April 1955. The LI, said Bernstein, Dahou, Debord, Fillon, Véra, and Wolman, was merely tracing plans for wall posters.

AT THE START

"At the start it was barely a group at all," Wolman said. We were in his third-story walkup in the rue du Temple in Paris, in an artist's flat with only a single touch to mark the year, which was 1985: the word processor he used for concrete poetry. "It was a gathering of people who struck sparks off one another. Some, like Mension, never contributed more than a line: 'No matter how you look at it, we'll never get out of this

. . . .

I AM THE FLY/ I am the fly / I am the fly in the ointment / I can spread more disease than the fleas which nibble away at your window display.

—"I Am the Fly," Wire, 1978

We're the young generation / And we've got something to say.

—"Theme from The Monkees," the Monkees, 1966

. . . .

alive.' But that line was not nothing." Wolman handed me a copy of *Internationale lettriste*, the LI's first publication, running to four issues from late 1952 (an illustrated brochure denouncing Isou) to June 1954 (a one-slogan illustrated street flyer); this was the second number, like the early versions of the later *Potlatch* simply a piece of paper mimeographed on both sides. February 1953: Mension's line was there, keeping company with a few others under the heading "fragments of research on a new comportment" (Wolman's "the new generation will leave nothing to chance," clumsier phrases from Debord and Serge Berna). Just above was "general strike," also credited to Mension, though perhaps the chopped sentences, each one looking for a referent or a wall, signal a group authorship—certainly, it's the voice of the group you hear.

there's no connection between me and other people. the world began on 24 december 1934. i'm eighteen, the splendid age of reform schools and sadism has finally replaced god. the beauty of man is in his destruction. i'm a dream that loves its dreamer. every act is cowardice if it requires justification. i've never done anything. the nothingness we perpetually seek is nothing but our life. descartes is worth as much as a gardener. only one movement is possible: that i be the plague and award the buboes. all means to oblivion are good: suicide, deathly pain, drugs, alcoholism, madness. but we also have to abolish conformists, girls over fifteen who're still virgins, the reputed well-adjusted, and their prisons. if some of us are ready to risk everything, it's because we now know there is nothing to risk, and nothing to lose. to love or not to love, this man or that woman, it's all the same.

The LI saw itself as a youth movement—the mean age in 1953 was about twenty-one—but not as a would-be mass movement with chapters and membership cards, like Isou's Youth Front. It was symbolic, even to itself—or only to itself, since no one else was looking. As a youth movement the LI was a provisional microsociety, made up out of reflections of a distorted future and echoes of an imaginary past. Some were common coin: promises of a world of everyday technological mastery, household conveniences and leisure machines, which anyone could find in the ads of the time, and what the LI called the "defused bombs" and "blunted knives" of dada and surrealism, which anyone could discover "under thirty years of dust and debris." But the rest came mostly from Debord, who constructed the symbolism of the group out of phrases and images cut from their contexts, puzzle pieces tossed on the table to find what referents they could, to change into metaphors or go blank. As Debord shaped the LI, the provisional microsociety was also a seance, a conversation between portents and ghosts, and he produced it as he would produce his *Mémoires*. He opened a route to the future for the LI with "Happiness is a new idea in Europe"; he blocked the road, turned the band back on itself, with a second line, a few words of premature requiem, pure bathos in Saint-Just's face, or forced out of his mouth—"Bernard, Bernard, this bloom of youth will not last forever."

Turning up again and again in the LI memoirs, always without attribution, in the group's writing the phrase first appeared in *Potlatch* no. 16, 26 January 1955, in Debord's "Educational Value," a detourned dialogue between unnamed authors. The quote was credited two issues later to an oration by the great French preacher Jacques Benique Bossuet (1627–1704), who gave elegies for long-dead saints as if he were present to celebrate their funerals. This one was for St. Bernard—Bernard de Clairvaux, who in 1146 launched the Second Crusade. "We will not go on that crusade," Bernstein wrote in *La Nuit* in 1961, when she and Debord were living in the Clairvaux dead end in the Marais district, and Debord too might have been answering St. Bernard's eight-hundred-year-old call in *In girum*: "Would we, perhaps, have been a little less lacking in pity if we had found activities that merited the use of our energy already awaiting us, already formed? But there was nothing of the kind. The sole cause we could support was one we had to define and lead ourselves."

So they did it through autoterrorism, intensifying the oppositions they carried within themselves. The contrived rage of "general strike" marked a negative that could be transcended only by contriving visions of a different life; the bathos of "Bernard, Bernard . . ." sent the visionaries into exile. That was the idea. On the symbolist terrain of the LI, Saint-Just's time-to-come, his promise of happiness, collapsed into Bossuet's promise of sorrow, his time-to-pass; the wish for novelty fought against the certainty that nothing was new under the sun. As a clash of metaphors it was almost an event, repeated every day. The LI believed the old world had to be changed because its time had stopped, but within the matrix of the group that meant to live in a new world, time moved too fast—and that contradiction was the LI's purchase on the world. For the sake of a future explosion, the members of the LI subjected themselves to the pressure of implosion. It was salutary, they thought, separating the true from the false, people no less than ideas. "Il s'agit de se perdre," Debord wrote in *I.L.* no. 2: "what's at stake is disappearance"—or, "self-destruction." "Our concern was not a literary school, a renewal of expression, a modernism," Debord and Wolman wrote in "Why Lettrism?," *Potlatch* no. 22, 9 September 1955. "At issue is a way of life, one which will continue to pass through many explorations, many provisional formulations, and which itself belongs only to the provisional . . . we are waiting for many people and events to come. We have the advantage of no longer expecting anything from known activities, known individuals, and known institutions."

It's not easy to go into exile within a world one means to change. If something more than madness or suicide is the real goal, isolation, especially the isolation of a group, has to be searched for. To find it, the LI didn't set up a commune in the countryside, or hole up in someone's parents' apartment, like the student Maoists in Godard's 1967 film *La Chinoise*, which should have been called "What I Did on My Summer Vacation." Instead, pursuing the dérive, the "technique of displacement without goals," the band drifted through the streets among everybody else. "The spectacle is permanent," Debord wrote in *I.L.* no. 2; Haussmann's Paris was a city founded in spectacle, so Debord and the rest took it as an image they could distort, that they could subject to a détournement in acts. Walking through the city in twos or threes or solo, looking for its "microclimates," its unmarked zones of feeling, they tried to hear their own voices beckoning from doorways still a block away, to catch the echo of a dead end in their mouths.

AS EVERYDAY

As everyday life it was a mystical quest: "We are bored in the city, there is no longer any temple of the sun." That was Chtcheglov's language: "And you, forgotten, your memories ravaged by all the sorrow of the map of the world, stranded in the Red Caves of Pali-Kao, without music and without geography, no longer setting out for the hacienda *where the roots call up the child and the wine is drunk down to fables from an old almanac.* Now that game is lost. You'll never see the hacienda. *The hacienda must be built.*" This was the language the LI used after Chtcheglov's exclusion: "we like to think that those who sought the Grail weren't dupes," they wrote in "36 rue des Morillons," *Potlatch* no. 8, 10 August 1954. "Their DÉRIVE is worthy of us . . . The religious makeup falls away. These knights of a mythic western were out for pleasure: a brilliant talent for losing themselves in play; a voyage into amazement; a love of speed; a terrain of relativity." This was the language Debord used in *In girum*, almost a quarter-century later: "It was a drift to great days, where nothing resembled the old—and which never stopped. Surprising meetings, stunning obstacles, grand betrayals, perilous enchantments."

As bathos it was just drunks trying to walk and think at the same time. As a use of time it was the shifting of the city back into the primeval forest, then into a haunted house more modern than anything modern architects ever dreamed of, a game of freedom in which the goal was not to score but to remain on the field, to consciously position oneself between past and future. "You can never know which streets to take and which to avoid," says the narrator in Paul Auster's 1987 novel *In the Country of Last Things*—she is speaking from the future, when the city has collapsed into an anarchy of killer

"It's unheard of, an adventure like this in the midst of the 20th century . . ."

—detail from Guy-Ernest Debord, *Mémoires*, 1959

gangs and flagellant sects, but the state of mind she is forced to bring to her city is the state of mind the LI chose to bring to its own. "Bit by bit," she says, "the city robs you of certainty. There can never be any fixed point, and you can survive only if nothing is necessary to you. Without warning, you must be able to change, to drop what you are doing, to reverse. In the end, there is nothing that is not the case. As a consequence, you must learn how to read the signs . . . The essential thing is not to become inured. For habits are deadly. Even if it is for the hundredth time, you must encounter each thing as if you have never known it before. This is next to impossible, I realize, but it is an absolute rule." And that too is Chtcheglov's kind of language, because on the dérive he took the lead. In the detourned characterizations of *In girum* Debord may be Zorro, Lacenaire, or even General Custer at Little Big Horn; Chtcheglov, except for a moment when Debord makes him into King Ludwig II, the mad castle builder of Bavaria, is always Prince Valiant.

"The *dérive* (with its flow of acts, gestures, strolls, encounters)," Chtcheglov wrote to Debord and Bernstein in 1963, "was *to the totality* exactly what psychoanalysis (in the best sense) is to language. Let yourself go with the flow of words, says the analyst. He listens, until the moment when he rejects or modifies (one could say *detourns*) a word, an expression, or a definition . . . But just as analysis [as a treatment complete in itself] is almost always *contra-indicated*, so the continuous *dérive*"—the everyday life of the Fourierist Disneyland that Chtcheglov had proposed ten years before—"is dangerous to the extent that the individual, having gone too far (not without bases, but . . .) without defenses, is threatened with explosion, dissolution, disassociation, disintegration. And so the relapse into what is termed 'ordinary life,' which is to say, in reality, 'petrified life' . . . In 1953-1954, we drifted for three or four months at a time: that's the extreme limit, the critical point. It's a miracle it didn't kill us. We had a constitution—a bad constitution—of iron."

In 1963 Chtcheglov was writing from an insane asylum; he was full of doubt. But in 1953 there was no doubt at all. "You don't fault a theme park for not being a cathedral" is common sense, whether applied to an adventure movie or to a nineteen-year-old member of a provisional microsociety; to expose that fault, to drop the old world into its maw, was the goal Chtcheglov had set for the LI—the search for the theme park where he and everyone else would live in their own cathedrals. He was sure the dérive was the way to find that new city, just as Debord was sure the dérive was the way to generate the conviction that the old city had to be destroyed, or the way to discover who was worthy of the task and who wasn't— as Debord loved to hear Lacenaire say in *Les Enfants du paradis*, "It takes all kinds to make a world—or unmake it." Debord hung his metaphors in the air; Chtcheglov was the first to live them out. "The powers that be," Debord said in *In girum*, "are still unable to measure what the swift passage of this man has cost them."

Making his movie in 1978, Debord bypassed the obvious confirmation: news footage of thousands of '68ers barricading streets Chtcheglov had once walked alone. Instead there was another comic strip: Prince Valiant is lost, fleeing thunder and rain, looking for shelter. "He finds a tavern frequented by travelers from distant, mysterious lands . . . and while outside the storm rages, here stories are told of fabulous places, of marvelous cities surrounded by great walls . . . meanwhile, a haggard-looking man approaches the tavern, bearing new drugs. (Next week: ROME FALLS.)"

On the dérive the members of the LI met, separated, spread out, came together, and tried to write down what they found, to map what they were calling the "psychogeography" of where they had been. They looked for new streets, which meant the oldest streets, as if the streets they thought they knew were judging their unreadiness to understand the secrets the streets contained. The dérive was a way of positing boredom: streets one had walked again and again. Détournement—which finally meant applying the reversible connecting factor to any posited subject or object—was a way of fighting off boredom, and of criticizing it. On the dérive, objective acceptance ("I love that street because it's beautiful") could turn into subjective refusal ("That street is ugly because I hate it"), which could turn into a glimpse of utopia ("That street is beautiful because I love it").

The LI wanted to create a city of possibilities in the heart of the city of the spectacle. First, though, the group had to create a city of negations: to escape the city's social elements of work and art, of production and ideology, to function as their anti-matter. The new city would be a psychogeographical amusement park; before that, it would be an affective black hole. "The spectacle says nothing more than 'That which is good appears, that which appears is good,'" Debord wrote in *The Society of the Spectacle*. In the LI's city there would be nothing that was not the case. Someday, the LI was sure, the one-eyed light of the spectacle would be sucked into the black hole as if it had never been.

ISOU

Isou would have smiled over Mension's "general strike"—after all, it was no more than a particularly mindless version of Youth Front, "Our Program" reduced to the "units of gratuitousness" Isou had identified as the only goods that youth possessed. It was old news—but there was a difference. Isou thought gratuitousness was worthless because it could not be integrated into the "circuit of exchange." Mension was insisting that no less than the stories the LI told around its table— the legends of preverbal sound poetry, the invasion of Notre-Dame, the blank movie, the raid on Charlie Chaplin—gratuitousness was a key to the black hole.

Isou thought units of gratuitousness had at least a pseudo-exchange value: they could be exchanged socially. Youth was drowning itself in violence and resignation because it was

Si vous vous croyez

DU GENIE

ou si vous estimez posséder seulement

UNE INTELLIGENCE BRILLANTE

adressez-vous à l'Internationale lettriste

édité par l'I. L. 32, rue de la montagne-geneviève, paris 5º

LI sticker, December 1955

"super-exploited by the seniority system"; that was why Isou called youth into the streets to change the world—to fight, as Debord would say in *In girum*, "for a place in a total revolution, or—they are sometimes the same—a better place on the wage scale." In the arithmetic of Isou's "nuclear economy," the sum total of the units of gratuitousness youth expended in compensation for its "nonexistence" precisely equaled what youth had to renounce in order to exist—to win any place, fixed or wished, in the social order. But in "general strike" the LI was posing a question Isou had ignored: what if one refused to renounce one's units of gratuitousness—acts that were not cowardly because they could not be justified—no matter what place in the social order they might be exchanged for? What if one experienced gratuitousness as freedom? What if one broke the circuit of exchange?

The LI, Debord said, lived "on the margins of the economy" and claimed "a role of pure consumption"; Isou said that without production there is no commodity one might consume. No commodity, the LI answered: time. It had stopped; the LI's concern was to make it pass. Running above "general strike" in *I.L.* no. 2 was "manifesto," signed by seven men and four women (Sarah, Berna, P.-J. Berlé, Brau, Dahou, Debord, Linda, Françoise Lejare, Mension, Papai, and Wolman), the grandest cohort the LI would ever muster, only three of whom would make it to the next year:

lettrist provocation always serves to pass the time. revolutionary thought lies nowhere else. we pursue our little racket in the restricted Beyond of literature. for lack of anything better, it is naturally to manifest ourselves that we write manifestos. a free-spirited way of life is a very beautiful thing. but our desires were fleeting and deceptive. it's said that youth is systematic. the weeks reproduce themselves in a straight line. our meetings are by chance and our chancy contacts are lost behind the fragile defense of words. the world turns as if nothing has happened. in sum, the human condition no longer gives us pleasure.

Like Mension, the group went to the edge of nihilism, tried to turn away, and found the way blocked:

. . . all those who sustain anything merely contribute to police work. we know that all extant ideas and forms of behavior are insufficient. present-day society is thus divided between lettrists and informers. . . . there are no nihilists, only impotents. almost everything is forbidden us. the détournement of minors

—and here the word means "subversion," "leading astray," "corruption," "seduction"—

and the use of drugs are pursued in the same way as all our more general efforts to transcend the void. many of our comrades are in jail for theft. we protest the punishment inflicted on those who have realized that it is absolutely unnecessary to work. we refuse to talk about it. human relationships must be grounded in passion, if not terror.

TWENTY-SIX

. . . .

PERPIGNAN, June 30 (France-Soir): *At 4:30 this morning an auto accident near the village of Saises took the life of the Reverend Father Emmanuel Suarez, head of the Dominicans, and of Father Martinez Cantarino, the general secretary of the order...*

—*"The Best News of the Week,"* Potlatch *no. 3, 9 July 1954*

. . . .

Twenty-six years later, in 1979, Wolman published a thick tabloid he called *Duhring Duhring*. On each of the sixty-four pages are fifty-four tightly cropped faces, more than three thousand in all: commonplace images of sitting politicians, dead statesmen, movie stars, subjects of famous paintings and sculptures, saints, comic-strip characters, revolutionaries, authors, every variety of celebrity. Each face is scored vertically with a blank strip, and then across the eyes with a word ("socialism," "classes," "owners," "workers," in one series; "embryo," "territory," "contempt," "narrative," in another). Many of the faces reappear throughout the production, picking up new words, and vice versa; the elements float across the newsprint.

The endless, seemingly random juxtapositions take in any story a daily might run. After a few pages, the reader is back in the middle of one of Debord's definitions from *The Society of the Spectacle*, the spectacle as the existing order's uninterrupted discourse about itself, even if that discourse is here reduced to babble, and its mouthpieces, the empowered and their stand-ins, the recuperators and the recuperated, left nearly unrecognizable, their identities scratched out by their social

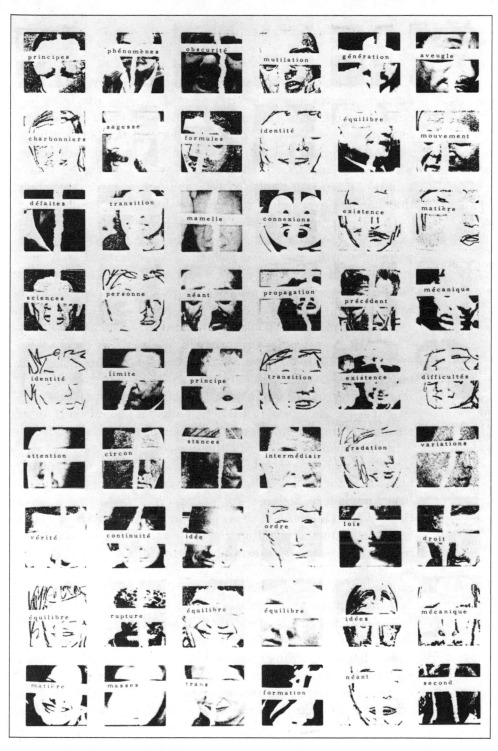

Page from (Gil) Joseph Wolman, *Durhing Durhing*, 1979

roles. It is a shaggy-dog story: if one puts down Wolman's all-purpose gazette and picks up any other, words and faces leap out of their official contexts, current events and settled history now a scrabble of BrezhnevinvasionUncleScroogerights-Napoleonstruggle, all referents dissolved into a meaningless whole. The only irony—the tail that wags the dog—is that if this is a picture of public speech, and public speech is babble, that babble nevertheless rules the world.

There is a motto on the first page: "we were against the power of words—against power." But *Duhring Duhring* is a permanent dada newspaper, which is to say immediately present, so I told Wolman I didn't understand the use of the past tense: "we were." "Because 'we' were the LI," he said. "Because that time was real time."

For a moment, in Wolman's flat in 1985, time went backward: "He was twenty-seven," read Wolman's *Potlatch* obituary. He and Debord founded the group; for years, they outlasted everybody else. But in January 1957, four months after representing the LI at the First World Congress of Free Artists in Alba, Italy, where the first plans for a new, truly international organization were made, Wolman too was excluded.

In Alba, Wolman set forth the perspectives of the LI to such would-be planners of imaginary towns as Constant Nieuwenhuys of Holland, Asger Jorn of Denmark, Guiseppe Pinot-Gallizio and Ettore Sottsass Jr. of Italy, and Pravoslav Rada of Czechoslovakia, most of them painters with agents and galleries: "The course of negation and destruction that in an ever-accelerating manner is overtaking all traditional forms of artistic creation is irreversible." Art was breaking up over a contradiction that was less aesthetic than social: "the result of new possibilities of action that can be seen all over the world."

A global upheaval in economics and science was imminent. In the East as in the West, the means of production remained in the hands of ruling classes, but the question of production was almost settled. Soon the only limits on production would be those of social control, and those limits would not hold. What was at stake were the means of transformation. Wolman was saying that work was going to wither away in the face of technology, that abundance would be measured not in commodities but in time, that leisure was the real revolutionary question. Leisure would soon be the axis of civilization: a realm of potential happiness so complete that it would test the power of all the mechanisms of alienation to dominate it. A war would be fought over the meaning of life. If leisure was conquered, civilization would turn into a prison disguised as a pleasure dome. But if leisure was not conquered, it would serve as a base for a practice of freedom so explosive that no known social order could ever satisfy it.

In other words, as a social possibility the modernist dream of unlimited mastery over the domain of necessity was already the only real aesthetic fact. Utopia, someone's utopia, was near. Traditional art existed to map utopia, to represent moments of possibility or totality that in the domain of necessity came and went as phantoms—"For art comes to you proposing to give nothing but the highest quality to your moments as they pass, and simply for those moments' sake," said Walter Pater in 1873—but now the field of utopia was anyone's everyday life, and moments could be made into history. That was why (as one could have read in *Potlatch* no. 5, a few inches down from the item on the Fujinomyia lipstick war) poetry had to be "seen in faces," and why it was necessary "to create new faces," why poetry had to be found "in the form of cities," and why the LI promised to "construire de bouleversantes," to construct by overturning: "The new beauty will be a beauty of SITUATION, *provisional* and lived." People would live in their own cathedrals, or they would live in their own prisons; self-contained by a page or a frame, the prison was now all any poem or painting could invoke. Traditional art could only recuperate possibility, separating it from totality. To communicate this fact, the page had to be blank, the canvas had to be blank, the screen had to be blank: proof that art could only be walked and talked.

Such a proof matched its field. Everyday life was also blank. It was a government of stadiums and television programs, habit and routine, received gestures orchestrating a hegemonic conversation in which no one's words were one's own. If art held itself back from the empty space of everyday life, it would disappear into its own emptiness—but if art disappeared, the impulse to create one's own utopia would go with it, and time would stop for good. The conclusion was plain: art could save the world, but only if artists allowed the world to save art.

One version of utopia, of the mastery of space and time, was already present, Wolman said: the basic modernist nightmare, fruit of all the plans drawn up in the 1920s for a new city that would have made Haussmann's Paris look like it was built by the Communards. On the terms of the spectacle, utopia was Le Corbusier's "Radiant City," the prison without walls—the "Christian and capitalist way of life" suspended in "definitive harmony," Wolman said, the city of guilt and work presented as an "unchangeable fact." Against this blinding light, Wolman used a line by Jorn to affirm the shadow city the LI had discovered on the dérive: "new, chaotic jungles, sparking experiences without purpose, devoid of meaning." This city would be made not for the circulation of commodities but for the passing of time. It would be a playground for acts that were not cowardly because they could not be justified, a shifting of settings and conflicts that would kill off the characters in a tragedy in twenty-four hours—and who could resist it? It sounded like fun, wrecking the world, putting it back together the next day. "We will not work to prolong the mechanical civilizations that ultimately lead to boring leisure," Chtcheglov had written. "We propose to invent new, changeable decors."

Haunted by key images from ancient times, our minds have remained far behind the sophistication of our machinery. Attempts to fuse modern science into new myths have gone nowhere. As a result, abstraction has invaded all the arts—contemporary architecture most of all. Pure plasticity, telling no story and making no movement, soothes the eye, and freezes it . . .

Past societies offered people an absolute truth and incontestable mythic symbols. The appearance of the idea of *relativity* in the modern mind allows one to glimpse the EXPERIMENTAL aspect of the

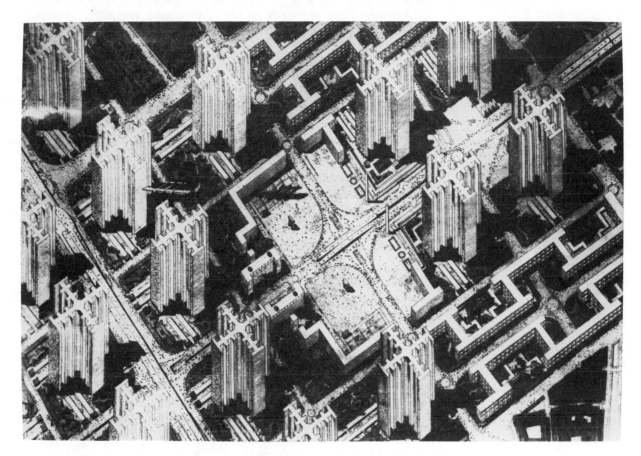

Le Corbusier, drawing for the Voisin Plan, 1925

next civilization, although that word doesn't quite serve: say, more fluid, more "fun." On the bases of this mobile civilization, architecture will be, at least in the beginning, a means of experimenting with a thousand ways of modifying life, with a view towards a synthesis today found only in legends.

This, Wolman was saying, was real leisure—leisure not as a compensation for work, not as a version of it, but as its annihilation—and this was why leisure was the real revolutionary question. To make this city of play, artists would have to reject the passive abstraction of all objectified, separate art, and leave their objects behind: "creation," Wolman told his audience, "can now be nothing less than" the "complete construction of an atmosphere."

Perhaps, in their own abstraction, Wolman's words floated in the air, to be carried off by whatever the weather was in Alba in September 1956—but if the LI's utopia was abstract, its anti-utopia was not. As Wolman spoke, bits and pieces of the Radiant City, the new buildings the LI had called vertical ghettos and apartment-house morgues, were being raised all over the world: from Le Corbusier's own "l'Unité d'habitation" in Marseilles, France, to the Godzilla homage of the Pruitt-Igoe housing complex in St. Louis, Missouri. Because this work served "the worst forces of repression," Wolman said, "it is going to completely disappear," and so soon the Situationist International was formed to make it happen, even if all the group had to offer were cleanly printed words against reinforced concrete, odd theories that might someday be realized as graffiti, and Wolman was left behind.

After his exclusion from the LI, Wolman earned his living as an artist, making objects and selling them, but he stuck to the LI's aesthetic—it was his as much as anyone's. He tried to construct by overturning what was already there; he practiced only détournement, the idea that in a world that had yet to be changed only a distortion of the images everyone took for granted could equal the weight of the blank page. Wolman went back to the papers; in 1963, on his way to *Duhring Duhring*, he discovered scotch art. He took Scotch tape, laid it down over headlines, lifted the tape, removed the words, and smeared them back into pages that might have been composed under water. He made his own papers, many organized around a specific date, be it his own wedding day, André Breton's death day, a May '68 day, the best news of the week, but in his hands the liquid streamers said that the events they spoke for were more controlling than anyone suspected, and less real: the worst news of the week. Time swirled, too fast for anyone to keep up with it; it stood still, denying the possibility that any new story might be told. The news was that there was no escape from history, even if history was only a noise.

Wolman did it for years. He said that words were meaningless and that they ruled the world: the spectacle was permanent. And yet Wolman's work communicated anything but surrender. It was a proof that what appeared to be was not, that the empowered facts of every day's headlines were part of an old-world art project no less arbitrary than anyone's poem. And it was this perspective that in 1979 led Wolman to fashion the line, "we were against the power of words—against power." More than twenty years after his exclusion from the LI, he was still working out the group's slogans.

"Why was he excluded?" I asked Michèle Bernstein, in 1957 one of those who voted Wolman out. "There are always two reasons for anything," she said. "There is always the good reason, and there is always the real reason. But even if I remembered the real reason, I wouldn't tell you."

BORN

Born in Paris in 1932, Bernstein grew up in Normandy; the war began when she was seven. Her parents had divorced long before, but her father was Jewish—though her mother remarried and gave Michèle the name of her gentile stepfather, that meant nothing to the Nazis. "Don't ever let anyone at school know you're a Jew," Bernstein's mother told her. The little girl's response sums up the woman she became: "Guess what!"

Gil J Wolman, untitled scotch art, 1974

she immediately announced to her friends in a big stage whisper, out of earshot of her teachers. "I'm a Jew!"

In 1985 she didn't tell the story idly. My wife and I were in Bernstein's tiny Paris pied-à-terre, a room decorated mainly with books and a sign on the wall: "RUE SAUVAGE." It was a relic from a street the LI once tried to save from demolition; the group thought the way the spirit of the street ("the most disruptive nocturnal perspective in the capital") lived up to its name made it a psychogeographical lighthouse. Bernstein handed me a copy of *Libération*, the leftist daily for which she wrote a weekly literary column. The front page carried the latest news on the TWA airliner that Arab terrorists had highjacked to Beirut a few days before. I read the story: under orders, it said, a German stewardess had selected those individuals with "Jewish-sounding names" from the passenger manifest, and they had been removed from the plane to a then-unknown fate. The selection had been opposed by some crew members, who feared that "innocent people"—that is, people who were in fact not Jews, but whose names "sounded Jewish"—might be lumped with the presumptively guilty: real Jews. "Are you flying home on TWA?" Bernstein asked sweetly. Yes, we said. "Got your yellow stars ready?"

She was small, with close-cut gray hair and a round face. She looked a bit like Gertrude Stein, with all of the imperiousness gone from the mouth, the eagerness to judge replaced by happy eyes. She was not an obvious match for the woman whose LI and SI writings, and her two novels, can be caught in a few words: cold, cruel, severe, unforgiving. The most striking essays practiced intellectual terrorism (notably "No Useless Leniency," *I.S.* no. 1, a defense of the strategy of, so to speak, recruitment through exclusion: "We have become stronger, and therefore more seductive"); the novels, both centering on "Geneviève" and "Gilles," versions of herself and Debord, her husband from 1954 to 1971, were about people living it out.

"I was a very greedy and devious girl," Bernstein said. "It's hard to imagine, now, that Gil and I were ever involved in anything as aggressive as l'Internationale lettriste. Most of us turned out to be rather nice people! But I was absolutely sure we would all be famous—and that we would replace the old world with a new one, that we would make the social revolution."

Bernstein enrolled at the Sorbonne; soon bored with her classes, she began wandering the streets, looking for kindred spirits. "One day I opened the door of a cafe—and I found my people. They were alcoholics—very young alcoholics, as we all were. They would come together in the afternoon; then there would be music, noise, talk, all through the night."

The cafe was Chez Moineau, 22 rue de Four, a block from Saint-Germain-des-Prés. People from all over the world passed through. It was a haven for refugees (Chtcheglov was from the Soviet Union), would-be artists, budding suicides, runaways and class cutters, petty criminals, dope pushers, bums, eccentrics (one old man regularly appeared in a Japanese warrior's helmet from which, by means of a wire, he flew a pack of cigarettes), and the new Lettrist International, which is to say a table, where sat those Debord judged ready to change the world. "Some, like Serge Berna, already had their legends," Bernstein said. "The rest became famous later on—oh, not all, not me, as you can see! It was not all lettriste. There were the nouveaux realistes and the realistes fantastiques. With us were Ivan Chtcheglov and Henry de Béarn—you can tell by the name, he came from a very noble family. Later he became a Gaullist; like so many, he finally became what he had been. Jean-Michel Mension"—Bernstein opened a book of Ed van der Elsken's photographs, the 1981 *Parijs!*, to the page of Mension and Fred running down the street in their colored hair ("The punks invented nothing!" she said)—"was only with us for a moment. He was from a Communist family. Today he is a bureaucrat in the Parti communiste.

"Chtcheglov and de Béarn were living in a loft, and every night the light from the Eiffel Tower would shine in their eyes. They decided to blow it up"—not as a political act, not as a nihilist affirmation, but because it kept them awake—"and they were arrested. With the dynamite. It was in all the papers. I don't know if they were really going to do it. Of course they had talked about it to everybody."

Van der Elsken had a living to make. Like every other photographer in Paris, he took a lot of pictures of lovers embracing on rainy streets, but Moineau's was his hangout as much as anyone's. Though Debord forbade him on pain of violence to shoot the LI, van der Elsken roamed the room, aiming into the mirrors that covered the walls. In some ways, the pictures he got say as much about the LI as the manifestos the group was writing at its table—a fact Debord acknowledged when he clipped images out of van der Elsken's first book, a photo-novel called *Love on the Left Bank*, and dropped them into *Mémoires*.

They are pictures of people at home in their milieu. Anonymous camera subjects step out of hundred-year-old bohemian clichés and become individuals, making demands on the people around them, and on whoever is looking at them. No matter how crowded a scene, there always seems to be more room in it; the hubbub never diminishes the autonomy of the noisemakers. Solitary figures look not isolated, but merely left alone. A terrific sense of expectancy moves in the room. There's a feeling that anything can happen, at any moment: a fight, an embrace, a fit, an oath, a new face, a new idea.

The people van der Elsken shot were mostly destitutes— acolytes of a cult of voluntary poverty. In *Potlatch* no. 22 ("Vacation Issue"), the LI published "The Division of Labor," an accounting of the temporary jobs its "theoreticians" found it necessary to take in order to stave off starvation while pursuing the theory of the abolition of work: "Interpreter, hairdresser, telephone operator, statistician, knitter, receptionist, boxer, writer-for-hire, real-estate agent, dishwasher, salesperson, mail carrier, African hunter, typist, filmmaker, turner, tutor, unskilled laborer, secretary, butcher, bartender, sardine packer." Throughout the LI and SI years, Bernstein worked as a racetrack prognosticator ("I made it all up)", a horoscopist ("That too"), a publisher's assistant, and finally a successful advertising director ("To us, you understand, it was *all* spectacle; advertising was not worse than anything else. We took our money where we could find it"). But that was later. In Moineau's, money came from theft, begging, passing out advertising leaflets, escorting tourists, hauling crates, poker, dealing drugs, chess, scholarships, parental allowances. The sort of fight Mension and Fred picked meant jail, which meant a bed and a meal. Some people had rooms; others slept in the metro, on park benches, in all-night cinemas, or in the cafe. Hashish was smoked openly in Moineau's; there was a lot of sexual conflict, a lot of fighting; the police made regular raids to round up girls under eighteen. People drank far more than they ate; the smiling, fiftyish barmaid, as van der Elsken put it, "cleaned up their vomit." One of his photos is unforgettable: a boy with his head down on a table, dead to the world, in front of him a dish with a few bills and a note. "I need 450 F [about $1.65] for a room to make love in," it reads. "All gifts accepted. Don't wake me up."

Photos of other delinquents of the time show very different people. The "Edwardians"—the Teddy Boys, working-class London youths whose early-1950s imitation of fin-de-siècle English dandies was taken by the press as an act of violence, a disruption of class codes prefiguring a refusal of class status—arrange their bodies into nihilist manifestos. Each is a match for the pose Debord assumed in *Ion*, as if cool were somehow imprinted in those born in the 1930s. But looking at the pictures now, one sees a cool so still it truly is a kind of violence. The impression is that the slightest shift of hand or mouth would not merely alter the image but shatter it, and maybe the frame—the social frame—too. One can look a little harder, and see that, for the Edwardians, cool means the transcendence of the desire for pleasure, a transcendence producing the greatest pleasure of all, oblivion.

For all their depths, though, there is something creepily false in these photos. It's the same quality captured a few years later in Larry Clark's pictures of Tulsa speed freaks, or in Jurgen Vollmer's pictures of the early Beatles in Hamburg. Here, one can watch the invention of pop culture, its reception, and its instant reinvention: a form of the reversible connecting factor. An image of negation is made in a song, in a movie (the first film to exploit the Spivs, precursors of the Edwardians, appeared in 1950), in a novel, in the cut of a coat, in a gesture; the new media transmit the image, and suddenly people all over the world are living it out. But because the content of the reversible connecting factor remains unexamined, not the sign of a new world but simply a sign of separation from the old, one can also watch the instant self-destruction of pop culture, and see cool freeze. The people in the pictures seem to be exchanging inheritance for genre, burying their nascent personalities in received images—images that might save them from a preordained future, that might burn off countless layers of conditioning and force an irruption of demand through centuries of acceptance, and all they do is fade into themselves. What wouldn't they have given, one might think, to speak even as incoherently as Mension did in "general strike"! To speak even that incoherently, though, they would have had to at least vaguely considered concepts like "oblivion." They would have had to have wanted to speak—to have been, like the LI, possessed by the need to explain themselves and to explain the world, a need that is antithetical to cool. They would have had to have understood that if they were making themselves up out of received images, as the LI tried to make itself up out of chosen images, then that was what they were doing.

They didn't, and this is why so many of the pictures of these people seem staged: they were, though not necessarily by the photographers. Vollmer's famous picture of John Lennon, posing in a Hamburg doorway around 1960 (reproduced on the cover of Lennon's 1975 lp *Rock 'n' Roll*), almost exactly recapitulates a once-famous newspaper photo of Edwardian Colin Donellan. Lennon cannot have missed it; his pose is almost evidence that, as a schoolboy, he had Donellan's picture pinned on his bedroom wall.

"Colin Donellan, at 22 a convicted thief and burglar, has, since the age of eight, been in the hands of the police," reads the caption in London's *Picture Post*, 10 October 1953. "He has been to approved [reform] schools, Borstals [juvenile prisons] of varying degrees of severity, and an adult gaol"; he stands with his back against the window of a men's wear shop, talking to a friend. Donellan is not looking at the camera; his clothes and hair are beautiful. He holds himself in menacing repose. In this carefully constructed moment, his eyes are empty; the scene is too perfect not to have been recorded. Donellan's picture is that of someone waiting; he has taken his own picture by waiting for it to be taken.

Here one sees a set; in Moineau's a setting. Before van der Elsken's lens, the spirit is that of movement, interest, uncertainty. The girls and boys in Moineau's seem oblivious of anybody but themselves; their peers seem to await a response, to offer themselves to a future they do not expect to make, to a history already judging them as deviants, anomalies, curios. Donellan and his pop-culture cousins seem to be auditioning for movies they've already seen; the people in Moineau's seem to be having fun.

. . . .

DALAI LAMA SAYS HE DIDN'T START RIOTS

The Dalai Lama, the exiled Tibetan leader, has rejected Chinese charges that he instigated the recent anti-Chinese riots in Lhasa and has accused Beijing of seeking a scapegoat for its own failures, a spokesman said yesterday.

Tahi Wangdi, the spokesman in New Delhi for the Dalai Lama, said, "No one has instigated the trouble from outside."

—San Francisco Chronicle,
3 November 1987

. . . .

1953

1953 began around a table and ended with the table in pieces. By August, the fast time caught in Wolman's letter to Brau had yielded to the deadly pace of *I.L.* no. 3, a lifeless broadsheet. "Indifference in the face of the suffocating values of the present is not permitted us, not when those values are guaranteed by a society of prisons, and we live on their doorsteps," Debord wrote dully in "To Be Done with the Comforts of Nihilism." "We don't want to participate at any price, or to accept our own silence, to accept . . . Red wine and negation in the cafes, the first truths of despair will not be the end of these lives, these lives so hard to defend against the traps of silence, against the hundred ways of TAKING SIDES." Bossuet's elegiac voice was already rising up, turning the echo of Saint-Just's voice in Debord's conclusion into a non sequitur: "We have to

Colin Donellan, 1953

Moineau's, 1953, by Ed van der Elsken

attest to a certain idea of happiness, even if we have known it to fail . . . We have to promote an insurrection that would matter to us." Debord might as well have called for a revival of the Spanish Civil War—which, just a hairline rule to the left, he and the rest of the LI did. "The Middle Ages begin at the border," they said in *I.L.* no. 3's one dashing phrase, "and our silence seals it." It was an admission that the LI's own terrain had turned up empty.

The group blew apart. Some quit; others were kicked out. Those who remained continued the search for the hacienda, drifting from one odd bar to another, writing down incidents they tried to make strange. Not a word appeared until June 1954, when Debord, Wolman, Dahou, and two or three others ran off the first fifty copies of the new *Potlatch* and began mailing them out to whoever they thought might most want to read it, or most not want to. The LI never published Chtcheglov's "Formula for a New Urbanism," which would not see the light of day until June 1958, in *I.S.* no. 1, and by then Chtcheglov was already crazy.

"He went mad," Bernstein said in 1983. "But he was not mad. He had been excluded—he was convinced the Dalai Lama was controlling what was happening to us. And then, one day, he had a fight with his wife. He broke up a cafe, smashed everything. His wife—who was a *swine*—called the police. She called an ambulance. Because she was his wife, she was able to commit him. He was taken away to an institution, and given insulin shock. And electroshock. After that, he was mad. Guy and I went to visit him: he was eating with his hands, with saliva dripping from his mouth. He was mad—the way you know when someone is mad. The letters he wrote to us were babble. And he is still there, if he is not dead. He was very shortly sent to a halfway house, where he had freedom, where he could come and go. But he had developed the disease where he could not live outside of the asylum, where he could not stand to be anywhere else, where he did not want to be anywhere else." Bernstein wrapped her arms around herself, making a straitjacket: "Whenever he came out, he became scared, and rushed back. So he took part in the asylum theater; he put on plays. And I think he is still there."

It is not hard to imagine that Chtcheglov's fall sealed the LI as a group. His destruction was an event, which gave the LI a tangible past, made the long year of doing nothing into a myth, into a story that could be told—made it real. The group had spent its time walking the streets, taking notes, then explaining its project to itself—that was all, from the attack on Chaplin to the first issue of *Potlatch*. "An art film on this generation," Debord explained in *On the Passage of a Few People Through a Rather Brief Moment in Time*, his film on those months, "can only be a film about the absence of its real works." But Chtcheglov's absence was a real work: if the momentary seizure of Notre-Dame was the LI's founding crime as legend (with Serge Berna, present in the cathedral, then within the LI, the group's link to its imaginary past), Chtcheglov's exclusion was the LI's founding crime as act—a symbolic murder, since to the LI exclusion meant civil death. It was no help that in 1957, with the formation of the SI, Debord made Chtcheglov a "member from afar," or that two decades later, in guilt and love, he made a film in which Chtcheglov was the hero; Chtcheglov's exclusion had consequences, and they could not be undone. Even as violence and dementia, those consequences were a form of history, an unsettled debt charged to whatever future the LI might ennoble or fail. Unwanted and unforeseen, those consequences were a proof that the LI could make history: events that could not be taken back. If, simply by pursuing its own philosophy of yes and no, explaining itself and acting on its conclusions, one day sitting down to vote on who should remain and who should not, the group could wreck a life, then it could wreck the world.

OUR TABLES

"Our tables aren't often round," the LI wrote in "36 rue des Morillons," "but one day, we're going to build our own 'castles of adventure.'" The group emerged from the year of the contin-

THE CHRONICLES OF ARTHUR *relate how King Arthur, with the help of a Cornish carpenter, invented the marvel of his court, the miraculous Round Table at which his knights would never come to blows . . . The carpenter says to Arthur: "I will make thee a fine table, where sixteen hundred may sit at once, and from which none need be excluded . . ."*

—*Marcel Mauss,* Essai sur le don (The Gift), *1925*

uous dérive with a sense of necessity, relaxing its ban on work and committing itself to a regular publication schedule. It stepped out again with a less abstract, more playful sense of reality, gleefully chronicling the best news of the week. The members of the LI remained planners of an imaginary city, but now they were also its critics—they saw that all cities were imaginary, complexes of desires turned into geography or suppressed by it, and they saw that all cities could be explored. Thus the LI toured Guatemala City in 1954, full of firing squads, setting up for vacationers, a cheap holiday in other people's misery; it visited the Catharist town of Beziers in 1209, on the day it was exterminated by the pope's armies in the Albigensian Crusade ("Kill them all," the papal commander said when a lieutenant asked him how believers in the True Church might be distinguished from the heretics, "God will recognize his own"); it crisscrossed the East End of London in 1888, guided by Jack the Ripper, "the psychogeographer of love." The imaginary city was Haussmann's Paris, a fantasy of commodities and their troops—and it was the belief that if one could find the right street, one could escape from that city into Chtcheglov's.

In the SI Debord called this instant route to total change the reversible connecting factor; in the LI he named it the "Northwest Passage." The metaphor wasn't geographical, it was psychogeographical—it was psychogeography itself. It belonged to the history of the modern city and to the prehistory of the dérive; Debord found it in *Confessions of an English Opium Eater*, the memoir Thomas de Quincey published in 1821.

"I remember long, wonderful psychogeographical walks in London with Guy," Alexander Trocchi said in 1983, a year before his death. "He took me to places in London I didn't know, that he didn't know, that he sensed, that I'd never have been to if I hadn't been with him. He was a man who could discover a city." The two met in 1955 in Paris, where Trocchi, born in 1925 in Glasgow, was serving one god as a pornographer for Maurice Girodias' Olympia Press, another as the editor of *Merlin*, a somber avant-garde quarterly. Joining the LI, Trocchi had to cut all ties, break with his friends and employers: "I stopped speaking to them. I was to enter into a closed society, a clandestine group, which was to be my whole world." He was near sixty when we met, and he looked forty; he was built strong, all power, his eyes set deep but piercing and clear. A huge, intimidating nose came out of his face like a claw. It was impossible to believe he had been a heroin addict for almost thirty years.

Though Trocchi left Paris in 1956 for the United States, when the SI was formed Debord counted him a founding, active situationist. In 1960 Trocchi published *Cain's Book*, an autobiographical novel in the form of a junkie's journal: "Il vous faut construire les situations," he wrote in the last pages. He was speaking of the fix: "systematic nihilism," but also "a purposive spoon in the broth of experience."

For a long time I have suspected there is no way out. I can do nothing I am not. I have been living destructively towards the writer in me for some time, guiltily conscious of doing so all along, cf. the critical justification in terms of the objective death of an historical tradition: a decadent at a tremendous turning point in history, constitutionally incapable of turning with it as a writer, I am living my personal Dada. In all of this there is a terrible emotional smear. The steel of the logic has daily to be strengthened to contain the volcanic element within. It grows daily more hard to contain. I am a kind of bomb.

This was the sort of person Debord wanted, but Trocchi never really returned. *Cain's Book* made him famous in bohemian circles in Britain, and in 1962, in London, he began Project Sigma, an attempt to unite every sort of dissident and experimental cultural tendency into an international corps of "cosmonauts of inner space." Debord published Trocchi's Sigma manifesto in *I.S.* no. 8, January 1963, but there followed the ambiguous note that it was "no longer as a member of the SI" that Trocchi pursued his "technique du coup du monde," his "invisible insurrection of a million minds"—to Debord, Trocchi's association with people like occultist Colin Wilson and Beat poet Allen Ginsberg, both of whom Debord had long since dismissed as "mystical cretins," was a resignation absent la lettre. To Trocchi, Debord's demurral was an exclusion, and he never got over it.

"Guy thought the world was going to collapse on its own, and we were going to take over," Trocchi said in 1983. "I wanted to do that—to take over the world. But you can't take over the world by excluding people from it! Guy wouldn't even *mention* the names of the people I was involved with—Timothy Leary, Ronnie Laing. I remember the last letter he sent me: 'Your name sticks in the minds of decent men.' He was like Lenin; he was an absolutist, constantly kicking people out—until he was the only one left. And exclusions were total. It meant ostracism, cutting people. Ultimately, it leads to shooting people—that's where it would have led, if Guy had ever 'taken over.' And I couldn't shoot anyone."

"It wasn't a question of loyalty," Trocchi said; he raised his hands. "Guy has my loyalty. I loved the man." Suddenly Trocchi turned away from me and shouted. *"Guy, Guy,"* he said, "WHAT IS IT? *I am talking to you now, even if you will never speak to me!"*

We were in a fifth-floor walkup in a seedy section of Kensington. Trocchi had plans for screenplays, movies, a memoir; he made his living dealing third-class rare books out of a tiny stall on Portobello Road. His apartment was littered with syringes and busted ampules. The walls were hung with founding situationist Constant's diagrams of his own new city: "In New Babylon, man has been freed from his burdens, builds life himself." I copied the words into my notebook: this, I thought, was where the great project of transforming the world had ended up.

Even in the moment, the irony failed to cut very deeply, perhaps because Trocchi had already circled away from the great project. He was speaking again of its smallest version, where the desire to take over the world was first the desire to be in the world, a desire driven by the conviction that one cannot truly be in the world until the alienation of each from all has been vanquished, until necessity has been banished, until the world has been changed. Trocchi was talking again about the dérive—there, he said, for as long as it lasted, you were in the world as if you were changing it, and there were intimations of utopia everywhere you looked. "The difficulties of the dérive are those of freedom," Debord wrote in 1956 in "Theory of the Dérive." "It all rests on the belief that the future will precipitate an irreversible change in the behavior and the decor of present-day society. One day, we will construct cities for drifting . . . but with light retouching, one can utilize certain zones which already exist. One can utilize certain persons who already exist." Even if he had been used, that was what Trocchi remembered most sweetly, so he talked about getting drunk, chasing oblivion into the black hole, the way out, the Northwest Passage. "There was a magical quality to Guy," Trocchi said. He was almost smiling; the flux of emotion in the previous half-hour had confused both of us, but now he was happy. "Distances didn't seem to matter to the man. Walking in London, in the daytime, at night, he'd bring me to a spot he'd found, and the place would begin to live. Some old, forgotten part of London. Then he'd reach back for a story, for a piece of history, as if he'd been born there. He'd quote from Marx, or *Treasure Island*, or de Quincey—do you know de Quincey?"

I used often, after I had taken opium, to wander forth, without much regarding the direction or the distance, to all the markets, and other parts of London, to which the poor resort on a Saturday night, for laying out their wages . . . Some of these rambles led me to great distances: for an opium-eater is too happy to observe the motion of time. And sometimes in my attempts to steer homewards, upon nautical principles, by fixing my eye on the pole-star, and seeking ambitiously for a north-west passage, instead of circumnavigating all the capes and headlands I had doubled in my outward voyage, I came suddenly upon such knotty problems of alleys, such enigmatical entries, and such sphinx's riddles of streets without thoroughfares, as must, I conceive, baffle the audacity of porters, and confound the intellects of hackney-coachmen. I could almost have believed, at times, that I must be the first discoverer of some of these *terrae incognitae*, and doubted, whether they had yet been laid down in the modern charts of London. For all this, however, I paid a heavy price in distant years, when the human face tyrannized over my dreams, and the perplexities of my steps in London came back to haunt me.

By the summer of 1954 this was part of the LI's myth—and just as the catacombs were really a symbol and the Northwest Passage was not really a place, the dérive too was now less a practice than a metaphor, capable of judging every word the LI wrote and, after that, every sentence the SI tried to pass. The LI believed in "continental drift" (geophysics today, but science fiction in 1954)—that is, as streets could be capes and headlands, and neighborhoods deserts or swamps, they all moved. They moved away from an unconsciously remembered wholeness—of "Pangaea," the original supercontinent of two hundred million years ago, or "Nostratic," the supposed common language of the Upper Paleolithic; of the Garden of Eden or Paris as a Commune—and into a dyslexia of separations. In his "Theory of the Dérive" Debord paused over a sociologist's study on "the narrowness of the real Paris in which each individual lives," citing the professor's diagram of all the movements undertaken by one student in the course of an entire year: "With no deviations, her itinerary delineates a small triangle, the summits of which are the School of Political Science, her residence, and that of her piano teacher." This, Debord said, was an example of "modern poetry, capable of provoking keen emotional reactions—in this case, indignation that it is possible to live like that."

A year or so later, Debord cut up maps of Paris and pasted them into psychogeographical maps; they differ from the imaginary maps geographers have made of the fragmentation of Pangaea into the continents we take for granted only because Debord's arrows point to unity as well as separation. But to recreate that unity—the whole world as a single round table—the separation had to be publicized. Before people would reject it, it had to be made undeniable. It had to be made into an event, and to be made into an event separation had to be intensified, turned into ruin and noise. The project could begin,

Debord wrote, with the construction of "an atmosphere of uneasiness": with a small group of people, who might hitch-hike "nonstop and without destination" during a transit strike to add to the confusion, or turn up on the streets in disguise, or publish plans for the raising of a house meant to be abandoned after its housewarming—"the greatest difficulty in such an undertaking is to convey through such apparently delirious proposals a sufficient degree of *serious seduction* . . . We need to work toward flooding the market—even if for the moment only the intellectual market—with a mass of desires whose realization is not beyond the capacity of man's present means of action on the material world, but only beyond the capacity of social organization as it stands."

If the LI, playing its game of freedom, could spread desires for a way of life neither government nor the market could ever satisfy, then people would overturn them—or ignore them, finding satisfaction in a drift through the city's Northwest Passage: "the future," Debord said, "belongs to the passerby." Psychogeography, as Asger Jorn defined it, was "the science fiction of urban planning"; maybe, to prove that separation was no more fated than the current status of the continents, you only had to tell the right story, and turn up the volume.

THERE IS

There is still sound in *Potlatch*, though you can't really speak of turning it up—it's already loud, in a peculiar way. With bits of news from the regular papers running into ultimatums and warnings, which shift into passwords, which themselves make up a secret language that presents itself as public speech, the loudness of the sound is in its aura of spontaneous generation. The voice seems to come out of nowhere, and no accounting of ancestors or familiars, even present on the page, can quite dim that sensation. The old news remains new because the world has turned as if none of it happened; the voice carries the shock of displacement, and it is strong enough to turn displacement into a value.

There's no formal displacement in *Potlatch*. With screaming juxtapositions and colored type overlays exploding incoherent essays printed upside down, Berlin dada journals were paper cabarets; this is not. This is just a sheet of carefully typed words forming grammatical sentences that make neat paragraphs following each other down conventionally sized pages. The displacement is invisible, a time-destroying voice coming off a stenciled piece of paper: a voice whose content is so disproportionate to its form that one or the other seems like a trick. Compared to *Potlatch*, the printed, illustrated numbers of *Internationale lettriste* are official culture; compared to them, *Potlatch* is a return to the clandestine newsletters that hundreds of French Resistance groups produced throughout the Occupation. "In a world where books have long lost all likeness to books," situationist familiar Adorno wrote then, "the real book can no longer be one. If the invention of the printing press inaugurated the bourgeois era, the time is at hand for its repeal by the mimeograph."

The LI put out *Potlatch* from 22 June 1954 to 22 May 1957; no. 29, the final issue, 5 November 1957, carried the legend "Bulletin d'information de l'Internationale situationniste," and the LI swallowed its tale. "We're not interested in a fond place in your memories," read "Potlatch, Directions for Use," no. 2, 29 June 1954. "But concrete powers are at stake. A few hundred people haphazardly determine the thought of the epoch. Whether they know it or not, they are at our disposal. By sending *Potlatch* to people effectively positioned, we can interrupt the circuit when and where we please." You found the thing on your desk, if you worked for a newspaper or the government, or maybe you found it in your mailbox: "Some readers have been chosen arbitrarily." ("You picked names out of the phone book?" I asked Wolman. "Let's not exaggerate," he said. "We didn't have a phone book. For that matter, we didn't have a phone.") Maybe you found it in the street, a throwaway, since the odds were at best one in two that those who got it read it: "You have a chance to be one of them."

As Debord would say, *Potlatch* was a gift, an offering of "nonsalable goods"—"previously unpublished desires and ques-

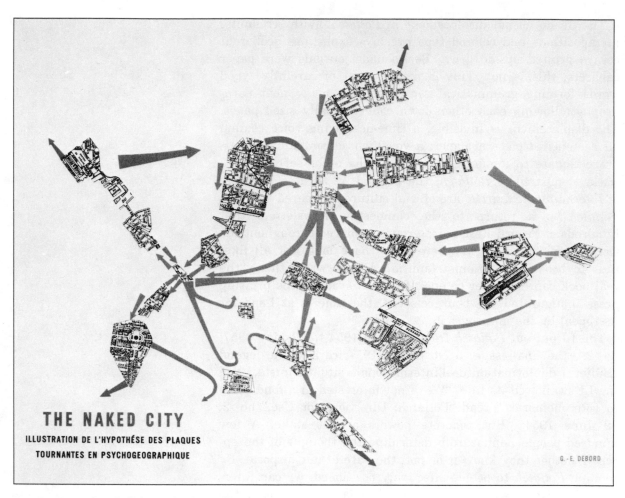

THE NAKED CITY

ILLUSTRATION DE L'HYPOTHÉSE DES PLAQUES
TOURNANTES EN PSYCHOGEOGRAPHIQUE

G.-E. DEBORD

Guy-Ernest Debord, "The Naked City," May 1957

tions, and only their thorough analysis by others can constitute a return gift." It was an attempt to start a conversation—a conversation, though, in which everyone would want to take part and that could only end in the discovery of a new language, with a new subject, which was to say a new idea of social life. "*Potlatch* is the most engaged publication in the world," no. 1 began, the letters slightly blurred, the keys of the typewriter obviously worn. "We are working toward the conscious and collective establishment of a new civilization."

The LI was playing with another metaphor. The ethnographic dictionary defined "potlatch" as "to consume," but the context the word called up was not commercial consumption but "consumed by the fire": it meant a gift that had to be returned until there was nothing left to give. It was a Chinook word, used by the Kwakiutl of British Columbia, the Tlingit of Alaska, Amerindian tribes first studied by anthropologists at the end of the nineteenth century.

These tribes, the anthropologists discovered, had a strange practice: one chief met another and offered gifts. The second chief had to respond in kind, but on a higher plane of value. That was the potlatch. The game might begin with the presentation of a necklace and end with the burning of a town—with a tribe burning its own town, thus raising the obligations of its rival to an almost impossible level. The potlatch was part of a festival, accompanied by storied songs, dances, and the conferral of new names on the great givers ("Whose Property Is Eaten in Feasts," "Causing Trouble All Around," "The Dance of Throwing Away Property"); it could be a symbolic exchange of courtesies and pieties, brought forth by a wedding or a funeral, and it could be a symbolic war, an exchange of challenges and humiliations. There was something in it of D. H. Lawrence's idea of democracy ("if you can call it an idea"): two people meeting on a road, and instead of passing by with eyes averted pausing, like Arthur and Lancelot, for a confrontation "between their very souls," thus setting free the "brave, reckless gods" within—"Now, damn the consequences, we have met." For one tribe to fail to rise to the provocation of another

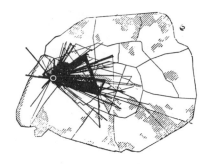

The movements of a student in the 16th arrondissement of Paris over the course of a year, as published in *I.S.* no. 1, June 1958

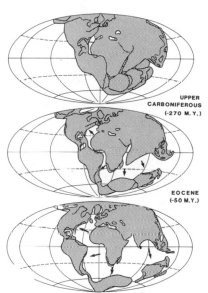

Continental drift showing (top) Pangaea, 270 million years ago, (middle) Laurasia and Gonwonaland, 50 million years ago, and (bottom) later land masses

was to admit that it valued property, mere things, more than honor; a chief who distributed the wealth of his tribe was said to "swallow the tribes" that received it. "The ideal," sociologist Marcel Mauss wrote in 1925 in *The Gift*, "is to give a *potlatch* and not have it returned."

This was no cultural anomaly, Mauss said: the potlatch was an echo of the Golden Age, a survival of a once-universal form of exchange—at its deepest level, it was a form of communication between people who held nothing back. It was a protean economy of emotion and play, as suffused with faith as the modern market was with cynicism, and it was absolute: "We are here confronted with total prestation [payment] in the sense that the whole clan, through the intermediacy of its chief, makes contracts involving all its members and everything it possesses."

It was no matter, to Mauss, that after all the skins and animals were gone the potlatch could end in an orgy of enslavement and human sacrifice—and no accident that Mauss was the nephew and collaborator of Emile Durkheim, theorist of the division of labor. Mauss saw the potlatch as a negation of division, as an affirmation of community. It was, he said, the first round table, "'from which none need be excluded'"—or could be.

Reading Mauss's book, polymath Georges Bataille found something very different: proof of a mythical id-economy of waste and loss hidden within the historical superego-economies of production and accumulation. In 1933, in "The Notion of Expenditure," he brought the potlatch into the present, not as a quaint memory of wholeness but as a permanent psychology of dissolution.

Bataille seized on the potlatch as an expression of humanity's ineradicable attraction to "recklessness, discharge, and upheaval"—"the immense travail," he stated flatly, "that constitutes life." He was writing self-consciously as a gnostic heretic, and that ineradicable attraction, he thought, was at the core of the heresy, deprived by Christianity and rationalism of all ordinary language, and now audible only in the bruitist languages of insanity, crime, dream, perversion, war, and revolution.

Bataille told a new story—a story not all that different from the story of the Martian genes in *Five Million Years to Earth*. Fleeing the absolutes of the potlatch, in which value derived from the possibility of total loss, humanity refounded civilization on the principle of utility and established a system of limits, where everything had its price. But whether civilization reproduced itself through barter, mercantilism, capitalism, or communism, it merely veiled humanity's inherent hatred of utility and limits, disguising its lust for "unconditional expenditure," for activities with "no end beyond themselves"—concealed the truth that oblivion was humanity's ruling passion. The self-destructive man might be legion, but even at his most lucid, Bataille said, he imagines himself outside the human community, a crazy man: "It does not occur to him that society can have, just as he does, an interest in considerable losses, in catastrophes that, *while conforming to well-defined needs*, provoke tumultuous depressions, crises of dread and, in the final analysis, a certain orgiastic state." In Mauss the potlatch was a shadowy performance of what, once, had been real life. Understood, it was a revelation of what real life would always be—even if that reality was now masked by a public culture of rational consumption, which hid the disfigurements of a secret culture, the bourgeois culture of family violence, adultery, incest, prostitution, lying, cheating, swindling, gambling, alcoholism, drug addiction, the modern dance of throwing away property.

All that was left of the public potlatch, Bataille said, was the humiliation the bourgeoisie offered the poor—a humiliation the poor could give back only through revolution, by offering themselves for destruction, asking for a greater destruction in exchange. But the triumph of the bourgeoisie was sealed by its culture, which ensured that the real life of expenditure and loss would be pursued "behind closed doors"—for the bourgeoisie distinguished itself from all other tribes "by the fact that it has consented to spend only for itself and only within itself."

The result, Bataille said, was the disappearance of "everything that was generous, orgiastic, and excessive," and its replacement by a "universal meanness"—the gift of a class so certain of its hegemony, so successful in identifying its history with nature, that it had finally dispensed with its mask, and against all that it still concealed happily exposed its "sordid face, a face so rapacious and lacking in nobility, so frighteningly small, that all human life, upon seeing it, seems degraded."

That was the ideal: the potlatch, the humiliation, that could not be returned. The poor, caught up in the promise that someday they too might spend only for themselves, could not respond. Neither could so-called revolutionaries, communists dedicated to production for the sake of use, blind to the passion for expenditure for the sake of loss. All, Bataille said, were prisoners of the fiction of utility—"and if a less arbitrary conception is condemned to remain esoteric, and if as such, in the present circumstances, it comes into conflict with an unhealthy repulsion, then one must stress that this repulsion is precisely the shame of a generation whose rebels are afraid of the noise of their own words."

Bataille was laying down a challenge; twenty-one years later, the LI picked it up. All of these meanings were present when the group chose the word "potlatch" to name its second life—and in 1954 the group could find a meaning in the word that might have gone unnoticed two or three decades earlier. Everything the LI had to say, all of its yesses and noes, rested on the promise of a world of abundance; the potlatch tribes, Mauss and Bataille had noted almost in passing, already lived in it. Because they were rich in meat and hides, they could afford to play a game of real life. Like the LI with its unexplained "creation of situations," the Kwakiutl and the Tlingit, with their ritualized exchange of affirmations and negations, reveled in abstraction; the potlatch was not merely a protean economy, it was a prophetic economy. As an absolute the potlatch was an exchange of everything that could not be put on the market; for it to function all commodities had to be taken off the market and raised above it, until the poorest trinket could symbolize the whole life of the tribe. So it would be, when the new civilization came into being; God would be dead, and everything would be sacred.

"Potlatch" was just a metaphor—a means of understanding the way the small becomes huge, of deciphering, say, the inexorably rising stakes of a confrontation between a husband and a wife ("the *potlatch* of complicity," Bernstein wrote in *La Nuit*), or the apparent lunacy of people burning their own town ("the *potlatch* of destruction," as the SI said of Watts), or the sudden expansion of a solitary refusal into an explosion: a few troublemakers, a few cops, a riot, the army, then the social order called into question. But metaphors are transformations, proofs of the arbitrary nature of language, grants of mystery to ordinary things—they are in other words incipient utopias. For the LI, the appeal of the potlatch metaphor was in its ability to simultaneously symbolize dissolution and community, in its suggestion that the commodity could lose the magic Marx had glimpsed in it. The table would once again be wood, still and powerless, but people would dance around it; that would be utopia, which would be a permanent potlatch of surprise. Walking the streets of the cities built for drifting, you'd meet other people; you'd exchange glances, then gestures, then words, arguments, agreements, insults, embraces. These situations would be open, made to be lived by their creators. Shaped by settings of reassurance and fear, there would be an intensity never before known in everyday life. You'd lose yourself in the oblivion of action; you'd know you were making it happen. Like John Wayne and Montgomery Clift in their fight at the end of *Red River*, you'd exchange love and hate, life and death; like the Tramp and the Flower Girl in the last shots of *City Lights*, you'd exchange terror and redemption; like Fred Astaire and Ginger Rogers dancing "Night and Day" in *The Gay Divorcee*, you'd exchange hesitations and commitments, repulsions and attractions. Arlene Croce describes it:

Abruptly she turns and crosses the set; he blocks her. She crosses and he blocks her. She turns away, he catches her wrist, their eyes meet and he dances ingratiatingly. Again she turns, again he catches her and she walks into the dance. When she stands away, he pulls her by the hand and she coils against him, wrapping herself in her own arm, as the free hand holds that wrist. In this position, together as if cradled, they just drift . . .

This would be the new beauty, provisional and lived. Anything could happen; you would find out what happened next. There would be no repetition. Time would move, and you would sense the passing of time, the accumulation of events that cannot be taken back—the "*necessary* alienation," Debord said—and with that sensation you would come alive, because you'd be making your own history. "The moment was temporary like everything is," Paul McCartney once said of his years as a Beatle. "Nothing in life really stays. And it's beautiful that they go. They have to go in order for the next thing to come. You can almost add to the beauty of a thing by accepting that it's temporary." To make this happen—that was what Debord meant by the wish "to realize the collective art of our time," what the LI meant by "the perfecting of a complete divertissement." From 1952 through May 1968, through all the furious, step-by-step demolitions of every dominant image of the good, behind them, all the obscure intimations of a new way of walking and a new way of talking, that was the situationist project—that was all it ever was.

I HAVE

I have tried to make the ethos the LI claimed into a narrative, to fill in the gaps, to make it at least half as clear as it was to Debord, Wolman, Bernstein, and the rest—inevitably, to make their old papers into something fit for rational consumption. They didn't. The voice in *Potlatch* is unfailingly logical, but it's the logic of people so caught up in their own vision that it can explain anything to them. For anyone else, there are gaps in the logic that can't be closed, and the controlling gap was implicit in the medium itself.

In 1985 Debord republished the complete run of *Potlatch* in a brightly typeset, cleanly designed book with a purple cover; it gives a sheen of likelihood, of investment and return, to words that first trumpeted their messages of destruction and rebirth in a realm outside apparent possibility, dim and smudged on loose sheets of mimeo. The elegance of print empowers the most impossible sentence, translates its noise into at least a facsimile of discourse, but noise and powerlessness were a lot of what *Potlatch* was about. Those values were self-evident in the original form; in a book, they have to dismantle the orderliness of official culture all over again. Reading *Potlatch* today—especially the first nine numbers, when a weekly schedule held and the LI tried to say everything at once—is first of all confusing; even if one plumbs every allusion, what remains is spooky.

"A new civilization," it says in no. 1; then in "All the Water in the Sea Couldn't . . ." Debord laconically summarizes the latest news on teenage suicides, the execution of anarchists in Spain, the execution of a rebel leader in Kenya, and the corruption of various French littérateurs. What the latter need, Debord says, "is the Terror"—which is what the former have already gotten. That's the implication, anyway (the reader is back in 1794, which has turned into 1954, except that 1954 has turned 1794 against its rightful inheritors); Debord does not explain.

A month later, with no. 5, 20 July 1954, the reader is back in the thirteenth century, which is also the future. "The Cathars Were Right," announces a headline, running above a *Combat* item on an American physicist's discovery of the antiproton, which subsumes a few brief dispatches on the CIA's coup against the democratic government in Guatemala; save for the headline and a subhead, there is no commentary from the LI.

"The proton is the nucleus of the hydrogen atom, and, in consequence, constitutes the basic element of all terrestrial matter," *Combat* says. "A proton and an antiproton—which will collide in mutual destruction. Thus the antiproton will be capable of annihilating all matter composed of protons. In essence, this will be 'anti-matter.' Nevertheless, it appears impossible for them to combine with enough force to destroy the planet." A nice touch, that "Nevertheless"—although perhaps no solace to deposed president Jacobo Arbenz and his supporters, the silent subjects of the LI's "Conclusion." *Le Figaro*: "The new government of Guatemala will disallow the right of illiterates to vote." *Paris-Presse*: "General Carlos Castillo Armas, head of the rebels who have gained victory in Guatemala, has been named president by the military junta." *L'Humanité*: "Castillo Armas defines his politics: 'The justice of the firing squad.'"

The *Potlatch* reader might have remembered the LI's report in no. 1: Arbenz instituted a modest land-reform program, the United Fruit Company complained, U.S. Secretary of State John Foster Dulles proclaimed what the LI called a "crusade" against what Dulles called "the forces of evil," the CIA organized a small group of Guatemalan military officers, and the LI called on Arbenz to "arm the workers." He didn't, troops were launched from Honduras, bombing commenced, the government fell, Arbenz escaped—so in no. 3 the LI brought on Saint-Just to curse him with the maxim that "Those who make a revolution by halves only dig their own graves." Someone's grave—the result was that, thirty years later, it was policy in Guatemala that any peasant found wearing glasses was to be shot on sight. That was the story the LI was telling in "The Cathars Were Right"—but what, the *Potlatch* reader might ask, did it have to do with the antiproton, and what did the antiproton have to do with the Cathars?

The LI was playing with history: "The Cathars Were Right" was a complex détournement, a set of reversals produced by the simplest juxtapositions. The only necessary tools were a few newspapers, a pair of scissors, a jar of paste, a sense of loathing, a sense of humor, and the notion that to be against power was to be against the power of words—it was a game, and like all games it had its rules. Détournement was a dis-course of noise made out of "prefabricated elements"; the origi-nal elements, Debord and Wolman wrote in 1956 in "Methods of Détournement," lose their original meanings in the flux of separation from their original contexts, but each element takes on a new meaning when combined with another, and the com-bination produces a meaning that supersedes its constituent elements. Titling is crucial; the most distant, out-of-place ele-ment is the most suggestive; the false author works on the conditioned reader like a psychoanalyst drawing out an analy-sand, playing on the reader's vague recollection of the original meaning of the most distant element, so that the small be-comes huge, an ancient memory a history—which is to say that, here, one was to vaguely recall that in the thirteenth century, in Languedoc, in southern France, the Christian here-tics known as Cathars believed in gnostic dualism.

The Cathars believed that the cosmos was divided equally between the good God, the God of the Spirit, and Satan, the evil God, "Rex Mundi," creator and king of the world. Heaven, the realm of the good God, was a place of affection and de-light, a festive hearth; the earth was altogether the realm of Satan, and the good God could not save it, because he had not made it. Everything terrestrial was evil: "nature and matter were not and could not be the work of the good God," Emman-uel Le Roy Ladurie writes in *Montaillou: The Promised Land of Error*, his 1975 study of the last Cathars. He cited a be-liever: "'It is the devil and not God who makes the plants flower and bear grain.'" And it was Satan who made the hu-man body grow and reproduce.

The Catharism of Montaillou was first and foremost a story, a myth. It was told over and over again, with variations, around the fire. To begin with there was the Fall. The Devil succeeded in leading astray some of the spirits surrounding the good God in Heaven. They fell from Heaven and were imprisoned here below by their seducer in ves-tures of earth, bodies of flesh, shaped in the clay of oblivion. These fallen souls sped madly from one deceased body to another, one ves-ture of decay into another.

This was life as a horror movie, a medieval *Night of the Living Dead*—but there was a way out. Someday the lost soul might find a body that could receive the Catharist sacrament of the consolamentum (consolation); then one would abjure all sin, a renunciation symbolized by one's refusal of sexual intercourse and the eating of flesh, and the soul's return to heaven, to the loving community where "the sacred was only the social, transfigured," would be assured. Those who were willing to become parfaits (the perfect) would assume the sacrament in the prime of life, in order to administer it to the credentes (believers), who would wait until they were on the verge of death to receive it—which meant that in the meantime the credentes could live a life of total liberty. Since in the end one would be absolved of all the sins one had ever committed, some Cathars believed what the Brethren of the Free Spirit, the Lollards, the Anabaptists, and the Ranters would preach in the centuries to come: that men and women could commit any sin, "and do whatever they please in this world." The world was matter and it was vile, human beings were matter and they were vile—but with the consolamentum and one's return to the world of the spirit, matter was naught. Only deliverance was true, and "until this moment"—which the consoled credente might hasten with the endura, a ritual suicide, a fast to the death—"all was permitted." And all was for the greater good: each pious death, regardless of the filth it left behind, promised the day when the split that rent the cosmos would close. Once all the souls that had fallen from heaven had gone home, there would be nothing left on earth but bodies without souls; with no more souls to enter them, they would decay into nothing, and that would be the end of the world.

So this was the original meaning of the most distant element of the LI's détournement of the news of the week: as the Cathars believed and scientists had finally proved, there was an absolute duality, a world of matter and a world of antimatter. But the juxtaposition of the antiproton and the Guatemalan coup produced new meanings. One could see that the Cathars themselves were antimatter—philosophically, because they were against matter; metaphysically, because as spirits imprisoned in a world of matter they could destroy that world; and historically, because finally it was not the world but the Cathars who were destroyed. Just as Arbenz's reforms threatened capitalism and an independent Guatemala threatened the empire of the United States, the beliefs of the Cathars were a threat to Rome, and Languedoc was an independent province, outside the Kingdom of France—and so with the pope's blessing the barons of the north embarked on the Albigensian Crusade, wiped out the Cathars, and soon fixed the borders of the modern nation where now, in 1954, one read "The Cathars Were Right." But ironies, like metaphors, are turns of phrase, inversions, reversals—one might think the formal division of the universe was not all the Cathars were right about. If they could incarnate antimatter, others could as well.

Dada sought the social atom in the destruction of ordinary language; Isou found its particles in the poetry of the final element, then set them free in the ether, where their charges reversed, repelling old meanings, attracting new ones. The LI was talking to itself. The Cathars were prophets of the destruction of the visible world; so was the LI, which called that world the spectacle.

THAT IS

That is a version of the content of the early *Potlatch*, but nothing like its voice. On its own page, "The Cathars Were Right" is funnier and more ominous than I can make it. My translation is slow and détournement is always quick—a new world in a double take, in the blink of an eye.

The *Potlatch* voice is that of a small group of nobodies scrabbling for bits and pieces of old moments of liberation, for the detritus of what could have been, and since it never was still could be—no matter how old the words, the LI could still be the first to blaze a trail into a new life. Originality was not the point—it was an ideology of creation in a society deter-

potlatch

POTLATCH POTLATCH POTLATCH POTLATCH POTLATCH POTLATCH POTLATCH POTLATCH POTLATCH POTLATCH

bulletin d'information du groupe français de l'internationale lettriste
paraît tous les mardis   n° 5 - 20 juillet 1954

LES CATHARES AVAIENT RAISON

Washington, 9 juillet - Toute la presse américaine publie aujourd'hui des photos
du physicien Marcel Schein, professeur à l'Université de Chicago, de son tableau
noir et de son "anti-proton", mystérieuse particule de matière cosmique qui au-
rait été détectée l'hiver dernier par un ballon sonde à 30 kilomètres au-dessus
du Texas.
Il s'agirait en fait d'une des plus grandes découvertes de la science moderne.
L'anti-proton, recherché depuis des années par les physiciens du monde entier,
serait l'opposé du proton.
Le proton est le noyau de l'atome d'hydrogène et, par conséquent, constitue l'é-
lément de base de tous les corps terrestres. Un proton et un anti-proton qui se
rencontrent se détruisent mutuellement. L'anti-proton serait donc capable d'an-
nihiler toute matière composée de protons. Ce serait essentiellement un "contre-
matière". Il paraît cependant impossible d'en réunir suffisamment pour détruire
la planète.   ("Combat" - 10 juillet)

                    CONCLUSION
                    - Le nouveau gouvernement du Guatemala vient de retirer le
                    droit de vote aux illettrés.   ("Le Figaro" - 9/7)
                    - Le général Carlos Castillo Armas, chef des insurgés qui
                    ont remporté la victoire au Guatemala, a été nommé président
                    de la junte militaire.   (Paris-presse - 10/7)
                    - Castillo Armas définit sa politique : " La justice du
                    peloton d'exécution."   ("L'Humanité" - 14/7)

LES GRATTE-CIELS PAR LA RACINE

Dans cette époque de plus en plus placée, pour tous les domaines, sous le signe
de la répression, il y a un homme particulièrement répugnant, nettement plus flic
que la moyenne. Il construit des cellules unités d'habitations, il construit une
capitale pour les Népalais, il construit des ghettos à la verticale, des morgues
pour un temps qui en a bien l'usage, il construit des églises.
Le protestant modulor, le Corbusier-Sing-Sing, le barbouilleur de croûtes néo-cu-
bistes fait fonctionner la "machine à habiter" pour la plus grande gloire du Dieu
qui a fait à son image les charognes et les corbusiers.
On ne saurait oublier que si l'Urbanisme moderne n'a encore jamais été un art
- et d'autant moins un cadre de vie - , il a par contre été toujours inspiré par
les directives de la Police ; et qu'après tout Haussmann ne nous a fait ces bou-
le vards que pour commodément amener du canon.
Mais aujourd'hui la prison devient l'habitation - modèle, et la morale chrétienne
triomphe sans réplique, quand s'avise que le Corbusier ambitionne de supprimer
la rue. Car il s'en flatte. Voilà bien le programme: la vie définitivement parta-
gée en îlots fermés, en sociétés surveillées; la fin des chances d'insurrection
et de rencontres; la résignation automatique. (Notons en passant que l'existence
des automobiles sert à tout le monde -sauf, bien sûr, aux quelques "économiquement
faibles" - : le préfet de police qui vient de disparaître, l'inoubliable Baylot,
déclarait de même après le dernier monôme du baccalauréat que les manifestations
dans la rue étaient désormais incompatibles avec les nécessités de la circulation.
Et, tous les 14 juillet, on nous le prouve.)
Avec le Corbusier, les jeux et les connaissances que nous sommes en droit d'atten-
dre d'une architecture vraiment bouleversante - le dépaysement quotidien - sont
sacrifiés au vide-ordure que l'on n'utilisera jamais pour la Bible réglementaire,
déjà en place dans les hôtels des U.S.A.
Il faut être bien sot pour voir ici une architecture moderne. Ce n'est rien

Front page of *Potlatch* no. 5, 20 July 1954

mined to suppress creation, and in that society détournement was a principle of freedom. There was nothing new under the sun; that meant the materials of transformation were already present, everywhere and anywhere, in today's papers, in yesterday's books, and so the *Potlatch* voice is huddled and all-powerful, satirical and sentimental, a midnight secret told as a noontime shout, self-referential within a global frame of reference. Legend and fact turn into one another; the mythic becomes prosaic, and vice versa; pronouncements on all things under the sun are made in tones of common knowledge just out of reach of common sense. In certain moods, one can feel a jarring, tearing momentum in the pages, the momentum of a dream as it rushes toward waking—the most violent screed seems reasonable, the most rational argument communicates as a rant, and as one picks out the names at the bottom of a manifesto, the questions ask themselves: who are these people? Don't they know what they're saying sounds like a joke? Why do they sound as if they've already got it?

The writers offer a world they reject—a world that almost everyone outside the LI acknowledges as both past and future. The writers offer a world they believe in, but that world is out of reach—out of reach then, and out of reach now. As one reads *Potlatch*, so is the world one has always taken for granted. The evanescent quality of Debord's later writing, his chiliastic serenity, is patent here: a voice speaking from a world one might want to make and then to live in, but also the voice of the mad professor in Eric Ambler's spy thriller *Cause for Alarm*. The LI offers ". . . A New Idea in Europe"; the old man, professor of classical mechanics at the University of Bologna until Mussolini's fascists drove him out, offers his unpublished masterpiece, hundreds of pages of whorls, faces, and high-school equations. The deposed professor has discovered a proof of perpetual motion; so has the LI. "Leisure is the real revolutionary question," says the LI, right out loud, nobody listening; "The cube root of eight," whispers the professor, "is God."

THE WORLD

The world the LI rejected was ultimately fixed in the pages of *Internationale situationniste*. As with the gap between the *Potlatch* voice and its medium, the idea of happiness discovered in the LI would over the years prove endlessly disproportionate to the ultimate medium: society as it was already ordered, everywhere. Thus from 1958 to 1969 the SI set forth an irrefutable analysis of the spectacle-commodity society ("The thought," Debord wrote in 1972, the year he formally dissolved what little was left of the group, *of the collapse of a world*"), and today the twelve numbers of the situationist journal read like a western version of *The Captive Mind*, with all of its weariness and resignation replaced by a sense of an impending explosion—"an explosion," as the SI once said of the art of the 1910s and 1920s, "which never took place."

The SI's writing is like a western version of Czeslaw Milosz's account of the surrender of Polish intellectuals to Stalinism in two ways: because it came from the West and focused on it, but also because what the SI wrote is a western, a cowboy melodrama staged in a cathedral—a cathedral now gothic, ordained by God and full of the smell of his corpse, now ruined and rebuilt from the ground up. "Our position is that of warriors between two worlds," Raoul Vaneigem told an SI conference in 1961: "one which we do not recognize, another which does not yet exist. We must precipitate the crash; hasten the end of the world, *the disaster in which the situationists will recognize their own*." Shifting a word or two, Vaneigem was quoting the papal commander who ordered the extermination of the Cathars, with the SI taking the place of God, but it was only détournement: "Any sign is susceptible to conversion into something else, even its opposite."

To write about the SI one has to use such slogans, or catch phrases like "the spectacle-commodity economy"—and to do so now is to loosen the SI's hold on the world it promised to destroy, a hold that seems so sure as one reads what the situationists wrote in their time. At the heart of the essays on

Watts or fallout shelters, the arguments are dressed in the armor of facts and scrupulous research, of history and sociology, but they are armed with the dispensations of poetry—the poetry of a title like "The Geopolitics of Hibernation," of its orchestration by an ad for the "Peace o' Mind" fallout-shelter company. As the symbolism of the shelter expands to take in Brasilia, a capital city protecting itself from its own country, or a state-sponsored nonalcoholic discotheque protecting its patrons from themselves, there is finally no ordinary argument at all, only an unstoppable recontextualization of anything an argument might touch. The analysis is irrefutable not because it is true, any more than it is refutable because it is false, but because it so happily used a private language to distort a public world; the whole of that world's negative truth could always be caught in an everyday moment.

Bernstein caught it in *Tous les chevaux du roi*, sending Geneviève, her narrator, off to a movie:

The afternoon loomed up empty before me. Luckily a theater on my street was playing a western so old I knew it had to be good. For a modest sum, I assisted in the invasions in China; in the efforts of an army triumphing without losses over backward terrorists, who hid in the underbrush, disavowed by everyone; in a presidential inauguration and an international tournament. Then the smile of Colgate toothpaste brought us to the feature; the lion roared on the screen; and the cowboy hero won his heroine in ninety minutes.

The declension of the last sentence is relentless: the alienated consumer of images brought into the spectacle as a participant in a war against herself, a war she will lose by identifying with the enemy, swallowing its images, and so consuming herself.

This was the bad world as the good—save for the blank irony of Bernstein's tone, the passage is seamless. But the bad world was not seamless. "Consumers themselves become spectacular, as do any objects of consumption," the SI wrote in "The Geopolitics of Hibernation," with "perfectly reified man [taking] his place in the show-window as a desirable image of reification"; the "internal defect of the system" was "that it cannot perfectly reify people." You could take your place in the show window, but you could not be at home there. So the bad world was full of cracks—and that was a story the SI told best in "The World of Which We Speak," combing the papers for evidence that, among other things, the spectacle of participation was really "The Technology of Isolation."

In contemporary society, the whole body of technology—above all the means of so-called communication—is oriented towards the maximum passive isolation of individuals, towards their control by a "direct and permanent relationship" *that only works in one direction*. Orders to which one cannot reply are broadcast by every sort of *leader*. Some applications of this technique can be seen as contemptible consolation prizes for what is fundamentally absent—or, on occasion, as evidence of the absolutism of what is missing.

If you're a TV fan, you'll want to know about the most amazing television set ever made—because it can go everywhere with you. It was invented by the Hughes Aircraft Corp. of the U.S.A., and the design is completely new—you wear it on your head. It weighs 950 grams; you wear it like a pilot's helmet, or a telephone operator's headset. It has a tiny plastic screen which looks like a monocle, held 4 cm in front of the eye . . . Only one eye is used to look at the screen; the manufacturers promise that with the other you can look anywhere else, or even perform manual labor or write. (*Journal du dimanche*, 29 July 1962)

The trouble at the coal mines has finally been settled, and it appears work will start again next Friday. Perhaps it's the feeling of having participated in the debate that explains the almost unbroken calm that has reigned at the pit-heads and in the miners' quarters for thirty-four days straight. Television and transistor radio contact maintained a direct and permanent relationship between the workers and their leaders—and, at the same time, forced them all to go home [to watch themselves on TV] when, before, they all used to gather at the union hall. (*Le Monde*, 5 April 1963)

There's a new cure for lonely travelers at the Chicago railroad station. For "a quarter" (1,25 F), a wax-covered robot shakes your hand and says: "Hello, my friend, how're you doing? It's been great seeing you. Have a good trip." (*Marie-Claire*, January 1963)

de l'histoire. Mais la logique rigoureuse de ces doctrinaires ne répond qu'à un aspect du besoin contradictoire de la société de l'aliénation, dont le projet indissoluble est d'empêcher la vie des gens tout en organisant leur survie (cf. l'opposition des concepts de vie et de survie décrite plus loin par Vaneigem dans *Banalités de base*). De sorte que le *Doomsday System*, par son mépris d'une survie qui est tout de même la condition indispensable de l'exploitation présente et future du travail humain, ne peut jouer le rôle que d'ultima ratio des bureaucraties régnantes ; qu'être, paradoxalement, la garantie de leur sérieux. Mais, dans l'ensemble, le spectacle de la guerre à venir, pour être pleinement efficace, doit dès à présent modeler l'état de paix que nous connaissons, en servir les exigences fondamentales.

A cet égard, le développement extraordinaire des abris anti-atomiques dans le courant de l'année 1961 est certainement le tournant décisif de la guerre froide, un saut qualitatif dont on distinguera plus tard l'immense importance dans le processus de formation d'une société totalitaire cybernétisée à l'échelle planétaire. Ce mouvement a commencé aux Etats-Unis, où Kennedy en janvier dernier,

Page from "The Geopolitics of Hibernation," *I.S.* no. 7, August 1962

"I no longer have any friends. I'll never talk to anyone again."
Thus began the confession of a Polish worker who had just turned on
the gas in his kitchen—recorded on his own tape recorder. "I am almost unconscious. There is no longer a chance that anyone will save
me. The end is near." These were the last words of Joseph Czternas-
tek. (*A.F.P.*, London, 7 April 1962)

THE GOOD

The good world for the LI was like heaven for the Cathars: a
world where "the sacred was only the social, transfigured." It
was what in the 1930s Russian critic Mikhail Bakhtin called
"carnivalization"—a way of being in the world that laughed
away "all that is finished and polished," "all pomposity,"
"every ready-made solution in the sphere of thought and world
outlook." How to get there was the subject of "Rational Embellishments to the City of Paris," *Potlatch* no. 23, 13 October
1955.

It began as a scholastic revision of an old surrealist paper,
Breton's 1933 "Experimental Researches (On the Irrational
Embellishment of a City)." Breton proposed a tradeoff between
spectacles ("Notre-Dame? Replace the towers with an enormous glass cruet, one of the bottles filled with blood, the other
with semen"); the LI was looking for an institutionalized disruption of everyday life, for Rimbaud's "rational disordering of
the senses" as a practical account of the errand, the appoint-
ment, the commute, the purchase. The LI leaped over Breton
and back to the spirit of "What is Dadaism and what does it
want in Germany?"; in the LI's new civilization, the practical
would be a question of the longest distance between two
points. The LI's ministry of leisure was issuing its first decrees.

—Open the metro at night after the trains stop running. Keep the
corridors and tunnels poorly lit by means of weak, intermittently
functioning lights.
—With a careful rearrangement of fire-escapes, and the creation of

. . . .

BBC ANNOUNCER:
*What is it that draws people like
"Mr. A." to this way of life?*

PSYCHIATRIST: *Most
normal adolescents go through
this phase . . . Some are almost
certainly attracted by its very il-
legality. The same with murder:
make it illegal, and it acquires a
mystique. Look at arson. I mean,
who can honestly say he's never
set fire to some great public
building? I know I have!*

*—Monty Python's Flying Circus,
"The Mouse Problem,"* The
Worst of Monty Python, *1970*

. . . .

walkways where needed, open the roofs of Paris for strolling.

—Leave the public gardens open at night. Keep them dark. (In some cases, a weak illumination may be justified by psychogeographical considerations.)

—Put switches on the street lamps, so lighting will be under public control.

The ministry moved on to the churches:

Four different solutions were advanced and recognized as legitimate until they can be tested by *experiment*, when the best idea will win out:

—G.-E. Debord declares himself in favor of the total destruction of religious buildings, of every faith. (No trace would remain, and the spaces would be used for other purposes.)

—Gil J Wolman proposes that churches be preserved but emptied of all religious significance. They should be treated as ordinary buildings. Let children play in them.

—Michèle Bernstein insists that churches be partially destroyed, so that the remaining ruins would reveal nothing of their original purposes . . . The perfect solution would be to raze the churches and reconstruct ruins in their places. The first of these two solutions is proposed simply for the sake of expediency.

—Lastly, Jacques Fillon wants to turn the churches into *haunted houses*. (Use their current ambiances, accentuating the panic-instilling aspects.)

Having completed Michel Mourre's interrupted sermon, the group went back to the secular.

—Keep the railroad stations as they are. Their rather moving ugliness greatly adds to the atmosphere of travel, which provides what slight attraction these buildings possess. Gil J Wolman demanded the complete suppression or falsification of all information about departures, destinations, schedules, etc.; this would encourage the dérive. After lively debate, the opposition backed down, and the project was adopted without dissent. Accentuate the aural ambiance of the stations by broadcasting arrival-and-departure information originating from numerous other stations—and from various ports.

—Suppression of the cemeteries. Total destruction of corpses and all tombstones: no ashes, not a trace, shall remain. (Attention must be drawn to the reactionary propaganda which, through the most elementary association of ideas, this hideous survival of past alienation represents . . .)

—Abolition of the museums, and the redistribution of masterpieces in bars (put the work of Phillipe de Champagne in the Arab cafes in the rue Xavier-Privas; put David's *Sacre* in the Tonneau in rue Montagne-Geneviève).

—Free and unlimited access to the prisons for everyone. Allow people to use them for vacations. No discrimination between visitors and prisoners. (To add to the fun, monthly lotteries would be held to pick visitors to be sentenced to actual jail terms.)

In "The Role of Writing," also in *Potlatch* no. 23, the LI had already proposed the "subversion" of various streets by means of graffiti specifically appropriate to them ("If we don't die here, will we go farther?" for rue Sauvage; for rue Lhomond, "Give it the benefit of the doubt"); now it affirmed the possibilities of creating civic confusion by the détournement of inscriptions on statues and monuments. It proposed an end to the "cretinization of the public" by various sorts of street names, announcing the erasure of all markers honoring "municipal officials, heroes of the Resistance," all those bearing words plainly "vile (e.g., rue de l'Evangile)," all those carrying the names "Emile" and "Edouard," and—

"What's interesting about this," said a friend of mine after looking over the LI's directives, "is how half of it remained a pipe dream, and how half of it came true."

"What do you mean?" I said, thinking of Bob Acraman's three-day vacation in a Nazi prison camp.

"Doesn't this remind you of anything? The graffiti? The gardens open at night, the lights flickering, people walking on roofs, streets with new names, all the transportation information completely scrambled? For a moment—really!—it seemed as if the prisons *would* open. The chapel in the Sorbonne was almost razed. There was even a leaflet demanding that Cardinal Richelieu be dug up and his bones tossed in the street. Of course there were new inscriptions on the statues. Probably the last thing to happen would have been taking the paintings out of the Louvre—it's easier to kill God than art. You see what I'm getting at?"

"What are you getting at?" I said, thinking of Johnny Rotten singing "Give the wrong time, stop a traffic line" as a route to anarchy in the U.K., about the weird split between the absolute demands in his voice and the triviality of his advice on how to realize them.

My friend had been to school in Paris; he was just remembering what it was like. "This is what happened in May '68," he said.

ANOTHER VERSION

Another version of the LI's "Rational Embellishments" happened at the University of Strasbourg in the fall of 1966. It was a small event, a series of student pranks, a sort of negationist panty raid—or, as a typical newspaper editorial put it at the time, "perhaps the first concrete manifestation of a revolt aiming quite openly at the destruction of society." A panty raid as the end of the world—that was the reversible connecting factor if anything was.

There were three planes on which the imaginary revolution in the Strasbourg laboratory took place: the artistic plane of a work called *The Return of the Durutti Column*, the literary plane of a text titled *On the Poverty of Student Life*, and the tactical plane of the events that followed and the response they provoked. But in outline the story was simple. Bored with their classes and disgusted by the pettiness of left-wing youth-group politics, in the spring of 1966 five students proclaimed their desire to see the government-sanctioned student union ruined, stood for election to its offices, and amidst the overwhelming apathy of their peers found themselves voted in to run the show. During the summer break, friends of the surprised winners made contact with the SI through its post office box in Paris—the only way the group made contact with anyone—and asked for a meeting. We have a piece of power, they said; we want to wreck it.

· · · · · · · · · · ·

IF YOU DON'T LIKE the news, go out and make some of your own.

—Scoop Nisker, radio signoff, KSAN-FM, San Francisco, 1969

· · · · · · · · · · ·

By 1957 a search for purity in motive and deed brought the Lettrist International to a state of immobilization, where there were only motives and no deeds; that was why the LI had to merge with others less pure, to take one step back. By 1966 the Situationist International reached the same pass. "The situationist project had taken on its definitive form," Christopher Gray wrote in 1974 in *Leaving the 20th Century*. "The SI was to be a small, tightly knit group of revolutionaries devoted to forging a critique of *contemporary*, that is to say consumer capitalism—and to publicizing this critique by every form of scandal and agitation possible. Everything depended on universal insurrection. Poetry could *only* be made by everyone." But the group had all but left the public space; the scandals it made took place only in its journal. With one-time allies like Henri Lefebvre spurned as imposters or thieves, with all the practicing painters and architects of the early SI years gone (some, like Jorn, resigned, the rest excluded), with anti-art exhibitions and plans to build new cities (or, failing that, to seize museums, even the headquarters of UNESCO) repudiated or forgotten, the SI had turned to a close reading of other people's gestures of refusal—their protests, riots, wildcat strikes, their acts of random violence. Though it was a reading of increasing empathy and excitement, sometimes perceiving the ideas in other people's minds far more completely than those people did themselves, coming off the page as a real conversation between actors and thinkers, it was of course a fabulist conversation, beginning in a refusal of art and now seeking its realization in events; even as the conversation expanded to take in the whole world, the news everyone talked about and the news no one but the speakers noticed, it became ever more aesthetic, a theory devouring its evidence. As they approached the climax of their story, the situationists were of the world but not in it: "What they had gained in intellectual power and scope," Gray wrote in a *Leaving* draft he did not publish, "they had lost, or so it seems to me, in terms of the richness and verve of their own everyday lives. Numbers were drastically reduced . . . Their organization was no longer meaningfully international. It was Parisian. There was no longer any of their previous experimentation with architecture or living space. Cultural sabotage too went by the board. They were permanently broke. The group turned inwards. There was little or nothing that didn't seem reformist. Everything went into the perfecting of their analyses, into the savagery of their anti-philosophy: into their magazine. The drunken, tearaway exhuberance of their Lettrist days was replaced by living up to the role of an incredibly austere rejection of everything apart from rejection." The Strasbourg students offered the SI a chance to go back to the world.

We want to cause trouble, the students said, as much as we can—how? Do it yourself, the SI said, reminding them of something Debord had written years before: "A revolutionary organization must always remember that its objective is not getting people to listen to speeches by expert leaders, but getting them to speak for themselves." You want to make trouble? Understand that just as everyday life is right here, in the successes and failures of our conversation, so are the premises for revolution. Revolution is not something that happens on the other side of the world, in China, Vietnam, Cuba—for you and for us that is just intellectual tourism, and as an opposition to the spectacle it can produce only a spectacle of opposition. So think globally, but act locally. Use the funds your fellows have so imprudently entrusted to your care; use the platform you've landed on. Write a critique of your own status, of students and the society they represent and serve—serve even when they flatter themselves they are its enemies. Disseminate your critique, and see what happens; if it is strong enough, something will. Use each edge of whatever scandal you can cause as a leg up on the next step; when one barrier breaks, go through it, and move on. Remember that though you are risking the careers society has planned for you, there is no protection in compromise, that the success of a scandal is the only safeguard for those who trigger it, that those who make a revolution by halves only dig their own graves. The students went back to Strasbourg; the fall term began.

The opening act featured sociologist Abraham Moles—a "pinhead" cybernetician, the SI named him two years before—who was chased from his lecture hall by a barrage of tomatoes. Next came Strasbourg student André Bertrand's *The Return of the Durutti Column*, a comic-strip account of the student-union takeover, named in homage to what Raoul Vaneigem had once proposed as the SI's "guiding image": a column of anarchist troops, as an ironically approving London *Sunday Telegraph* report on the Strasbourg affair explained, led by the Catalan revolutionary Buenaventura Durruti (Bertrand couldn't spell), which in the early days of the Spanish Civil War "went from village to village destroying the entire social structure, leaving the survivors to rebuild everything from scratch." The strip closed with the promise that students would "soon be able to procure the most scandalous publication of the century . . . 'On the Poverty of Student Life, considered in its economic, political, psychological, sexual, and especially intellectual aspects, with a modest proposal for its remedy' . . . a cardiogram of everyday reality which will allow you to choose your side: for or against the present misery, for or against the power which, by taking your history from you, prevents you from living. IT'S YOUR MOVE!"

In an elegantly printed edition of ten thousand copies, a green-jacketed pamphlet appeared soon after—credited to the Association fédérative générale des étudiants de Strasbourg under the auspices of the Union nationale des étudiants de France, but in truth written by situationist Mustapha Khayati when the student conspirators proved unable to come up with their own statement—and what made it different from other radical manifestos of the time was that it was well-written, logical, all-encompassing, and devoid of intent to please, casting scorn on its audience like Huelsenbeck slashing his riding crop on the stage of the Cabaret Voltaire. "Apart from the policeman and the priest, it is safe to say that the student is the most universally despised creature in France," the text began, and it went on to say why: in the society of the spectacle, the student was the "perfect spectator."

The words moved fast. Making slogans out of lines from Marx's "Critique of Hegel's Philosophy of Right" ("to make shame more shameful still by making it public"), the essay boiled nearly a decade of situationist writing down to twenty-eight virulent pages, coolly and cruelly satirizing the university ("the institutional organization of ignorance"), professors, the "Idea of Youth" (a capitalist "publicity myth"), the "celebrities of Unintelligence" (Sartre, Althusser, Barthes), modern culture ("In an era when *art is dead*" the student was "the most avid consumer of its corpse"), not to mention the work ethic, the government, the economy, the church, and the family. As the silent partner of bourgeois hegemony, the traditional left went on the same scrap heap, from bereft anarchist combines to empowered Leninist, Stalinist, or Maoist Communist parties ("'at the head' of the revolution" because it had "decapitated the proletariat")—but, Khayati said, "Let the dead bury the dead." There was a new proletariat, defined not by labor or penjury, but made up of everyone "who has no power over his own life and knows it." There was a new revolt, against all hierarchy and ideology, for autonomy and a history purposefully made: a war against the poverty of the commodity, for the riches of time. The revolt was still partial and confused, losing itself in the "pure, nihilist rejection" of juvenile delinquents or in "the mass consumption of drugs" ("an expression of real poverty and a protest against it: a fallacious religious critique of a world that has itself superseded religion"); it was also gaining consciousness of itself, seeking its theory as its theory found its practice. You could see it all over the world—in the West, Khayati said, with the Free Speech Movement in Berkeley in 1964 (in 1966 that was an obvious note to sound), or in the East, with Jacek Kuroń and Karol Modzelewski's antibureaucratic, anticlerical 1965 "Open Letter to the Polish Communist Party" (that was not obvious at all in 1966, though in 1980 the document would be read as a phantom charter for Solidarity)—to anyone who knew how to look, the facade of the old world was cracking and the moment had come to smash it, to "create at last a situation that goes beyond the point of no return," to realize the goal of a poetry made by all in a permanent revolutionary festival, to "live without dead time and indulge untrammeled desire." The text ended, and the discourse shot off into wonderland; the pamphlet lay in your hand, grinning like the Cheshire cat. The reaction could not have been more extreme if the student union had spent its money on guns.

Professors, university administrators, city officials, labor-union leaders, editorialists, Communist Party functionaries, the business community, parents, priests, and left-wing and right-wing student groups united to denounce the misappropriation of public funds and the betrayal of positions of public trust—to combat, they said, the collapse of decency, morality, order, the university, and Western civilization itself. A smaller number rallied to the defense of the reprobates; the press waved the filmy bloody shirt of a demonic, fanatic, always mysterious band carrying the incomprehensible name "Situationist International" ("How many are there?" asked *Le République lorrain*. "Where do they come from? No one knows"). The student-union officers capitalized on hysterical coverage in the international media to spread their publications across Europe, renamed the Association fédérative générale "The Society for the Rehabilitation of Karl Marx and Ravachol" (the latter a nineteenth-century anarchist bomber, whose song "Le Bon Dieu dans le merde" had been reprinted in *I.S.* no. 9 in 1964— "If you want to be happy / Name of God! / Hang your landlord, cut the priests in two / Name of God! / Damn the churches down / God's blood! / And the good Lord in shit"), then scheduled a plebiscite on its dissolution, invited supporters to occupy the student office building, abandoned student stores and restaurants while urging students to steal books and food, and declared the campus psychiatric clinic a front for mind control, cut off its funding, and announced its abolition. At the University of Strasbourg in the fall of 1966, there was only one conversation, governed by the same principle of expansion that governed the conversation in Berkeley in the fall of 1964 or Poland in August 1980, in Durruti's Barcelona in July 1936 or

Huelsenbeck's Berlin in January 1919: on Monday people began to question rules and regulations, the next day the institutions behind the rules, then the nature of the society that produced the institutions, then the philosophy that justified the society, then the history that created the philosophy, until by the end of the week both God and the state were in doubt and the only interesting question was the meaning of life.

Though all of the actions of the rogue body were legal, after six weeks of chaos the courts stepped in, closed the student union, and stripped the Strasbourg Five of their offices. "Disarmingly lucid," the British section of the SI, Gray and three others, said of the judge's summation—in *Ten Days that Shook the University*, the U.K. edition of the Strasbourg publications—for the judge had got it right:

One only has to read what the accused have written for it to be obvious that these five students, scarcely more than adolescents, lacking all experience of real life, their minds confused by ill-digested philosophical, social, political, and economic theories, and bored by the drab monotony of their everyday life, make the empty, arrogant, and pathetic claim to pass definitive judgements, sinking to outright abuse, on their fellow-students, their teachers, God, religion, the clergy, and the governments and political systems of the entire world. Rejecting all morality and restraint, these students do not hesitate to commend theft

—"'They believe that all things are common, whence they conclude that theft is lawful for them,'" the British added in a footnote, quoting the Bishop of Strasbourg in 1317, on the Brethren of the Free Spirit—

the destruction of scholarship, the abolition of work, total subversion, and an irreversible proletarian revolution with "unlicensed pleasure" as its only goal.

This was détournement in acts, the British announced: proof of the "ability to both *devalue* and *'reinvest'* the heritage of a dead cultural past . . . a student union, for example, recuperated long ago and turned into a paltry agency of repression, can become a beacon of sedition and revolt." To Khayati, on the scene and speaking to reporters as "K.," it was "a little experiment"; to the British it was "a modest attempt to create the praxis by which the crisis of this society as a whole can be precipitated . . . A situation was created in which society was forced to finance, publicise and broadcast a revolutionary critique of itself, and furthermore to confirm this critique by its reactions to it."

ONCE

Once it was a famous victory; more than twenty years later, the critique is frozen by its own rhetoric. Its very urgency, its leap toward a day that came and passed, stops its time and casts its words backward. But André Bertrand's *The Return of the Durutti Column* now reads like a lost issue of *Potlatch*—or, rather, like the return gift *Potlatch* asked for. It doesn't matter that Bertrand could not have seen the LI's newsletter, which by 1966 had disappeared without a trace; enough of the *Potlatch* voice went into *Internationale situationniste* for Bertrand to recreate it whole. All of the LI's adolescent self-regard is in his comic strip; so is the LI's heedless simultaneity, its menace, and its faith in the cryptic slogan.

On the Poverty of Student Life was a polemic; *The Return of the Durutti Column* is a story, like Debord's *Mémoires* told through the cut-and-paste of détournement, and told in a similar tone—as if it were the tale of a grand quest, recounted long after the fact by an old man to an awestruck child. There are craven villains, played by professors, bureaucrats, leftists of every stripe; there are "dashing adventurers," the Strasbourg usurpers, the formal narrative of their exploits marked off in boxed captions to facsimiles of documents, a few newly drawn cartoons, but mostly to photos and art works scavenged from magazines and books, and now talking in comic-strip balloons. "The never-ending festival and its Dionysian debaucheries accompanied them everywhere," says the sagaman of the heroes; there follows the text of a long letter from their landlord, accusing them of ending a party by pissing off a second-story balcony.

Bertrand was a situationist fan; not making art but playing with it, he worked with a fan's obsessiveness, with a fetishistic love of forgotten signs and talismans. Thus he began at the beginning, in the middle of *Hurlements en faveur de Sade*, collapsing it into a single panel: in white speech balloons against a black screen, the Strasbourg cabal hatches its plan. The new Durutti Column enters a Trojan horse; then Lenin gets a balloon ("I could give a flying fuck about the JCR," he says of a Trotskyist youth group), then Ravachol, speaking his own words: "I will never go back. The harm men do to each other fills me with horror; I hate their civilizations, their virtues, and their gods far too much ever to sacrifice anything to them." "Little by little," the chronicle of the vandals continues, "they became aware of those with whom they could make the wrecking of the social machine into a pitiless game. Thus it was that they began their palavers with the 'occult International'"—the latter, the unnamed SI, pictured in one of the group's favorite images, the banquet scene from the Bayeux Tapestry. Musing on Marx and the "critique of everyday life," the king in Delacroix's *Death of Sardanapal* placidly readies himself for the funeral pyre as eunuchs throttle his naked wives and concubines. Every few panels, children recite the LI's primitive theories as the SI followed them up: by stealing goods simply to give them away, says a toddler, delinquents transcend the modern society of abundance and rediscover the first social order, "the practice of the gift." A five-year-old explains that there is no need to produce or acquire, no need for competition or conflict—and "therefore no more need for laws, no more need for masters." The coup is sealed with a grotesque medieval drawing of golem-like beggars, all of them drunk, one with twisted fingers as long as his rotting skull.

As it was distributed throughout Western Europe, in Great Britain and the United States, *The Return of the Durutti Column* was a four-page foldout or a feature in an underground newspaper. One has to imagine it as it first appeared in Strasbourg, when the scandal had yet to take place—when the comic strip was a riddle blown up into huge posters and plastered as a mural across the city walls. One has to walk down the one-way street of the dominant idea of happiness ("Freedom," John Kenneth Galbraith said in disgust twenty years later, when all roads seemed to lead to Rome and none away from it, "consists of the right to spend a maximum of one's money by one's own choice"); one has to imagine the street turned into a free field of noise.

Obscenities scream over the traffic. Next to a billboard selling the Colgate smile there is a poster of two toothbrushes happily discussing the coming war against something called "the old world." There is a photo-cartoon arguing for money as the root of all evil and a second proposing a potlatch in its place. Along with the usual ads guaranteeing an elevator ride to the top of the social hierarchy, there are others explaining how to cut the cords. Covered in bubble bath, a starlet promotes not the film you've seen a hundred times but the end of the Christian era; then in a grainy, purloined movie still, two mounted cowboys talk philosophy. This last was the most distant element: out of all the panels in Bertrand's production, it alone still communicates the deadpan, dreamtime incongruousness the whole show had in 1966. It was true fan's work; it came from Bernstein's novel *Tous les chevaux du roi*.

Once the SI had paid its bills with paintings Jorn and others turned over for sale; in 1960 there was no money. Michèle must write a novel, Debord said. I cannot write a novel, she said—I have no imagination. Anyone can make art, Debord said. But situationists cannot practice a dead art, Bernstein said, and the novel is dead if anything is. There is always détournement, Debord said. So Bernstein contrived a book out of every fragment of popular fiction: a prefabricated bestseller, rooted in a parody of Choderlos de Laclos' 1782 classic *Les Liaisons dangereuses*, not coincidentally a 1959 hit film starring Jeanne Moreau. The book sold well enough for its publisher to request another, which Bernstein swiftly provided with *La Nuit*, using the same characters and the same plot, this time parodying the nouveau roman; a few years later, when Bernstein brought her publisher the manuscript of Debord's "La Société du Spectacle," he bought it too—though concerned that readers might take the title as a promise of show-business gossip.

No mention of Bernstein's books ever appeared in any situationist publication; "They were jokes," she said in 1983. Set in 1957, just before the founding of the SI, they are more than that: precise, flat, disturbing studies of restlessness and sloth, of people who have found a way to turn life into a game, where it is reduced to seduction and manipulation, a slow dance of self-deception, destruction, and waste. The tension is between Gilles, the gamesman, and Geneviève, his wife and pupil; the story is about Gilles's need for pupils, for acolytes— for concubines to complement his wife, whose role it is to choose them. A sense of common dissatisfaction—the disenchantment of "a generation not lost, but tired"—hangs over the tale, cut off from anything that might free it from the bedrooms and cafes where it appears as simple neurosis and pretension; against the prison of private life, the phrase "Tous les chevaux du roi" represents redemption. The situationists loved Lewis Carroll, but the line is not an allusion to Humpty Dumpty; it comes from an old French ballad about a queen and her common lover, who one night steals into the king's castle and lies with the queen in her bed: together they make a river, "and all the king's horses could not cross it." It is as deep and singular an image of revolution as there has ever been, but in *Tous les chevaux du roi* so distant an element it is barely an image at all.

Geneviève has found Gilles a woman named Carole, young, blonde, and credulous; in *La Nuit*, off at her western, the cowboys on the screen somehow remind her of Gilles and Carole, already lost in their new affair. But the central scene of the doubled story takes place early in *Tous les chevaux du roi*: the three sit in Gilles and Geneviève's apartment, getting to know each other. Carole is confused; she understands that Geneviève has a normal job, but Gilles doesn't seem to do any work at all. She asks him what he does; the answer Bernstein put in

Gilles's mouth—as rendered by Bertrand and put in the mouth of a cowboy, then translated for *Ten Days that Shook the University* by situationists Donald Nicholson-Smith and T. J. Clark—translated from French into English, but also out of Bernstein's commercial vernacular and back into the LI's secret language—sums up better than anything else the project Guy Debord began in 1952, a project that by the end of 1966 had only one more act to go. "What is it that you really do? I don't understand," says Carole. "What's your scene, man?" says a cowboy in a white hat. "Reification," say Gilles and a cowboy in a black hat. "It's an important study," Geneviève says. "Yes," says Gilles. "I see," says Carole. "It's very serious work with thick books and a lot of paper spread out on a big table." "Yeah?" says the first cowboy. "I guess that means pretty hard work with big books and . . ." "No," says Gilles. "I walk. Mainly, I walk." "Nope," says the second cowboy. "I drift. Mostly, I just drift."

THE REST

The rest of the story can almost be subsumed under what once passed for official history. It is mostly arithmetic: more than three hundred books about May '68 were published in the year after that interesting event, and some were even published in the twenty years after that. Amazing, how quickly everyone from conservative philosopher Raymond Aron to media-crowned student-revolt spokesman Daniel Cohn-Bendit got their books on the market—it's as if they knew how short the halflife would be. Like Marcel Janco in his last year, they were working against the clock—a dada clock, the same clock Janco began fighting in 1916, the clock that had already beaten him before that year was out. With most of their lives ahead of them, Cohn-Bendit and those with whom he shared the event wrote as if they knew nothing would ever measure up to what they had just seen and done—as if they knew that in a few years almost nobody, maybe not even themselves,

Panels from André Bertrand, *Le Retour de la colonne Durutti*, October 1966 ▶

…C'EST L'ARGENT EN EFFET LE MOTIF DE TOUTES LES DISCORDES, DE TOUTES LES HAINES, DE TOUTES LES AMBITIONS, C'EST EN UN MOT LE CRÉATEUR DE LA PROPRIÉTÉ. SI L'ON N'ÉTAIT PLUS OBLIGÉ DE DONNER QUELQUE CHOSE EN ÉCHANGE DE CE QUE NOUS AVONS BESOIN POUR NOTRE EXISTENCE, L'OR PERDRAIT SA VALEUR ET PERSONNE NE CHERCHERAIT ET NE POURRAIT, S'ENRICHIR, PUISQUE RIEN DE CE QU'IL AMASSERAIT NE POURRAIT SERVIR À LUI PROCURER UN BIEN ÊTRE SUPÉRIEUR À CELUI DES AUTRES. DE LÀ, PLUS BESOIN DE LOIS, PLUS BESOIN DE MAÎTRES

LA PRÉSIDENCE PASSE ENCORE, MAIS LA TRÉSORERIE IL N'EN ÉTAIT PAS QUESTION. ILS CONVAINQUIRENT AISÉMENT UNE PASSANTE, QUE LE HASARD AVAIT MIS SUR LEUR TROTTOIR, DE PRENDRE LE RÔLE PLUS COMPROMETTANT DE TRÉSORIÈRE.

LEUR CONNAISSANCE DE LA VIE NE DEVAIT RIEN À LEUR PRÉSENCE ÉPISODIQUE DANS L'ENCEINTE DES FACULTÉS NI AUX QUELQUES DIPLOMES QU'ILS AVAIENT ACQUIS PAR LES MOYENS LES PLUS DIVERS ET LES MOINS AVOUABLES.

DE QUOI T'OCCUPES TU EXACTEMENT ?

DE LA RÉIFICATION.

NON, JE ME PROMÈNE, PRINCIPALEMENT JE ME PROMÈNE.

JE VOIS, C'EST UN TRAVAIL TRÈS SÉRIEUX, AVEC DE GROS LIVRES ET BEAUCOUP DE PAPIERS SUR UNE GRANDE TABLE.

MES PRINCIPES ET MES GOÛTS FIRENT MON BONHEUR DEPUIS MON ENFANCE. ILS FURENT TOUJOURS L'UNIQUE BASE DE MA CONDUITE ET DE MES ACTIONS : PEUT-ÊTRE IRAI-JE PLUS LOIN, JE SENS QUE C'EST POSSIBLE, MAIS POUR REVENIR, NON. J'AI TANT D'HORREUR POUR LES PRÉJUGÉS DES HOMMES, JE HAIS TROP LEUR CIVILISATIONS, LEURS VERTUS ET LEURS DIEUX, QUE JE N'AI JAMAIS PEUR...

RAVACHOL JULES, DIT KOENIGSTEIN FRANÇAISE, NÉ LE 11 OCTOBRE 1854. TAILLE 1m 666 ; PROFESSION : TEINTURIER RELATIONS : RÉVOLUTIONNAIRES. CAUSE DE LA DÉTENTION : DESTRUCTION D'IMMEUBLES ET DÉTENTION D'ENGINS EXPLOSIFS.

L'EXCELLENCE DE CE SAVOIR THÉORIQUE NE POUVAIT ALLER SANS UNE PRATIQUE APPROPRIÉE. ILS AVAIENT PEU À PEU SU RECONNAÎTRE CEUX AVEC QUI LA DÉTÉRIORATION DE LA MACHINE SOCIALE SERAIT UN JEU IMPITOYABLE. C'EST AINSI QUE LES POURPARLERS AVEC L'« INTERNATIONALE OCCULTE » S'ENGAGÈRENT.

would care one way or another. But if May '68 has nearly vanished from official history, the part played by the situationists was all but excised from the beginning. That is because they made so many enemies—and because the absolute demands they made on the event left behind definitions of its success and failure so extreme that no reasonable account could address them without appearing sentimental, crazy, or ashamed. And that is why even the official history the SI made has remained a kind of secret history.

The event itself, though, did not play by the rules of history. There was no economic crisis; no question of political legitimacy had been raised by anyone with a forum commensurate to such a question. There was a modern, well-functioning capitalist welfare state, led by a man of enormous resilience and prestige, and there was, as a natural, hegemonic fact, the ever-present sense of what Lefebvre would later call the negation modernity carries within itself: a sense, as situationist René Viénet wrote just after May '68, that "the *familiar* in alienated life, and in the refusal of that life, is not necessarily *known*." In other words, there was a sleeping sense of mystery and displacement to which modernity could not afford to grant a language, and if that language was the one the situationists had been trying to create for so long, betting that the sleeping sickness could be cured as soon as its language was found, this was nothing new. What was new, in the year before the explosion, was a certain increase in pressure.

In the year after the Strasbourg scandal more than 300,000 copies of *On the Poverty of Student Life* found their way into print. Small groups modeling themselves on the Strasbourg example formed at colleges across France, and beseiged the SI with pleas for instruction: the SI's only instruction was that they act autonomously, that they promote an insurrection that would matter to them, and some did. The Enragés, a handful of SI fans who named themselves after a radical faction led by Jacques Roux during the French Revolution, came together in early 1968 at Nanterre, a suburban extension of the University of Paris housing a prestigious, leftist faculty: Lefebvre,

Alain Tourraine, Jean Baudrillard, Edgar Morin. The Enragés painted slogans on the walls ("LIVE WITHOUT DEAD TIME," "BOREDOM IS ALWAYS COUNTERREVOLUTIONARY," "EVERY-THING DISPUTABLE MUST BE DISPUTED," "I TAKE MY DESIRES FOR REALITY BECAUSE I BELIEVE IN THE REALITY OF MY DE-SIRES") and disrupted classes for two months straight. "The other day you consigned me to the trashcan of history," Morin said to his students one morning. "HOW DID YOU GET OUT?" one of them screamed back. "I would prefer," Morin said evenly, "to be on the side of the trashcans rather than on the side of those who handle them"—and just like that he turned into the embodiment of Bataille's hideous bourgeoisie, the mask dropped from his suddenly sordid face, and he found himself standing in front of a hooting crowd that had fallen in love with the noise of its own words. "And in any case I prefer to be on the side of the trashcans rather than on the side of the crematoria!" Morin shouted, but nobody was listening. Morin imagined himself in Germany in the mid-1930s, when Nazi students drowned out professors who would soon be wear-ing yellow stars; the Enragés imagined themselves at the Con-vention in 1793, on top of the Mountain.

Many students were outraged; some were thrilled. Some, led by Cohn-Bendit, seized the chance to launch calls for educa-tional reform and the sexual integration of dormitories; that gave the press a scandal. Mass meetings were held; people be-gan to criticize their studies, then the university, then the idea of the university itself. The Enragés hung a huge banner over the entrance to the campus: "NEVER WORK." Soon nobody did—the trouble continued, the press coverage grew, and on May 2 the Nanterre dean closed the college. That same day he scheduled disciplinary proceedings against Enragé René Reisel, Cohn-Bendit, and six others for May 6, at the Sorbonne in Paris—and "What followed," read the *Le Monde* account of the night of May 6, "surpassed in scope and violence everything that had happened in an already astonishing day."

The conflict, as it unfolded over the next weeks, was less be-tween people in revolt and the government they no longer acknowledged than between organized forces of orderly protest and the presence of dissolution. The public space was suddenly empty, a free field: practical proposals for the postponing of exams and the liberalization of university entrance requirements fought against the weird abstraction of reversible slogans ("THE MORE YOU CONSUME THE LESS YOU LIVE"), slogans that in the moment did not seem weird or abstract at all. Carefully monitored, nonviolent marches turned into a potlatch of tear gas, clubs, and incendiary bombs on one side, paving stones, barricades, burning cars, and Molotov cocktails on the other: "a kind of street fighting that sometimes reached a frenzy, where every blow delivered was immediately returned, and where ground that had scarcely been conquered was just as quickly retaken." A one-day general strike called by the Communist Party trade-union bureaucracy (the pretext was a protest against police brutality, the motive a wage increase) became an open-ended general wildcat strike of ten million people against—against what? The workers who occupied their factories and soldered the doors closed were not acting in solidarity with the people rioting in Paris; like the people in Paris, they were taking the breakdown of authority as a chance to act for themselves. In a signal way, there were no words to match the gestures everyone understood. There was only public happiness: joy in discovering for what drama one's setting is the setting, joy in making it.

On May 14 the Enragés and the SI federated. René Reisel was elected to the Occupations Committee of the Sorbonne, which at his insistence was constituted as a revolutionary council: an assembly in permanent session, open to all, every delegate subject to daily reelection or rejection. Some speakers asked for a humanization of the pedagogical apparatus; Reisel, a teenager, spoke for the abolition of the university, the commodity, the class system, wage labor, "the spectacle," "survival," the "suppression of art" and its "realization," the expropriation of all property and power, and the recreation of the polity as a federation of autonomous councils answerable only to themselves. Acting in the name of the assembly, the Enragés and the SI began to link up with occupied factories, issued leaflets, and sent telegrams:

POLITBURO OF THE COMMUNIST PARTY OF THE USSR THE KREMLIN MOSCOW/ SHAKE IN YOUR SHOES BUREAUCRATS STOP THE INTERNATIONAL POWER OF THE WORKERS COUNCILS WILL SOON WIPE YOU OUT STOP HUMANITY WILL NOT BE HAPPY UNTIL THE LAST BUREAUCRAT IS HUNG WITH THE GUTS OF THE LAST CAPITALIST STOP LONG LIVE THE STRUGGLE OF THE KRONSTADT SAILORS AND OF THE MAKHNOVSCHINA AGAINST TROTSKY AND LENIN STOP LONG LIVE THE 1956 COUNCILIST INSURRECTION OF BUDAPEST STOP DOWN WITH THE STATE STOP LONG LIVE REVOLUTIONARY MARXISM STOP OCCUPATION COMMITTEE OF THE AUTONOMOUS AND POPULAR SORBONNE.

That same day, May 17, they walked out of the Occupations Committee, damning its timidity and factionalism; along with some forty others the dozen Enragés and situationists formed the Council for Maintaining the Occupations, and until June 15 spread hundreds of thousands of copies of its posters, manifestos, and comic strips across the country and, translated into half a dozen languages, around the globe. "What we have done in France," the Council said on May 30,

is haunting Europe and will soon threaten the ruling classes of the world, from the bureaucrats of Moscow and Peking to the millionaires of Washington and Tokyo. *Just as we have made Paris dance*, the international proletariat will again take up its assault on the capitals of all nations, on all the citadels of alienation. The occupation of factories and public buildings throughout the country has not only blocked the functioning of the economy, it has brought about a general questioning of the society. A deeply-rooted movement is leading almost every sector of the population to seek a real change in life. It is now a revolutionary movement which lacks only *the consciousness of what it has already done* in order to triumph.

The result, after de Gaulle rallied the voting majorities (after changing his mind about resigning—and, he and the SI agreed, leaving the nation to civil war), was educational reform for students, and a wage increase for factory workers. If, as René Viénet wrote, commodity time stopped in May, free time moved too fast to keep or master; almost instantly, the noise that for a few weeks sounded like the beginning of a new language turned into babble, and today it is hard to read.

What is not hard to read is the account of what everyday life was like during the brief suspension of what almost everyone had taken everyday life to be. In 1954 the Lettrist International had committed itself to the perfecting of a complete divertissement; in 1968 Debord, the only member of the Situationist International left from those days, was able to recognize it.

The movement was a rediscovery of collective and individual history, a recognition of the possibility of intervening in history, an awareness of participating in an irreversible event ("Nothing will ever be the same again"); people looked back in amusement at the *strange existence* they had led a week before . . . people found themselves at home everywhere. The *recognized desire* for dialogue, for completely free expression, and the taste for true community found their terrain in the buildings transformed into open meeting places . . . the wandering of so many emissaries and travelers through Paris, through the entire country, between the occupied buildings, the factories, and the assemblies carried this true practice of communication. The occupations movement was plainly a rejection of alienated labor; it was a festival, a game, a real presence of real people and real time.

IN MANY

In many of the more than three hundred books, many people tried to say the same thing: after all, they had seen it, done it, lived it out. They were trying to hold onto it as it vanished—of all the graffiti, Debord wrote, "perhaps the most beautiful simply said, 'QUICK.'" As a momentary illusion, it was easy to dismiss—easy, even, to forget. As the realization of fantasies of a new city, fantasies that had been contrived and acted out fifteen years before, it was impossible to forget—and impossible to match. "Nothing will ever be the same again"—the slogan cut back against those who embraced it, cut them in half. "Years, like a single instant prolonged to this moment, come to an end," Debord said in 1959, on the soundtrack to *On the Passage of a Few People Through a Rather Brief Moment in Time*: he was speaking of 1953. "What was directly lived reappears frozen in the distance, inscribed in the fashions and illusions of an era carried away with it," said a man in the voice of a radio newscaster. Debord spoke again, then a young woman: "What should be abolished continues, and we continue to wear away with it . . . the years pass and we have not changed anything."

"Once again morning in the same streets," Debord said as he put daybreak footage on the screen. "Once again the fatigue of so many nights passed in the same way. It is a walk that has lasted a long time." "Really hard to drink more," said the newscaster; the screen went white. Then, in historical time, came the event: "the 'sunrise,'" Debord said in "The Beginning of an Epoch," in *I.S.* no. 12, September 1969, "'that, in a flash, all at once, traces the shape of the new world.'" It was a turning point in history where history refused to turn; as a beacon of the future it revealed nothing so vividly as the past.

EPILOGUE

Punk song: a man stands in a room, bare save for a mattress, a few bottles, a few books. From his window he can see a crowd gathered before a huge, new public building. The setting is uncertain; you can't tell if this is taking place in the present, in some tired near-future, or if the sodden familiarity of the scene locates the action well back in the past. A dignitary steps down from a reviewing stand to snip a ribbon. As the crowd presses up for a better look, the man in the room begins a keening sound: the strangled no of someone who's spent too much time talking to himself, a voice that gives off not the slightest hope of winning a response. Stamping one foot, the man edges toward hysteria, then escapes it as his cursing takes on a hint of form.

He's screaming quietly at his walls, at the people he has to look at, hating them and hating himself, wishing that the crowd were a loving community and that he could join it, though with his every jagged intonation—"and we bow to re–pub–lic . . . we bow to em–ploy–er . . . we bow to *God*" (a horrible, helpless loathing for the last word)—he drives himself out even of any fantasized community, past any possible communication. He loses his breath for a moment, loses his train of thought, then regains it; the listener, who feels almost ashamed to be listening, begins to realize that, at least to the man in the room, this cry-and-thump is some kind of music.

The singer has made his way down to the street; he stands on the fringes of the crowd, peering from behind a corner of the new building, still making his noise. *Don't look at him*, says a woman to her child. *Fucking drunks*, says her husband. The man leans out from the corner, as if expecting someone to actually acknowledge his presence. The way he carries his tune,

THE SECTORS OF A city are, at a certain level, legible. But the meaning they have had for us, personally, is incommunicable, like the clandestinity of private life, of which we possess nothing but pitiful documents . . . And only a few encounters were like signals emanating from a more intense life, a life that has not really been found.

—*Guy Debord*, Critique of Separation, *1961*

all hesitations and broken cadences, tells how he holds his body: ready for abuse, maybe wishing for it. Abuse is a kind of communication: a perversion of community that in an inverted way might suggest community when nothing else does. So the man bears down harder; this is now a public assault, no matter that the public ignores it. It's a riot, a rising, even if there is only one rioter—*so far*, he thinks. "Little girls, lit–tle girls, we're innocent until pro–ven guilty," he chants over and over. For a moment, he gives the words so much weight they sound as if they're about to mean something; then the moment passes, and he sounds like a child molester. By then everyone else has gone home.

It is—it might as well be—1985. In Washington, following his overwhelming reelection as president of the United States, Ronald Reagan addresses members of his administration. "We made beautiful music together in the last four years," he says, "but from here on in, it's shake, rattle, and roll." In Guatemala, mercenaries working with government troops to root out resistance to the state in place since Big Joe Turner first took "Shake, Rattle and Roll" to the top of the charts wear t-shirts printed with a version of an old slogan: "KILL 'EM ALL, LET GOD SORT 'EM OUT." In Berkeley, near a crowded coffee bar, I finish the morning paper in which I've read these stories, and watch former mental patients force themselves on the busy bohemian bourgeoisie, begging quarters, tearing at their clothes, calling down the wrath of God. One man, who on any day can be seen carefully retracing his steps across the whole north side of town (never the south side—there is a border in the city only he can see), carries his trademark unstrung bow and quiver full of sticks; another has a series of messages neatly painted on his ruined pants and shoes. As I look, the wasted derelicts, none of them old, all of their clocks stopped, change into Ranters shouting obscenities in seventeenth-century English churches, Free Spirit adepts crouching in doorways in fourteenth-century Swabia: weird cultural survivals, time walkers, loop tracers. I'm carrying too many books in my head, product of living too long with my own—but how many, really, is too many, when the Cathars are still making news? The heresies and blasphemies that flowed from Abiezer Coppe's mouth like lava in London in 1649 ("and lo a hand was sent to me, and a roll of a book was therein . . . it was snatcht out of my hand & the Roll thrust into my mouth; and I eat it up, and filled my bowels with it, where it was bitter as worm wood; and it lay broiling, and burning in my stomack, till I brought it forth in this forme. And now I send it flying to you, with my heart") today signify the extremes of a great social revolution, but they had their source, for Coppe, in Tourette's Syndrome and coprolalia; there is a textbook case right here. A man rises to his feet, spinning, and the word "shit" comes down like rain, ten times, a hundred times; then in under a minute the man announces himself as every well-known rock 'n' roll performer the name of whose group, or whose own first or last name, begins with the letter "J." "I'm Jimi Hendrix, I'm Joe Walsh, I'm Junior Walker, I'm Jimmy Jones, I'm Michael Jackson, I'm Johnny Rotten, I'm Elton John, I'm Steve Perry, I'm Ian Anderson, I'm Jeff Beck . . ." I go home and listen to "The Building."

The song comes from *it falleth like the gentle rain from heaven—The Mekons Story*, a collection of fragments and detritus that traces the first six years of an English punk band, founded in Leeds in 1977, temporarily defunct as of 1982. The record presents itself as a chronicle of possibility and failure. Vision collapses into bile, shared rage into private shame, wit into self-mockery, melody and beat into the drunken, electronically slurred narration that stitches the pieces together. Merely one of thousands of groups to come together on the terrain cleared by the Sex Pistols, the Mekons were best known as the band that took punk ideology most seriously: "Those who couldn't play tried to learn, and those who could tried to forget." They quickly blew their only chance to submit to the strictures and rewards of a major label, and disappeared into a pop wilderness mapped by none so well as themselves; on *The Mekons Story*, you can hear it all happen.

Released in 1978, the Mekons' first, small-label recordings— "Never Been in a Riot," "Where Were You?," and "32 Weeks"—

were preposterously rough, left-handed screeches about, respectively, a wish for trouble, a wish for affection, and the number of weeks of low-wage labor required to pay for various household objects, like refrigerators. They were self-conscious affirmations of punk crudity, stabs in a dark brought forth by turning out the lights, and they attracted attention in the small but growing punk community. Made in 1982, when "punk" was just another chapter in the history of rock 'n' roll and no one was paying attention to the Mekons, "The Building"—no instruments, no band, just Mekon Mark White's throat and foot—is beyond crudity. As a smear of oblivion and public life, silence and public speech, it is the antithesis of self-consciousness, of ideology or even style: it is an event, even if as such it's the tree falling in the forest, the building collapsing only in the singer's mind. Naked, demanding that the world be changed, "The Building" is the first punk song, a rant going back far beyond the Sex Pistols; naked, damning the fact that the world is more like it is now than it ever was before, it's also the last.

THE WHOLE

The whole of the story I have tried to follow is in this song. The primitivism of the music dissolves the temporal claims of the story and simultaneously subsumes its detail, assumes all of its debts: that is why the performance is so strong. It turns Jean-Michel Mension's "general strike" into the punk song it almost was and punk songs back into the graffiti Mension almost wrote. All at once, certain that to speak a language everyone can understand is to say nothing, the man in the room calls up Hugo Ball flapping his wings in the Cabaret Voltaire, Wolman hissing and barking in the Tabou, the glossolalia of Debord's *Mémoires*, Johnny Rotten's unspeakable confusion in the last minute of "Holidays in the Sun." All at once, now certain that to denounce the old world is to kill it and that to prophesy a new world is to call it into being, the man reenacts Huelsenbeck's hateful Berlin speeches, Michel

Mourre's sermon in Notre-Dame, the LI's decrees in "Rational Embellishments to the City of Paris," the SI's carnivalization of May '68, the plea for destruction in "Anarchy in the U.K." He reenacts none of them in the event, but just before they happened, and just after they made what history they made—after they happened out of it. Leaving these pseudo-events suspended in time, the man reenacts the judgment of history on all such attempts to make it, on all attempts to get out of the century, whether backward or forward: the judgment that save for madness or suicide there is no way out of one's time. But of course this is not all that is happening in the song. So quiet, "The Building" is an echo of an explosion that actually took place.

"We wanted to create a situation where kids would be less interested in buying records than in speaking for themselves," Malcolm McLaren said of the Sex Pistols, and one result of "Anarchy in the U.K." was a sort of giant answer record, an assemblage made of thousands of pieces, in dozens of languages, all over the world. It was a potlatch of yesses and noes that sounded like a conversation in which everything was at stake—a potlatch that, for a time, sounded like a conversation in which everyone was taking part.

This is what you can still hear in some of the artifacts the punk conversation left behind—in the Adverts' "One Chord Wonders," X-ray Spex's "I Am a Cliché," the Gang of Four's "Return the Gift." Destroying all limits on everyday speech, turning it into public speech, the conversation discovered a new subject: everyday life, which was revealed as public life. In this answer record, the most obvious facts of love or money, of habit or news, were neither obvious nor facts, but interested constructions, mysteries of credulity and power. In misery or delight, one could dramatize submission or resistance, false consciousness or negation. As in "Anarchy in the U.K.," streets became potential fields of action, and ordinary buildings world-historical. As in "Holidays in the Sun," the world-historical became a joke, then a horror movie. As in "Bodies," the private self became the body politic, and that transformation produced an urgency, a spirit of collective vehemence—the thrill of speaking out loud driven by its own danger—that no record had quite contained before.

It was, in a haphazard way, an art project. It had its proximate roots: in 1968 McLaren and his partner-to-be Jamie Reid were on the fringes of King Mob, a group Christopher Gray formed in London after his exclusion from the SI. Taking its name from the murderous crowds that rampaged through London during the anti-Catholic Gordon Riots of 1780, opening prisons and putting criminals on the streets, the band attacked the spectacle-commodity society by smashing up Wimpy bars. In surging letters three feet high it painted the city walls with cryptic slogans: sometimes lines from Coleridge's "Dejection: An Ode" ("A GRIEF WITHOUT A PANG, VOID, DARK, AND DREAR, A STIFLED, DROWSY, UNIMPASSIONED GRIEF"), sometimes just "I CANT BREATHE." The group threw a potlatch in Selfridges', with a man dressed up as Santa Claus giving away the department store's toys to throngs of happy children; it accomplished Strasbourg-style détournement when the children were forced to witness the shocking sight of one of Santa's helpers placed under arrest. In the pages of the short-lived sheet *King Mob Echo*, all the old talismans appeared once more: a reprint of Vaneigem's celebration of dada, a photo of Rosa Luxemburg in her canal coffin, the colloquy between Suso and the Free Spirit, a letter to the London Central News Agency from Jack the Ripper ("I love my work"), cartoons of naked Ranters preaching, even a bitter rejection of "alternative culture" ("the Cabaret Voltaire on ice") signed with the pen-name "Richard Huelsenbeck." Then the times changed, the context in which all these things could communicate not pedantry but novelty vanished, and what once were metaphors became fugitive footnotes to a text no longer in print.

As with the already-old slogans the LI put on Paris walls in 1953, those who tried to carry this conversation into the next decade soon found that the phrases they were condemned to use were barely language at all. Damning his "revolting celebrity" as the black hand behind May '68, Debord wrote an end to the SI, hoping to destroy the revolutionary commodity it had become. The SI's multitude of new fans, he said, would never learn the answer to their most important question: what metallic color had been chosen for the cover of *I.S.* no. 13? "The more our theses become famous, we ourselves will become *even more inaccessible*, even more clandestine," he said, and though he kept his word, it was only his; the year was 1972, and there was no more "we." McLaren opened his King's Road boutique and sold his May '68 t-shirts. Reid started *Suburban Press*, a mimeographed journal devoted to an SI-style critique of the planned London suburb of Croydon. Gray put together *Leaving the 20th Century*; Reid designed it. And Reid printed up little red stickers, which he posted in supermarkets—

but nobody was frightened. The last days, anyone could have figured, referred only to those of the story he was telling.

By 1975 the old talismans had come loose from their events; they were toys. Together, McLaren and Reid began to fool with them. Playing with legends of freedom picked up in art school, in news reports about May '68, in *The Return of the Durutti Column,* in tales recounted in Gray's book—playing with situationist notions of boredom as social control, leisure as work, work as a swindle, architecture as repression, revolution as festival—playing with the dadaist aggression and arrogance in the SI's writing, with its millenarian strain, the sense that the world could be changed in an instant—and playing with the inversions of the new social facts, with mass unemployment in a welfare state as a new kind of leisure, and that kind of leisure as the bad conscience of a new kind of boredom—they invented a pop group. With "I am an antichrist," the first line of the group's first song, they restaged the invasion of Notre-Dame. Just as that forgotten event led to the foundation of a small band that went on to imagine and spark a wildcat general strike, a wildcat general strike is what McLaren, Reid, and Johnny Rotten restaged in the words and sounds that followed.

It was the restaging of another art project—for that, before and after all the elegant and absolutist theory, before and after the long and inspired argument with history, was what the situationist project had been. If the spectacle was bad art, the creation of situations was the good. "We have to multiply poetic subjects and objects," Debord wrote in 1957, as the LI dissolved itself into the SI, "and we have to organize games of these poetic objects among these poetic subjects. This is our entire program"—and the entire program it was. In *Internationale situationniste* the facts of life were removed into a poetic dimension, where they could be reseen, and remade, by anyone, by everyone; during May '68, it had seemed as if the game had begun. If you looked you could see it happen: every gesture was extended, every street redrawn, every building demolished and rebuilt, every word part of a new language. But this is also what happened with punk.

LISTENING

Listening to "Anarchy in the U.K." years ago, all I wanted to know was why the record was so powerful. I have an idea now.

In my account of what McLaren and Reid made of the SI's old art project—by 1975, dead letters sent from a mythical time—Johnny Rotten appears as a mouthpiece; I prefer to think of him as a medium. As he stood on the stage, opened his mouth, and fixed his eyes on the crowd, various people who had never met, some who had met but who had never been properly introduced, some who had never heard of some of the others, as Johnny Rotten had heard of almost none of them, began to talk to each other, and the noise they made was what one heard. An unknown tradition of old pronouncements, poems, and events, a secret history of ancient wishes and defeats, came to bear on Johnny Rotten's voice—and because this tradition lacked both cultural sanction and political legitimacy, because this history was comprised of only unfinished, unsatisfied stories, it carried tremendous force.

All the demands that dada made on art, that Michel Mourre made on God, that the LI and the SI made on their time, came to life as demands on the symbolic milieu of pop music—demands that produced a voice it had never used. Because these demands were so disproportionate to the strictures the pop milieu had come to accept—strictures that produced entertainment as alienation and art as hierarchical dispossession—the milieu exploded. Because the milieu enclosed pop culture, obscure and hermetic incidents and ideas were taken up by countless ordinary people, and those incidents and ideas made a code those people did not know they were deciphering, a code which deciphered them.

With Debord, Huelsenbeck, Ball, Wolman, Chtcheglov, Mourre, Coppe, and more fighting for Johnny Rotten's microphone, the pop market was flooded with desires it was not built to satisfy. Traditional rock 'n' roll desires to make noise, to step forward, to "announce yourself," were transformed into the conscious desire to make your own history, or to abolish the history already made for you. The situationists bet that such a pass would lead people to go off the market, but that is not what happened—rather, people drove deeper into the market, and the result was topsy turvy. Remade as punk, pop music returned a gift it never knew it had received—returned it on a higher plane of value, producing richer works of art than dada, the LI, or the SI ever did. But the gift also fell short of the gift to which it found itself returned, because in the tradition in question, art had never been the goal, but "only an occasion, a method, for locating the specific rhythm and the buried face of this age . . . for the possibility of its being stirred." Remaining always within the pop milieu, the symbol factory, punk was only art—and so as language, thought, or action it was swallowed by the chiefs who began the game. Measured against the demands its precursors made, punk was a paltry reflection; measured against the records the Sex Pistols and their followers made, the leavings of dada, the LI, and the SI are sketches of punk songs; all in all it is the tale of a wish that went beyond art and found itself returned to it, a nightclub act that asked for the world, for a moment got it, then got another nightclub. In this sense punk realized the projects that lay behind it, and realized their limits.

The story continued; it also changed. Because the story punk was telling was so old and so foreign—a story about art and revolution now playing itself out in a realm of amusements and commodities—every sound and movement seemed completely new. But the very intensity of this illusion, its vertigo, drove the story into the past, in search of an anchor.

"Nothing is true; everything is permitted." So said Nietzsche, and Mourre, and numerous punks, and Debord, quoting Rashid al-Din Sinan, Islamic gnostic, leader of the Levantine Assassins, Sinan as he lay on his deathbed in 1192, unless it was 1193, or 1194—and apochryphal or not, the words make up the first line in the canon of the secret tradition, a nihilist catchphrase, an entry into negation, a utopianism, a shibboleth. If this was all Johnny Rotten's songs finally said, the story would turn back on itself and die, choking on its own clichés. But in his most convulsive moments, Johnny Rotten said something more—what Hasan i-Sabbah II, chief of the Assassins in Iran, and Sinan's spiritual master, said in 1164.

In that year, Hasan i-Sabbah II, legatee of the first Hasan i-Sabbah, founder of the Assassins, announced the millennium. In Alamut, the mountain fiefdom he ruled, he threw down the

Koran and proclaimed the end of the law. With his subjects, in the Holy Hour, he turned his back on Mecca. In the midst of Ramadan, the Holy Fast, they feasted and rejoiced. "They spoke of the world as being uncreated and Time as unlimited," wrote a chronicler; because "in the world to come there is no action and all is reckoning," they declared that on earth "all is action and there is no reckoning."

This is absolute freedom, the prize seized by the Cathars, the Brethren of the Free Spirit, the Lollards, John of Leyden, the Ranters, and Adolf Hitler: the end of the world. This is the fire around which the dadaists and Debord's strangely fecund groups held their dances, and which consumed them—a fire, though, that can be heard in the words they left behind because of the noise the Sex Pistols made. In the dadaists' manifestos and poems, in the LI's détournement of the best news of the week, in the SI's détournement of the news of the world, the fire is a reference point, properly footnoted but carefully marginalized; in the Sex Pistols' music, no footnotes at all, the fire is central. The ancestors danced around it; their inheritors dove in.

In the act, the story doubles back and rewrites itself. All of the freedom of that twelfth-century blasphemy, and all of its terror, is in the Sex Pistols' music, far more than it is in their precursors' writing. This is what is happening in the last minute of "Holidays in the Sun," and it is why no sane person would want to listen, or sing, for a minute more.

This is the secret the Sex Pistols told, and it is half of the story. The other half is a secret the Sex Pistols didn't tell. Their ancestors did tell it, because they lived it out—or, because they were not punks but primitive philosophers, they glimpsed the secret before the fact, as Debord did. "This is our entire program," he went on in 1957, "which is essentially transitory. Our situations will be ephemeral, without a future: passageways."

I was drawn to this message, coded but not stated in punk, because in a small and anonymous way I lived it out myself.

In the fall of 1964, in Berkeley, at the University of California, I was, day after day, for months, part of the crowd that made up the Free Speech Movement. In that event, which began as a small protest over rules and regulations, and which I now understand as a conversation, everything was at stake and, in one way or another, everyone took part. "I came here to go to business school," a friend said—he couldn't have been less interested in politics, in questions of how and why people make judgments on the ordering of their shared space and time, on what counts and what doesn't according to those judgments—"and all we ever do is talk about this goddamn FSM!"

It was a period of doubt, chaos, anger, hesitation, confusion, and finally joy—that's the word. Your own history was lying in pieces on the ground, and you had the choice of picking up the pieces or passing them by. Nothing was trivial, nothing incidental. Everything connected to a totality, and the totality was how you wanted to live: as a subject or as an object of history. In enormous gatherings, people spoke out as they never had before; they did the same in gatherings of two or three.

As the conversation expanded, institutional, historical power dissolved. People did and said things that made their lives of a few weeks before seem unreal—they did and said things that, not long after, would seem even more so. A school became a terrain on which all emotions, all ideas and theories, were tested and fought over; it was scary and it was fun. Dramas were enacted; people gathered around poisonous speeches; one found oneself in Homeric times, and the metaphor was physical, the body politic. In the university's Greek Theater, the entire community came together; before sixteen thousand people the president of the university gave a long, calming speech, so full of reasonableness it defused every mental bomb anyone had brought to the event. Then Mario Savio, the stuttering Demosthenes of the Free Speech Movement, walked toward the podium to deliver a response, police seized him and dragged him away, and what was left was nothing: it was as if the president of the university had never opened his mouth.

There was only chaos. People who moments before had been lulled into a lovely sleep screamed their lungs out. It was the loudest noise I've ever heard, or made.

Soon enough, the battle was resolved—won—in a great, formal debate by professors over rules and regulations. The rules were changed, and everyone went back to real life. But though the Free Speech Movement would occasionally be cited in years to come as a harbinger of the storm of protest that swept the campuses of the United States in the late 1960s and early 1970s, as a prefiguration of the protest against the Vietnam War, in fact the event, its spirit, in which people acted not for others but for themselves, with no sense of distance or separation, completely disappeared, as if it had never been.

For better or worse—it wasn't my choice—this event formed a standard against which I've judged the present and the past ever since. Even though the event left nothing behind one could touch—no monuments, not even a plaque—I never got over it. Time passed and I tried to hold on to it, as an incomplete but indelible image of good public life. As an image it reappeared in different shapes, in different times. I recognized it from afar in May '68, when, in my own town, the open discourse and experimental action of the Free Speech Movement had long since been transformed into ideology and manipulation: during a Berkeley demonstration held in solidarity with the rioters in Paris, activists mistakenly distributed the leaflets denouncing the atrocities committed that night by the local police an hour or so before the police showed up. So I looked back, wanting more of what I'd briefly seen, seeking an anchor, and recognized the public life of a few years before in accounts of what revolutionary councils had been like in Petrograd in 1917, Berlin in 1918, Hungary in 1956—but reading the books, the event I'd been part of seemed almost as old.

I recognized this public life in punk—right away, with no idea why. As a fan I felt the way John Peel felt as a disc jockey: shocked. After so much had happened, after so much had stopped so fast, after so little had happened for so long, it felt as if the sound were coming from another planet, it seemed so remarkable that it was happening at all. But as I looked into this new event, the shock doubled. The event was a strand in a real tradition, partly grasped by its many authors, mostly not; the tradition had its own imperatives, which operated in a manner independent of what anyone might choose to make of them.

I found a tale composed of incomplete sentences, voices cut off or falling silent, tired repetitions pressing on in search of novelties, a tale of recapitulations staged again and again in different theaters—a map made altogether of dead ends, where the only movement possible was not progress, not construction, but ricochet and surprise. And so, pursuing this story, when I finally came across Debord's homily on the ephemeral, his theory of "situations without a future," I was drawn to it as I had been drawn to the noise in punk: to his frank and determined embrace of moments in which the world seems to change, moments that leave nothing behind but dissatisfaction, disappointment, rage, sorrow, isolation, and vanity.

This is the secret the Sex Pistols didn't tell, which they only acted out: the moment in which the world seems to change is an absolute, the absolute of passing time, which is made of limits. For those who want everything, there is finally no action, only an endless, finally solipsistic reckoning. Thus Debord, over and over, quoting that sentimental line of Bossuet's, "Bernard, Bernard, this bloom of youth will not last forever"— words that, combined with those that follow them (which, once, out of all the times he used the phrase, Debord also quoted), are not sentimental at all. "Bernard, Bernard, this bloom of youth will not last forever," Bossuet said to the dead saint. "The fatal hour will come—the fatal hour, which, with an inexorable sentence, will cut short all false hopes. On our own ground, life will fail us like a false friend. The wealthy of this earth, who lead a life of pleasure, who imagine themselves to possess great things, will be astonished to find their hands empty."

THERE IS

There is a hint of transformation here, of resentment, leading—who knows where? There is the certainty of failure: all those who glimpse possibility in a spectral moment become rich, and though they remain so, they are ever after ever more impoverished. That is why, as I write, Johnny Rotten is a pop star who cannot make his fans forget the Sex Pistols, why Guy Debord writes books about his past, why the Hacienda is a nightclub in Manchester, England, and why, a few years before he died, Dr. Charles R. Hulbeck again became Huelsenbeck, left the U.S.A., and went back to Switzerland, hoping to rediscover what he'd found there more than fifty years before (not believing for a minute that he would), trying, he said, "to go back to some kind of chaos," half-convinced that "liberty really never existed anywhere."

If all of this seems like a lot for a pop song to contain, that is why this story is a story, if it is. And it is why any good punk song can sound like the greatest thing you ever heard, which it does. When it doesn't, that will mean the story has taken its next turn.

WORKS CITED

This book does not pretend to be a history of any of the movements it addresses; the restricted list that follows does not provide anything like a comprehensive or even schematic bibliography, discography, or filmography of those movements. It is meant simply to keep the record straight.

Films are listed by title, with the name of the director following. Recordings are listed by artist, with label, date, and country of release (if not U.S.) in parentheses; singles are noted in quotation marks, with lps and eps italicized; punk performers are noted by home town; only original releases are cited. Interviews from which short quotes from punk performers have been taken are generally not listed here, nor are daily newspaper reports.

Adorno, Theodor. *Minima Moralia: Reflections from Damaged Life* (1951), trans. G.F.N. Jephcott. London: Verso, 1978.

Adverts (London). "One Chord Wonders"/"Quickstep" (Stiff, 1977, U.K.). "Gary Gilmore's Eyes"/"Bored Teenagers" (Bright/Anchor, 1977, U.K.). *Crossing the Red Sea with the Adverts* (Bright/Anchor, 1978, U.K.).

Ambler, Eric. *Cause for Alarm* (1938). Harmondsworth, U.K.: Penguin, 1961.

Anscombe, Isabelle. *Punk*. New York: Urizen, 1978.

Arendt, Hannah. "Organized Guilt and Universal Responsibility" (1945), in *The Jew as Pariah*, ed. Ron Feldman. New York: Grove, 1978.

Arp, Jean (Hans). "Dadaland" (1938–1962), in *Arp on Arp: Poems, Essays, Memories*, ed. Marcel Jean, trans. Joachim Neugroschel. New York: Viking, 1972.

—— and Richard Huelsenbeck. *Dada in Zürich*, ed. Peter Schifferli. Zurich: Sansouci, 1966.

Ascherson, Neal. *The Polish August: The Self-Limiting Revolution*. New York: Viking, 1981.

Association fédérative générale des étudiants de Strasbourg. *De la misère en milieu étudiant, consideré sous ses aspects économique, sexuel et notamment intelletuel et de quelques moyens pour y remédier*. Strasbourg: AFGES, 1966. Reprinted Paris: Champ Libre, 1977.

―――― *Le Retour de la colonne Durutti*. Strasbourg: AFGES, 1966. André Bertrand's comic strip as fold-out pamphlet. Courtesy Steef Davidson.

Atkins, Guy. *Asger Jorn: The Crucial Years, 1954–1964*. London: Lund Humphries, 1977.

Au Pairs (Birmingham). "You"/"Kerb Crawler" (021, 1981, U.K.).

Auster, Paul. *In the Country of Last Things*. New York: Viking, 1987.

―――― *The Locked Room*. Los Angeles: Sun & Moon, 1986.

Ball, Hugo. *Flight Out of Time: A Dada Diary* (1927, *Die Flucht aus der Zeit*), ed. John Elderfield, trans. Ann Raimes. New York: Viking, 1974.

Bataille, Georges. "The Notion of Expenditure," trans. Allan Stoekl. *Raritan*, 3 (Winter 1984). Originally published in *La Critique sociale* (Paris), 7 (January 1933).

Berger, John. "Lost Prophets." *New Society* (London, 6 March 1975). Review of Christopher Gray, *Leaving the 20th Century*.

―――― and Alain Tanner. *Jonah Who Will Be 25 in the Year 2000*, trans. Michael Palmer. Berkeley: North Atlantic, 1983. Screenplay of 1976 film including interview with director Tanner about May '68.

Bernstein, Michèle. *La Nuit*. Paris: Buchet-Chastel, 1961.

―――― "The Situationist International." *Times Literary Supplement* (3 September 1964).

―――― *Tous les chevaux du roi*. Paris: Buchet-Chastel, 1960.

Berreby, Gérard, ed. *1948–1957: Documents relatifs à la fondation de l'Internationale situationniste*. Paris: Allia, 1985. Anthology including most lettrist publications by LI members; all LI publications; Asger Jorn, *Pour la forme* (1958); and color facsimile of Jorn and Guy-Ernest Debord, *Fin de Copenhague* (1957).

Berry, Chuck. "Johnny B. Goode," with studio dialogue, on *Rock 'n' Roll Rarities* (Chess, 1986, previously unreleased version, recorded 1957). "Johnny B. Goode" (Chess, 1958).

Bertrand, André. See Association fédérative générale des étudiants de Strasbourg.

Bettleheim, Bruno. *Surviving and Other Essays*. New York: Vintage, 1980.

Boomtown Rats (Dublin). "I Don't Like Mondays" (Columbia, 1980).

Brau, Eliane. *Le Situationnisme ou la nouvelle internationale*. Paris: Nouvelle Editions Debresse, 1968. Commentary on Lettrist International by a participant.

Brau, Jean-Louis. *Cours, camarade, le vieux monde est derrière toi! Histoire du mouvement révolutionnaire étudiant en Europe*. Paris: Albin Michel, 1968. Extensive discussion of lettrist movement and LI by a participant. Includes Front de la jeunesse, "Notre programme," as appendix.

——— *Instrumentation verbale* (Achèle, 1965, France). Courtesy Larry Wendt. See also Dufrêne, François.

Brown, Bernard E. *Protest in Paris: Anatomy of a Revolt*. Morristown, N.J.: General Learning, 1974.

Buster, Prince. *Judge Dread Featuring Prince Buster—Jamaica's Pride* (Melodisc, c. 1965, U.K.). Includes Judge Dread trilogy: "Judge Dread," "The Appeal," and "Judge Dread Dance" ("Barrister Pardon").

Buzzcocks (Manchester). *Spiral Scratch* (New Hormones, 1977, U.K.).

Chopin, Henri, ed. *Du Revue-Disque 33* (Multi-Techniques, 1968, France). Includes Gil J Wolman, "Mégapneumes 67, 'La Mémoire.'" Courtesy Larry Wendt.

Clanton, Jimmy. "Go, Jimmy, Go," with studio dialogue, on *The Ace Story Volume Two* (Ace, 1980, U.K., recorded 1959).

Clark, Larry. *Teenage Lust: An Autobiography*. New York, 1983.

——— *Tulsa*. New York, 1971.

Clark, T. J. *The Painting of Modern Life: Paris in the Art of Manet and His Followers*. New York: Knopf, 1984.

Clash (London). "White Riot"/"1977" (CBS, 1977, U.K.). *The Clash* (CBS, 1977, U.K.). "Complete Control" (CBS, 1977, U.K.).

Cohn, Nik. *Awopbopaloobop Alopbamboom: Pop from the Beginning*, rev. ed. London: Paladin, 1972. Originally published 1969 as *Pop from the Beginning* (U.K.) and *Rock from the Beginning* (U.S.).

Cohn, Norman. *The Pursuit of the Millennium: Revolutionary Millenarians and Mystical Anarchists of the Middle Ages* (1957), rev. ed. New York: Oxford, 1970. Includes appendix of numerous Ranter texts. "Conclusion" of 2nd ed. (London: Mercury, 1962), which differs significantly from this edition, was also used.

Cortinas (Bristol). "Fascist Dictator" (Step Forward, 1977, U.K.).

Costello, Elvis (London). *This Year's Model* (Columbia, 1978).

Croce, Arlene. *The Fred Astaire and Ginger Rogers Book*. New York: Dutton, 1972.

Curtay, Jean-Paul. *La Poèsie lettriste*. Paris: Seghers, 1974. Includes appendices with poems by major lettrists.

Dada Berlin. Paris: Musée d'art moderne de la ville de Paris. Anthology notable for Raoul Hausmann, "Club Dada Berlin, 1918–1921," written 1966.

Dada for Now: A Collection of Futurist and Dada Soundworks (Ark, 1985, U.K.). Includes contemporary recreations by Trio Exvoco of Hugo Ball sound poems and of the Huelsenbeck–Janco–Tzara "L'Amiral cherche une maison à louer" (all composed 1916).

Dada Zeitschriften. Hamburg: Nautilus, 1978. Facsimile reproductions of dada journals, including *Cabaret Voltaire* (Zurich, 1916), *Club Dada* (Berlin, 1918), *Der Dada* (Berlin), 1–3 (1919–20), and trial sheets for uncompleted *Dadaco* (Munich, 1920).

Davidson, Steef. *The Penguin Book of Political Comics*, trans. Hester and Marianne Velmans. New York: Penguin, 1982. Includes numerous situationist, King Mob, and situationist-influenced comics and cartoons.

Debord, Guy (-Ernest). *Considérations sur l'assassinat de Gérard Lebovici*. Paris: Gérard Lebovici, 1985. "Debord's patron and friend Gérard Lebovici—a French film producer whom [Debord] met in 1971—not only supported Debord's work by financing what was effectively a situationist press, Champ Libre, he also bought a cinema—the Studio Cujas in St. Germain—which projected Debord's cinematographic production on a continuous and exclusive basis. This lasted only through 1984, however, when following the mysterious and still unsolved murder of Lebovici in a parking garage off the Champs Elysées, Debord withdrew his films in a gesture of protest and mourning classically situationist in its decisiveness. Incensed by the murder of his friend and by the manner in which the press reported it [in effect, blaming it on Debord as "bad company" and spuriously linking Debord to the French terrorist group Action directe], he then wrote [a book] in which he announced that 'the outrageous manner in which the newspapers have discussed [Lebovici's] assassination has led me to decide that none of my films will ever be shown again in France. This absence will be the most fitting homage.'"—Thomas Y. Levin, "Dismantling the Spectacle," in *On the Passage of a Few People through a Rather Brief Moment in Time: The Situationist International, 1957–1972*, ed. Elisabeth Sussman. Cambridge: ICA/MIT, 1989. In a letter to Levin later in 1987, Debord replied to the question of whether his films might still be screened outside France: "Never again, and nowhere."

———— *Contre le cinéma*. Aarhaus, Denmark: Institute scandinave de vandalisme comparé, 1964. Scripts of Debord's first three films with visual descriptions plus technical notes; introduction ("Guy Debord et le problème de maudit") by Asger Jorn.

———— *Oeuvres cinématographiques complètes: 1952–1978*. Paris: Champ Libre, 1978. Scripts of Debord's five films (*Hurlements en faveur de Sade*, 1952; *Sur le passage de quelques personnes à travers une assez courte unité de temps*, 1959; *Critique de la séparation*, 1961; *La Société du Spectacle*, 1973; *Réfutation de tous les jugements, tant élogieux qu'hostiles, qui ont été jusqu'ici portés sur le film "La Société du Spectacle"*, 1975; and *In girum imus nocte et consumimur igni*, 1978), with visual descriptions.

———— *Preface à la quatrième édition italienne de "La Société du Spectacle."* Paris: Champ Libre, 1979. Trans. Frances Parker and Michael Forsyth as *Preface to the Fourth Italian Edition of "The Society of the Spectacle."* London: Chronos, 1979, 1983.

———— "The Situationists and the New Action Forms in Politics and Art," in Internationale situationniste, *Destruktion AF RSG 6*. Odense, Denmark: Galerie EXI, 1963. Exhibition catalogue in French, Danish, and English.

———— *La Société du Spectacle*. Paris: Champ Libre, 1971. Originally published Paris: Buchet-Chastel, 1967. Trans. as *Society of the Spectacle*. Detroit: Black & Red, 1977.

———— with Asger Jorn. *Mémoires*. Paris: Internationale situationniste, 1959; constructed 1957. See also Jorn, Asger.

Decline ... of Western Civilization, The. Directed by Penelope Spheeris. 1980. Includes performance by Darby Crash and the Germs.

Dils (Los Angeles). "I Hate the Rich"/"You're Not Blank" (What, 1977). "Class War"/"Mr. Big" (Dangerhouse, 1977).

Drabble, Margaret. *The Ice Age*. New York: Knopf, 1977.

Dufrêne, François, ed. *L'Autonomatopek 1* (Opus International, 1973, France). Includes Jean-Louis Brau, "Turn Back Nightingale," Isidore Isou, "Lances rompues pour la dame gothique" (1945), and Gil J Wolman, "Ralentissez les cadences, mégapneume." Courtesy Larry Wendt.

Enfants du paradis, Les. Directed by Marcel Carné, script by Jacques Prévert. 1944.

Essential Logic (London). "Wake Up" (Virgin, 1979, U.K.).

Fairport Convention. "Tale in Hard Time," on *What We Did on Our Holidays* (Island, 1969, U.K., released as *Fairport Convention* in U.S.).

Firesign Theater. *Don't Crush That Dwarf, Hand Me the Pliers* (Columbia, 1970).

Five Million Years to Earth (Quatermass and the Pit). Directed by Roy Ward Baker, script by Nigel Kneale. 1967.

Foster, Stephen C., ed. *Lettrisme: Into the Present*, special issue of *Visible Language* (Cleveland), 17 (Summer 1983).

Front de la jeunesse. See Brau, Jean-Louis.

Gang of Four (Leeds). "At Home He's a Tourist"/"It's Her Factory" (EMI, 1979, U.K.). *Entertainment!* (EMI, 1979, U.K., later Warner Bros., U.S.).

Gillett, Charlie. *The Sound of the City: The Rise of Rock and Roll* (1970), rev. ed. New York: Pantheon, 1983.

God and the State (Los Angeles). *The Complete Works of God and the State* (Independent Project, 1985, recorded 1983).

Gordon, Kim. "'I'm Really Scared When I Kill in My Dreams.'" *Artforum* (New York, January 1983).

Gray, Christopher, ed. and trans. *Leaving the 20th Century: The Incomplete Work of the Situationist International*. U.K.: Free Fall, 1974.

Great Rock 'n' Roll Swindle, The. Directed by Julien Temple, script by Malcom Forger. 1980.

Grosz, George. *A Little Yes and a Big No*, trans. Lola Sachs Dorina. New York: Dial, 1946.

Hausmann, Raoul. *Courrier Dada*. Paris: Terrain Vague, 1958.

——— "Dadaism and Today's Avant-Garde." *Times Literary Supplement* (3 September 1964).

——— *Poèmes phonetiques complètes* (S Press Tapes, West Germany). Includes "Phonemes," composed 1918–19, recorded 1956–57; "Soundreel," composed 1919, recorded 1959; and "Interview avec les lettristes," 1946.

Heatwave (London), 1–2 (July and October 1966). Mimeographed journal published by group of same name, including Christopher Gray and others, before affiliation with Situationist International.

Horkheimer, Max, and Theodor W. Adorno. *Dialectic of Enlightenment* (1944), trans. John Cumming. New York: Herder and Herder, 1972.

Huelsenbeck, Richard, ed. *Dada Almanach*. Berlin: Erich Reiss, 1920. Facsimile edition, New York: Something Else, 1966.

——— ed. *Dada: Eine literarische Dokumentation*. Hamburg: Rowohlt, 1964.

——— "Dada, or the Meaning of Chaos." *Studio International* (London, January 1972). Edited version of talk given at Institute of Contemporary Arts, 1 October 1971.

——— *Deutschland müss untergehen!* Berlin: Malik, 1920. Courtesy Klaus Humann.

——— *En Avant Dada: Die Geschichte des Dadaismus*. Berlin: Paul Steegemann, 1920. Facsimile edition, Hamburg: Nautilus, 1978. Trans. Ralph Manheim in Motherwell, ed., *The Dada Painters and Poets*.

——— *Memoirs of a Dada Drummer*, ed. Hans J. Kleinschmidt, trans. Joachim Neugroschel. New York: Viking, 1974. Text of 1957 *Mit Witz, Licht und Grütze*, plus numerous essays including "On Leaving America for Good" (1969).

Internationale situationniste. *Internationale situationniste: 1958–1969*. Paris: Champ Libre, 1975. Facsimile edition of complete run of principal situationist journal.

——— *La Véritable Scission dans l'internationale: Circulaire publique de l'Internationale situationniste*. Paris: Champ Libre, 1972. Includes Guy Debord and Gianfranco Sanguinetti, "Thèses sur l'Internationale situationniste et son temps," with appendices on Situationist International after May '68. Trans. as *The Veritable Split in the International*. London: Pirhana, 1974.

Ion (Paris, April 1952), no. 1.

Isou, Isidore. *L'Agrégation d'un nom et d'un méssie*. Paris: Gallimard, 1947.

———— *Contre le cinéma situationniste, néo-nazi*. Paris: GB/NV/MB, 1979.

———— "Les Créations du lettrisme." *Lettrisme* (Paris), 4th series, 1 (January 1972). Lengthy mimeographed catalogue of lettrist approaches to the arts.

———— "The Creations of Lettrism." *Times Literary Supplement* (3 September 1964). Greatly abridged version of the above.

———— *Introduction à une nouvelle poèsie et une nouvelle musique*. Paris: Gallimard, 1947.

———— *Oeuvres de Spectacle*. Paris: Gallimard, 1964. Includes the screenplay of *Traité de bave et d'éternité* and "Le Manifeste du cinéma discrépant."

Jackson, Michael. *Thriller* (Epic, 1982).

Joel, Billy. "The Longest Time," on *An Innocent Man* (Columbia, 1983).

Jorn, Asger. *Pour la forme: Ebauche d'une méthodologie des arts*. Paris: Internationale situationniste, 1958. Writings from 1954–1957. Includes Guy-Ernest Debord, "The Naked City." Reprinted in its entirety in Berreby, *1948–1957*.

———— with Guy-Ernest Debord. *Fin de Copenhague*. Copenhagen: Bauhaus Imaginiste, 1957. Overpainted collage satire of advertising, mass media, and city planning, purportedly assembled and printed in forty-eight hours on the basis of a single visit to a single newsstand; rough sketch for Debord's *Mémoires*. Facsimile reprint in Berreby, *1948–1957*; facsimile edition, Paris: Allia, 1986. See also Debord, Guy.

Jung, Carl G. "The Concept of the Collective Unconscious" (1936), in *The Viking Portable Jung*, ed. Joseph Campbell, trans. R.F.C. Hull. New York: Viking/Penguin, 1971.

Joy Division (Manchester). *An Ideal for Living* (Enigma, 1978, U.K.). *Unknown Pleasures* (Factory, 1979, U.K.).

Karp, Walter. "Coolidge Redux." *Harper's* (October 1981).

KILL IT. London, 1977. On "snuff rock"—program notes for C. P. Lee's play *Sleak* in form of punk fanzine.

King Mob. "It Was Meant to Be Great But It's Horrible: Confessions, S. Claus, 1968." London, 1968. Broadside preceding King Mob demonstration in Selfridges'. Courtesy Fred Vermorel.

———— *King Mob Echo* (London, April 1968). Courtesy Simon Frith.

———— "Posters Rejected by the L.S.E., October 25th to October 27th." London, 1968. Anti-leftist-hierarchy posters: revival of Abiezer Coppe's coprolaliac Ranterism. Courtesy Fred Vermorel.

———— "Two Letters on Student Power." London, November 1968. By

Christopher Gray and "Richard Huelsenbeck." Courtesy Simon Frith.

Kleenex (Zurich). "Beri-Beri"/"Ain't You"/"Heidi's Head"/"Nice" (Sunrise, 1978, Switzerland). "You (friendly side)"/"Ü (angry side)" (Rough Trade, 1979, U.K.). See also Liliput.

Kleinschmidt, Hans J. "Berlin Dada," in Stephen C. Foster and Rudolf Kuenzli, eds., *Dada Spectrum: The Dialectics of Revolt*. Madison, WI: Coda/Iowa City: Iowa, 1979.

Knabb, Ken, ed. and trans. *Situationist International Anthology*. Berkeley: Bureau of Public Secrets, P.O. Box 1044, Berkeley, CA 94701, 1981. Basic English-language collection of situationist writing; includes most major situationist essays and several important LI essays.

Kraus, Karl. *In These Great Times: A Karl Kraus Reader*, ed. Harry Zohn, trans. Joseph Fabry, Max Knight, Karl F. Ross, and Zohn. Manchester, U.K.: Carcanet, 1984. Includes "Promotional Trips to Hell," on Verdun vacations (1921).

Lanzmann, Claude. *Shoah: An Oral History of the Holocaust*. New York: Pantheon, 1985.

Le Roy Ladurie, Emmanuel. *Montaillou: The Promised Land of Error*, trans. Barbara Bray. New York: Vintage, 1979.

Lefebvre, Henri. *Critique de la vie quotidienne*, rev. ed. Paris: L'Arche, 1958. Different from *Introduction à la critique de la vie quotidienne*, below.

―――― *Everyday Life in the Modern World* (1968), trans. Sacha Rabinovitch. London: Allen Lane/Penguin, 1971.

―――― *Introduction à la critique de la vie quotidienne*. Paris: Grasset, 1947.

―――― *Introduction à la modernité*. Paris: Minuit, 1962.

―――― *Position contre les technocrates*. Paris: Gonthier, 1967.

―――― "'7 Manifestes Dada,' par Tristan Tzara." *Philosophies* (Paris), vol. 1 (March 1924).

―――― *The Survival of Capitalism*, trans. Frank Bryant. London: Allison and Busby, 1976.

―――― *Les Temps des mépris*. Paris: Stock, 1975. Interview with Lefebvre.

Lerner, Robert E. *The Heresy of the Free Spirit in the Later Middle Ages*. Berkeley: University of California Press, 1972.

Lèvres nues, Les (1954–1958). Paris: Plasma, 1978. Facsimile edition of Belgian post-surrealist journal, edited by Marcel Marien, with which Lettrist International collaborated. Numerous LI contributions.

Lewis, Bernard. *The Assassins: A Radical Sect in Islam* (1967), 2nd ed. New York: Oxford, 1987.

Lewis, Jerry Lee. "Great Balls of Fire," three versions, with studio dialogue, on *The Sun Years* (Sun/Charly, U.K., 1982, recorded 1957).

Liliput (Zurich). "Split"/"Die Matrosen" (Rough Trade, 1980, U.K.). "Eisiger Wind" (Rough Trade, 1981, U.K.).

Lippard, Lucy R., ed. *Dadas on Art*. Englewood Cliffs, N.J.: Prentice-Hall, 1977. Includes "Invest in Dada!," trans. Gabrielle Bennett of Richard Huelsenbeck, Johannes Baader, and Raoul Hausmann, "Legen sie Ihr Geld in dada an!," originally published in *Der Dada* (Berlin), 1 (1919).

Llosa, Mario Vargas. *The War of the End of the World*, trans. Helen R. Lane. New York: Farrar, Straus, 1984.

Lunsford, Bascom Lamar. "I Wish I Was a Mole in the Ground," on *Anthology of American Folk Music, vol. 3: Songs*, comp. Harry Smith (Folkways, 1952, originally released in 1928 on Brunswick). Lunsford first recorded song in 1924.

Marien, Marcel. "Le Chemin de la croix (vii)." *Les Lèvres nues* (Brussels), 4 (January 1955). Includes text of Serge Berna/Michel Mourre 1950 Notre-Dame sermon, with commentary. Collected in *Les Lèvres nues (1954–1958)*.

Marx, Karl. "A Contribution to the Critique of Hegel's Philosophy of Right. Introduction (1843–44)," in *Early Writings*, ed. Quintin Hoare, trans. Gregor Benton. New York: Vintage, 1975.

———— "The Fetishism of the Commodity and Its Secret" (1867), in *Capital*, vol. 1, trans. Ben Fowkes. New York: Vintage, 1977.

Mauss, Marcel. *The Gift: Forms and Functions of Exchange in Archaic Societies* (1925), trans. Ian Cunnison. New York: Norton, 1967.

Mekons (Leeds). "Never Been in a Riot"/"32 Weeks"/"Heart and Soul" (Fast Product, 1978, U.K.). "Where Were You?"/"I'll Have to Dance Then (On My Own)" (Fast Product, 1978, U.K.). *The Quality of Mercy Is Not Strnen* (Virgin, 1979, U.K.). *it falleth like the gentle rain from heaven—The Mekons Story 1977–1982* (CNT, 1982, U.K.).

Meltzer, Annabelle. *Latest Rage the Big Drum: Dada and Surrealist Performance*. Ann Arbor: UMI Research, 1980.

Milosz, Czeslaw. *The Captive Mind* (1951, 1953), trans. Jane Zielonko. New York: Vintage, 1981.

Monty Python's Flying Circus. *The Worst of Monty Python's Flying Circus* (Pye/ATV, 1970).

Motherwell, Robert, ed. *The Dada Painters and Poets: An Anthology* (1951), 2nd ed. Boston: Hall, 1981. Basic English-language collection.

Mourre, Michel. *Malgré le blasphème*. Paris: René Julliard, 1951.

Trans. A. W. Fielding as *In Spite of Blasphemy*. London: John Lehmann, 1953.

Naumann, Francis M. "Janco/Dada: An Interview with Marcel Janco." *Arts Magazine* (November 1982).

"Notre-Dame Scandal, The." *Transition* (Paris), 6 (1950).

Orioles. "It's Too Soon to Know" (It's-a-Natural, 1948).

Penguins. "Earth Angel (Will You Be Mine)" (Doo-tone, 1954).

Police Academy 2: Their First Assignment. Directed by Jerry Paris, 1985.

Pomerand, Gabriel. *Saint ghetto des prêts*. Paris: O.L.B., 1950.

Pomerantz, Marsha. "Back to Chaos." *Jerusalem Post Friday Magazine* (16 March 1984). On Marcel Janco's revival of Cabaret Voltaire.

Potlatch: 1954–57. Paris: Gérard Lebovici, 1985. Nos. 1–29 of Lettrist International newsletter, with introduction by Guy Debord.

Public Image Ltd./PiL (London). *Metal Box* (Virgin, 1979, U.K.).

Quantick, David. "Punky Adventures on the Wheels of Peel." *New Musical Express* (London, 15 February 1986). Interview with John Peel.

Raabe, Paul, ed. *The Era of German Expressionism*, trans. J. M. Ritchie. Dallas: Riverrun, 1980. Includes Richard Huelsenbeck, "Zurich 1916, as it really was" (1928) and Raoul Hausmann, "Club Dada. Berlin 1918–1920" (1958).

Raincoats (London). "Fairytale in the Supermarket" (Rough Trade, 1979, U.K.).

Raspaud, Jean-Jacques, and Jean-Pierre Voyer. *L'Internationale situationniste: Protagonistes/chronologie/bibliographie (avec un index des noms insultés)*. Paris: Champ Libre, 1972. Schematic ref.

Reid, Jamie. *Up They Rise: The Incomplete Works of Jamie Reid*. London: Faber, 1987. Graphics 1971–1987, with interviews and commentary by Jon Savage.

Richman, Jonathan/The Modern Lovers. "Road Runner," on *Beserkley Chartbusters* (Beserkley anthology, 1975). *The Modern Lovers* (Beserkley, 1976, produced 1971 by John Cale). Including "Pablo Picasso," copyright © 1975 by Modern Love Songs, used by permission of Joel S. Turtle, Administration: "Some guys try to pick up girls and get called assholes/ This never happened to Pablo Picasso." "I'm Straight," on *Troublemakers* (Warner Bros. Special Products anthology, 1980, recorded 1972).

Richter, Hans. *Dada: Art and Anti-Art* (1964). New York: Oxford University Press, 1978.

Riha, Karl, ed. *113 dada Gedichte*. Berlin: Klaus Wagenbuch, 1982.

Robinson, James M., ed. *The Nag Hammadi Library in English*. Includes "The Gospel of Truth, I, 3 (29–30)," trans. George W. MacRae. San Francisco: Harper & Row, 1977.

Rosenberg, Harold. "Criticism-Action," in *Act and the Actor* (1970). Chicago: University of Chicago Press, 1983.

—— "Surrealism in the Streets," in *The De-Definition of Art* (1972). Chicago: Chicago, 1983.

Roxy London WC 2 (Jan–Apr 77), The (EMI, 1977, U.K.). Ambient recording: "the complete construction of an atmosphere." Includes performances by Adverts, Eater, Slaughter & the Dogs, Wire, and X-ray Spex.

Schneider, Peter. *The Wall Jumper*, trans. Leigh Hafrey. New York: Pantheon, 1983.

Sex Pistols (London). "Anarchy in the U.K."/"I Wanna Be Me" (EMI, November 1976, U.K., withdrawn January 1977, reissued and best heard as 12-inch single on Barclay, 1977, France). "God Save the Queen"/"No Feelings" (A&M, May 1977, U.K., pressed, destroyed). "The week they were all assaulted—beaten, razored—when they truly could not go out except in clandestinity—the polarization in England was beyond belief. It was a *crunch*. There was an enormous support all over England for the Sex Pistols—not just among teenagers, but among very young kids, 10, 12—and from all sorts of people who were definitely *not* kids, such as myself—and as well from people who were a good bit older than I: people who really seemed to think that Johnny Rotten *was* the Antichrist—that out of all this chaos and destruction, 'the last days,' would come the millennium: the return of the '60s"—Denis Browne, assistant to Alexander Trocchi, 1983. "God Save the Queen"/"Did You No Wrong" (Virgin, May 1977, U.K.). "Pretty Vacant"/"No Fun (live)" (Virgin, July 1977, U.K.). "Holidays in the Sun"/"Satellite" (Virgin, October 1977, U.K., withdrawn after legal complaints over misappropriation of sleeve art). *Never Mind the Bollocks Here's the Sex Pistols* (Virgin, November 1977, U.K., Warner Bros., U.S.). Includes A-sides of singles plus, among other tracks, "Bodies." *The Great Rock 'n' Roll Swindle* (Virgin, 1979, U.K.). Includes "Johnny B. Goode" and "Road Runner" with studio dialogue, "Whatcha Gonna Do About It," "(I'm Not Your) Stepping Stone," "Don't Give Me No Lip Child," "Belsen Was a Gas" (live, recorded 14 January 1978 in San Francisco), and alternate version of "Anarchy in the U.K." *Gun Control—Winterland 1/14/78* (Ruthless Rhymes bootleg). *We Have Cum for Your Children—Wanted: The Goodman Tapes* (Skyclad bootleg). Includes 1976–77 live recordings, rehearsals, TV performances, and interviews, including the 1976 "Fuck" interview.

Sex Pistols. Target Video, 1988. The final concert in San Francisco, 14 January 1978.

Shattuck, Roger. "Paris Letter." *Accent: A Quarterly of New Literature* (Urbana, August 1948). On lettrism and existentialism.

Sheppard, Richard, ed. *New Studies in Dada: Essays and Documents.* Hutton, Driffield, U.K.: Hutton, 1979. Notable for Karin Füllner, "The Meister-Dada: The Image of Dada through the Eyes of Richard Huelsenbeck," numerous obscure and untranslated documents by Huelsenbeck, Joahnnes Baader, and Raoul Hausmann, and a lengthy chronology by Stephen C. Foster and Rudolf Kuenzli.

Situationist International (U.K.). *Ten Days That Shook the University: The situationists at Strasbourg.* London: Situationist International, 1967. Translation of *De la misère en milieu étudiant,* with introduction, and postscript, "If you make a social revolution, do it for fun." Illustrations from *Le Retour de la colonne Durutti.*

Slash (Los Angeles), 10 and 11 (May and July 1978). Interview with Malcolm McLaren.

Slits. "Once upon a time in a living room" (Y/Rough Trade "official bootleg," 1980, recorded 1977, U.K.).

Spellman, Benny. "Lipstick Traces (On a Cigarette)" (Minit, 1962).

Spencer, Neil, and Paul Rambali. "Malcolm and Bernard: Rock 'n' Roll Scoundrels." *New Musical Express* (London, 9 August 1980). Interviews with Malcolm McLaren and Bernard Rhodes.

Suburban Press (London), 1–6 (1970–1974). Journal on suburbia and consumer life published by Jeremy Brook, Jamie Reid, and Nigel Edwards. Courtesy Jon Savage.

Suicidal Tendencies (Los Angeles). "Institutionalized," on *Suicidal Tendencies* (Frontier, 1983).

Thompson, Gudrun. "Manners for Muggings." *Damage* (San Francisco, June 1981).

Time Zone (New York). "World Destruction" (Celluloid, 1984).

Trocchi, Alexander. *Cain's Book* (1960). New York: Grove, 1979.

——— "A Revolutionary Proposal: Invisible Insurrection of a Million Minds." *City Lights Journal* (San Francisco), 2 (1964). Originally published as "Technique du coupe du monde" in *Internationale situationniste,* 8 (January 1963).

——— *Sigma Portfolio.* London: Sigma, 1965. Twenty-six items assembled by Trocchi, including his "Potlatch—an interpersonal log" (1964).

Twenties in Berlin, The: Johannes Baader, George Grosz, Raoul Hausmann, Hannah Höch. London: Annely Juda Fine Art, 1978. Includes interview with Vera Broido-Cohn on Baader.

USA for Africa. "We Are the World" (Columbia, 1985).

van der Elsken, Ed. *Love on the Left Bank.* London: André Deutsch, 1957.

——— *Parijs! Fotos-1950–1954.* Amsterdam: Bert Bakker, 1981.

Vanderhaeghe, Guy. *My Present Age.* New York: Ticknor & Fields, 1985.

Vaneigem, Raoul. *Le Mouvement du Libre-Esprit: Généralités et té-moignages sur les affleurments de la vie à la surface du moyen-age, de la renaissance, et, incidemment, de notre époque.* Paris: Ramsay, 1986.

—— *Traité de savoir-vivre à l'usage des jeunes générations* (1967), 2nd ed. Paris: Gallimard, 1981. Trans. Donald Nicholson-Smith as *The Revolution of Everyday Life.* Scattle: Left Bank and London: Rebel, 1983.

Ventura, Michael. *Shadow Dancing in the U.S.A.* Los Angeles: Tarcher, 1985.

Vermorel, Fred and Judy. *Sex Pistols: The Inside Story* (1978), rev. ed. London: Omnibus, 1987.

Viénet, René, *Enragés et situationnistes dans le mouvement des occu-pations.* Paris: Gallimard, 1968. Narrative with numerous docu-ments and illustrations. Trans. (narrative only) Loren Goldner and Paul Sieveking as *Enragés and situationists in the Occupa-tions Movement, France, May–June 1968.* Heslington, York, U.K.: Tiger Papers, c. 1972.

Vollmer, Jurgen. *Rock 'n' Roll Times: The Style and Spirit of the Early Beatles and Their First Fans.* New York: Google Plex, 1981. Photographs from Hamburg and Paris.

Walker, Benjamin. *Gnosticism: Its History and Influence.* Welling-borough, Northamptonshire, U.K.: Aquarian, 1983.

Warner Communications. "Entertainment—An Essential Part of Life," in *Annual Report.* New York: Warner Communications, 1977.

Wenner, Jann. "Peter Townshend," in *The Rolling Stone Interviews.* New York: Paperback Library, 1971.

Willett, John. *Art and Politics in the Weimar Period: The New Sobri-ety, 1917–1933.* New York: Pantheon, 1978. Includes Kurt Tuchol-sky, "Danton's Death."

Williamson, Sonny Boy. "Little Village," with studio dialogue, on *Bummer Road* (Chess, 1970, recorded 1957).

Wilson, Edmund. "Night Thoughts in Paris, 1922," in Loren Baritz, ed., *Sources of the American Mind,* vol. 2. New York: Wiley, 1966.

—— *To the Finland Station* (1940). New York: Farrar, Straus, 1972.

Wire (London). "I Am the Fly" (Harvest, 1978, U.K.).

Wolcott, James. "Kiss Me, You Fool: Sex Pistols '77." *Village Voice* (21 November 1977).

Wolman, Gil J (as Joseph Wolman). *Durhing Durhing* (Paris, Septem-ber 1979).

—— *Improvisations—Mégapneumes* (Barclay, 1965, France). Cour-

tesy Larry Wendt. See also Chopin, Henri, and Dufrêne, François.
——— *Résumé des chapitres précédentes*. Paris: Spiess, 1981. Artistic autobiography by détournement: works, writings, reviews; includes numerous examples of scotch art.
X-ray Spex (London). "Oh Bondage Up Yours!"/"I Am a Cliché" (Virgin, 1977, U.K.). *Germfree Adolescents* (EMI, 1978, U.K.).

SOURCES AND CREDITS

This section includes credits and permissions for the use of illustrations, song lyrics, and other copyrighted works, as well as source notes to material cited in the text that does not, as it were, float in the air. Translations not credited are by the author.

PROLOGUE

p. 1. Ray Lowry, first panel of "note oilskin base," *New Musical Express* (19 May 1984), reprinted by permission of the artist.

p. 4. Walter Mehring, "Dadayama," trans. Alan C. Greenberg in his *Artists and Revolution: Dada and the Bauhaus, 1917–1925* (Ann Arbor: UMI Research Press, 1979), pp. 197–198.

pp. 8, 11, 13. "Anarchy in the U.K.," "God Save the Queen," "Pretty Vacant," by Steve Jones, Paul Cook, John Lydon, and Glen Matlock. All Sex Pistols songs quoted in this book are copyright © 1977 by Glitterbest Ltd., all rights reserved, used by permission.

p. 22. "La Légende dorée," *Les Lèvres nues* no. 3 (October 1954), p. 36; Berreby, p. 286.

p. 24. Lefebvre, *Les Temps des mépris*, pp. 39–40.

p. 24. "While present-day." "Maintenant, l'I.S.," *I.S.* no. 9 (August 1964), p. 5.

THE LAST SEX PISTOLS CONCERT

p. 27. "warning to those." Vaneigem, "Commentaires contre l'urbanisme," *I.S.* no. 6 (August 1961), p. 37; Gray, p. 130.

p. 29. Matt Groening, comic strip, "Storefront of Doom," *L. A. Reader* (3 August 1984), copyright © 1984 by Matt Groening, reprinted by permission of the artist.

p. 33. John Berger, "Lost Prophets," p. 600.

p. 34. Atelier populaire poster, "une jeunesse que l'avenir inquiète trop souvent" (phrase taken from a speech by President Charles de Gaulle, 24 May 1968).

p. 35. Jamie Reid, Sex Pistols flyer, reprinted by permission of the artist, courtesy Jon Savage.

p. 40. Anonymous Slits flyer, courtesy Jon Savage.

p. 41. Quantick, "Punky Adventures on the Wheels of Peel," p. 12.

pp. 43–44. Warner Communications, "Entertainment," pp. 10–11, courtesy Bruce McGregor.

p. 44. Photograph of the Penguins, courtesy Michael Ochs Archives.

pp. 44–45. "British ad in 1957." From Jorn and Debord, *Fin de Copenhague*.

p. 45. Drabble, pp. 59–60.

p. 47. Camus, *The Rebel* (New York: Vintage, 1956), p. 276.

p. 52. "Le Bruit et la fureur," *I.S.* no. 1 (June 1958), p. 6; Knabb, p. 42.

pp. 54–55. Anonymous leaflet, "For a Dignified and Effective Demonstration," courtesy A. Hares, Mattoid, London.

p. 56. Wenner, "Pete Townshend," pp. 108, 127.

pp. 62–63. "Road Runner," words and music by Jonathan Richman, copyright © 1975 by Modern Love Songs, used by permission of Joel S. Turtle, Administration.

p. 66. Vaneigem, *Traité*, pp. 180–181; *Revolution*, p. 134.

pp. 66–67. T. V. Smith, "One Chord Wonders," reprinted by permission of the songwriter.

p. 68. Adorno, p. 59.

p. 71. Photograph of Lora Logic, courtesy Rough Trade Records.

p. 72. Vaneigem, *Traité*, p. 15; *Revolution*, p. 12.

pp. 76–77. On "snuff rock," *KILL IT*, n.p.

pp. 78–79. Muddy Wehara, comic strip, "No Future for You," first published in Japanese in *Music Magazine* (Tokyo, June 1986), trans. Toru Mitsui, courtesy Wehara and Mitsui.

p. 81. "Screwing the System with Dick Clark," in Lester Bangs, *Psychotic Reactions and Carburetor Dung*, ed. Greil Marcus (New York: Knopf, 1987), p. 137.

pp. 90–91. Africa Bambaataa and Bill Laswell, "World Destruction," copyright © 1984 by OAO Music/BMI.

p. 93. Norman Cohn, p. 280.

p. 93. "Dismemberment murder" from LeMoyne Snyder, *Homicidal Investigation* (1959), courtesy Charles C Thomas, Publisher, Springfield, Illinois.

p. 98. Marx, "Contribution," *Early Writings*, p. 254.

p. 99. Debord, *Société*, thesis no. 34.

p. 102. Milosz, p. 55.

p. 102. Ascherson, p. 16.

pp. 103–105. Debord, *Société*, nos. 30, 4, 8, 9.

p. 106. Marx, *Capital*, pp. 163–164.

p. 113. Huelsenbeck, *Deutschland muss untergehen!*, pp. 7–8. Trans. Jeffrey Faude.

p. 113. Steve Jones, Paul Cook, John Lydon, and John Beverly, "Bodies."

p. 114. "WONDER OF WONDERS." *Club Dada* (Berlin, 1918), in *Dada Zeitschriften*.

p. 115. Marx, "Contribution," pp. 246–247.

p. 115. Huelsenbeck, *En avant dada*, in Motherwell, p. 44.

p. 117. Photograph of Luxemburg, as used in *King Mob Echo*, taken from J. P. Nettl, *Rosa Luxemburg* (London: Oxford University Press, 1966).

p. 117. Steve Jones, Paul Cook, John Lydon, and John Beverly, "Belsen Was a Gas."

pp. 118–119. Debord, *In girum*, *Oeuvres*, pp. 224–225, 252–253, 237–238.

pp. 120–121. For "Nazi Execution of Two Russian Partisans" see *Flesh and Blood* (Cupertino, Cal.: Genotype, 1980), p. 128 (as "Nazi execution of two Ukrainian children"); for the story behind the photograph see "Echo of '41 in Minsk: Was the Heroine a Jew?," *New York Times* (15 September 1987), p. 1.

p. 122. Lanzmann, pp. 142, 143.

pp. 122–123. "Three Glorious Days in a Nazi Prison," *San Francisco Chronicle* (11 September 1980), p. 17, reprinted by permission of United Press International, copyright © 1980.

pp. 124–125. T. J. Clark, pp. 209, 236, 233–234, 210.

p. 125. "I will never forget." Quote from *Peter Kropotkin's Revolutionary Pamphlets*, ed. Roger N. Baldwin (New York: Dover, 1970), p. 239.

p. 125. "Sur la commune" (18 March 1962), reprinted in *I.S.* no. 12 (September 1969), p. 109; Knabb, pp. 314–315.

p. 128. Debord, *Société*, no. 43.

p. 130. Matt Groening and Steve Vance, greeting card, "Confessions of a Crazed Shopper," copyright © 1984 by Matt Groening and Steve Vance, reprinted by permission of Paper Moon Graphics.

p. 135. Arendt, p. 233.

pp. 136–138. Karp, pp. 31–32.

pp. 139–140. Atilla Kotányi and Vaneigem, "Programme élémentaire du bureau d'urbanisme unitaire," *I.S.* no. 6 (August 1961), pp. 16–17; Knabb, pp. 65–66.

p. 140. Debord, *Société*, no. 17.

p. 141. "reversible connecting factor." Debord, "The Situationists and the New Action Forms in Politics and Art," p. 9.

p. 142. Lefebvre, *Position*, p. 195.

p. 143. Poster advertising *I.S.* no. 11, courtesy International Instituut voor Sociale Geschiedenis, Amsterdam.

pp. 146–147. Lefebvre, *Les Temps des mépris*, pp. 157–160.

p. 149. T. J. Clark, p. 236. "For the petit-bourgeois consumer of culture in the twentieth century, the available form of popular art has been black American music, and that is where my notion of collective vehemence was picked up—from kinds of blues singing and shouting, from improvised ensemble playing, from Charlie Parker's way with the themes and harmonies of white popular music, from Little Richard and Fats Domino. But this kind of list is more than usually misleading here: the effect we are talking about does not for the most part lead to 'masterpieces,' and can be found almost anywhere, often surrounded by pure shlock" (p. 310, n. 61).

pp. 151–152. Kurt Tucholsky, "Danton's Death," trans. John Willett in his *Art and Politics in the Weimar Period*, p. 57, copyright © 1978 by Pantheon Books, a Division of Random House, Inc.

FACES

p. 155. Photograph of Johnny Rotten by Dennis Morris, reprinted by permission of the photographer.

p. 156. Photograph of Hennings, courtesy Hans J. Kleinschmidt.

p. 157. Photograph of Ball, courtesy Hans J. Kleinschmidt.

p. 158. Photograph of Huelsenbeck from *Phantastische gebete*, 2nd ed. (Berlin, 1920), courtesy Hans J. Kleinschmidt.

p. 159. Frame enlargement of Chtcheglov from Debord's film *In girum*, in *Oeuvres*.

p. 160. Frame enlargement of Bernstein et al. from Debord's film *Sur le passage*, in *Contre le cinéma*.

p. 161. Photograph of London punk from Val Hennesey, *In the Gutter* (London: Quartet/Namara Group, 1978), p. 73, copyright © 1978 by Val Hennesey.

p. 162. Portrait of Saint-Just from Ernest Hamel, *Histoire de Saint-Just* (Brussels, 1860), frontispiece.

LEGENDS OF FREEDOM

p. 165. Debord, page from *Mémoires*.

p. 166. Vaneigem, *Traité*, p. 276; *Revolution*, p. 205.

p. 167. Debord, page from *Mémoires*.

p. 169. Illustrations from "L'Urbanisme unitaire à la fin des années 50," *I.S.* no. 3 (December 1959), pp. 14–15.

pp. 170–171. Debord and Wolman, "Mode d'emploi détournement," *Les Lèvres nues* no. 8 (May 1956), p. 2; Berreby, p. 302; Knabb, p. 8.

pp. 171–172. Ivan Chtcheglov (as Gilles Ivain), "Formulaire pour un urbanisme nouveau" (1953), *I.S.* no. 1 (June 1958), pp. 15–20.

p. 172. Auster, *The Locked Room*, pp. 58–59.

p. 173. Trocchi, "Potlatch—an interpersonal log," *Sigma Portfolio*, item no. 4, p. 4.

p. 173. "time frightens." Debord, with Gianfranco Sanguinetti, "Thèses," in *La Véritable Scission dans l'internationale*, p. 45.

pp. 173–174. Debord, *Sur le passage*, *Oeuvres*, pp. 17, 22; Knabb, pp. 29, 30.

p. 174. Wolman, "liberté PROVISOIRE," *I.L.* no. 2; Berreby, p. 154.

p. 174. Debord, *Sur le passage*, *Oeuvres*, pp. 21–22; Knabb, p. 30.

p. 175. Illustration with caption from *I.S.* no 8 (January 1963), p. 42; trans. Gray, p. 69.

pp. 176–178. Quotes and illustration (p. 177) from "Le Déclin et la chute de l'économie spectaculaire-marchande," *I.S.* no. 10 (March 1966), pp. 3–11; Knabb, pp. 153–159.

p. 178. Illustration from *I.S.* no. 9 (August 1964), p. 37.

p. 179. "Les Mauvais Jours finiront," *I.S.* no. 7 (April 1962), p. 12; Knabb, p. 84.

p. 179. Debord and Wolman, "Mode," p. 8; Berreby, p. 308; Knabb, p. 18.

p. 179. Anonymous detourned comic strip, courtesy Lang Thompson.

pp. 179–180. "L'Opération contre-situationniste dans divers pays," *I.S.* no. 8 (January 1963), p. 28; Knabb, p. 113.

pp. 179–180. Debord, *Préface*, p. 19.

p. 181. "the domain." "Problèmes préliminaires à la construction d'une situation," *I.S.* no. 1 (June 1958), p. 12; Knabb, p. 44.

p. 181. "The situationists." "All the King's Men," *I.S.* no. 8 (January 1963), p. 31; Knabb, pp. 115–116.

p. 182. Debord, "Rapport sur la construction des situations et les conditions de l'organisation et de l'action de la tendance situationniste internationale" (June 1957), paper prepared for the founding conference of the SI in Cosio d'Arroscia, Italy, July 1957; Berreby, p. 618; Knabb, p. 25.

p. 183. Debord, page from *Mémoires*.

THE ART OF YESTERDAY'S CRASH

p. 189. Work by El Lissitzky from Sophie Lissitzky-Kuppers, ed., *El Lissitzky* (London: Thames & Hudson, 1980), reprinted by permission of VEB Verlag der Kunst Dresden.

p. 190. Vargas Llosa, pp. 15–16.

p. 190. "La Révolution d'abord et toujours!," *La Révolution surréaliste* no. 5 (Paris, 15 October 1925), p. 31. Later published with "What is Dadaism and what does it want in Germany?" in *Heatwave* no. 2 (London, October 1966), pp. 10–13.

p. 191. "My first article." Lefebvre, *Les Temps des mépris*, pp. 38–39.

p. 191. Lefebvre, "'7 manifestes dada,'" pp. 28–30/443–445.

p. 191. Lefebvre, *Position*, p. 229.

p. 192. Huelsenbeck, "Dada, or the Meaning of Chaos," p. 26.

pp. 192–193. Arp, "Dadaland," p. 234.

p. 194. Photograph of Cabaret Voltaire by Monica Cardenas, courtesy Elisabeth Kauffmann Zürich.

p. 194. Arp, "Dadaland," p. 232.

pp. 194–195. Huelsenbeck, *En avant dada*, in Motherwell, p. 23.

pp. 195–196. Ball, 20 September 1915, p. 28; 4 October 1915, p. 30; 11 October 1915, pp. 32, 49.

p. 200. Poly Styrene, "Oh Bondage Up Yours!," copyright © 1977 by Essex Music International/Copyright Control.

p. 201. Ball, 27 March 1917, p. 101.

p. 202. "he and his brother Jules." Naumann; all other sources give "Janco's brother George" because of an error in Ball's diary.

pp. 204–205. Ball, pp. 51–52, 54, 57; 9 January 1917, p. 96.

p. 206. Huelsenbeck, *Memoirs of a Dada Drummer*, flyleaf, prob. 1916, pub. *Dada* no. 3 (Paris, December 1918).

p. 207. Huelsenbeck, "Das Cabaret Voltaire," *Der Querschilt* no. 7 (Berlin, 1927), quoted in Karin Füllner's "The Meister-Dada," in Sheppard, *New Studies in Dada*, p. 22. Trans. Michelle Krisel.

pp. 207–208. Ball, 18 June 1921, p. 210; Elderfield, p. xxvii.

p. 209. Advertisement for Dada Haarwasser, courtesy Kunsthaus Zürich.

p. 210. Ball, 5 April 1916, p. 59.

p. 210. Debord, *Critique de la séparation, Oeuvres*, pp. 48–49.

p. 210. Hausmann, "Dadaism and Today's Avant-Garde," p. 800.

p. 211. Debord, with Pierre Canjeurs, "Préliminaires pour une définition de l'unité du programme révolutionnaire," paper prepared for unconsummated linkage between the SI and the French group Socialisme ou barbarie (June 1960); Knabb, p. 308.

p. 212. "the ideals of culture." Ball, 16 June 1916, p. 67.

p. 212. Arp, "und dazu das Dada-wort von Hans Arp" (15 January 1966), Arp and Huelsenbeck, *Dada in Zürich*.

p. 213. Ball, p. 8.

p. 213. Ravien Siurlai, *Die Aktion* (Berlin, 5 June 1912).

p. 214. Ball, 5 March 1916, p. 55; 9 July 1915, p. 25.

p. 215. Ball, 16 June 1916, p. 67; 9 July 1915, p. 25.

p. 216. Marinetti, untitled "Parole in libertà," from *Parole consonanti vocali numeri in libertà* (Milan, 11 February 1915), courtesy Beinecke Rare Book and Manuscript Library, Yale University.

p. 217. Lenin on music, as quoted by Maxim Gorky, in Wilson, *To the Finland Station*, p. 450.

pp. 217–218. Huelsenbeck, *En avant dada*, in Motherwell, p. 32.

pp. 218–219. Huelsenbeck, *Memoirs*, pp. 8, 9–10.

p. 220. Huelsenbeck, "Dada, or the Meaning of Chaos," p. 27; *Memoirs*, p. xxxiii.

pp. 221–222. Ball, pp. 66–67; 18 June 1916, p. 67; 24 May 1916, p. 64.

p. 223. Photograph of Tristan Tzara, courtesy Fondation Arp, Clamart, France.

p. 223. Mask of Tzara by Marcel Janco, courtesy Dadi Janco, Janco Dada Museum, Ein Hod, Israel.

p. 223. Photograph of war victim from Ernst Friedrich, *Krieg dem Krieg!* (Berlin, 1924), facsimile edition as *War against War!* (Seattle: Real Comet Press, 1987), p. 220, reprinted by permission of the publisher.

p. 223. Photo collage by Hannah Höch, *Fröliche Dame*, private collection, used by permission.

p. 224. Robinson, p. 43.

p. 224. Walker, pp. 105–106.

pp. 225–226. Huelsenbeck, *En avant dada*, in Motherwell, p. 26.

p. 227. Collage of text by and photo of Hugo Ball from *Dadaco* (Munich, 1920), in *Dada Zeitschriften*.

p. 229. Karl Kraus, insert following p. 90; p. 89.

p. 230. Huelsenbeck, *En avant dada*, in Motherwell, p. 26. Including passages trans. John Rockwell, from facsimile edition, p. 34.

p. 232. "What is Dadaism," in Huelsenbeck, *En avant dada*, in Motherwell, pp. 41–42.

p. 233. Photo collage by John Heartfield from *Dadaco*.

p. 234. Huelsenbeck quoted in Hans J. Kleinschmidt, "Berlin Dada," in Stephen C. Foster and Rudolf Kuenzli, eds., *Dada Spectrum: The Dialectics of Revolt* (Madison, Wis.: Coda, 1979), p. 164.

p. 234. Huelsenbeck, "Was woltc expressionismus," 12 April 1918, *Dada Almanach*, p. 34, trans. Ralph Manheim in Motherwell as "Collective Dada Manifesto," misdated 1920, pp. 242–243.

p. 234. Huelsenbeck, "Erste dadarede in Deutschland," February 1918, *Dada Almanach*, pp. 105–106.

p. 235–236. Jung, "The Concept of the Collective Unconscious," pp. 66–67.

p. 237. Photograph of Senator Alben Barkley, courtesy National Archives, Washington D.C.

p. 238. Huelsenbeck, "On Leaving America for Good" (1969), in *Memoirs*, p. 187.

p. 239. Vaneigem, *Traité*, p. 185; *Revolution*, p. 137; *King Mob Echo*.

p. 241. For Janco's *Cabaret Voltaire*, see *Marcel Janco* (Tel Aviv: Masada, 1982), p. 20.

p. 242. Ball, p. 67.

THE CRASH OF YESTERDAY'S ART

p. 245. Isou, "Creations," pp. 796–797. Much of the following biographical information on Isou is drawn from Jean-Paul Curtay, *La Poésie lettriste*; most of the more scandalous items are from Nicholas Clarion, "The Messiah of Lettrism," *Commentary* (August 1949), pp. 183–184.

p. 248. Diagram from Isou, *Introduction*, in Curtay, p. 249, used by permission.

p. 249. Photograph of Isou from his *Fondements pour la transformation intégrale du théatre* (Paris: Bordas, 1953), frontispiece.

p. 251. Maurice Nadeau, "Les 'lettristes' chahutent une lecture de Tzara au Vieux Colombier," *Combat* (22 January 1946), p. 1.

p. 253. "estheperist poetry." Isou, "Creations," p. 796.

p. 254. "Hausmann lay dying." Nicholas Turbrugg, "The Limitations of Lettrism—An Interview with Henri Chopin," in Foster, p. 64.

p. 255. Pages from Pomerand, *Saint ghetto des prêts*. Commentary by Curtay, "Super-Writing 1983—America 1683," in Foster, p. 29.

p. 260. Deborah Chessler, "It's Too Soon to Know," copyright © 1948 by Edward M. Morris Co./BMI.

p. 262. Photograph of the Orioles and Deborah Chessler, courtesy Jonas Bernholm of Mr R&B Records.

p. 264. Photograph from trial of the Lagnyites, *Combat* (8 May 1951), p. 1.

p. 264. Photograph of Starkweather and Fugate, UPI/Bettmann Newsphotos.

p. 267. Front page of Kingston newspaper, courtesy the *Daily Gleaner*.

pp. 269–271. "Notre programme" (Isou), *Front de la jeunesse* no. 1 (1950), in Brau, *Cours, camarade*, pp. 288–290. Trans. Adam Cornford.

p. 273. Adorno, p. 93.

p. 274. Brau, *Cours, camarade*, p. 166. A few months before his death in 1985, Brau encountered Isou at the opening of an exhibition; they had not spoken for years. "You told us you would give us immortality," Brau said. "Where is it?" Then they went for a drink.

p. 274. "It began at the beginning." See Wolman, "Introduction à Wolman" ("Isou était une fin, au début il y avait Wolman"), and with Jean-Louis Brau (signed as "***") and CP-Matricon, "Pour un mort synthetique," both *Ur* no. 1 (Paris, 1950), in Wolman, *Résumé*, pp. 10–12, 17–19, and Wolman, "La Mégapneumie," *Ou* no. 32 (Brussels, June 1967), in Wolman, *Résumé*, p. 16.

p. 275. "a giant sigh." David Seaman, "Letterism—A Stream That Runs Its Own Course," in Foster, p. 18.

p. 275. Tabou poster from Wolman, *Résumé*, p. 13. Reconstruction of events in the Tabou is based on Brau, *Instrumentation verbale*, and Wolman, *Improvisations—Mégapneumes*.

p. 276. Photograph of Wolman from *Ion*, courtesy Luc Sante.

p. 277. Isou, "Les Grandes Poètes lettristes," *Bizarre* no. 32–33 (1964), in Wolman, *Résumé*, p. 10.

THE ASSAULT ON NOTRE-DAME

p. 279. "Today Easter Day." In Marien, "Le Chemin de la croix (vii)," p. 36; Berreby, p. 26. Trans. Adam Cornford.

p. 281. Photograph of Notre-Dame conspirators from *Combat* (12 April 1950), p. 2.

p. 282. "Lettre de André Breton," *Combat* (12 April 1950), p. 2; trans. in "The Notre-Dame Scandal," *Transition* no. 6 (Paris, 1950), p. 135.

p. 283. Postcard by Postmoderns Post Cards.

p. 283. Dr. Micoud quoted in "Quand la Justice est en folie," *Combat* (19 April 1950), p. 1, and "The Notre-Dame Scandal," pp. 136–138.

p. 284. Mourre, *In Spite of Blasphemy*, pp. 206–207. Numerous short quotes from this book are not cited here when they follow the course of Mourre's narrative.

p. 285. Mourre, pp. 214, 227.

p. 288. Mourre, p. 28.

pp. 292–293. Mourre, p. 115.

p. 295. Mourre, p. 170.

p. 300. Lerner, pp. 134–138.

p. 301. Advertisement, courtesy Kit Rachlis and the *Village Voice*.

p. 302. Norman Cohn, p. 177; *King Mob Echo*.

p. 303. David E. Apter, "The Old Anarchism and the New," in Apter and James Joll, eds., *Anarchism Today* (Garden City: Doubleday, 1971), p. 13.

p. 303. Nik Cohn, *Awopbopaloobop*, p. 219.

p. 305. Mourre, p. 205.

p. 306. Hausmann, "Club Dada Berlin 1918–1921" (26 July 1966), in *Dada Berlin*, p. 5.

p. 307. Pico della Mirandola, in Lerner, p. 241.

p. 307. James Wolcott, "Kiss Me You Fool: Sex Pistols '77," *Village Voice* (21 September 1977), p. 53.

p. 309. "You don't fault a theme park." Richard Corliss, "Keeping the Customer Satisfied," review of *Indiana Jones and the Temple of Doom*, in *Time* (21 May 1984), p. 83.

pp. 310–311. "All the King's Men," *I.S.* no. 8 (January 1963), pp. 31–32.

p. 312. "Notre collaborateur Benjamin Péret injuriant un prêtre," *La Révolution surréaliste* no. 8 (Paris, 1 December 1926), p. 13.

p. 312. Péret, *Combat* (14 April 1950), p. 2.

p. 312. "no precedent." Mourre said the same. "Do you realize?" he told Dr. Micoud, "I'm the first who ever dared do that! Get up and speak in Notre-Dame! In that nave!" "The Notre-Dame Scandal," p. 137.

p. 313. Marx, "Contribution," pp. 243–244.

p. 313. Debord, *Société*, no. 138.

p. 315. Versions of Baader's announcement in Berlin Cathedral: Alfred Barr, *Fantastic Art, Dada, Surrealism* (New York: Arno, 1968, orig. 1936), pp. 24–25; Richter, p. 127; Hausmann, "Club Dada. Berlin, 1918–1920," in Raabe, p. 227; Sheppard, *New Studies*, pp. 172–173.

p. 315. Hausmann, *Courrier Dada*, pp. 74–75, trans. in Richter, p. 125.

p. 316. Vera Broido-Cohn, in "Johannes Baader," *The Twenties in Berlin*, p. 4.

p. 317. Photograph of Grosz, courtesy Estate of George Grosz, Princeton, New Jersey.

p. 317. *Time* cover, 30 November 1981, copyright © 1981 Time Inc., all rights reserved, reprinted by permission.

p. 318. Grosz, untitled collage on paper, present whereabouts unknown, taken from Joshua Kind, "The Unknown Grosz," *Studio International* (London, March 1967), p. 144.

p. 320. Baader, Hausmann, Huelsenbeck, "Legen sie ihr geld in dada an!," *Der Dada* no. 1 (Berlin, 1919), in *Dada Zeitschriften*, trans.

Gabrielle Bennett in Lippard, pp. 55–56.

p. 321. Photograph of Baader from Huelsenbeck, *Dada Almanach*, following p. 32.

p. 322. Norman Cohn, pp. 148–149.

p. 322. "Lieu de recontre supposé des internationaux-situationnistes à Paris," sidebar to "Nos buts et nos méthodes dans le scandale de Strasbourg," *I.S.* no. 11 (October 1967), p. 25, quoting passage from Norman Cohn, 2nd ed., pp. 318–319.

THE ATTACK ON CHARLIE CHAPLIN

p. 323. See various reports from Cannes by R.-M. Arlaud, *Combat* (14–22 April 1951), p. 2.

p. 323. Maurice Schèrer, "Isou, ou les choses telles qu'elles sont," *Cahiers du cinéma* no. 10 (Paris, March 1952), pp. 27–32.

p. 326. Photograph of Berna from *Ion*, courtesy Luc Sante.

p. 328. Photograph of Pomerand from *Ion*, courtesy Luc Sante.

p. 330. Photograph of Debord from *Ion*, courtesy Luc Sante.

p. 332. Atkins, pp. 57–58.

pp. 333–336. Debord, *Hurlements, Oeuvres*, pp. 7–14.

p. 335. Debord and Wolman, "Pourquoi le lettrisme?," *Potlatch*, p. 154.

pp. 340–341. "Finis les pieds plats," *I.L.* no. 1 (November 1952); Berreby, pp. 147, 262 (reprint of leaflet). Trans. Sophie Rosenberg. See also Wolman, *Résumé*, pp. 26–29; *Combat* (30 October 1952), p. 1; and *Combat* (1 November 1952), p. 2. The LI's critique of Chaplin and *Limelight* was matched a few months later by Pauline Kael, in "Some Notes on Chaplin's *Limelight*," her first published review: "The minority audience was always fascinated by the stills which revealed the beauty of Chaplin—the depth and expressiveness beneath the tramp make-up; the majority was perfectly satisfied with the mask of comedy. In a chance glimpse we thought we perceived a tragic countenance under the mask. Now Chaplin has given us too long a look—the face has been held in camera range for prolonged admiration—and the egotism of his self-revelation has infected the tragic beauty. The illusion, the mystery, are gone—and with them, possibly a good section of the minority audience as well." *City Lights* no. 3 (San Francisco, Spring 1953), p. 56.

p. 342. Jim Ryan, "Fast Living Update," reprinted by permission of the artist, all rights reserved.

p. 343. "Position de l'Internationale lettriste," letter refused by *Combat* (2 November 1952), in *I.L.* no. 1; Berreby, p. 151. Trans. Sophie Rosenberg.

p. 343. *I.S.* no. 1 (June 1958), facing p. 30.

LIPSTICK TRACES (ON A CIGARETTE)

p. 345. Frame enlargement of Michèle Bernstein from Debord's film *Sur le passage, Contre le cinéma*.

p. 346. Vaneigem, *Traité*, p. 186; *Revolution*, p. 138.

p. 346. "the violence of the delinquents." "Les Mauvais Jours finiront," *I.S.* no. 7 (April 1962), p. 16.

p. 347. ". . . une idée neuve en Europe," *Potlatch*, pp. 45–46.

p. 348. Wolman to Brau, in Brau, *Cours, camarade*, p. 66. Trans. Sophie Rosenberg.

p. 348. "the first revolution, the LI told itself." "The Apostles were devoted to each other because they felt they were discovering truths hitherto unknown . . . of such groups Isaiah Berlin has written: 'Those who have never been under the spell of this kind of illusion, even for a short while, have never known true intellectual happiness.'" Noel Annan, "Et Tu, Anthony," *New York Review of Books* (22 October 1987), p. 6.

p. 349. Photograph of Mension and Fred by Ed van der Elsken, from *Parijs!*, reprinted by permission of the photographer.

p. 350. "the catacombs of visible culture." "L'Aventure," *I.S.* no. 5 (December 1960), p. 3.

p. 351. "A la Porte" (29 June 1954), *Potlatch*, p. 19.

p. 351. Debord, *In girum*, *Oeuvres*, pp. 236, 244.

p. 352. "leaving traces." "manifeste," *I.L.* no. 2 (February 1953); Berreby, p. 154.

p. 353. Vanderhaeghe, pp. 90–91.

p. 356. Debord, "Déclaration sur l'experience de la dérive," quoted in Jorn, *Pour la forme*, p. 126; Berreby, p. 539.

p. 357. Colin Newman and Graham Lewis, "I Am the Fly," copyright © 1978 by Carlin Music Corporation, used by permission of Carbert Music Inc. and Carlin Music Corporation (U.K.), Administration, all rights reserved.

p. 357. Tommy Boyce and Bobby Hart, "Theme from *The Monkees*," copyright © 1966 by Screen Gems–EMI Music Inc.

p. 358. Mension, "grève générale," *I.L.* no. 2; Berreby, p. 155.

p. 359. Debord, "La Valeur éducative," *Potlatch*, pp. 101, 123.

p. 359. Debord, *In girum, Oeuvres*, p. 240.

p. 360. Debord and Wolman, "Pourquoi le lettrisme?," *Potlatch*, p. 162. Trans. Sophie Rosenberg.

p. 361. Chtcheglov, "Formulaire," *I.S.* no. 1, p. 15.

p. 361. "36 rue des Morillons," *Potlatch*, p. 54.

p. 361. Debord, *In girum, Oeuvres*, p. 247.

p. 362. Auster, *In the Country of Last Things*, pp. 6–7.

p. 362. Chtcheglov, "Lettres de loin," *I.S.* no. 9 (August 1964), p. 38.

p. 363. Debord, *In girum, Oeuvres*, pp. 246–247.

p. 364. Debord, *Société*, no. 12.

p. 364. LI sticker, courtesy Michèle Bernstein.

pp. 365–366. Quotes from "manifeste," *I.L.* no. 2 (February 1953); Berreby, p. 154.

p. 367. Page from Wolman, *Durhing Durhing*, courtesy Jacques Spiess.

p. 368. "He was twenty-seven," "La Rétraite," *Potlatch* no. 28 (22 May 1957); *Potlatch*, p. 231.

p. 368. Wolman, "Intervention de Wolman" (September 1956); Berreby, pp. 596–598.

p. 369. "the new beauty." Debord, contribution to "fragments de recherches pour un comportement prochain," *I.L.* no. 2 (February 1953); Berreby, p. 155.

p. 370. Chtcheglov, "Formulaire," *I.S.* no. 1, pp. 15–17.

p. 371. Le Corbusier drawing, courtesy Fondation Le Corbusier.

p. 374. Wolman, scotch art, courtesy Michèle Bernstein and the artist.

p. 379. "La Division du travail" (9 September 1955), *Potlatch*, p. 169.

p. 380. Debord, "Pour en finir avec le confort nihiliste," Berreby, p. 156.

p. 381. Photograph of Colin Donellan by Slim Hewitt, *Picture Post* (London, 10 October 1953), courtesy Bettmann Archives/BBC Hulton.

p. 382. Photograph of Moineau's by Ed van der Elsken, from *Parijs!*, reprinted by permission of the photographer.

p. 384. Debord, *Sur le passage, Oeuvres*, p. 25.

p. 384. *Potlatch*, p. 54.

p. 386. Trocchi, *Cain's Book*, pp. 236, 218.

p. 388. Debord, "Théorie de la dérive," *Les Lèvres nues* no. 9 (November 1956), p. 10; Berreby, p. 316.

p. 389. Thomas de Quincey, *Confessions of an English Opium Eater* (New York: Penguin, 1979).

p. 389. Debord, "Théorie," p. 6; Berreby, p. 312.

p. 389. Debord, "Introduction à une critique de la géographie urbaine," *Les Lèvres nues* no. 6 (September 1955), p. 14; Berreby, p. 291.

p. 390. "an atmosphere." Debord, "Théorie," p. 9; Berreby, p. 315.

p. 390. "the greatest difficulty." Debord, "Introduction," pp. 12, 13; Berreby, pp. 289, 290.

p. 391. Adorno, p. 51.

p. 391. Debord, "Le Rôle de 'Potlatch' autrefois et maintenant," *Potlatch* no. 1, new series (Amsterdam, 15 July 1959); Berreby, p. 253.

pp. 392–393. Illustrations: Debord, "The Naked City" (Paris: MIBI, May 1957), in Jorn, *Pour la forme*, and Berreby, pp. 536–537, courtesy Mark Francis and the Musée national d'art moderne, Paris; illustration from *I.S.* no. 1 (June 1958), p. 28; Alfred Wegener's concept of continental drift, adapted from Claude Allègre, *The Behavior of the Earth* (Cambridge: Harvard University Press, 1988), p. 6.

pp. 392–393. D. H. Lawrence, *Studies in Classic American Literature* (New York: Viking, 1964, orig. 1923), pp. 44–45.

pp. 392–393. Mauss, p. 103, n. 128; p. 108, n. 171.

pp. 394–396. Bataille, "The Notion of Expenditure," pp. 78, 63, 72–74, 64.

p. 398. Croce, p. 35.

pp. 399–400. "Les Cathares avaient raison," *Potlatch*, pp. 33–34.

p. 401. Debord and Wolman, "Mode," pp. 4–5; Berreby, pp. 304–305.

p. 402. Le Roy Ladurie, pp. 332, 325, 252–353, 327.

p. 404. Front page of *Potlatch*, courtesy Gil J Wolman.

p. 406. Vaneigem, in "La Cinquième conférence de l'I.S. a Göteborg," *I.S.* no. 7 (April 1962), p. 27.

p. 407. Bernstein, *Tous les chevaux du roi*, p. 43.

p. 408. "Géopolitique de l'hibernation," *I.S.* no. 7 (April 1962), p. 9; Knabb, p. 81.

p. 408. "Le Monde dont nous parlons ('La Technique de l'isolement')," *I.S.* no. 9 (August 1964), pp. 6–7; Gray, p. 82.

p. 409. Illustration from "Géopolitique de l'hibernation," *I.S.* no. 7, p. 4.

p. 410. Breton, contribution to "Sur certaines possibilities d'embellissement irrationnel d'une ville," *Le Surréalisme au service de la révolution* no. 6 (Paris, May 1933), p. 18.

p. 412. "Project d'embellissements rationnels de la ville de Paris," *Potlatch*, pp. 177–180. Trans. Adam Cornford.

p. 414. Gray, p. 84.

p. 415. Gray, unpublished notes, courtesy Alexander Trocchi.

p. 415. Debord, "For a Revolutionary Judgment of Art" (February 1961); in Knabb, p. 312.

p. 416. AFGES, *Le Retour de la colonne Durutti* (André Bertrand), p. 4.

p. 416. AFGES, *De la misère en milieu étudiant* (Mustapha Khayati), Knabb, pp. 319–337.

p. 419. Judge Llabador quoted in SI (U.K.), *Ten Days*, p. 1.

p. 419. "They believe." SI, *Ten Days*, p. 24, taken from Norman Cohn.

p. 424. Bernstein, *Tous les chevaux du roi*, pp. 29–30, and as in SI, *Ten Days*, p. 18.

p. 425. Bertrand, *Le Retour de la colonne Durutti*, p. 3, courtesy Steef Davidson.

p. 426. Viénet, p. 15.

p. 427. Morin quoted in "Le Commencement d'une epoch" (Debord), *I.S.* no. 12 (September 1969), pp. 20–21; Knabb, pp. 243–244.

p. 429. "POLITBURO." Viénet, p. 275; Knabb, p. 345.

p. 429. "What we have done." Comité Enragés-Internationale situationniste, Conseil pour le maintien des occupations, "Addresse à tout les travailleurs" (20 May 1968), Viénet, pp. 283–284; Knabb, p. 350.

p. 430. "Le Commencement" (Debord), pp. 3–4.

p. 431. Debord, *Sur le passage, Oeuvres*, pp. 28, 29.

p. 431. "Le Commencement" (Debord), p. 34.

EPILOGUE

p. 433. Debord, *Critique, Oeuvres*, p. 45.

p. 434. Mark White, "The Building," copyright © 1982 by CNT Productions.

p. 435. Abiezer Coppe, *A Fiery Flying Roll* (1649), quoted in Norman Cohn, p. 321.

p. 439. "Last Days" sticker, courtesy Jon Savage.

pp. 442–443. Lewis, pp. 71–73.

p. 446. Debord, "La Valeur éducative," quoting Bossuet, *Oraisons funèbres* (1688), *Potlatch* no. 16 (26 January 1955); *Potlatch*, p. 101.

p. 447. Huelsenbeck, "On Leaving America for Good," in *Memoirs*, p. 189.

p. 447. Ray Lowry, first panel of "note oilskin base," *New Musical Express* (19 May 1984), reprinted by permission of the artist.

ACKNOWLEDGMENTS

Over the last years I benefited from the generosity of many people. For their support; their provision of hard-to-find books, articles, handbills, posters, artworks, comics, documents, records, and tapes; their readings of drafts; their hospitality, conversation, or doubts, I thank Dave Allen, Thomas Ammann, Andrew Baumer, Jonas Bernholm of Mr R&B Records, Sara Bershtel and Wendy Wolf of Pantheon Books, Paule-Léon Bisson-Millet, Adam Block, Liz Bordow, Bill Brown, Denis Browne, Mattias Bruner, Bart Bull, Hugo Burnham, Robert Christgau, Bob Cobbing, Michael Conen and Lexy Green of Asta's Records in Oakland, Michael Covino, Elvis Costello, Jean-Paul Curtay, Steef Davidson, Paul de Angelis of E. P. Dutton, Carola Dibbell, Down Home Music of El Cerrito, Melanie Fechner, Dan Franklin and David Godwin of Secker & Warburg, Ken Friedman, Gill Frith, Bernard Gendron of the Center for Twentieth Century Studies at the University of Wisconsin–Milwaukee, Andy Gill, John Goddard of Village Music in Mill Valley, Matt Groening, Lawrence Grossberg, Tristan Haan of the International Instituut voor Sociale Geschiedenis in Amsterdam, Niko Hansen, A. Hares of Mattoid in London, Dick Hebdige, Marina Hirsch, Peter Howard of Serendipity Books in Berkeley, Klaus Humann, David Joselit and Elisabeth Sussman of the Institute of Contemporary Art in Boston, Scott Kane and Robin Schorr of KALX-FM in Berkeley, Elisabeth Kauffmann of Elisabeth Kauffmann Zürich, Mick Kidd of Biff Comics in London, Jon King, Doug Kroll, John Lee of Moe's Books in Berkeley, Michael Lesy, Tom Levin, W. T. Lhamon, Lora Logic, Ray Lowry, Tom Luddy, Daniel Marcus, Eleanore and Gerald Marcus, Marlene Marder, Dave Marsh, Bruce McGregor, B. K. Moran, Lynda Myles, Scott Piering, Carolyn Porter, Cynthia Rose, Jim Ryan, Luc Sante, Berigan Taylor of Berigan's in Oakland, Paul Thomas, Lang Thompson, Nanos Valaoritis, Anne Wagner, Ed Ward, Steve Wasserman, Muddy Wehara, Larry Wendt, Dave Wheeler and B. George of the ARChive of Contemporary Music in New York, Tony Wilson of Factory Records, and Langdon Winner. I remember the encouragement of my dear friend and editor, the late Bill Whitehead.

I would never have gotten anywhere without the aid, the bookshelves, and the translations, written or person to person, of Frances

Cahn, Adam Cornford, Jeffrey Faude, Jo Anne Fordham, Alice Yaeger Kaplan, Marian Kester, Michelle Krisel, Sophie Rosenberg, Kristin Ross, Fred Vermorel, and Tom Ward. Nor without the scrutiny of the producers and magazine editors who gave me a chance to fool with my themes in public: at *Another Room*, Lucy Childs and Michael Mallery; at *Artforum*, Ingrid Sischy, David Frankel, and Melissa Harris; at the *Boston Phoenix* (and later at the *Village Voice*), Kit Rachlis; at the *L. A. Weekly*, Michael Ventura; the staff of *Music Magazine* in Tokyo; the staff of *New Formations* in London; at *New West/California*, Jon Carroll, Nancy Friedman, Janet Duckworth, and Bill Broyles; the staff of "Nightline"; at *Raw*, Art Spiegelman and Françoise Mouly; the staff of *Rock & Roll Confidential*; at *Rolling Stone*, Barbara Downey Landau and Jann Wenner; with "Surface Tension" in Sydney, Tony MacGregor and Virginia Madsen; at *Touch* in London, Jon Wozencroft; at *Threepenny Review*, Wendy Lesser; at *Triquarterly*, Jonathan Brendt, Jon Schiller, and Anne-Marie Zwierzyna; at the *Village Voice*, M. Mark and Doug Simmons. I received sober advice and undreamed-of enthusiasm from my agent, Wendy Weil, her coworkers Julian Bach and Norin Lucas, and her representative Anthony Goff in London. Nancy Laleau, my typist, was a good sport.

Were it not for Lindsay Waters of Harvard University Press I doubt this book would have been finished. Joyce Backman edited it and Gwen Frankfeldt designed it in the spirit in which it was written. I value the support of Paul Adams, Nancy Clemente, Susan Metzger, and Claire Silvers; most of all I value the fact that they had a more than merely professional interest in what I tried to do.

I owe a special debt to those members of the Lettrist International and the Situationist International who offered me friendship, papers, artifacts, and querulousness: T. J. Clark, Donald Nicholson-Smith, the late Alexander Trocchi, Gil J Wolman, and most of all Michèle Bernstein. I owe a great deal to David Orr of the Pace Trust in Louisville; to Robin Cembalest, for her indefatigable photo research and her charming presence; to the libraries of the University of California at Berkeley; to Toru Mitsui; to Howard Hampton; to Geoff Travis of Rough Trade Records in London; to Emily and Cessie; and to Jenny.

A few people did not simply help, give advice, read drafts, or come up with documents, though they did all of that; in the words of one of them, they were co-conspirators. They are Simon Frith, Jim Miller, John Rockwell, and Jon Savage. They can't be thanked, only recognized.

INDEX

ABOUT THE AUTHOR

Greil Marcus was born in San Francisco in 1945 and studied political thought at Berkeley, where he taught American Studies in 1971–72. He is the author of *Mystery Train: Images of America in Rock 'n' Roll Music* (1975) and the editor of *Stranded* (1979) and *Psychotic Reactions and Carburetor Dung*, by Lester Bangs (1987). He lives in Berkeley with his wife and two daughters.